CHILLING EFFECTS

In *Chilling Effects*, Jonathon W. Penney explores the increasing weaponization of surveillance, censorship, and new technology to repress and control us. With corporations, governments, and extremist actors using big data, cyber-mobs, artificial intelligence, and other threats to limit our rights and freedoms, concerns about chilling effects – or how these activities deter us from exercising our rights – have become urgent. Penney draws on law, privacy theory, and social science to present a new conformity theory that highlights the dangers of chilling effects and their potential to erode democracy and enable a more illiberal future. He critiques conventional theories and provides a framework for predicting, explaining, and evaluating chilling effects in a range of contexts. Urgent and timely, *Chilling Effects* sheds light on the repressive and conforming effects of technology, state, and corporate power and offers a roadmap of how to respond to their weaponization today and in the future.

Jonathon W. Penney is a legal scholar and social scientist at Osgoode Hall Law School, York University, Toronto. His award-winning research on privacy, technology, and human rights has received national and international attention, including coverage in the *Washington Post*, the *New York Times*, *Reuters International*, *WIRED*, *The Guardian*, *Le Monde*, and beyond.

Praise for Chilling Effects

Chilling Effects couldn't be more vital and timely. The government is orchestrating a massive wave of chilling effects to promote authoritarian aims, and the law is ill-prepared to address the harm. Penney demonstrates why chilling effects are one of the most pernicious threats to free speech and democracy. This book is the definitive account of chilling effects – the most comprehensive and incisive analysis to date. In addition to providing a clear and deep understanding of chilling effects, Penney develops compelling legal reforms to prevent chilling effects from subverting our freedom.

Daniel J. Solove, author of On Privacy and Technology
and the Bernard Professor of IP and Technology
Law at George Washington University Law School

With the voice of a storyteller and the persuasive power of a sociologist and legal theorist, Jonathon Penney helps us understand why and how the powerful can chill our behavior, morphing, manipulating, and changing what we say and do and who we aspire to be as individuals, groups, and society. This book is a masterclass on the social force and meaning of chilling effects at the behest of governments, companies, and cyber mobs. We must pay attention to Penney's lessons, lest we become less free and our democracies wither.

Danielle Keats Citron, Jefferson Scholars Foundation
Schenck Distinguished Professor in Law, University of
Virginia School of Law, Vice President, Cyber
Civil Rights Initiative

Jonathon Penney's *Chilling Effects* is one of the most important books on privacy and civil liberties written this decade. Penney advances the our understanding of how threats to our rights affect our behavior and thinking, by offering a nuanced theory of chilling effects as conformity, by rooting that theory in solid empirical social science, and by offering comprehensive solutions to limit chilling effects and protect our fragile democratic freedoms. An instant classic, *Chilling Effects* belongs on the bookcase or nightstand of every scholar of civil liberties – and of every citizen who cares about democracy.

Neil Richards, Koch Distinguished Professor in Law, Washington University

Amidst profound ongoing concerns around online censorship, threats to privacy, and harassment, Jonathon Penney offers an imaginative and elegant framework to understand how we might mitigate their proliferation. This book lights a path from today's narrow legal doctrines towards more comprehensive protection for our hard-won personal freedoms.

Jonathan Zittrain, Professor of Law, Computer Science,
and Public Policy, Harvard University

Jonathon Penney has written an enormously thought-provoking book of urgent relevance to our contemporary political condition. Courts declining to hear claims about privacy and surveillance harms owe us all a much better explanation of what they are doing.

Julie E. Cohen, Mark Claster Mamolen Professor
of Law and Technology, Georgetown Law

AI-enhanced censorship is being deployed by both governments and big tech, and it can control and silence us in new and unprecedented ways. Jonathon Penney writes an authoritative account of this dangerous moment, blending legal expertise, social science acumen, and tech savvy. Beautifully written, erudite, and comprehensive, *Chilling Effects* is essential reading for anyone wishing to endure this era with our fundamental freedoms and democracies intact.

Bruce Schneier, renowned security technologist and
author of *Rewiring Democracy: How AI Will Transform
Our Politics, Government, and Citizenship*

It is now widely understood that we live in a matrix of real-time digital surveillance in which every aspect of our lives is subject to algorithmic analysis on behalf of big tech platforms and government security agencies. But what does this new ecosystem portend for the future of rights, democracy, and the social bonds that tie us together in mutually supportive communities? In this masterpiece of interdisciplinary research, the world's leading authority on "chilling effects," Jonathon Penney elaborates on the ways in which digital surveillance are casting a shadow over our lives in ways that are corrosive to civic deliberation, inducing conforming and compliant behavior on a mass scale. This thoughtful, extremely informative book is a must read for anyone interested in the insidious ways in which the proliferating means of digital surveillance systems are undermining rights, freedoms, and democracy and – more importantly – how to resist them.

Ron Deibert, Professor of Political Science and
Director of the University of Toronto's Citizen Lab

Jonathon Penney has an unparalleled talent to describe the nature, manifestation, and consequences of surveillance and their chilling effects. With ease the book paints a clear picture of how chilling effects intersect with power, suppression, and control. We all need – now more than ever – this insightful guide on how to protect privacy, freedom, equality, and democracy in the digital age.

Sandra Wachter, Professor of Technology and
Regulation, Oxford Internet Institute,
University of Oxford

The concept of chilling effects is surprisingly underdeveloped and misunderstood. In *Chilling Effects*, Jonathon Penney has given us the definitive work on the concept with a bold new vision of how to understand them as pressure to conform and comply. This book is a vital contribution to our understanding of free expression and surveillance and a must read for a better democracy.

Woodrow Hartzog, Professor of Law, Boston University School of Law

Jonathon Penney's writing is theoretically rich and normatively compelling. At a moment where state and corporate power are increasingly aligned, this book provides an intellectual toolset for resistance, unpicking all the ways in which laws and digital surveillance combine to compel and encourage compliance and conformity. In short, a book for *this* age.

Vicki Nash, Professor, Oxford Internet Institute, University of Oxford

As we usher in a world of AI-powered surveillance, *Chilling Effects* offers an important analysis of the ways in which such surveillance can shape our behavior. Its message that this is not just about privacy harms, but the health of democracy and civil society more broadly, could not be timelier.

Lisa Austin, Professor, University of Toronto Faculty of Law

Jonathon Penney powerfully reframes "chilling effects" for the digital age, revealing how surveillance and social pressure push people to conform and self-censor. With compelling examples and a bold new theory, this book is essential reading for anyone concerned about the future of democracy and the battles over freedom of expression that will shape it.

Urs Gasser, Dean, School of Social Science and
Technology, Technical University of Munich

I don't know anyone who has thought harder and deeper about chilling effects than Jonathon Penney. An important book for anybody interested in privacy, surveillance, data protection, or freedom of expression. I highly recommend it.

Frederik Zuiderveen Borgesius, Professor of ICT and
Law, iHub, Radboud University

Chilling effects have never been more urgent or relevant, given the current political and media climate, and this book arrives at precisely the right time. With remarkable theoretical clarity, and building on his earlier influential work, Jonathon Penney expands the chilling effects framework into a powerful model of social compliance and behavioral control. He offers a rigorous and comprehensive foundation for an emerging field that scholars, practitioners, and advocates alike cannot afford to ignore.

Michael Latzer, Professor and Chair, Media Change &
Innovation Division, IKMZ – University of Zurich

Chilling Effects

REPRESSION, CONFORMITY, AND POWER IN THE DIGITAL AGE

JONATHON W. PENNEY

York University

CAMBRIDGE
UNIVERSITY PRESS

Shaftesbury Road, Cambridge CB2 8EA, United Kingdom

One Liberty Plaza, 20th Floor, New York, NY 10006, USA

477 Williamstown Road, Port Melbourne, VIC 3207, Australia

314–321, 3rd Floor, Plot 3, Splendor Forum, Jasola District Centre, New Delhi – 110025, India

103 Penang Road, #05–06/07, Visioncrest Commercial, Singapore 238467

Cambridge University Press is part of Cambridge University Press & Assessment, a department of the University of Cambridge.

We share the University's mission to contribute to society through the pursuit of education, learning and research at the highest international levels of excellence.

www.cambridge.org
Information on this title: www.cambridge.org/9781108725309

DOI: 10.1017/9781108641784

© Jonathon W. Penney 2026

When citing this work, please include a reference to the DOI 10.1017/9781108641784

First published 2026

A catalogue record for this publication is available from the British Library

A Cataloging-in-Publication data record for this book is available from the Library of Congress

ISBN 978-1-108-48587-6 Hardback
ISBN 978-1-108-72530-9 Paperback

Contents

Preface and Acknowledgments

This book is based on research I began over a decade ago, when I was still a doctoral student, but so many people – family, friends, colleagues, collaborators, and mentors – have shaped my thinking, research, and teaching on the subject, and supported my work, since those early days. My academic career, and this book, would not have been possible without them.

Let me begin with a few mentors that deserve special mention: Vicki Nash, Neil Richards, Danielle Keats Citron, Ron Deibert, and the late Greg Lastowka. Each have deeply influenced my thinking – not surprising as each are leaders in their respective fields; in Greg's case, was, before his untimely passing – but it was their kindness, generosity, and thoughtfulness with time and support that set them apart, and demonstrated to me that to be a truly great scholar one must also lift up those around you. These mentors helped me grow both as a scholar and as a person. *Thank you.*

The privacy law scholars community, with its annual Privacy Law Scholars Conferences in North America and Europe, has been deeply influential on the ideas in the book and immensely supportive. While there are far too many to mention here, there are a few that must be named: Neil Richards, Danielle Keats Citron, Daniel Solove, Julie Cohen, Ari Waldman, Woodrow Hartzog, Sandra Wachter, Karen Levy, Lisa Austin, Margot Kaminski, Chris Hoofnagle, and Gavin Phillipson.

I am very fortunate to have spent time at a number of incredible schools, research labs, and communities that greatly benefited my research and the book. That list includes the Citizen Lab based at the Munk School of Global Affairs and Public Policy, University of Toronto; the Berkman Klein Center for Internet and Society at Harvard University; the Cyber Civil Rights Initiative; the Institute for Rebooting Social Media at Harvard; the Oxford Internet Institute at the University of Oxford; the Citizens and Technology Lab at Cornell University; the Center for Information Technology Policy at Princeton University; the Shorenstein Center on Media, Politics and Public Policy at the Harvard Kennedy School; Columbia Law School, Harvard Law School, and the Faculties of Law at Oxford and Victoria

University Wellington; the Schulich School of Law at Dalhousie University, and my current home, Osgoode Hall Law School at York University in Toronto. Among the benefits have been research collaborations with amazing colleagues, many of whom I am privileged to count as friends, including Noura Aljizawi, Siena Anstis, Kendra Albert, Samantha Bradshaw, Danielle Keats Citron, J. Nathan Matias, Konrad Kollnig, Ram Shankar Siva Kumar, Gabby Lim, Bruce Schneier, Alexis Shore-Ingber, Aurelia Tamò-Larrieux, and Lucas Wright. Work colleagues past and present have also been critical in supporting my research and career: Saptarishi Bandopadhyay, Jamie Baxter, Benjamin Berger, Kim Brooks, David Blaikie, David Chodikoff, Barnali Choudhury, Mary Condon, Lynda Corkum, Stephen Coughlan, Carys Craig, Elaine Craig, Rob Currie, Giuseppina (Pina) D'Agostino, Allen Davis, Valerio De Stefano, Richard Devlin, Michael Deturbide, Trevor Farrow, David Fraser, John Grant, Roslyn Levine, and François Tanguay-Renaud.

Many have provided excellent feedback, constructive criticisms, or helpful advice. Kendra Albert, David Abrams, Alex Abdo, Siena Anstis, Lisa Austin, Jack Balkin, Nick Barber, Katy Bass, Samantha Bradshaw, Susan Benesch, Elissa Berwick, Elettra Bietti, Michael Birnhack, Marc Blitz, Frederik Zuiderveen Borgesius, Ian Brown, Ryan Budish, Danielle Keats Citron, Ignacio Cofone, Julie Cohen, Masashi Crete-Nishihata, Jakub Dalek, Ron Deibert, Joan Donovan, Brenda Dvoskin, David Erdos, Suzy Frankel, Mary Anne Franks, Urs Gasser, Lex Gill, Sue Glueck, Eric Goldman, Scott Hale, Woody Hartzog, Philip Howard, Kirsty Hughes, Michael Ignatieff, RonNell Andersen Jones, Thomas Kadri, Paul Kelly, Cynthia Khoo, Jeff Knockel, Mordechai Kremnitzer, Ram Shankar Siva Kumar, Michael Latzer, Emily Laidlaw, Vili Lehdonvirta, Yafit Lev-Aretz, Karen Levy, Gabby Lim, Asaf Lubin, Gianclaudio Malgieri, Alex Marthews, Alice Marwick, Kirsten Martin, J. Nathan Matias, Hideyuki Matsumi, Viktor Mayer-Schönberger, Vicki Nash, Tom Nichols, Peter Ormerod, Eric T. Meyer, David O'Brien, Taylor Owen, Chris Parsons, Frank Pasquale, Bilyana Petkova, Gavin Phillipson, Neil Richards, Ira Rubenstein, Mols Sauter, Teresa Scassa, Bruce Schneier, John Scott-Railton, Evan Selinger, Andy Sellars, Weiwei Shen, Dan Solove, Katherine Strandburg, Jay Stanley, Daniel Villar-Onrubia, Sandra Wachter, Ari Waldman, Yana Welinder, Ryan Whalen, Christopher Wolf, Joss Wright, Lucas Wright, Felix Wu, Wenming Xu, Marcelo Thompson, Elana Zaide, Ben Zevenbergen, Jonathan Zittrain, and Ethan Zuckerman all provided invaluable feedback on drafts of this book, draft papers, research, and/or talks it is based on, or helped me think through issues relating to the book. I also thank Neil Richards and Sandra Wachter for the opportunity to speak to their students about my research at Washington University School of Law and the Oxford Internet Institute, University of Oxford, respectively. I am especially grateful to Jonathan Zittrain, Urs Gasser, Adam Holland, Rebecca Tabaskey, and the rest of the amazing team at Harvard's Berkman Klein Center for Internet and Society for supporting me, and my research, over so many years; and the University of Toronto's Citizen Lab – another incredible place I am proud to call home – which likewise supported me and provided countless opportunities to workshop research or ideas that now inform the book. Thank you Ron, Céline, Adam, and the rest of the "CitLab" family.

I must also thank my editor Matt Galloway at Cambridge University Press, who went above and beyond with generous support, patience, and indispensable advice along the way. Jadyn Fauconier-Herry, Claire Sissen, and Jaisakthi Arul at the Press were also essential in the book's editing and production process.

Friends near and far have also been invaluable: Kendra Albert, Elissa Berwick, Ryan Budish, Aaron Campbell, Masashi Crete-Nishihata, Rob Danay, Tyson Dyck, Pelin Gure, Andrew Inch, Paul Kelly, Hardave Kharbanda, Ram Shankar Siva Kumar, Jon Lanman, Gabby Lim, James MacDuff, Adam Malcolm, Nathan Matias, Darren and Jessica Morofke, Michael Pal, Doug Publicover, Graham Reynolds, Mark Sakamoto, Neil Thomas, Paolo Torchetti, Peter Tsuluhas, Luis Villa, Joss Wright, and Jeff Wright all provided essential help or advice at different times. Family has also been indispensable. My mother Linda, whose love for books, travel, and ideas, led her to work hard to instill a passion for reading and learning in all three of her children. Growing up around stacks of books, wasn't it inevitable that we'd write a couple to add to the piles, Mom? My father Walter, whose work ethic, incisive logic, and focus are hard to match, taught me the value of tireless persistence and hard work, much like the quiet dignity in difficult labour I saw from my grandfathers Fred Snow, a coalminer in Glace Bay, and Tom Penney, a fisherman in Cook's Harbour. My siblings Vanessa and Jordan, both gifted researchers and writers, helped in key moments (and endlessly exacerbated my middle child syndrome). I owe a great debt to Kerban and Yavuz Hanoz, who go above and beyond to support my family, work, and success. And Suna's sister Lale, who has been like a little sister to me since we all met that first summer in New York City, has helped us out in difficult times.

I am grateful, most of all, to my amazing wife and two children – the three rocks in my life, or better yet, the gemstone and two little gleaming pebbles. They know my love, and the trials and tribulations of my book writing, the best – because they've had to live through it all! My two magical daughters, Leyla and Ela, who bring joy, laughter, and light to our days and remind me what really matters. I cannot wait until you are both old enough to read this! When you do, please remember to never lose your sense of wonder, amazement, and imagination about the world – it keeps us going. And then, remind me of the same. And Suna – my wife, best friend, most thoughtful critic, fiercest defender, and the love of my life – without whom, and her unrelenting support over so many years, this book might have remained merely scattered papers, words, and ideas. And with whom, the book, and everything else, is so much better, and has so much more meaning. This book is dedicated to her.

Parts of this book were adapted from several articles but its ideas and central theory represents a substantial evolution and development in my thinking.

Those articles include: *Understanding Chilling Effects*, 106 University of Minnesota Law Review 1451 (2022); *Privacy and Legal Automation: The DMCA as a Case Study*, 22 Stanford Technology Law Review 412 (2019); *Internet Surveillance, Regulation, and Chilling Effects Online: A Comparative Case Study*, 6(2) Internet Policy Review (2017); *Chilling Effects: Online Surveillance and Wikipedia Use*, 31 Berkeley Technology Law Journal 117 (2016).

Abbreviations

AI	Artificial Intelligence
DC	District of Columbia
DOJ	Department of Justice
EU	European Union
FBI	Federal Bureau of Investigation
FTC	US Federal Trade Commission
GDPR	General Data Protection Regulation
NSA	National Security Agency
UK	United Kingdom
US	United States

Introduction

WE ARE LIVING IN A CHILLING NEW ERA

It was a bright cold day in April, and each of these stories was in the news: An American permanent resident, who possesses many of the same legal and constitutional rights of citizens – including freedom of speech – is detained and rendered to a secret facility by United States federal authorities for promoting and engaging in university campus protests – activities all protected by the US Constitution.[1] A member of Congress calls for the Federal Bureau of Investigation (FBI) and Department of Justice to criminally investigate protests at retail locations for a business owned by one of the world's most wealthy and powerful men – a titan of the technology industry who is now also a controversial and powerful White House official – in many ways, a "shadow" president in Donald Trump's new administration.[2] A US attorney based in Washington, DC sends target letters threatening to prosecute anyone that "obstructs" the work of a secretive government agency that has been systematically dismantling critical government infrastructure, including the administration of social security, health, and nuclear management.[3] Private sector data contractors are conducting large-scale online surveillance to help government authorities map and track a person's "activity, movements, and relationships."[4] And as most social media companies increasingly engage in vast surveillance for profit,[5] others like X (formerly known as Twitter) – one of the most popular social media platforms in the world, and now owned by that same powerful White House official – have been transformed into massive pro-government propaganda machines, where lies, disinformation, harassment, abuse, and hate are not just rampant but amplified.[6]

What links each of these cases is not just that they all happened within the same few weeks, but the fact they are all examples of government, commercial enterprise, and technology being intentionally wielded to create a profound *chilling effect* on people's fundamental rights and freedoms.[7] By "chilling effect," I meant just as the words suggest – a cooling or inhibiting effect where people are deterred or discouraged from speaking or acting freely due to some threat – like the threat of surveillance or prosecution by federal authorities or threats of violence and harassment by

"

malicious actors on social media. These cases are not comprehensive. They are a mere sample of the many ways state, corporate, and technological power is presently being weaponized in unprecedented ways to chill and repress us.

How did we get here? It is impossible to create a precise road map for this chilling new era and when it began, though there have been important milestones. Edward Snowden's revelations about mass government surveillance were undoubtedly a critical early one. Though over a decade ago, most privacy lawyers and scholars still remember where they were when stories about Snowden's national security leaks first broke. The former National Security Agency (NSA) contractor had exposed to the world a trove of classified US Government documents disclosing the existence of highly secretive and extensive mass surveillance programs being used by US intelligence agencies and their partners in the West.[8] Starting in June 2013, the *Guardian* and *Washington Post* would publish a series of stories detailing these top- secret surveillance tools and programs. There was the PRISM surveillance program, which involved the NSA and FBI tapping directly into the main servers of nine leading US internet and social media companies – Microsoft, Yahoo, Google, Facebook, PalTalk, AOL, Skype, YouTube, and Apple – and extracting audio and video data, chat logs, images, emails, and other documents to track targets.[9] There was the NSA surveillance tool XKEYSCORE, which allowed the agency to collect, analyze, and probe massive troves of online content and metadata concerning "nearly everything a user does on the internet."[10] There was ECHELON, a global surveillance collaboration between the US, Canada, the United Kingdom, Australia, and New Zealand involving tapping into digital telecommunications with intercept stations around the world.[11] It was as if the dystopian futures of total surveillance, manipulation, and control envisioned in George Orwell's *Nineteen Eighty-Four*[12] or Aldous Huxley's *Brave New World*[13] were no long mere visions, but our lived reality; except it wasn't just big government behind it all, but big business – especially big tech.[14] It was shocking, at least at the time. In retrospect, the national security surveillance programs disclosed by Snowden arguably pale in comparison to the Trump administration's more recent use and abuse of law, surveillance, and technology to chill and repress.

Nevertheless, I remember where I was that June – in my small shared apartment in Cambridge, Massachusetts, and in the process of packing my bags. I was nearing the end of a fellowship at Harvard's Berkman Klein Center for Internet & Society, a research center that's been at the forefront of technology law and policy issues for decades – including privacy, a key focal point of my research. My plan had been to soon return to Oxford University, where I was then still a doctoral student. As I read about the fascinating but deeply troubling revelations about mass online government surveillance contained in the Snowden leaks, certain questions were burning in my mind: How would this surveillance impact on people's behavior? Would it have a *chilling effect* on people's rights and freedoms in the US and around the world? I had been wrestling with similar questions in my doctoral work at Oxford, but now the Snowden revelations had created a unique opportunity to study the questions in real time. I would not have to design an experiment to carry out in some cloistered university lab. We were all living in a mass surveillance experiment now.

In research that began at Harvard that spring and continued at Oxford the following year, I would conduct a study to answer these very questions – by exploring the impact these NSA surveillance programs had on people's use of Wikipedia, the immensely popular online encyclopedia. I was not prepared for what I would find: clear and compelling evidence of chilling effects due to the threat of NSA surveillance, whereby tens of millions of people, maybe more, were being chilled from freely searching and informing themselves online.[15] My study, which I will talk about in more detail in Chapter 1, would be among the very first in the world to document real world chilling effects caused by mass surveillance.[16] My findings would receive extensive media coverage in the US and around the world. When I began fielding media calls and emails not just from the United States or Canada, but from places as far flung as India, Russia, South Korea, and New Zealand, it became clear how the findings had struck a deeper, even universal chord: people were deeply worried and troubled about online surveillance and its impacts *everywhere*.

As the widespread coverage and international interest suggested, my study offered compelling insight as to what is at stake in the threat chilling effects pose to human rights and democracy, both today and tomorrow. For that reason, the study would also thrust me into the middle of high stakes litigation between the Wikimedia Foundation – the nonprofit organization that runs Wikipedia – and the US Government after lawyers for the Wikimedia Foundation and the American Civil Liberties Union (ACLU) asked me to act as an expert witness in support of their lawsuit. I did so *pro bono* because I believed in the importance of the rights at stake.[17] On the day that the lawsuit was filed just a few years later, a case that challenged the constitutionality of various NSA surveillance programs, Wikipedia founder Jimmy Wales and Wikimedia Foundation Executive Director Lila Tretikov would write in an op-ed in the *New York Times*:

> The notion that the N.S.A. is monitoring Wikipedia's users is not, unfortunately, a stretch of the imagination. One of the documents revealed by the whistle-blower Edward J. Snowden specifically identified Wikipedia as a target for surveillance, alongside several other major websites like CNN.com, Gmail and Facebook. The leaked slide from a classified PowerPoint presentation declared that monitoring these sites could allow N.S.A. analysts to learn "nearly everything a typical user does on the Internet."
>
> The harm to Wikimedia and the hundreds of millions of people who visit our websites is clear: Pervasive surveillance has a chilling effect. It stifles freedom of expression and the free exchange of knowledge that Wikimedia was designed to enable.[18]

Indeed, if people are chilled from seeking out information, freely reading, and informing themselves on sensitive and contentious matters of public policy like terrorism and national security, that is deeply corrosive to freedom and democracy. Their lawsuit – *Wikimedia Foundation v. NSA* – remains ongoing. But in the decade since the Snowden leaks, the threats did not subside, but only grew in size and scope.

GROWING THREATS

With the Snowden revelations still fresh in memory, *The Guardian* and the *New York Times* would break another explosive surveillance and data-tracking story just a few years later in March 2018. This one involved a murky and now infamous British political consulting and data science firm called Cambridge Analytica and the social media giant Facebook.[19] Cambridge Analytica had inappropriately harvested data from the Facebook profiles of more than 87 million people – collecting and retaining profile pictures, posts, comments, personal preferences, group memberships, any and all personal information data it could access – the vast majority of whom had not consented to even the firm's access to the data, let alone how it would be ultimately used. Cambridge Analytica used that misappropriated data to build "psychographic profiles" of voters to target them with tailored ads, messaging, and other influence operations both to help Donald Trump's campaign in the 2016 US presidential election and pro-Brexit groups in the United Kingdom's referendum on European Union membership that same year.

Not surprisingly, like the mass government surveillance that I explored in my own Wikipedia study, the large-scale corporate surveillance and data-mining operation in the Cambridge Analytica scandal also had substantial chilling effects. In a study of over 2,200 American social media users a few months later, researchers found that 42 percent of these users reported that the Cambridge Analytica scandal had caused them to change their behavior on Facebook, including 25 percent self-censoring their posts; 19 percent posting less; 19 percent changing privacy settings; and another 10 percent deleting or deactivating their accounts.[20] Another 26 percent in the study indicated that the Cambridge Analytica scandal had caused them to change their behavior on "other social media," including 20 percent being more careful about what they post; 12 percent posting less; and 4 percent deactivating or deleting their accounts. Furthermore, 39 percent indicated that their posting and sharing on social media was "way less personal." Overall, 79 percent said they were "very" or "somewhat" concerned about the privacy of their information on social media, and 82 percent said they self-censor on social media due to privacy concerns. *The Atlantic*, reporting the findings, observed that "people are changing the way they use social media," including being far less personal in their posting online, and the privacy invasions of scandals like Cambridge Analytica were likely to blame.[21]

Less than two years later, the *New York Times* would break a story about another shadowy company – one that may, the *Times* predicted, "end privacy as we know it."[22]

That company, Clearview AI, had developed a revolutionary facial recognition technology (FRT) application powered by cutting-edge artificial intelligence (AI) and machine learning capabilities. It claimed that it could identify anyone based on a single photo or image with astonishing accuracy that no other facial recognition software could match: a 98.6 percent accuracy rate.[23] Perhaps the best measure of its capabilities has been the company's success – thousands of police services around the world have used it, and many more are eager to try.[24] Kashmir Hill, the journalist who would ultimately break the story about Clearview AI for the *Times*, was originally skeptical but later convinced through countless demonstrations and by using the tool herself of its immense capabilities – and immense threat to privacy and potential for chilling effects.[25] But what was chilling about Clearview AI wasn't *just* the powerful AI-driven facial recognition surveillance system it was secretly marketing to law enforcement around the world, but *how* it developed that technology. As it turns out, the company trained the AI powering its surveillance system using billions of facial images it illegally "scraped" – extracted at scale using automated programs – from social media platforms like Facebook, Instagram, and LinkedIn.[26] If the surveillance, facial identification, and tracking capabilities that Clearview AI touts sound dystopian and far-fetched, like something right out of those same science fiction novels, they are equaled only by its creepy and villainous origin story: a deeply chilling surveillance technology developed through mass global privacy violations. That brings to mind science fiction like Mary Shelley's *Frankenstein* as much as Orwell's *Nineteen Eighty-Four*. Yet, the threat to privacy – and potential for widespread societal chilling effects – posed by a new generation of companies like Clearview AI, using and abusing AI, FRT, and other emerging technologies for profit, was very real.

Take the story of Derrick Ingram. Ingram, a 28-year-old Black Lives Matter activist living in New York City, found himself barricaded in his Hell's Kitchen apartment in the early hours of August 7, 2020, surrounded by dozens of officers from the New York Police Department (NYPD).[27] The officers claimed they had a warrant for his arrest – supposedly based on his use of a megaphone at a protest months earlier.[28] While Ingram frantically consulted with various public defender lawyers on the phone as he live-streamed the encounter, he could hear police drones buzzing overhead. In the end, Ingram was not arrested and though charges were later filed against him, those charges were also eventually dismissed. But what was just as troubling as the stark show of police force that day, was how police had located him. It turns out that video of the police standoff showed officers outside his home reviewing a document entitled *Facial Identification Section Informational Lead Report*, which included a photo of Ingram from his own publicly accessible Instagram account.[29] That photo, which captured a clear image of his face, was taken at a bar following a protest and posted the same day – August 6, 2020 – the day before the police standoff at his home. In fact, the NYPD would later confirm that it used FRT in its investigation but would not provide any more details.[30] But it seems improbable that the photo did not play a role, given the timing. A later report by *BuzzFeed* would confirm that the NYPD had contracted the services of Clearview AI at the time.[31]

The ongoing threats of police investigations, rearrest, and targeted surveillance have chilled Ingram's activism and his life. He has moderated his social justice protesting and campaigning and now describes himself as far less "reactionary."[32] He has withdrawn from social events and also declined work opportunities, including what he described as a "dream job" offer, just because he was still struggling psychologically with these threats, and believed he would fail if he took on the work.[33] "People know my address now … I'm scared every day, but I don't have the means to relocate," Ingram has said.[34] Clearview AI had boasted it could identify a person with a single photo. It appeared to have helped the NYPD do so with Ingram. The threat and chilling effects were real and profound.

And it's not just individuals or activists who are impacted. It is entire communities. Like the border town of Chula Vista, California, where poorer immigrant communities find themselves in the flight path of the town's growing fleet of drones.[35] In October 2018, Chula Vista became the first city in the US to launch a "Drone as First Responder" program, wherein 911 dispatchers can send drones as first responders to deal with emergencies, including crimes in progress and other threats to public safety.[36] Since then, drones have flown 20,000 times in the town. While some residents support the drone program, others report impacts that suggest broader chilling effects due to the privacy threats. Some residents report they feel "constantly watched."[37] Others report being afraid to use their backyards or other public spaces out of fear they are under surveillance. Another resident reports suffering persistent anxiety and sleep deprivation.[38] And these chilling effects are not endured uniformly, but impact certain communities more than others. *WIRED* magazine analyzed data for the drone flights and found a pattern: the poorer the neighborhood, the more it is exposed to drones.[39] Those poorer neighborhoods tend to be populated by working class black, Hispanic, and immigrant populations.[40] Those living homeless in the town report feeling as if they live in a "surveillance dystopia," as drones regularly fly low over their encampments.[41] In a drone town, a lack of a home means no privacy and thus no relief. In other words, the drone surveillance is impacting the entire town, but these resulting chilling effects disproportionately impact poor, working class, and racial communities. These differential impacts are another reality of chilling effects.

Nor is it only overreaching government, law enforcement, or commercial enterprise contributing to the problem. New technologies are also enabling abusers, who chill victims through targeted threats, stalking, harassment, and cyber-mobs. And the victims of these threats are disproportionately women and racial and sexual minorities.[42] Take the story of Stephanie Feldman, a novelist and editor. Feldman was at work when she first learned someone had stolen her online identity and had launched a persistent online harassment campaign that would chill her, and her friends and colleagues, with impacts that still affect her life today.[43] The perpetrator had created a Twitter account – the social media platform now known as X – to impersonate her using only a photo and a login, nothing more. The perpetrator proceeded to portray Feldman as a feminist who supported "white genocide" – killing all white males – that inevitably unleashed a campaign of threats, harassment, and abuse from a virtual cyber-mob directed toward Feldman herself.[44] The attacker also went after her publisher and employer, trying to get her fired.[45] For months after the attack, Feldman received daily threats and hate mail that caused her to fear for her safety. She began to self-censor both her writing and online communications and withdrew from social media and the internet altogether.[46] She even became too fearful to promote a new book that she had edited online, afraid it would lead to further attacks on her or the writers that contributed to it.[47] In some US states, laws like the Texas Heartbeat Act are being specifically designed to weaponize chilling effects to eviscerate even constitutionally protected rights by outsourcing to private parties not just legal prosecution, but also targeted stalking and harassment campaigns just like this.[48] Like Feldman, victims of such state-directed or supported campaigns of stalking and harassment are not only chilled from speaking or exercising their rights, but living.

None of this is coincidental. Today, surveillance and censorship is on the rise everywhere.[49] More data is being collected, analyzed, mined, and stored about us and our daily activities than at any other time in history.[50] We now speak of "big data" – massive data sets generated from billions of daily online transactions; emails; texts; digital media; searches; comments; likes; posts; health records; social media activities; streaming services; scientific data; GPS trackers; smart phones; smart appliances; and new surveillance and sensory technology, among many other things.[51] These data sets are larger, more varied, and more complex than at any other time in history.[52] For instance, by 2003 all human activity in history had created a total of five exabytes (10^{18} bytes) of data. As of 2013, that amount was being generated every two days. Today, big data is even bigger – every day, the internet alone processes 1,826 petabytes of data; Google processes 3.5 billion searches; Facebook users upload 300 million photos and make over 500,000 comments and nearly 300,000 status updates.[53] Advanced new data-mining techniques, enabled by AI, machine learning, and automation, have been developed to analyze and excavate these massive data sets to predict and influence our behavior to advance both state and corporate interests.[54] These same advanced technologies and techniques are being used in astonishing and disturbing new ways to analyze and employ data to track, censor, manipulate, and control us,[55] automate legal and regulatory enforcement,[56] or to promote corporate interests.[57] Meanwhile, ubiquitous computing, social media use, and the internet of things, have made targeted spying, stalking, harassment, and cyber-mobbing not only easier, but far too common.[58]

Not surprisingly, concerns about the impact of these developments on privacy, speech, and other fundamental rights and freedoms – particularly their chilling effects on these rights and freedoms – have taken on greater urgency and importance.[59] Indeed, beyond law and social science, the term "chilling effects" has taken hold in "everyday discourse."[60] And the COVID-19 pandemic – resulting in citizen health tracking and surveillance infrastructure – and sweeping recent legal changes – like the widespread criminalization and restriction of abortion and other reproductive freedoms following the US Supreme Court's decision in *Dobbs* – have only compounded these chilling effect concerns.[61] Thus the scale of impact is likely far broader than individuals, groups, or even communities, affecting entire populations – as my research on the chilling effects of government surveillance on Wikipedia use has shown. Even those fortunate enough to escape repressive or authoritarian regimes abroad are no longer safe. For instance, my colleagues at The Citizen Lab, an interdisciplinary laboratory based at the Munk School of Global Affairs & Public Policy, University of Toronto – where I have been a long-term research fellow – have extensively documented how authoritarian governments are increasingly engaging in forms of transnational campaigns of targeted surveillance, stalking, and harassment to chill the speech and activism of dissidents and diaspora communities.[62] Chilling effects are local, and global.

A LONG HISTORY

Yet, these concerns about chilling effects are certainly not new, nor is overreach by government, commercial enterprise, and abusers in weaponizing chilling effects to repress and victimize. Modern history is littered with examples. Between 1917 and 1921, two-thirds of US states enacted intentionally vague and broadly construed anti-sedition laws in order to criminalize and chill the speech and activities of labor unions and the broader labor movement.[63] During the "red scare" of the McCarthy era – which I will talk about in more depth in Chapter 1 – in addition to states passing repressive, vague, and overreaching anti-communist statutes to chill left-wing groups and their activities, state and federal authorities also targeted them with persistent surveillance and regularly released publicly lists of alleged communists and socialists. The aim was to weaponize employers and the general public into blacklisting, firing, and socially punishing those named, to create a broader climate of fear and chilling effects.[64] As historian Lawrence Cappello has observed, all of these vague laws, surveillance, and tactics to create vast chilling effects were later repurposed in the 1950s and 1960s to victimize and chill the civil rights movement, and later saw use in the Watergate scandals of the 1970s, Iran-Contra of the 1980s, and the overreach of national security surveillance and law enforcement in the early twenty-first century following the 9/11 terrorist attacks.[65]

To be clear, while many of these examples highlight governments and police weaponizing chill, corporate actors have long done so too. There is also a long history of companies using legal threats to chill and deter critics.[66] For instance, "SLAPP" lawsuits are an explicit example of this. The term "SLAPP suits" – Strategic Lawsuits Against Public Participation – was coined by two University of Denver professors in the 1980s to refer to lawsuits threatened or filed by companies to chill people from speaking publicly on matters in the public interest – something they observed among large construction companies that regularly threatened citizens and activists who publicly criticized them for environmental abuses.[67] SLAPP suits are an explicit case of chilling effects being weaponized to preserve or extend corporate power, with perpetrators usually powerful companies or business persons who use them to suppress news reporting or to silence people who wish to speak out on corporate corruption, criminality, and other wrongdoing. The researchers documented tens of thousands of such cases in the US, but surely the number is even greater today, as SLAPP suits are now a global problem.[68] Similar legal threats have been employed by companies in many other contexts. For instance, Big Tobacco used persistent threats to chill government efforts to regulate or ban tobacco products,[69] while pharmaceutical companies have also been prolific in their legal threats to chill those who support industry regulation.[70] Businesses are also often complicit when governments weaponize chill to repress and control. State abuses were regularly carried out with private sector collaborators during the McCarthy, Civil Rights, and Watergate Eras.[71] And the antiabortion movement has a long history of weaponizing violence and violent threats to chill abortion access often enabled by corporate complicity or silence.[72]

This long history continues to unfold today. The Snowden leaks, Cambridge Analytica, and Clearview AI stories all involved similar joint ventures between powerful technology companies working closely with governments – what Bruce Schneier calls the surveillance-industrial complex[73] – to likewise enable more invasive mass surveillance and thus wider chilling effects. And as the stories recounted at the outset of this chapter suggest, we are likely at the dawn of an even more dangerous period where law, surveillance, and many other forms of state, technology, and corporate power are merged and weaponized to achieve society-wide chilling effects.[74] For instance, as I write, the second Trump administration, with the help of Elon Musk and other technology industry titans, is wielding technology in systematic and surprising new ways to monitor, influence, and repress. Overreaching new laws are being enacted across the US and around the world to chill the speech, reproductive freedoms, and other fundamental rights of women and sexual minorities,[75] while corporate actors secretly fund these efforts.[76] And right wing activists use online platforms to launch angry cyber-mobs to "doxx" (disclose their names, location, and other personal information), harass, stalk, threaten, and abuse them.[77] Feldman is an example of that kind of weaponized chill, which aims not only to obliterate people's rights, but chill and repress already marginalized and disempowered people and communities.

PERSISTENT SKEPTICISM

Yet even as concerns about chilling effects today grow, and there is increasing recognition that chilling effects are destructive to freedom and democracy, widespread skepticism persists about their existence and impact. Though the idea of "chilling effects" is not new – it has been a part of US constitutional law since the Second World War – lawyers, legal scholars, privacy theorists, and social scientists often question whether chilling effects even exist, or if they do, whether their impacts are anything more than temporary, trivial, or ephemeral.[78] Skepticism among courts has persisted too, especially concerning chilling effects due to privacy threats like surveillance or personal threats like stalking and harassment. Judges tend to downplay, dismiss, or ignore such chilling effects entirely, or in other cases, create legal rules or barriers to make bringing claims based on such chilling effect concerns more difficult.[79] For example, in its 2013 decision in *Clapper v. Amnesty International*, the US Supreme Court dismissed chilling effects caused by government surveillance as "self-inflicted injuries" that were too "subjective" and "speculative."[80] And in its 2023 high-profile decision in *Counterman v. Colorado*,[81] the Court overturned a conviction under a Colorado anti-stalking law while entirely ignoring how the perpetrator's own stalking and harassment had had a profound chilling effect on the victim, a musician, causing her to live in constant fear of physical attack, cancel concerts, and ultimately abandon her singing career as a result.[82] Even in the high stakes litigation between the Wikimedia Foundation and the US Government in *Wikimedia Foundation v. NSA*,[83] in which I have been involved as an expert witness, the courts have been persistently dismissive of the lawsuit's claims of surveillance chilling effects as too speculative, despite compelling evidence of chilling effects. Such skepticism is not unique to American law. Lawyers, legal scholars, and judges in Canada, the United Kingdom, Europe, Australia, New Zealand, and beyond – nearly any jurisdiction that has recognized chilling effects in law and jurisprudence – have expressed similar skepticism.

Not only does skepticism persist, but how we conceptualize chilling effects is also a big problem. The conventional understanding is that a chilling effect is when a person, deterred by fear of some legal harm or punishment, engages in *self-censorship*, that is, censors themselves and does not speak or engage in some activity, despite that activity being lawful, even desirable.[84] This conventional focus on self-censorship and speech is not surprising – the idea of "chilling effects" first came to prominence in US constitutional law in a series of cases decided in the 1950s and 1960s, wherein the Court invoked the concept in striking down various overreaching McCarthy and Civil Rights Era laws for chilling First Amendment protected speech and other expressive activities.[85] And prominent First Amendment scholars – like Frederick Schauer, whose 1978 account of chilling effects is still today described as "definitive"[86] – have also helped explain and elaborate the Court's "chilling effects doctrine," which has tended to focus almost exclusively on legal and regulatory chilling effects and self-censorship: how vague and uncertain laws – and uncertainties inherent in the legal process – combined with the risk or threat of legal harms like criminal or civil penalties could chill First Amendment protected speech and behavior. Such law-centered claims are now widely recognized as First

Amendment injuries, with courts regularly invalidating statutes and regulations for having a chilling effect on First Amendment protected speech.[87] So, this understanding is predominant in US law as it's the conceptualization embraced by the US Supreme Court, as well as prominent legal scholars who have also adopted it and helped shape and define it. It is also predominant internationally, in many of those same countries noted earlier – wherever American law and jurisprudence has had influence.

Yet, this conventional conceptualization is too narrow, legalistic, and empirically weak, leaving us with little insight as to the *true* scope of chilling effects and their impacts and harms. It is too narrow because it focuses only on legalistic forms of chilling effects and thus cannot explain chilling effects in a range of other contexts – like those caused by surveillance or personal threats and abuse online. It is empirically weak as much of its assumptions about how and why people are chilled find little support in empirical evidence. And it neglects critical insights from a range of social science fields about how chilling effects involve not just an absence – self-censorship, which is a lack of speaking or doing – but also *shape* behavior. While self-censorship is an important dimension of chilling effects, it is only one dimension of the phenomena. In fact, chilling effects predominantly involve not just a deterrent effect, but a shaping effect – people speaking, acting, or doing in a way that conforms to, or is in compliance with, perceived norms, not simply self-censoring to avoid a legal harm. To borrow a term from Julie Cohen, chilling effects are also *productive.*[88] They not only involve the silencing of speech, but also the production of conforming and compliant speech and behavior. As such, this legalistic and unsupported conventional view cannot help us understand chilling effects and their true threat, and instead only feeds greater skepticism. That, in turn, makes it more difficult for victims to go to court to vindicate their rights in the face of invasive and repressive chilling effects due to surveillance and other targeted threats, and for policymakers to enact law reforms to address them.

Part of the problem is that there has been a significant dearth of theoretical and empirical studies of chilling effects, at least until recently. Legal scholars who were interested in the concept did not have the knowledge or training to do the empirical work necessary to study this behavioral phenomenon. And the social scientists who did have the training were less interested in chilling effects, given its legal origins and dimensions. Fortunately, that is changing. There is today a growing body of interdisciplinary research that theorizes and explores chilling effects not as a legal doctrine but as a behavioral phenomenon in a variety of contexts, like chilling effects due to government[89] and private sector surveillance,[90] data collection, processing, and profiling,[91] and targeted personal threats, harassment, and abuse.[92] The central focus of this new work – which should be recognized as an emerging but distinct field of interdisciplinary social scientific and legal inquiry – has moved on from the question of whether chilling effects exist to exploring and understanding them, and how to respond.[93] And what I argue in this book is that this new research, when synthesized with insights from a variety of other fields of social and behavior science, shows that chilling effects are best understood as a powerful form of *conformity* and *compliance* effects with deeper psychological foundations. This theory builds on insights concerning the chilling effects of privacy and personal threats by scholars and theorists like Julie Cohen, Daniel Solove, Neil Richards, Margot Kaminski, Ryan Calo, Bruce Schneier, and Danielle Citron and links this behavioral phenomenon that lawyers have called "chilling effects" to a broader social and behavioral scientific literature on conformity and compliance and their evolutionary foundations.[94] And what this extensive body of behavioral theory and research tells us is that when facing certain perceived threats – like surveillance and observation; uncertainty about the law or other behavioral norms; or threats to personal safety – people do not act or speak freely but instead engage in self-censorship and conformity. That is, they act the way they believe others would act in the same circumstance or how they believe they are expected to act – they conform and comply.

So, chilling effects are a more powerful form of conformity and compliance effects. As we will see, people engage in behavioral conformity in response to personal threats for a variety of reasons. But a central one is for safety and security. There is strength in numbers. Conforming to the group, expected behavioral norms, or the expectations of broader society, ensures greater protection from threats, and reduces the risk of harm and likelihood of ostracism and alienation. This is also why conformity – and chilling effects – are a behavioral tendency with a deeper psychological foundation.[95] Throughout human history and evolution, those of us who engaged in conformity in response to threats were more likely to survive, because acting in compliance with norms of the group or community enhanced the likelihood of surviving the threat.[96] Breaking norms and behavioral expectations may leave you ostracized and alone – and more vulnerable to threats. Hence, this behavioral tendency has become hardwired into human psychology through evolutionary processes over a very long time. Thus, people can be chilled and engage in conformity and compliance both consciously and subconsciously. We often do it deliberately to avoid threats, but we also do it subconsciously – we can be chilled and we don't even know it.

What makes chilling effects *different* from garden variety social conformity is that they involve some of the most powerful kinds of threats. The central factors in a conformity theory of chilling effects tracks the central factors in conformity and compliance: observation; uncertainty; personalization; and power and authority. But when it comes to chilling effects, it is not merely observation by peers – that you find in psychology experiments exploring the conforming effects of mere observation – but systematic and persistent surveillance by powerful entities like government and law enforcement.[97] The uncertainty triggering chilling effects is often not simply uncertainty about behavioral norms, but uncertainty and ambiguity about legal requirements backed by significant criminal and civil penalties coupled with the threat of social ostracism and alienation associated with lawbreaking. The personal threats are not just single threats of violence, but often large-scale campaigns of harassment, stalking, and intimate privacy violations, and abuse, sometimes enabled or directed by government itself.[98] In other words, chilling effects are a *more* powerful form of conformity and compliance that are magnified by the power and authority of government, law enforcement, and well-resourced commercial enterprise. Chilling effects are thus qualitatively and quantitatively different from typical forms of conformity and compliance due to the magnitude of threats at stake, but to understand them you must also understand conformity and compliance.

This *conformity* theory of chilling effects, which I explain and advance in this book, has a number of important theoretical, empirical, normative, and legal advantages. First, it is neither singular nor narrow, and unlike conventional theories focused on law or privacy alone, it is better grounded in social science and empirical literature. As such, it also has greater predictive and explanatory power. It offers a more comprehensive theory that better accounts for and explains chilling effects due to different kinds of threats.[99] And combined with insights from social and deterrence theory, it can predict the scope and magnitude of chilling effects in these different contexts too. Beyond more robust theoretical understanding, this also has important legal and public policy implications, including for chilling effects standing and doctrine. Second, it demonstrates more clearly how privacy and chilling effects theory are inextricably linked. If privacy theory is concerned with preserving social conditions for autonomy and self-development, then understanding chilling effects – which fosters competing social conditions favoring self-censorship, social conformity, and compliance – is essential.[100] Third, by theorizing chilling effects not just in relation to individual-level self-censorship but also broader social conditions and power dynamics, it provides a normative foundation to distinguish "good" and "bad" chilling effects, and also navigate competing ones – which also has implications for law and policy.

Most importantly, this theory of chilling effects helps us understand the far-reaching scale and scope of chilling effects, and how they are toxic and corrosive to democracy and civil society. It helps us understand how chilling effects deeply impact individuals – that we are wired, psychologically, to be chilled, and thus it can affect us even without our awareness. We are chilled into silence consciously, but also subconsciously. Chilling effects shape us, our psychology and personal identity, ultimately producing more docile people and populations that are easier to control. It helps us understand how these impacts are *compounding*, because that is also how conformity and compliance work. That is, as more threats are added, the chill becomes greater. This means that when a person is faced both by a surveillance threat, uncertainty, and personal threats, the chilling effect will necessarily be greater than a case where the person faces only one of these threats. It also helps us understand how chilling effects, and the threats that cause them, can help explain the increasing tribalism and extremism we see today, both online and offline. That's because conformity can sometimes encourage one to self-censor and remain silent – behavior more often associated with chilling effects – if that is the expected norm. But it can also mean more polarizing and extreme speech or behavior, if that is the group norm that a person conforms with in the face of a threat. So, chilling effects can lead to both individual and even societal-scale censorship, but also more extremist behavior too.

Lastly, this theory better captures the broader social context of chilling effects and their relationship to existing social, economic, and political structures, power, and hierarchies, which is essential to understanding how chilling effects impact democratic societies. A behavioral phenomenon – caused by state and corporate actions – that encourages the production of speech and behavior that is more compliant and conforming has obvious implications in an era of surveillance capitalism and the emergence of mass citizen-tracking systems.

We need to change our thinking. We need to reject conventional approaches. We need to better understand chilling effects, the threats they pose, and what factors – like surveillance and other public and private sector actions – cause or magnify them. That is what this book is about – changing how we think about chilling effects so we are better prepared to stop them, and their corrosive impacts both on people and society. That's because a world rife with chilling effects – due to overreaching surveillance, targeted legal threats, vast algorithmic data collection and processing, and ubiquitous online threats and abuse fostered by big government and big business – is just as dystopian as the nightmarish totalitarian futures imagined by writers like Orwell and Huxley.

STRUCTURE OF THE BOOK

Let me say a little about the structure of this book (and my argument) before we begin. The book is divided into three parts. Part I consists of the first two chapters and essentially sets out and critically analyzes conventional understanding and theories of chilling effects. Chapter 1 examines the leading theory of chilling effects – as fear of legal harm – a legalistic account most often employed by lawyers and judges. I argue this predominant conventional account is too narrow, legalistic, and deeply flawed theoretically and empirically, and cannot explain, predict, or understand chilling effects in a wide variety of contexts. As such, it only contributes to skepticism about chilling effects, rather than dispelling them. Chapter 2 critically examines privacy-based conventional theories, which approach chilling effects as a result of privacy harms. While privacy-based theories of chilling effects improve on legal accounts, they are also too narrow and cannot explain chilling effects in a variety of contexts, including forms of privacy-related chilling effects. Moreover, courts and judges have also remained deeply skeptical of privacy-based theories. To address these limitations and fully understand the threat chilling effects pose to freedom, fundamental rights, and democracy we need a new understanding of chilling effects that moves beyond conventional accounts.

In Part II, I elaborate this new understanding. This part consists of three chapters. Chapter 3 lays the theoretical and empirical foundation for connecting chilling effects with a broader body of social science and behavioral theory, in particular, research on social influence, like conformity and compliance. Chapter 4 elaborates a new theory of chilling effects – as conformity and compliance. I argue that chilling effects are best understood as a more powerful form of conformity and compliance – just like conformity, chilling effects reflect a behavioral tendency to self-censor and conform in the face of threats like surveillance, uncertain laws, or personal threats. The chapter also elaborates what I call the four "chilling effect" factors: observation; uncertainty; personalization or personal threats; and power and authority, which help predict and explain chilling effects. Chapter 5 demonstrates the explanatory power of this new understanding by elucidating a taxonomy of broad range of different types of chilling effects and explaining them using the theory.

Part III explores the implications of this new understanding and consists of five chapters. Chapter 6 uses this new understanding to elaborate the dangers of chilling effects both on an individual level and societal scale. Chapter 7 explains what chilling effects theory – based on the new theory advanced in this book – is for. That is, I illustrate its useful functions and applications, including demonstrating how chilling effects are weaponized against disfavored groups or to support systems of power and control; correcting flawed popular assumptions about chilling effects; and improving our understanding of privacy. Chapter 8 sets out a framework for predicting and evaluating chilling effects, including balancing them against competing chilling effects claims or competing values or public policy concerns, like speech and national security. Chapter 9 makes the case for critical changes in chilling effects law and doctrine based on the new understanding advanced in this book. Lastly, Chapter 10 predicts the "future" of chilling effects – which today looks darker and more dystopian than ever – and proposes a comprehensive law and public policy reforms and solutions to stop it.

PART I

Conventional Chilling Effects Theories and Their Limits

What are chilling effects? Chilling effects are a behavioral phenomenon. They speak to how people behave in certain situations, like when deciding how to act in light of a law that might prohibit their planned activities or when aware they are being watched by others. Conventional understanding conceptualizes chilling effects in terms of deterrence and self-censorship, and is usually very legalistic. To be "chilled" in response to some threat or concern, like an unclear law, means we are *deterred* from speaking, acting, or exercising our rights and freedoms, the way we otherwise would have, but for the threat. A key result of this deterrent effect is *self-censorship* – we exercise self-restraint, refraining from speaking or engaging in some activity, even if we believe that the activity is not only lawful, but desirable in the circumstances.

On this conventional understanding, the reason we are deterred and end up self-censoring is a kind of rational fear of legal or privacy harms with the decision to self-censor a calculated decision to avoid those harms. For example, we may be chilled by a vague or overly broad law because we fear, with good reason, that our speech or actions may violate the law, leading us to engage in a rational choice to self-censor in order to avoid legal liabilities, punishment, or other legal harms. Or we are chilled because of potential harms that might stem from privacy threats. For example, we might be chilled by government or corporate surveillance because we fear the data and information collected about us could be leaked, shared, or disclosed later, to embarrass us or damage our reputation, so we make a conscious and rational decision to avoid speaking or sharing information that could be collected and retained.

So, the conventional understanding is that a chilling effect is a rational choice and deterrent effect, with self-censorship the key outcome, due to fear of legal or privacy harms. This understanding is reflected in the term itself – "chilling effects." A risk of a legal harm "chills" or deters us. We are frozen. We do not speak. We do not act. We are silent. This conventional understanding is predominant in law, apparent in how both lawyers and courts invoke and reason about chilling effects – particularly the United States Supreme Court – and in the leading theories of chilling effects. It is also prevalent in public policy, mainstream media, and popular culture invocations. This is not surprising, as this conventional understanding captures important dimensions of chilling effects and resonates with popular fears about the totalitarian potential of technology, government, and big business exemplified in literary classics like Orwell's *Nineteen Eighty-Four* or Huxley's *Brave New World*. Both novels foretell dystopian futures, wherein totalitarian regimes deploy technology and mass surveillance to guarantee total population control through widespread self-censorship, among other things. In Orwell's Oceania, chilling effects are ubiquitous.

But conventional understanding of chilling effects today is also deeply flawed, incomplete, and neglects important insights from social theory necessary to understand chilling effects, their impacts, and implications. This is the case I make in this Part. In Chapters 1 and 2, I analyze and critique the leading conventional theories of chilling effects – chilling effects as fear of legal harm and fear of privacy harm – and illustrate their limitations. I tackle each, in turn, and argue they are too narrow, cannot account for or explain chilling effects in a range of different contexts, and neglect insights from a range of social science fields about how chilling effects *shape* behavior.

1

Law's Flawed Theory and Its McCarthy Era Origins

Today's leading conventional theory is chilling effects as fear of legal harm. It is largely a product of law and the legal profession – lawyers, judges, and legal scholars. It has three central tenants. First, chilling effects are a *deterrent effect* arising due to people's *fear of legal harms*. That is, a person is chilled or deterred from speaking or engaging in lawful activities – such as First Amendment protected speech – out of fear of legal harm or punishment,[1] combined with uncertainties in the law and legal process, and the costs of defending legal claims.[2] The "legal harm" here could include any kind of legally mandated punishment, such as a fine, imprisonment, imposition of civil liability, or deprivation of a benefit.[3] To be clear, this fear, and the response, is both rational and calculated. That is, the reason that someone might be deterred from speaking or doing is a rational choice made to avoid the potential legal harm. Second, this leading conventional theory focuses predominantly on *self-censorship* as the outcome of chilling effects. That is, an *absence* or lack of speaking, acting, or doing – a silencing, in the speech context, or an inhibiting effect, if speaking of action more generally. Third, chilling effects also concerns *lawful* activity – be it speech or conduct – which is how it can be distinguished from deterrence of illegal conduct in the law more generally.[4] A classic example would be a vague or overly broad statute that would chill or deter someone from speaking or acting as they were uncertain whether their speech could fall within the scope of the statute and whether they could successfully defend their case within an uncertain legal system. As a result, a person exercises a kind of self-restraint and censors themself – deciding not to speak up or engage in some activity. The fear leads the person to self-censor as a calculated decision not to act in order to avoid the legal harm.

This modern conceptualization of chilling effects emerged in mid twentieth-century American law during the McCarthy Era – a period in the late 1940s and 1950s marked by public fear and hysteria about the supposed threat of communism, led on the national stage by the bullying anti-communist demagogue Senator Joe McCarthy, from whom the period takes its name.[5] This origin story is no coincidence. The vast network of repressive anti-communist laws enacted across the country during the "Red Scare" threatened citizens with significant penalties and

19

punishments for exercising basic rights and freedoms – such as freedom of speech, thought, and association.[6] Some laws, such as the 1940 Smith Act, aimed to effectively criminalize the Communist Party and association with it.[7] Other laws enabled the anti-communist crusaders' primary *modus operandi*: the "spotlight of pitiless publicity,"[8] that is, a systematic program of identification, exposure, and public/private sector reprisals carried out through countless local, state, and federal investigations, public hearings, loyalty oaths, mandated disclosure, blacklisting, denial of government benefits, and dismissal or forced resignation from employment.[9] Tens of thousands of citizens were persecuted, lost their livelihoods, and had their reputations and lives ruined often for doing nothing more than expressing sympathy for left-wing causes or associating with political groups later deemed "subversive" by the government.[10]

Not surprisingly, these laws helped create a broader climate of fear and intimidation – and chilling effects. A 1954 national opinion survey found 41 percent of Americans felt that "some [or all] people do not feel as free to say what they think as they used to," suggesting a significant societal chilling effect.[11] Though the US Supreme Court's initial response to these laws was disturbingly tepid and deferential, it eventually shifted course as the excesses of McCarthyism became more pervasive and clear.[12] As the Court began to scrutinize these laws more closely, it found chilling effects a compelling and flexible concept to convey the impact these overreaching laws and government measures had on people's rights, especially First Amendment speech, and to justify declaring them constitutionally invalid.[13]

The concept of chilling effects would endure beyond the McCarthy Era, in part because new threats to speech and other fundamental freedoms inevitably also endured. For instance, as the anti-communist crusade began to subside in most parts of America by the late 1950s, in the Southern states – where some of the most repressive anti-communist laws had been enacted – governments and law enforcement repurposed those laws to target and suppress the civil rights movement.[14] These tactics accelerated after the Supreme Court's landmark decision in *Brown v. Board of Education*,[15] which held that legally mandated racial segregation in public schools was unconstitutional.[16] Courts would similarly employ chilling effects reasoning and arguments in ensuing years, scrutinizing these and other laws and government tactics aimed at suppressing and deterring civil rights activism.[17]

Today, this conventional and legalistic conceptualization of chilling effects is the predominant public and scholarly understanding. It is apparent in varying forms in legal scholarship examining chilling effects more generally,[18] and law and economics in particular.[19] And as one of the most "pervasive concepts" in First Amendment law,[20] it is considered and applied by lawyers and judges every day across the country, and regularly invoked by courts to invalidate laws.[21] This predominance is largely because this is the conceptualization the US Supreme Court embraced in its jurisprudence, though First Amendment scholars such as Schauer, who would develop and explain the theory underlying the Court's doctrinal reasoning,[22] also helped ensure its preeminence. As an account of chilling effects focused on overreaching government laws and actions, it also fits well with an American cultural and constitutional ethos premised on liberty, individualism, and limited government.[23] There is also an argument that the influence of conventional understanding can be linked to conceptualizations of power exercised through sovereignty, law, and punishment that have been with us for centuries.[24] In other words, its influence is present and ongoing both in law and the public imagination.

With these American and Western legal and cultural origins, this conceptualization has also become the predominant one employed by lawyers, legal scholars, and courts around the world, with Canada, the United Kingdom, Europe, Australia, New Zealand, India, Malaysia, and South Africa being good examples, but not the only ones.[25] My home country of Canada offers a compelling example. Legal scholarship has tended to focus on conventional debates on how uncertain laws, regulations, and legal doctrines have a chilling effect on speech.[26] In the past, the Supreme Court of Canada has invoked chilling effects in many cases, often along these lines – such as citing it to justify modifying defamation law,[27] or to strike down vague and overly broad prohibitions on hate speech as unconstitutional violations of free expression.[28] In each case, the Court employed a conventional understanding of chilling effects that is hardly distinguishable from that employed by the US Supreme Court. This is typical. Nearly every jurisdiction in which the idea of chilling effects has been recognized in the law has likewise adopted this conventional approach, including the common law world and beyond.[29]

Yet, despite its far-reaching impact and global influence, this leading conventional theory is deeply flawed. When its premises and assumptions are interrogated, they do not hold up. The empirical evidence simply does not support the claim that fear of legal harms is what animates chilling effects in most cases, at least not this legal fear alone. It is thus also too narrow. In focusing exclusively on concerns about government laws and overreach, it misses chilling effects in a range other contexts, particularly those due to private sector practices. Its individualistic focus means it also misses the broader collective impacts of chilling effects, such as those associated with mass surveillance. Lastly, it neglects key insights from social science and social theory about the nature and impact of chilling effects. In short, we need a different approach to fully understand chilling effects.

THE CHILL OF THE MCCARTHY ERA

Though chilling effects came to prominence in the US Supreme Court, it was not the first to employ the term in the modern era. Rather, it was Paul Freund, a Harvard Law School professor, who first used the term "chilling effects" in an influential 1951 law review article entitled *The Supreme Court and Civil Liberties*.[30] In analyzing how the Supreme Court had been addressing civil liberties issues, especially the

First Amendment, he explained, soberly and methodologically, how vague or overly broad laws could "chill" or deter conduct that is both constitutionally protected and socially desirable, as people would play it safe and self-censor, rather than risk punishment.[31] To avoid these negative impacts, he reasoned, the public interest in free expression would be served if such statutes were held invalid as contrary to the First Amendment.[32]

At the time he was writing, the anti-communist furor of a new "Red Scare" was in full swing.[33] At the federal level, various agencies and bureaucracies had been conducting investigations of disloyalty and communist subversion for years, including the Federal Bureau of Investigation and the infamous House Un-American Activities Committee, founded in 1938.[34] Similar investigations were likewise being conducted at the state level.[35] A year earlier, in February 1950, Senator Joseph McCarthy made his sensationalist claim that he possessed a list of over 200 communists and communist sympathizers in the federal government – then controlled by Truman and the Democratic Party – which he intended to root out and expose through Senate investigations.[36] In fact, countless repressive anti-communist laws and ordinances had already been enacted across the country by the time Truman was elected president in 1945,[37] including the notorious Smith Act, which made it unlawful to advocate for the overthrow of the government or to be a member of any such subversive group.[38] Many more such laws would follow.[39]

Oddly, Freund did not mention any of this broader context, though he was doubtlessly aware of it. In a brief paragraph raising "basic questions" about the Smith Act, he acknowledged the "fearful" task facing the Supreme Court in addressing the legality of the Act in a forthcoming case, wherein the Court would have to weigh "tensions" and "claims of public order" against what Freund called the "exhortations" of the "nonconformist,"[40] a rather stilted and cautious terminology given the countless people whose lives had already been ruined due to persecution under the law, often for no more than their political affiliations.[41] On this count, Freund's recommendation that the Court should avoid looking "absurd in the sight of history" suggests awareness that the "Red Scare" would pass and its legal excesses – like the Smith Act – would be judged by history in a far different light.[42] But why was he so oblique? Perhaps Freund was himself afflicted by the very chilling effects of which he wrote. After all, teachers and university professors across the country, including at Harvard, were subject to extensive federal and state investigations into communist ties or sympathies in the late 1940s and 1950s.[43] By 1955, 36 percent of academics reported that their colleagues were censoring themselves on controversial and unpopular topics.[44]

Freund's discussion of chilling effects was also not an extensive elaboration. He did not set out these details as to the broader legal or societal climate. He did not even expressly lay out all of his premises and assumptions. It was simply an *argument* – based on chilling effects reasoning. Yet there are elements here that would later become conventional understanding of chilling effects in law. Freund, after all, was a leading constitutional law expert, described by the late Justice Lewis Powell, Jr., as the "foremost constitutional scholar of his day."[45] When he wrote, people noticed, including the US Supreme Court. In fact, through clerking and his time at Harvard as both a professor and student, Freund had developed personal relationships with several of the justices.[46] On this occasion his argument also did not go unnoticed.

FROM ARGUMENT TO DOCTRINE

Less than a year later, Justice Felix Frankfurter, who decades earlier taught Freund when the latter was a student at Harvard,[47] referenced Freund's notion of a "chill" in a 1951 case, *Wieman v. Updegraff*.[48] At issue in that case was an anti-communist Oklahoma loyalty statute, typical of the period, that required all state employees – including the plaintiff college teachers – to swear a "loyalty oath" that, among other things, they had not associated with any "subversive" groups in the previous five years.[49] While the plurality decided on procedural grounds, Justice Frankfurter, writing a concurring opinion, went further. He relied on Freund's chilling effect argument. He found the loyalty statute would "chill" the "free play of spirit" teachers must cultivate, contrary to First Amendment protections.[50] Though he did not cite Freund, he was surely the source of the idea. A few years later, Chief Justice Earl Warren would likewise invoke Freund's chilling effects reasoning in a case involving film licensing and censorship.[51] Only this time, Freund's article was explicitly cited.[52]

These would not be the U.S Supreme Court's last reference to chilling effects. Indeed, in the Court's hands the idea of legal "chilling effects" would take on far greater prominence, with Justice William J. Brennan, among the most influential jurists of twentieth century,[53] taking the lead.[54] In a series of cases in the late 1950s and continuing through the 1960s – many involving overreaching McCarthy Era laws and government measures later repurposed in the South to suppress civil rights activists – the Court would develop chilling effects from a First Amendment argument into a broader "chilling effects doctrine."[55] That doctrine essentially involves various rules and principles that treat laws that may chill speech with a "high level of suspicion," and is now fully entrenched in First Amendment law.[56]

A classic example of the Court's chilling effects doctrine can be seen in Justice Brennan's 1964 opinion in *New York Times Co. v. Sullivan*, a famous case involving free speech and the civil rights movement.[57] In that case, L. B. Sullivan, the police commissioner in Montgomery, Alabama, had successfully sued the newspaper for libel in Alabama state court after it published a full page advertisement criticizing the Montgomery police for their treatment of Martin Luther King., Jr. and civil rights protesters.[58] However, the Supreme Court concluded that the broad Alabama libel law, on which the plaintiff's lawsuit was based, was invalid, as it would likely have an unconstitutional "chilling effect" on First Amendment protected speech:

> A rule compelling the critic of official conduct to guarantee the truth of all his factual assertions – and to do so on pain of libel judgments virtually unlimited in amount – leads to a comparable "self-censorship"... Under such a rule, would-be critics of official conduct may be deterred from voicing their criticism, even though it is believed to be true and even though it is, in fact, true, because of doubt whether it can be proved in court or fear of the expense of having to do so. They tend to make only statements which "steer far wider of the unlawful zone."[59]

Key ideas expressed in this passage would later become conventional aspects of chilling effects theory – a concern for self-censorship; a deterrence theory of chilling effects; and fear of a legal harm, causing the chill, that arises due to the costs and uncertainty of the legal system. However, it would not be until Frederick Schauer published his oft cited account over a decade later that the behavioral theory underlying chilling effects doctrine would be more thoroughly elaborated.

SCHAUER'S CHILLING EFFECTS THEORY

Schauer, a legal scholar best known for his work on the First Amendment,[60] would offer the first comprehensive theoretical treatment of chilling effects in 1978. His article *Fear, Risk, and the First Amendment: Unraveling the Chilling Effect*, extensively analyzed relevant First Amendment cases and developed the Supreme Court's doctrinal reasoning about chilling effects into a fuller account that blended legal theory and law and economics.[61] Though Schauer was not the first or last First Amendment scholar to analyze chilling effects theory,[62] his account is today considered the "leading" theory and "definitive" treatment.[63] In Schauer's hands, chilling effects reasoning and doctrine, largely shaped by the U.S. Supreme Court until that point, would become a full fledged theory that synthesized legal theory and rational decision theory, a branch of law and economics. Schauer's work would give chilling effects more legal, theoretical, and scholarly heft, and link it to a movement in legal scholarship that would soon dominate the legal field – law and economics.[64]

Indeed, Schauer's main contribution was to provide a proper theoretical foundation for the behavioral assumptions underlying chilling effects doctrine, and what is conventional understanding of chilling effects today. Chilling effects, conventional understanding holds, is based on a deterrence theory – a person is deterred from speaking or doing out of fear of some harm, in this case, legal harm. To explain *how* people arrive at the decision to self-censor, in light of legal harms, he drew on rational decision theory. He posited that a person engages in a form of rational cost-benefit analysis – an assessment of risk – before speaking or acting and decides to avoid doing so, as a way of avoiding the feared legal threat or harm.[65] This way of thinking about individual decision making and choice is consistent with rational decision theory, a central tenant of law and economics.[66] This is what I meant earlier when I said the "fear" in conventional theories is both rational and calculated.

Schauer also articulated the normative foundation for the conventional understanding of chilling effects, which is less often explored in legal scholarship and rarely so in jurisprudence. This conceptualization of chilling effects largely rests on liberal theory and its various classic themes. These normative commitments are also apparent in Schauer's 1978 article, though he expounds them in greater depth elsewhere.[67] He cites some of the classics in the liberal tradition,[68] including John Milton's *Areopagitica* and John Stuart Mill's *On Liberty*,[69] and more contemporary liberal theorists like Ronald Dworkin and Alexander Meiklejohn. The key rationales for being concerned about chilling effects very much track classic First Amendment rationales and normative commitments. First, freedom of speech and expression is a net positive for society, providing an essential truth identification function[70] or underpinning self-government.[71] Schauer echoes these sentiments, citing each of these "positive virtues" of freedom of speech.[72] Second, is commitment to skepticism about state interventions, especially in matters of free expression, embodied in Mill's famous "harm principle."[73] Third, is the classical liberal commitment to individual liberty and freedom – what some theorists call autonomy – which has both an individual and societal value.[74] Though Schauer does not mention the importance of autonomy, he does nod towards the "transcendent value" of speech and "individual liberty."[75] And certainly other works on chilling effects and the First Amendment elaborate that rationale.[76] A chill on speech by government laws offends each of these normative commitments, undermining the benefits of speech, limited government, and individual liberty and freedom.

This is only a brief outline, but it is easy to see how this conventional theory of chilling effects theory would be embraced in American constitutionalism, given its individualistic and libertarian orientation. This account, and its normative foundations, provides powerful normative justification to closely scrutinize state efforts to regulate speech and similar constitutionally protected activities, especially those inconsistent with Mill's harm principle. It also justifies legal rules like the judicially shaped "chilling effects doctrine," which encourages courts to treat such state efforts with suspicion, in line with classic liberal or libertarian skepticism for such state interventions.

THEORETICAL AND EMPIRICAL PROBLEMS

There are, however, significant problems with a chilling effects theory based on rational fear of legal harm, including theoretical, empirical, and normative limitations. Many of these problems center around the deterrence theory upon which this conventional chilling effects theory sits, which is likewise based on rational decision theory from law and economics. In the decades since the Supreme Court first embraced chilling effects First Amendment claims and Schauer published his account,[77] researchers from a range of social science fields have systematically tested the theory's assumptions and effectiveness, and they are often not empirically supported.

First, an extensive collection of experimental studies in psychology and other disciplines show that people do not make decisions as deterrence theory assumes.[78] People do not regularly engage in rational cost calculations and even when they do, situational pressures may mean it is not necessarily rational.[79] People are often also not sufficiently aware of the law or state activities such that any possible legal harm or sanction could impact their decision about speaking or acting.[80] It *may* be that many people are reasoning to avoid other kinds of harms, like privacy harms. I address that point later in in Chapter 2 – though this claim *still* assumes a cost-benefit analysis that empirical studies suggest is not likely happening.

Second – and perhaps because of these flawed assumptions – there is little empirical evidence that deterrence actually works.[81] That is to say, the evidence suggests that a rational or calculated fear and avoidance of known legal sanction or harm – like a statute imposing a legal punishment – is rarely a central or even important reason why most people might modify their behavior to comply with the law.[82] This is not to say that deterrence and related chill never happens – not at all. As I will argue later, when people or groups are specifically targeted with legal threats, this like of personalization can have profound chilling effects. The point here is that in most cases, where you do not have that kind of targeting, evidence supporting deterrence is "modest to negligible"[83] and, in the cases where deterrence *does* impact, it requires a very specific set of conditions that are not often present in day to day contexts.[84] This empirical weakness and specificity for deterrence theory also means that this theory of chilling effects as fear of legal harm, based on deterrence, has little predictive power. It is, as Darlow and Robinson say of deterrence theory, "unpredictable."[85] So, the leading conventional chilling effects theory, which rests on a legalistic deterrence theory, is both empirically weak and unpredictable. It cannot, for instance, predict chilling effects, nor their scope and magnitude.

Third, this legalistic theory is too narrow and has little explanatory power for chilling effects in a range of different contexts – beyond say legal statutes or regulations – where there is no obvious legal harm for people to fear and thus chill their behavior. One compelling example of this is chilling effects associated with surveillance. There are now several empirical studies demonstrating how online surveillance can have a chilling effect on people's behavior online, including the information they read, search for, or access.[86] But this theory of chilling effects based on rational and calculated fear of legal harm cannot account for these impacts, as there is no obvious "legal harm" that would cause the chill.

For instance, take my study that I talked about at the outset of the book. That study explored the impact that NSA surveillance programs had on people's use of Wikipedia – the online encyclopedia. Given Wikipedia's immense popularity as a source for information in the United States and globally,[87] I hypothesized that people may be chilled from accessing more privacy-sensitive content on Wikipedia due to awareness that their activities may be monitored by one of the many NSA surveillance programs disclosed by Snowden and intensely covered by other U.S. and international media in June 2013 and months thereafter.[88] Not only that, but documents leaked by Snowden, and also covered by *The Washington Post* that June, confirmed that Wikipedia was one of the sites explicitly targeted by the NSA's PRISM surveillance program.[89]

To test that hypothesis, I examined Wikipedia article "view count" data for a group of privacy-sensitive Wikipedia articles – those articles on terrorism-related topics like "dirty bomb," "suicide attack," and "Al Qaeda"; essentially Wikipedia content that may raise privacy concerns for internet users if they knew the government was monitoring their online activities – as they would following the Snowden revelations. The data basically offered a measure of how many people viewed the Wikipedia articles in any given month. By examining this data for the months before, during, and after June 2013, I could spot any changes in view counts or viewing trends either consistent or inconsistent with a chilling effect. To get a scale of the readership and popularity of Wikipedia, my data set for these privacy-sensitive Wikipedia articles constituted nearly 81 million total article views over the course of the 32-month period I studied.[90] In other words, there were tens of millions of people captured in the data.

The results evinced clear and compelling evidence of surveillance chilling effects whereby likely tens of millions of people, maybe more, were being chilled from reading, searching informing themselves freely online due to the NSA surveillance.[91] First, the data showed a large, sudden, and statistically significant drop of 693,617 total article views in June 2013, a 25 percent drop off from the month before. This was consistent with a chilling effect in June 2013 due to public awareness about government surveillance due to reporting on the Snowden leaks in the U.S. and internationally that month. However, there was *also* a statistically significant change in the long term overall trend in monthly Wikipedia article views – that went from increasing 41,421 views month to month before June 2013 to a decrease of 67,513 in views per month after. Both of these findings can be seen in the visualization at Figure 1.1:

The vertical line represents mid-June 2013, helping illustrate the impacts of the surveillance revelations before and after that month. The 25 percent drop off in June 2013 can be clearly seen, with the pre-June trend line peaking with over 3,000,000 views and then a significant drop off in June, with the post-June trend line starting far lower – beginning just over 2,300,000 article views. The change in overall change in viewing trends is also easily seen. Pre-June, total article views increase monthly peaking just before June 2013 while after, there is the 25 percent drop in June, and then even after that, article views continue to decline month to month.

Further analyses confirmed this chilling effect. First, I repeated the same analysis for the *most* privacy-sensitive Wikipedia terrorism related articles within the broader set. Next, I repeated the analysis on three other groups of Wikipedia articles just to compare view trends over the same months – including articles concerning "security," "infrastructure," and the most popular Wikipedia articles over the same

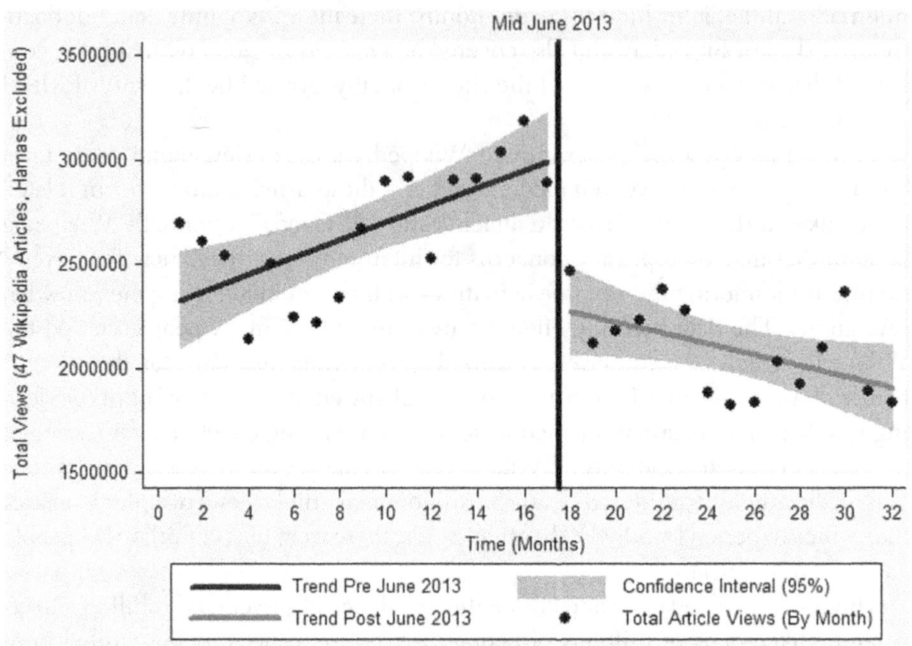

FIGURE 1.1 Chilling effects visualized. Pre and post June 2013 article view trends. The sudden drop in views and trend shift – from increasing monthly views over to decreasing after June 2013 – is consistent with a significant and lasting chilling effect.

32 month period.[92] If it was a chilling effect I was seeing in the data, then these even more privacy concerning articles would show more impact. While the comparator groups of Wikipedia articles, which included more benign content that would not raise privacy concerns, would not show any viewing impacts or changes around June 2013. And that is precisely what I found – the more privacy sensitive articles showed even greater impact, with views dropping 26 percent in June coupled with an even steeper monthly trend reversal.[93] And the comparator Wikipedia articles showed no June 2013 impacts.

When designing the study, I thought that if I found any evidence of a chilling effect, it would be in the month of June 2013, when media coverage of Snowden's disclosures was most intense thus chilling people from reading privacy sensitive articles on Wikipedia. However, I did not expect the chill to be so severe – the 25 percent and 26 percent drop offs I found were substantial. But most eye-opening was the longer term impact of the chilling effects. The overall Wikipedia article view trend reversal continued not just a few months following June 2013, but for more than a full year to August 2014 – the month I stopped collecting data and began writing up my results. But the trend in the data suggested the chilling effect due to the online government surveillance continued for months and months thereafter – possibly with a permanent impact.

My findings would also corroborate those of an earlier 2015 Massachusetts Institute of Technology (MIT) study on Google search traffic by Alex Marthews and Catherine Tucker. They similarly found a statistically significant reduction in Google searches after the June 2013 Snowden revelations for certain search terms that would raise privacy concerns for Internet users aware of NSA surveillance online.[94] Specifically, following the widespread media coverage of the Snowden disclosures in *The Guardian* and *Washington Post* that June, across 41 countries included in the Google search data set, including the United States, they found a statistically significant 4 percent reduction searches involving terms that internet users perceived may get them into "trouble" if the government were monitoring their online activities.[95] Those search terms included, for example, terms like "white powder," "dirty bomb," and "assassination."[96] Among non-American internet users, they found also found a statistically significant reduction in searches involving search terms that users perceived may personally embarrass them – terms like "abortion," "suicide," "and "viagra."[97] As with my Wikipedia study – awareness of online surveillance, or its possibility, discouraging internet users from searching for certain sensitive topics and content, is powerful evidence of a surveillance chilling effect.

I'll talk more about the implications of these findings later in the book. For now, the important point here that they pose a very big problem for the conventional legal theory of chilling effects. Why? That theory simply cannot explain these results, and the chilling effects they document, as there are simply no clear legal harms or threats involved. There is nothing illegal about searching on Google or other Wikipedia articles. Nor were there any media stories of internet users being arrested for accessing Wikipedia articles or any similar online content or information over the course of the 32 month study. At the very most, there was a vague and uncertain possibility of legal harms – like prosecutions in the future based on data collected and some as yet unknown statue or law – but such a vague future threat would not be enough for the cost benefit analysis assumed by traditional forms of deterrence theory. In short, there was no legal harm to cause the chilling effect observed. Something else is going on here, which a law-focused account cannot explain.

A final problem with this conventional chilling effects theory focused on legal harms is that it is normatively thin. As earlier noted, its liberal or libertarian foundations and skepticism for state regulations offer, as earlier noted, justification for limits on overreaching laws and governmental activities – as the chilling effects doctrine does within First Amendment jurisprudence. However, it has little to say about corporate or commercial actors whose activities also have chilling effects on people's behavior – like corporate surveillance or invasive forms of data collection.[98] These private sector activities likewise often pose no threat of "legal harm," so the theory both cannot explain these effects nor does it offer a justification for curtailing them. As such, this theory has very little to say about extractive and exploitative commercial surveillance practices, and their broader context in today's information economy.

Schauer anticipates some of these problems and thus in his work limits the focus of chilling effects theory to *lawful* activities and First Amendment protected speech, assuming as a premise the position that *more* speech is necessarily a positive for society.[99] But speech can also cause societal harms, especially if it is corporate speech and protected by the First Amendment based on chilling effect concerns. In fact, scholars like Amanda Shanor, Robert Post, and Mila Sohani have documented how corporations have employed the First Amendment, and the chilling effects doctrine itself, toward neo-liberal and de-regulatory ends – like having courts strike down or gut positive regulations.[100] For instance, in its controversial decision in *Citizens United v. FEC*[101] striking down third party election spending restrictions under the First Amendment, the Supreme Court's conservative majority cited "chilling effects" on corporate speakers *fourteen times* and used chilling effect concerns as a central justification for its ruling. Here, chilling effects have been weaponized to undercut legislation that benefits society, in this case protecting critical democratic processes from the corrupting influences of wealthy companies and individuals. From this angle of view, this conventional theory not only offers to way to critique these developments, but actively enable them.

Lawful activities, including speech, can have also have chilling effects – like forms of threatening speech and harassment, something that has been magnified in today's social media environment. As Danielle Keats Citron has argued, cyber-harassment and other forms of online abuse – like targeting an individual persistently with threats, defamation, and privacy invasions can cause severe distress, even fear of physical harm.[102] That, in turn, has a "totalizing and devastating" chilling effect on victims, chilling not only their speech but often their entire lives.[103] Again, this theory offers no way to resolve a conflict between *these* chilling effects and those that might arise due to state legislation – like a cyber-harassment law – enacted to address them.[104] In short, today's leading conventional theory of chilling effects, based on a fear of legal harms, helps us navigate chilling effects arising due to state actions – mostly legislative actions – but little else. It is simply too narrow, theoretically and normatively.

2

Privacy's Useful but Limited Theory

In Chapter 1, we examined the leading conventional theory of chilling effects – as a rational and calculated fear of legal harm. It trained our eyes on the legal, statutory, and regulatory impact of government, and theorized chilling effects as a deterrent effect leading to self-censorship. But we learned this formulation is far too narrow – it could not explain chilling effects beyond the impact of laws, and offered no insights as to chill associated with privacy-invasive government actions – like surveillance – or those of businesses and commercial enterprise. It also neglected the insights of social science and social theory that would help us understand the impact of chilling effects beyond self-censorship alone.

A second privacy-focused conventional understanding addresses some of these shortcomings – chilling effects as a response to privacy threats and harms. Here, chilling effects are sometimes a result of a visceral, even psychological, fear of these threats and harms or in other cases more rational – a deliberate choice to avoid these harms or their risk in the future. This conceptualization emerged largely in American legal scholarship in the early twenty-first century, especially following the new privacy threats of the post-9/11 era. Daniel Solove, a leading privacy scholar, offered the first extensive elaboration, although other influential privacy scholars like Julie Cohen and Neil Richards have each advanced similar theories and conceptualizations. This understanding moves us beyond mere legal harms, to theorize chilling effects due to privacy threats like surveillance, data collection, and invasive information practices, and their implications.[1] Privacy theories of chilling effects also better account for the new social, commercial, security, and technological realities of the early twenty-first century – the context in which Solove first set out his account – including the emergence of the internet and digital media, and the new privacy challenges these technologies posed. And, at least in the cases of Solove, Cohen, and Richards, better account for social theory and behavioral science.

Yet, critical problems persist. I refer to this privacy-focused chilling effects theory and others like it as *conventional* because while it moves us beyond legal harms, it often retains other central tenets of conventional understanding, including rational decision-making, deterrence theory, and self-censorship. The theory does not so much depart from conventional understanding of chilling effects as fear of legal harm, as simply expand it to encompass privacy harms and concerns. As such, the theory inherits many of the same limitations.

NEW CENTURY, NEW THREATS

This new privacy-focused account of chilling effects, by no coincidence, would emerge at a time of complex new privacy threats. As the internet and other new communication technologies emerged in the late 1990s, American legal scholars like Julie Cohen, Jeff Rosen, Anita Allen, Paul Schwartz, and Solove grappled with the new challenges these technologies posed to privacy. Allen, for instance, wrote of privacy "as a matter of escaping as well as embracing encumbrances of identity" and lamented the "rapid erosion" of privacy new technologies were ushering in.[2] Similarly, Cohen, Rosen, Solove, and Schwartz worried about the rise of "networked society" and the negative effects of new privacy invasive technologies and information, collection, and retention practices among government and industry.[3]

The terrorist attacks on September 11, 2001 were also a transformative event. Following the attacks, governments around the world established new large-scale surveillance programs, infrastructure, and data collection practices to identify and track terrorism and other national security threats.[4] These expansive new surveillance and data collection powers, combined with internet and other emerging digital technologies, posed complex new threats to privacy, autonomy, and freedom, not just in the private sphere – as Samuel Warren and Louis Brandeis and others in the Anglo-American tradition had theorized[5] – but in public spaces as well.[6]

Continental thinkers like Hannah Arendt, Jürgen Habermas, and Michel Foucault offered American legal scholars new ways to think about these emerging surveillance practices and privacy challenges, and how they impact freedom, autonomy, and self-development.[7] Arendt, for instance, wrote of the importance of sanctity in the private sphere to full engagement in public life. Privacy was the "dark and hidden side of the public realm."[8] To "have no private place," she wrote, was to be "no longer human."[9] Indeed, Habermas and Arendt's construction of the public sphere as a space free from coercion and authoritarian control both influenced and reflected a European concern with public sphere privacy, but also resonated with American privacy scholars concerned with government overreach.

The work of Foucault also resonated. Decades earlier, he had used Jeremy Bentham's famous "Panopticon" prison design – where prisoners were always possibly being watched, but could not know – to forge a powerful metaphor to understand surveillance in modern society.[10] In Foucault's panopticon society the threat of constantly being watched helped to discipline and control people. With governments and the private sector now harnessing digital technology to track and observe in powerful and pervasive new ways, these ideas were prescient. The panopticon has since become one of the most widely cited metaphors.[11] For example, sociologist David Lyon, founder of the surveillance studies field, would draw heavily on Foucault's work to understand the post-9/11 surveillance paradigm.[12]

CHILLING EFFECTS AND PRIVACY

This is the context in which a new theoretical approach to chilling effects – as fear of privacy threats and harms – took shape in American law and legal scholarship. Daniel Solove's work has been critical to moving chilling effects theory and scholarship beyond the legalistic conventional account. Though others had theorized the chilling effects of privacy threats before him, Solove was the first to offer a more comprehensive account in a series of articles in 2006 and 2007, and later expanded in his 2010 book *Understanding Privacy*.[13] Solove's work on chilling effects reflects his broader pragmatic approach to privacy, which is widely cited and influential.[14] He rejects attempts to singularly define or conceptualize privacy, preferring instead a framework that analyzes the subject pluralistically and contextually via taxonomies and categorizations of various activities that raise privacy problems, issues, and harms.[15] In delineating that framework, Solove explores chilling effects and their impacts while elaborating risks and harms associated with post-9/11 privacy threats like surveillance, data collection, and other data and information practices.[16]

Solove did not offer a monolithic chilling effects theory. Rather, in the course of elaborating his "taxonomy" of privacy harms in various contexts, and in linking privacy harms to First Amendment values, he discussed and theorized chilling effects. In doing so, he built on existing conventional understanding and expanded it to include new forms of chill and self-censorship associated with privacy threats, like surveillance and data collection practices.[17] He theorized chilling effects in two main ways. First, on an individual level, where people are chilled from exercising their rights and freedoms not due to fear of legal harm or punishment but as a response to increased risk of future privacy-related harms – like harms to reputation if private or embarrassing information collected about a person under surveillance is publicly disclosed or shared[18] or increased risk of identity theft or fraud due to misappropriated information.[19] Sometimes chilling effects are a product of a more visceral fear of such privacy harms, but at other times, it is more of a rational response, like avoiding certain activities due to increased risk of future privacy harms.

Second, Solove also explored broader societal-level impacts. Citing Foucault and the "panopticon effect," he theorized that widespread surveillance and data collection about people creates a broader atmosphere comparable to "environmental pollution" that promotes self-censorship or chilling effects.[20] Here, people under surveillance perceived a "power imbalance" in society and are chilled by increased risk of "abuses of power" – like "fear" of reprisals for protesting government or engaging in unpopular or unconventional things – creating an overall inhibiting effect.[21] Furthermore, being under observation increases the possibility of being "caught" in some form of immoral or illegal activity that could lead to either privacy or legal harms,[22] like avoiding engaging in certain activities "for fear that they will wind up on a watch list or suspicious persons list."[23] In each of these examples, the chilling effect remains a deterrent effect, but arises due to fear of privacy harms.

Solove also enriched the normative dimensions of chilling effects theory. Given his extensive analysis of chilling effects in constitutional jurisprudence, he understood well how they implicate First Amendment interests like freedom of speech, expression, and association.[24] In making this connection, he was also able to elaborate how chilling effects impacted foundational privacy interests that also require these things, particularly in private and intimate contexts. For example, he drew on Cohen, Schwartz, and Ruth Gavison among others, to understand how chilling effects threatened a person's "moral autonomy"[25] and "self-determination."[26] Chilling effects threatened each of these core privacy values.

Other leading privacy scholars like Cohen, Richards, and Calo have theorized chilling effects due to information privacy invasions – like surveillance and observation.[27] They have likewise strengthened its normative foundations, connecting chilling effects to similar critical interests fundamental to privacy, like intellectual freedom, creativity, personhood, and self-development. For example, Cohen's critical early work on internet privacy theorized anonymity as a shield from the chilling effects of digital surveillance.[28] And Richards' powerful concept of intellectual privacy – which concerns an intimate zone where one has the freedom to read, think, and communicate privately – highlights the importance of guarding against certain privacy-related chilling effects to ensure personal freedom, autonomy, and self-development.[29] It also shows how chilling effects have implications, on a societal level, for deliberation in healthy democratic societies.[30] Indeed, by theorizing surveillance chilling effects not just as an individual concern but a societal one as well, Solove, Richards, Cohen, and others provide a stronger justification to take action on chilling effects that impact behavior beyond just speech alone.

This is an important shift. Foucault's idea of a panopticon society, after all, rested on an assumption of a broad societal chilling effect: The threat of constant surveillance deterred people from acting freely. But First Amendment "chilling effects" scholars like Schauer did not readily make this connection, given their primary concern with overreaching laws and their impact on individuals and speech, rather than broader privacy and societal effects. Nor have the courts. Unlike the first conventional theory we discussed in Chapter 1 – chilling effects as fear of legal harms – which was embraced by the US Supreme Court and developed into First Amendment doctrine, courts have been much more ambivalent about recognizing chilling effects associated with privacy harms.

This is where these privacy-focused works on chilling effects have made a critical contribution. And a societal view of privacy, central to each of these scholars' work, led them to theorize the role of chilling effects beyond simple individualistic legal harms.

LIMITATIONS

But there are important problems here as well. A theory of chilling effects as a fearful or rational avoidance response to privacy threats and harms remains largely consistent with conventional understanding of chilling effects discussed in Chapter 1, and so inherits many of the same limitations. As noted earlier, this conceptualization still relies predominantly on forms of deterrence theory. Solove writes that "[d]etermining the existence of a chilling effect is complicated by the difficulty of defining and identifying deterrence."[31] And elsewhere, he wrote that the value in guarding against chilling effects is not just apparent by focusing on the individual who is "deterred from exercising their rights," but harms to society as well.[32] While chilling effects certainly do include a deterrence dimension – people *are* discouraged from certain speech or activities – focusing primarily on that neglects the productive side of chilling effects, the more inhibited and conforming speech and activities. There is no question that Solove explores how surveillance can cause conformity, but he still largely theorizes chill in terms of deterrence and fear of privacy harm.

First, in reasoning about chilling effects, Solove at times appears to accept the idea that people engage in decision-making comparable to a rational cost–benefit analysis, determining privacy "risks" before acting,[33] the only difference here being the assessment involves not just risks of legal harms but privacy ones as well. Cohen, among the most persistent critics of conventional conceptions of privacy, argues that most privacy scholars ignore how subjectivity is "shaped" by social and cultural processes,[34] and thus privacy theories based on an assumed autonomous subject able to assess risks and consent to privacy choices are inevitably flawed.[35] As earlier noted, deterrence theory's assumption that people engage in such rational decision-making is not well supported by empirical research. Moreover, there is also a substantial body of research illustrating what behavioral economist Alessandro Acquisti has deemed the "privacy paradox" – where people who self-report caring about privacy in practice are not willing to pay for it or will trade it away for small rewards.[36] But simply because people reason *badly* about privacy and chilling effects does not mean it is not happening. In fact, there are reasons to question the paradox and Acquisti himself has also found evidence to be skeptical due to the highly contextual nature of privacy itself.[37] In short, evidence suggests privacy reasoning is complex and context-specific and is thus very unpredictable – at least using behavioral economic models and theories.

However, the fact that privacy reasoning may not be predictable through economic models does not mean that it is not happening. There will no doubt be cases where, as Solove reasons, increased risks of privacy harms – like disclosure of embarrassing information or fear of identity theft – will have chilling effects; this does not need to be a product of a precise cost–benefit analysis, but simply based on a reasonable fear or concerns about how personal information might be used or disclosed in the future, or how information collection might increase risk of such disclosure. At the very least, we can say that an account that relies on a theory of assessment of privacy risks, will be less helpful in explaining cases of chilling effects where people are not aware of the privacy risks or threats at stake, and therefore are acting without any deliberate assessment of privacy risks and harms; and even when aware will have little predictive or explanatory power as to the existence, scope, or magnitude of chilling effects for different contexts given the complexity and uncertainties in privacy reasoning.

Second, while this theory has more explanatory power for chilling effects beyond mere fear of legal harms, it still has important limitations here too. A theory of chilling effects as a fearful or avoidance response to privacy harms, for instance, can explain the results of my Wikipedia study discussed earlier. There were no apparent legal risks for internet users to read the Wikipedia articles after Snowden revelations about National Security Agency surveillance online, so Schauer's account could not explain the results. By contrast, there certainly could be *privacy* concerns about that surveillance, like a concern that reading these articles on topics associated with "terrorism" may lead one to end up on a terrorism watch list – a privacy harm. Or perhaps information about these reading habits could be later disclosed or shared with third parties, leading to reputational damage or possible blackmail. This is no problem for a privacy theory of chilling effects.

However, such privacy theories have difficulty explaining chilling effects in other contexts where there is no such obvious privacy harm, like those done for social reasons. For example, a growing body of research in social psychology has documented what has been called a "watching eye" effect, wherein artificial surveillance cues – like simply a set of "watching" human eyes in the presence of participants – can have a chilling effect on their behavior. That is, the awareness of surveillance – even where participants *know* it is artificial and nobody is *actually* watching – promotes socially conforming or compliant behavior in a wide range of contexts.[38] This chilling effect leads participants to conform to pro-social norms like telling the truth, avoiding cheating, avoiding acting unconventionally, avoiding expressing views inconsistent with the perceived views of the group majority, and in other studies chilling antisocial behavior as well. A typical experimental set up in this research involves participants carrying out activities or interacting with other people in the presence of an image of a pair of eyes.[39] Interestingly, research shows that even where the "watching eye" is clearly artificial (e.g., the "gaze" deployed is simply a photo or image of an eye) these effects on behavior remain.[40] If the "watching eye" effect is real, it poses a problem for theories of chilling effects as fear of privacy harm, because there is no apparent privacy harm or threatened privacy harm here. There is no government conducting surveillance or harvesting, processing, and retaining information or data. There is also no private sector company doing the same. There is no apparent fear of future reprisal or data that could be disclosed to embarrass or harm the individual. A theory based on privacy threats or harm alone cannot explain these chilling effects.

Lastly, this privacy-focused conventional theory also has normative limitations. Solove and other privacy scholars have certainly added normative heft to chilling effects theory, speaking to how privacy-related impacts can negatively affect not just speech, but also other core individual interests – like personal freedom, intellectual privacy, autonomy, and self-development. On a societal scale, these impacts threaten deliberative democracy, creativity, and diversity of viewpoints in society. These impacts can be caused not just by government surveillance, but private sector surveillance and data gathering as well. So Solove's theory, and conventional theories like it, also provides a normative and theoretical foundation to critique private sector practices beyond state actions. This, too, is an important advancement from Schauer's exclusive focus on overreaching laws and government action.

However, like Schauer's account, a privacy theory of chilling effects like this offers no way to navigate cases of competing chilling effects. An example of this would be a privacy statute that might promote privacy – and thus guard against surveillance-related chilling effects – but might also impact – or chill – speech. In fact, First Amendment scholars like Eugene Volokh have argued that such privacy and data protection measures are unconstitutional restrictions on First Amendment speech.[41] Volokh openly acknowledges that forms of privacy invasion – like public exposure or disclosure of "embarrassing personal information" – can have a chilling effect on speech and public engagement, but he privileges speech, arguing it ought to be free of the chill of privacy restrictions or vague exceptions to such legislation.[42] Though Volokh's arguments have not gone uncontested,[43] versions of these same arguments are regularly advanced to oppose new privacy and data protection laws today. A comprehensive chilling effects theory ought to provide some normative guidance – via empirical or theoretical dimensions – to resolve these conflicts. However, a privacy- focused chilling effects theory offers no guidance beyond recognition of privacy-related issues, in addition to legal ones.

In fairness to Solove – and other scholars wrestling with chilling effects, privacy, and US law – his reasoning about chilling effects and privacy was constrained by the limits of First Amendment doctrine and the predominant conventional view shaped by Schauer. Indeed, when moving beyond those doctrinal limits, Solove clearly departs from a conventional chilling effects understanding – like when he speaks of the "panopticon effect" and how large-scale or mass surveillance can create broader societal dampening or inhibitory effects. Most importantly, Solove also sought out insights from fields beyond legal scholarship and economics, often relying on sociological insights from surveillance studies and continental philosophy to speak to *what* privacy-related chilling effects produce, something Schauer and conventional accounts largely neglect. This is an essential insight from Solove's critical work on chilling effects that brings us beyond the limits of deterrence-based theories.

MOVING BEYOND CONVENTIONAL THEORIES

I have argued that the two conventional theories of chilling effects – based on legal harms and privacy harms – have significant limitations. The former is primarily a deterrence-based theory and assumes a rational assessment of legal risks, yet empirical research shows these assumptions are not well supported. The latter, though more sophisticated, still often relies on similar deterrence assumptions – with chilling effects a rational means of avoiding risks associated with privacy threats and harms. Both lack explanatory power for chilling effects beyond contexts where more concrete and tangible harms – be they legal or privacy – are not present. And both have normative limitations as well.

Finally, these theories are primarily based on a narrow conception of chilling effects. These theories made assumptions about *why* people are chilled – by vague statutes or surveillance, for instance – and then examined the legal implications of this. And in doing so, they have focused predominantly on an *absence*, that is, self-censorship – people want to speak or do and decide not to do so – to the exclusion of examining more fully the broader implications of the more cautious, conforming, and compliant speech. A key part of these limitations was born out by criticisms that often relied on insights from other fields of social science and research to question the assumptions of conventional chilling effects theories, and provide more insight on the implications of what chilling effects *produce*.

Indeed, the US Supreme Court has itself admitted that chilling effects doctrine rests on certain behavioral assumptions and that if those assumptions are proven incorrect one day, it may abandon the doctrine.[44] I have argued in both Chapters 1 and 2 that those behavioral assumptions are no longer sound. In the ensuing chapters, I set out a new understanding of chilling effects – one more grounded in social science – and argue that chilling effects theory and doctrine, if not abandoned, needs to be substantially reformed.

PART II

A New Understanding

In this Part, I argue that a chilling effect is best understood as an act of conformity or compliance – though a more powerful form – in response to a perceived threat. Chilling effects mainly arise in contexts of uncertainty – such as uncertainty in the law or surveillance; observation – when people know they are being watched or are aware of the possibility; and personal threats – like receiving personal legal threats or threats of violence. And the actors responsible for chilling effects typically possess both power and authority, like government, police, or big business. When faced with these kinds of threats – observation, uncertainty, personal threats, and power/authority – social science tells us that people tend to engage in social conformity and compliance: They are far more likely to act the way they believe others would act in the same circumstance. That is, they engage in conformity.

Here, the person is chilled from speaking or doing as they wished, and instead conforms their behavior to comply with what they perceive to be the social norm in that context. Most often, this will mean complying with the law as the law can be said to reflect or express widely accepted social norms, even if they believe what they wanted to do was both legal and desirable in the circumstances. Or, in the example of surveillance, they avoid engaging in an activity, believing that doing so they may be cause or accused of breaking a social norm or rule, which can lead to other personal threats – like social ostracism or sanction. This might mean conforming speech so as not to contradict the majority opinion, refusing to engage in an activity that might be flagged as unconventional or antisocial, or redirecting and engaging in a different activity that would be considered more socially acceptable.

Why do people conform in these scenarios? There are many reasons why people engage in conformity. But the most important factor is threat perception – people conform out of fear and anxiety in response to threats to them personally or the group with which they identify, and conformity provides a sense of safety, protection, and support, among other benefits. Our tendency to conform when facing threats has a deeper psychological foundation, likely for evolutionary reasons – those who conformed in the past were more likely to survive, thrive, and prosper. Sometimes we engage in conformity subconsciously – we are not even aware that we are doing it. We are wired to be chilled, so to speak.

Chilling effects are a product of the same behavioral response that leads us to conformity, the only difference is that the threat that causes chilling effects isn't simply peer pressure or groupthink – although these do contribute to chilling effects – but threats posed by the most powerful actors in society: laws enforced by police; surveillance conducted by government or big business; or, online, the threats, stalking, and abuse by cyber-mobs and similar armies of trolls. Our response is conformity and compliance, that is to say, chilling effects. I elaborate this new conformity theory of chilling effects in the following chapters.

3

Social Chilling Effects

Many of the shortcomings in the conventional understanding of chilling effects stem from its neglect of insights from social science. But why would judges, lawyers, and legal scholars overlook whole fields of social research and theory? There are many reasons. One reason, Julie Cohen argues, is unlike theorists in other fields, legal theorists are largely committed to liberal theory and are thus uncomfortable discussing how social conditions shape individual behavior and choice.[1] They thus tend to overlook the power and influence of cultural norms and practices. As Ari Waldman has observed, social theory remains largely "under-developed" in legal scholarship.[2]

But there *are* conditions particular to chilling effects theory and doctrine that have led to a conventional understanding that has entrenched this neglect. Schauer's account, which as we saw in Chapter 1 has largely defined conventional understanding, was deeply influenced by law and economics. Chilling effects theory, he wrote, was "at bottom, just a branch of decision theory."[3] Decision theory is the theory of rational decision-making, or rational choice, a central focus of law and economics then, and now.[4] This is no coincidence. By the late 1970s, when Schauer wrote, law and economics was already ascendant, well on its way to becoming the predominant paradigm in the American legal academy.[5] In the decades since, it has enjoyed "powerful" and "widespread influence" in legal scholarship,[6] and has likewise captured key segments of policy-making and legal practice as well.[7] This influence has spread from North America to Europe and beyond.[8]

But law and economics is not simply a legal theory or approach to legal analysis. It also advances a theory of human behavior and social ordering. The neoclassical paradigm of law and economics, which emerged in the 1960s and 1970s, approached individuals as self-interested rational actors seeking to maximize their personal wealth or preferences, with decisions made based on a rational cost–benefit analysis.[9] It also adhered to legal centrism, the notion that government provides the only source of order and enforced rules in society.[10] Schauer, consistent with this paradigm, theorized that people are chilled or self-censor via a rational decision-making process, wherein people weigh the benefits of speaking against risks or costs.

A legal threat or harm would be detrimental to a person's self-interest, so they would self-censor as a result. Schauer's account likewise adheres to legal centrism, focusing almost exclusively on the chilling effect of statutes and legal rules. In short, this theory of human behavior and social order, like law and economics itself, has achieved "unparalleled dominance" in the legal academy,[11] applied by judges, lawyers, and scholars to a range of different legal contexts.[12] Chilling effects is simply one more area of law its influence has impacted.

That impact, however, ensured that chilling effects theory and doctrine has remained largely disconnected from a broader range of social theory. That's because law and economics, for its first two decades, largely ignored social and behavioral theories and insights from other social science fields.[13] Exemplifying the hubris of the field, Judge Richard Posner, one of the most influential law and economics scholars, wrote in 1989 that the economic theory of human behavior was the "most fruitful in the history of social science" and that insights from other social science fields were unnecessary "bells and whistles" that would just hinder progress.[14] It was not until the 1990s that law and economics finally "discovered" these social theories and insights.[15] That discovery was thanks in large part to the pioneering work of socio-legal scholar Robert Ellickson who showed not only that social conformity – enforced through extralegal social measures – can shape, influence, and even *control* people's behavior, but in many cases, do so far more effectively than even the law.

In this chapter, we elaborate on the social dimensions of chilling effects. A wealth of social science has explored behavior very much akin to chilling effects – people engaging in self-censorship, self-restraint, and speaking or acting differently – but not in typical chilling effect scenarios involving overreaching laws or surveillance. Rather, the behavioral phenomenon is investigated mainly in social contexts as social conformity and compliance, though the clear similarities with the legal concept of chill have led some social scientists to also describe the documented behavior as "chilling effects." The point is that conformity is essential to understanding chilling effects because, as we will see, conformity and chilling effects are the same behavioral response to perceived threats, just the threats concerning the former are mainly social, while the latter is not just social, but legal, privacy, and personal threats.

THE RANCHERS OF SHASTA COUNTY

In 1981, Ellickson, then a law professor at University of Southern California, set out to study the issue of ranchers' liability for livestock trespass damages.[16] A devoted law and economics scholar, he had done so, in part, because Ronald Coase – one of the founders of the law and economics field – had famously used the issue to explain what became known as the Coase Theorem, a central proposition of law and economics.[17] The Coase Theorem essentially holds that because individuals are rational self-interested actors, they would always negotiate an efficient allocation of resources, no matter what the law says.[18] Coase used as his central illustrative example the issue of cattle trespass liability as between two neighbors – a rancher raising cattle and a farmer growing crops – who come in conflict when the rancher's cattle trespass on the farmer's lands, damaging crops. According to his theorem, Coase claimed, the rancher and the farmer would, via rational decision-making and cost–benefit analysis, negotiate a settlement of the dispute, including transfer of cash for fence payments, that would result in the *same* affordances – like the quality and amount of fencing erected between properties – regardless of whether the law imposed liability for cattle trespass or not.[19] The point was that government intervention was unnecessary as the parties would adjust and arrive at the same optimal amount outcome either way.[20]

Ellickson was interested in testing Coase's Theorem, but not with statistical analysis or economic modeling. Instead, he wanted to test it in the real world: Was this really how ranchers and farmers behaved? To answer that question, he conducted an in-depth ethnographic study of actual ranchers and farmers living in Shasta County, a remote and rural county in Northern California.[21] He chose Shasta County because a local county board, empowered by California law, had at times imposed cattle trespass liability in some regions of the county, but not others – the very legal rule Coase had used in his famous example.[22] Ellickson probed the historical, geographical, legal, and social landscape of the county, and conducted extensive interviews with local ranchers, farmers, and county officials.[23] What he found was far removed from the world assumed by Coase and neoclassical law and economics scholarship.

It turns out not only do ranchers and farmers not adjust their behavior based on cattle trespass liability rules, as Coase's Theorem predicted, but they also managed and resolved all such disputes between neighbors almost entirely ignorant of the law.[24] In fact, Ellickson found the law was "practically irrelevant" and when they did turn their mind to it, they often got it wrong.[25] So, ranchers were not acting based on rational assessment or the nature of cattle trespass liability rules.[26] Not only that, the other behaviors that Coase predicted – like cash payments between neighbors to jointly pay for fencing – *never* happened.

So what, then, governed these disputes between neighboring ranchers in Shasta County? Social norms. Though there is no fixed definition, social norms can generally be understood as informal rules and standards of conduct understood by members of a group or community; they reflect the group's shared expectations about how to behave and how not to, and thus social norms guide behavior without the force of laws.[27] In Shasta County, ranchers were strongly committed to local norms of "neighborliness" or cooperation among neighbors.[28] When it came to cattle trespass, for example, a central such neighborly norm was that a rancher was responsible for the acts of their own livestock.[29] Adherence to this convention was independent of any legal entitlements – it applied whether or not the law imposed liability for cattle trespass – and was a matter of morality for ranchers in the county.[30] It was about being a good neighbor. A good neighbor was morally obliged to erect a fence to protect their neighbor's crops, and quickly retrieve cattle when notified by a neighbor that they had gone astray and were found trespassing. No self-respecting rancher would accept pay for such labor either, nor would they offer it. Such cold distant business-like behavior could poison a neighborly relationship.[31] Ranchers not only ignored trespass law and other legal rights, but any steps taken toward formal legal processes – like hiring a lawyer – were frowned upon.[32] There was, in fact, a deeply entrenched social norm against litigation.[33] Good neighbors do not litigate. They cooperate.

These neighborly social norms were enforced through extralegal social threats and conventions – basically, threats to person and property, which had a powerful conforming and compliance effect on the ranchers. Key to norm enforcement was what Ellickson deemed "self-help," that is, the victim takes action and "gets even" – settles scores or accounts with the perpetrator. Nearly all disputes in Shasta County were resolved through self-help. The most common form was gossip. Many ranchers were part of families that had been living in Shasta County for several generations, and planned to stay indefinitely. People tended to know each other, and word got around quickly. So, ranchers were strongly motivated to adhere to norms, believing, for example, that if they did not, they would be gossiped about and their family name and reputations would be ruined in the community.[34]

When more milder forms of self-help like gossip failed, a victim was justified in resorting to more serious forms of self-help sanction – like threatening physical violence; usually this involved threats to maim or kill, and in some cases actually maiming or killing, the offending livestock.[35] Though Ellickson was not able to conclude how often violent self-help was employed by ranchers, fear of extralegal physical retaliation and violence was a major factor in maintaining order in rural Shasta County, with most ranchers admitting that they worked to keep control of their cattle in order to avoid physical violence and harm to their livestock.[36]

Ellickson's findings disproved Coase's Theorem. But even more than that, they introduced to mainstream scholarship an essential insight of sociological approaches to law about how social norms and their extralegal enforcement through perceived threats can shape, regulate, and control conduct not just outside the law and formal legal institutions, but far more effectively as well.[37] In doing so, he undercut a central assumption in Coase's work, and the then law and economics neoclassical paradigm, that formal laws were the sole source of rules and social order. In Shasta County, norms and their enforcement through extralegal threats provided social order, while the law was practically irrelevant. As we will see, behavioral conformity and compliance in response to these kinds of threat perceptions – to person, reputation, or property – are key to understanding chilling effects as well.

CONFORMITY, COMPLIANCE, AND SOCIAL THREAT

The Shasta County ranchers offer an excellent example of social influence – how a person's behavior is influenced by the behavior of others.[38] There are different forms of social influence. One is the concept of compliance, where one changes their behavior or beliefs in response to an express request, demand, or threat by another.[39] Compliance means to acquiesce to the threat. Obedience, another form of social influence, involves changing behavior in acquiescence to a threat or demand from a figure of authority.[40] However, by far the most common and familiar form, and the one most apparent in our rancher parable, is conformity – where one changes or shapes their behavior or beliefs to match the behavior or beliefs of others – to match the norm of the group.[41] In Shasta County, the vast majority of ranchers behave in conformity with local norms to avoid potential threats to reputation and physical retaliation if they violate those very norms.

"SOCIAL" CHILLING EFFECTS

Everyone no doubt will recall a time when they decided against saying something or doing something because doing so might be offensive or viewed as inappropriate in the circumstances. So, you remain silent or maybe say something different instead. Often people self-censor like this willingly – people generally do not want to be offensive, for instance – but sometimes, people do so unwillingly or begrudgingly, feeling they are under social pressure to do so. This behavior – engaging in self-censorship to conform – is not so different from Shasta County ranchers refusing to complain about minor cattle trespassing incidents, so as not to violate neighborly rancher norms. Even these simple acts of self-censorship are comparable to the chilling effects and self-censorship that Schauer and other legal scholars have written about in relation to vague and uncertain laws. But they are not legal- or privacy-related chilling effects, they are *social* – where you self-censor or change your behavior for social reasons so as not to violate a social expectation or norm, leading to social disapproval, and even damage to your reputation, depending on the context. When people complain about "political correctness" what they are really complaining about is conformity – the social pressure they feel to conform with social norms of speech and behavior in different groups and contexts.

Though social scientists do not always use the term "chilling effects,"[42] a range of behavioral social science fields, including social psychology, sociology, behavioral economics, and communications, among many others, pursue research on forms of self-censorship, self-restraint, and socially conforming or compliant behavior – all of which match or are analogous to the notion of "chilling effects" that lawyers or journalists talk about. The key difference, however, is that these "social" chilling effects are investigated not as the product of law or overreach by government or big business, but as extralegal social factors, with conformity and compliance the result.

In fact, I have already talked about one such example in social psychology, where social norms play an essential part in creating a kind of "social" chilling effect.

In Chapter 2, I discussed the "watching eye" effect; awareness of surveillance leads participants to engage in more socially conforming or compliant behavior. So, what causes this chilling effect? There are different theories, but social norms are a key part of the story. The leading theory is that negative behavioral motivations, that is, fear of negative social sanction – being caught violating social norms – explains the chilling and conforming effect. In other words, the watching eye reminds participants of the possibility of being watched – much like Bentham's Panopticon – which heightens the possibility that they face social sanction if they break social norms, and they seek to avoid negative judgments or evaluations by others. The watching eyes can also encourage participants to be more self-aware and evaluate their own behavior, in light of the same constraining social norms, also leading to conforming and compliant behavior.[43] There is also an element of uncertainty, which also suggests *informational* influence in the conformity. In many of the watching eye experiments the participants are presented with a social dilemma, problem, or puzzle, which creates some uncertainty for them about how to act or behave, leading them to conform – likely as a means to resolve uncertainty and avoid social disapproval. The conforming behavior in watching eye research manifests in different ways. In some cases, it leads people to conform to typical pro-social norms such as telling the truth, sharing, cooperating, and being more generous. In others, it leads them to avoid antisocial behavior like cheating, lying, acting unconventionally, or expressing views inconsistent with the perceived views of the group majority.

Importantly, there is a deeper psychological foundation for the chill of observation in the watching eye research. Indeed, even where participants *know* the observation or surveillance is artificial and nobody is *actually* watching they are nevertheless chilled and engage in more socially conforming and compliant behavior. Indeed, this research and other observational studies in psychology have confirmed that simply being under the gaze of watching eyes created more negative psychological states in participants, including fear, anxiety, anger, distress, and nervousness, prompting conformity and compliance.[44] While under observation, people at a deeper psychological level feel under threat, and conformity is their instinctual response.

Another example is a body of research that explores what happens when these social chilling effects become too prevalent within a group, community, or population. This can lead to a range of harmful outcomes, one where dissenting voices are increasingly silenced or chilled in the group due to social conformity over time creating what political scientists call a "spiral of silence."[45] Communications scholars like Elizabeth Stoycheff and Ben Marder have described these impacts as "chilling effects," and documented the phenomena in online contexts as well.[46] The same way people are chilled by the presence of human observers they are likewise chilled by the presence and observation of others online, engaging in forms of self-censorship and conforming their online speech and behavior to the perceived norms of the audience.

These are just a few examples of research exploring social forms of chilling effects. There are many others. The central point is that the thread linking them is they all investigate behavior that is identical or directly analogous to forms of chilling effects decreed by lawyers, judges, journalists, and the like, but explore and explain that behavior in terms of social conformity and compliance. So, if conforming effects and chilling effects are similar, related, or possibly even the same thing, understanding the former can help us better understand the latter. On this count, among the foundational works in this body of literature on conformity – and its power to shape behavior the way chilling effects do – was Solomon Asch's famous experiment on social conformity in the 1950s. In Asch's experiment, a group of eight students were given a simple task of matching one of three "comparison" lines drawn on a large white card with a "standard" line drawn on another.[47] The match was easy to make as the aim of the study was to test how often participants would disregard their own private judgment about the correct answer and conform with the incorrect answer given by the group. Remarkably, Asch found that three-quarters of participants conformed at least once, and overall, participants conformed to the group over a third of the time.[48]

These results were both surprising and disturbing. We like to think of ourselves as rational and independent individuals who "think for ourselves" and do not "follow the herd." Yet, Asch's experiment did not involve uncertainty. The participants *knew* the answer given by the group was wrong and yet participants *still* conformed. And the reason was almost surely due to social influence. That's because those participants in the experiment's control group not facing social pressures – those given the same line-matching task but not subject to group pressure – got the answer correct 100 percent of the time.[49] So, participants conformed due to social pressures – to avoid breaking the norm of the group, and the social consequences of doing so.

And Asch's findings were not a creature of a laboratory. Nor were they specific to only one cultural group. Versions of his conformity experiment have been replicated and his findings reproduced in countless social and cultural contexts – over 130 times in seventeen different countries.[50] And while there are important variations among different cultures,[51] the main thrust of his findings hold up, with people conforming between 20 and 40 percent of the time. The power and reach of social influence and conformity cut across culture, geography, and language.

These impacts are directly analogous to the chilling effects typically associated with state and corporate activities, like people self-censoring or refraining from engaging in some activity due to an uncertain law. In Shasta County, conformity and compliance enforced through extralegal means – threats to person and property – governed how ranchers behaved and settled cattle trespass disputes, essentially operating and governing like law purports to do, but in many ways far more effectively.

Ranchers were expected by the broader rancher community to engage in social conformity – to conform to neighborly social norms. In most cases, the social pressure
to do so was implicit – ranchers erected fences and looked after their cattle without
request or demand. And like the participants in Asch's famous experiment, they
conformed to avoid the social consequences of breaking expected norms. So, the
sanctions for violations were *social* not *legal* and yet they were able to control and
govern behavior in the county while laws were largely irrelevant.

There are clearly stark similarities between chilling effects and conforming effects.
In fact, I will argue in the next chapter that they are one and the same. Yet, questions remain. Why do people engage in conformity – leading to chilling effects – in
the face of legal threats or forms of government and corporate surveillance? How
do social norms and factors in conformity impact on chill in these and other circumstances? Indeed, while the different forms of "social" chilling effects discussed
in this chapter provide an important foundation for a more robust understanding of
chilling effects, including answers to these questions, much of this literature does
not address the impact of law or forms of police, corporate, or governmental surveillance – the types of actions we typically associate with chilling effects. I do so in
Chapters 4 and 5.

4

A Conformity Theory of Chilling Effects

In Chapter 3, we examined "social" forms of chilling effects and highlighted the impact of social influence and conformity on people's behavior. This is not to privilege conformity and norms absolutely over other factors that impact how people decide to act in the face of a law or privacy threat like surveillance. When it comes to legal compliance, for example, research suggests that social norms, moral values, and perceptions as to legitimacy and fairness of the law itself all influence whether people obey the law,[1] as well as both deterrence and expressive effects.[2] So, understanding how law, social influence, and people interact more generally is complex and simple or singular answers do not push the ball forward.[3]

However, the picture is somewhat simpler when it comes to chilling effects. That's because chilling effects arise in more specific circumstances. Nearly all chilling effect concerns or claims arise in one of these four circumstances: First, in contexts of uncertainty – like when a person is uncertain about the law's requirements or the possibility of law enforcement action. Schauer theorized about these kinds of legal and regulatory chilling effects and the US Supreme Court fashioned a "chilling effects" doctrine to address them in First Amendment law. Second, chilling effects due to surveillance – such as when people are aware that they are being tracked or monitored by government or are aware of the possibility of it. These are the kinds of chilling effects Solove and other privacy law scholars have written about. Third, personalized threats – threats or actions that are more targeted or personal, like a personally received legal threat or threat of violence. The notion of self-censorship or chilling effects in the face of coercive threats is ancient, for good reason. Today legal scholars and social theorists have extended this idea to new digital contexts – like the chilling effect of online abuse and harassment. Lastly, chilling effects are most often caused by actors with power and authority – like government, law enforcement, or big business – such as a large company that operates a popular social media platform.

These four examples are all typical scenarios often invoked by lawyers, journalists, policymakers, and anyone else concerned about chilling effects. But they are not *only* that. These scenarios all happen to also reflect the four key factors

49

that social scientists find cause or contribute to social conformity and compliance: uncertainty, observation, personal threats, and authority. That is to say, people's tendency to engage in social conformity is *greatest* in these very scenarios. When we are uncertain, feel we are being watched or under surveillance, and are personally threatened – and the actor doing so possesses power or authority – a wealth of behavioral social science tells us that social norms become a predominant influence on our behavior, creating a chilling effect: People are chilled from speaking or acting as they otherwise would, and instead behave in conformity with the perceived social norm in that context. In other words, chilling effects are best understood through the lens of conformity as a behavioral response to perceived threats and these factors are really just "chilling effect" factors that provide guidance as to when chilling effects – which really are conformity and compliance effects – are most powerful.

I am not the first to link chilling effects to forms of conformity. As we will see, scholars and experts like Julie Cohen, Neil Richards, Margot Kaminski, and Bruce Schneier have all done so in respect of surveillance, and drawn on social theory and behavioral science, as I do, in making that link. I build on their insights to propose a new more comprehensive theory of chilling effects that explains them not just as an outcome of surveillance, but many other forms of personal threats as well. This chapter sets out this theory and explains how it works.

CONFORMITY AND CHILLING EFFECTS

Asch's famous experiments on social conformity in the 1950s showed how strikingly similar chilling effects and conforming effects were. Due to conformity, people self-censored – remained silent, that is, were chilled from expressing their own strongly held personal beliefs about what is right and wrong. But not only that, they also engaged in socially conforming speech and behavior that directly disregarded or contradicted their personal beliefs about right and wrong. Despite knowing better, they still just followed the herd. Conformity likewise shaped and controlled behavior in Shasta County. In fact, conformity had an even greater impact on people's behavior than the law itself. If conformity can shape behavior more effectively than the law, then surely it also plays a role in chilling effects?

Indeed, it does. In fact, social psychologists in the 1950s immediately related Asch's findings to the broader social and political climate of the times – the McCarthy Era in America, which as we saw was a period of intense and unprecedented social and political conformity – and chilling effects. Asch's work offered a new way to understand those broader currents. The same era that saw the popularization of the concept of chilling effects itself, also produced insights on the psychology of mass conformity. That is no coincidence. The concepts are inextricably linked. Chilling effects are not only related or analogous to conformity – they are one and the same – chilling effects are conformity and compliance effects, with one critical difference: They are a much more powerful version of these impacts as they are most often a product of powerful state and corporate actors, acting with legal, governmental, or market authority, and enhanced by technology and data.

Why chilling effects are more powerful when dealing with state or corporate actors is all about threat perception and how it drives more powerful forms of conformity. In Chapter 3, we noted that in Shasta County, most ranchers conformed with local norms mainly to avoid threats to reputation and violent retaliation, including threats to person and property. Similarly, the observational chilling effects seen in the "watching eye" research have deeper psychological foundations, with people feeling fear and anxiety – threatened – while being watched by others. Such threat perception is central to understanding chilling effects in typical scenarios involving law, government surveillance, and other kinds of threats. We will return to this point later.

Asch's famous experiments help highlight two critical points. First, that chilling effects and conforming effects are the same thing. Second, chilling effects have a *productive* dimension – in Asch's experiments, participants were not only chilled from expressing their own beliefs; rather, they gave answers that conformed with the speech and expression of the majority. Chilling effects produce silence but also behavior and speech in conformity with expected norms. This latter point will become important for understanding the implications of a conformity theory of chilling effects. However, we need to first examine what I call the four main chilling effect factors – observation; uncertainty; personalization; and power/authority, which are also, as we noted earlier, central factors that contribute to, amplify, and magnify conformity and compliance.

THE FOUR CHILLING EFFECT FACTORS

1 *Observation*

When people are aware they are being observed by others or are aware of the possibility of it, they are chilled from freely speaking and acting. This is one of the most prevalent critiques and concerns about modern government and corporate surveillance and data harvesting. These chilling effects are in fact a social conformity and compliance effect. A famous example of this phenomenon is what has been called the "Hawthorne effect" – named for the Illinois-based Hawthorne plant of the Western Electric Company where it was first documented.[4]

The Hawthorne telephone and office equipment manufacturing plant, located just outside Chicago, employed 30,000 men and women.[5] Management planned a series of experiments at Hawthorne to boost the productivity of workers. Management thought that better lighting would be one way to do so. So, they singled out a group of workers to test their hypothesis. They put these workers in a separate room, increased the lighting, and then did the same with another group of workers, the control group, but in their separate room, they kept the lighting the same. They were surprised to find that productivity increased for workers in *both* rooms. Thinking they had erred, they had psychologists design a series of additional experiments over the next several years that tried to vary other work conditions to improve productivity, from more coffee breaks, shifted work hours, free lunches, to overtime pay, different work locations, even dimming the lights. But over and over again, in every experiment, productivity increased in both the testing group and the control group of workers. They even went back and reinstated the original work conditions, and still, productivity increased for all workers participating in the study.[6] The obvious conclusion was that none of the conditions were impacting productivity, but the fact that these workers had been singled out and put under observation for the study. Knowing they were under surveillance, they changed their behavior and worked even more diligently than normal, boosting productivity.

What the Hawthorne plant researchers had stumbled upon unintentionally is the social fact that people change their behavior when they know they are being watched; a proposition so widely documented it is now an accepted "truism" of social science.[7] Social conformity best explains the Hawthorne effect. With the workers aware that they were under surveillance as participants in the study, they changed their behavior to conform with the norm expected of them by management – working diligently and avoiding time-wasting. Hence, productivity increased no matter the work condition. More recently, an extensive review and meta-analysis of "Hawthorne effect" studies and similar observational effects literature found extensive evidence of chilling effects, in terms of conforming and compliance – with people's awareness of being watched reducing antisocial behavior like lying or cheating while promoting more pro-social behavior with passive observers, where tasks were more consequential, and where participants faced social dilemmas.[8]

Computer and electronic forms of observation and monitoring have these same chilling and conforming effects. For instance, studies have found that computer monitoring of employees increases productivity and reduces "social loafing" – the tendency for some people to put in less effort when working as part of a group.[9] The workers subject to computer monitoring, concerned about social disapproval and negative evaluation, are chilled into conforming with positive or expected work norms – working harder and avoiding piggybacking on others' work.[10] These results make sense from a social psychology and conformity perspective. If people are concerned about social sanction and their long-term reputation and place in social groups or other perceived threats – like job loss or demotion if caught loafing – more consequential contexts – like observation or surveillance by larger audiences, for example – force participants to focus more on those long-term interests.[11] They are chilled and conform accordingly.

However, there is also a deeper psychological foundation for this chilling and conforming tendency, given the anxiety and distress often triggered by the thought or perception that we are being watched by others. In the computer and electronic observational studies, as with other observational studies, being under the scrutiny of computer-enhanced monitoring and observation triggered immense anxiety and distress among participants – in this case, the possibility of demotion or job loss, magnifying chilling and conforming effects. The "watching eye" effect research, discussed earlier, demonstrates the power of observation and these deeper psychological foundations – even where participants *know* the surveillance is artificial and nobody is *actually* watching they are nevertheless chilled and engage in more socially conforming and compliant behavior. This research and other surveillance and observational studies in psychology have confirmed that simply being under the gaze of watching eyes created more "negative" psychological states in participants, including anxiety, anger, distress, and nervousness, prompting conformity and compliance.

These chilling and conforming effects, and discomfort while being watched, are precisely the kinds of impacts privacy scholars and surveillance theorists have long raised about modern state and corporate surveillance. Alan Westin wrote of the need for "solitude" and a place of "emotional release" that is "freed" from surveillance and the "observation" of others.[12] Ruth Gavison similarly wrote of the importance of private respite from the "inhibitory effects" of the "casual observation."[13] Ryan Calo, in his work on "subjective" privacy harms, wrote of chilling effects as stemming solely from unwanted observation.[14] Solove likewise acknowledged these social psychological effects leading to chilling effects, noting not only that awareness of surveillance makes a person "feel extremely uncomfortable," but also alters behavior leading to self-censorship and inhibition.[15] As a result, surveillance is a "tool of social control" that enhances the "power of social norms" when people are being observed.[16]

More recently, work by legal scholars, surveillance theorists, and communications scholars like Frederik Zuiderveen Borgesius, Michael Latzer, Mario Büchi, Joanna Strycharz, and Claire M. Segijn have explored the systematic observation of people or populations through data collection and analysis – dataveillance.[17] This new body of research gives special attention to the role of corporate and commercial practices and elaborates further the systematic observation inherent in today's algorithmic collection, retention, and analysis of data and "digital traces" by state and corporate actors, which is often pervasive, automatic, and continuous.[18] For instance, Büchi, Latzer, and Noemi Festic propose a new theoretical model for dataveillance, arguing that people's "sense" of dataveillance is the main cause of chilling effects.[19] But what does it mean to have a sense of dataveillance? Very simple – it just means people's awareness that they are constantly being closely observed, tracked, and analyzed by data collection and processing. In other words, it is our first chilling effect factor – people's awareness of being observed. The only difference is that the observation is being carried out through systematic and automated algorithmic data collection and processing.

Like our conformity and compliance theory, these theorists also ground their model in social psychology, specifically, the theory of planned behavior – wherein people's attitude toward engaging in certain activities – like digital communications – is a product of salient and readily accessible information and beliefs about the consequences of doing so.[20] On this theory, where an activity may lead to risks or harmful consequences, a person may avoid or mute their activities – like inhibiting their communications. This sounds like a deterrence theory, but it isn't. Rather, it operates much like the Hawthorne effect or the pair of eyes in the watching eye research: Something that increases people's sense or awareness that they are systematically observed through data – like widespread media coverage of the Snowden revelations about mass surveillance or the Cambridge Analytica scandal concerning targeted surveillance and algorithmic profiling – leads to chilling effects. Thanks to these high-profile and widely covered scandals, these forms of observation and surveillance are no longer just viewed as "creepy" government or industry practices by the general public; but serious and invasive privacy threats.[21] These are important insights that enrich our understanding of chilling effects, especially in the context of data surveillance and processing. And it is a model that is more informed by social science than conventional theories. In fact, the theory of planned behavior, on which Büchi, Latzer, and Festic rely, is an example of the more automatic form of thinking that we will talk about later in this chapter, which underlies chilling effects in some contexts. My only critique is that this dataveillance theory is incomplete – it neglects other central factors that likewise contribute to chilling effects, like personalization, uncertainty, and power/authority. We talk about these next.

2 *Uncertainty*

Uncertainty is another central chilling effects and conformity factor. In Asch's experiment, people conformed to the group a third of the time even though they knew that the group's answer was wrong. As it turns out, we are even *more* vulnerable to social influence when uncertain. In fact, social psychology has long established that the more uncertain we are about a situation or choice the more susceptible we are to social influences in our decision-making, leading us to conform.[22]

The pioneering work of Muzafer Sherif in the 1930s, one of the founders of modern social psychology, was among the first to document this behavioral tendency.[23] In his classic study using "auto-kinetic effects" – an optical illusion where an object that is stationary appears to move – he placed people individually in a dark room and asked how far they believed a point of light moved.[24] Alone, people reported varying degrees of movement, showing the ambiguity of the task – there was no correct answer. He then ran the experiment again. This time people observed the point of light in groups of three, and reported out loud. Each time he ran the experiment in groups, participants tended to report the same distance as others in the group. In short, he showed people were resolving the ambiguity and uncertainty in the experiment by seeking information about social consensus, or social norm, and then *conforming* their answer according to that norm.[25]

Incredibly, these group norms were also *internalized* by participants. That is, people continued to conform to the norms even after the groups left and individuals continued to participate alone in future rounds of the experiment. They remained even when the experiment was redone a year later. This demonstrated that people had internalized the social norm, that is, had come to personally accept it as correct.[26] The experiment led both to what social psychologists call "public conformity" – conforming behavior publicly in the presence of others – as well as "private conformity," doing so while alone or in private.[27] With public conformity, a person might secretly or privately admit that they were just pretending to believe the consensus answer in order to conform with the group norm – but private conformity means that they have really come to believe it. They're convinced.

This simple experiment demonstrates how uncertainty magnifies social influence and conformity. In Asch's experiment, participants discounted their own private judgment about what they were certain was right in order to conform to the group norm just over a third of the time. Here, when faced with an ambiguous problem, *all the participants* eventually conformed to the group by the third round of the experiment. Put another way, people are chilled from acting independently based on their own judgment, and instead act in accordance to the social norm.

So, uncertainty increases conformity and compliance. Consistent with a theory of chilling effects as conforming and compliance effects, uncertainty is *also* a predominant feature of situations in which chilling effects arise or are typically invoked. A simple and classic example from law would be a statute that is vague and uncertain in its scope and application, making decision-making about how to act in light of the law more difficult. As Schauer had argued in his leading account, uncertainty and the possibility of error in the legal process is central to chilling effects. Another form of uncertainty contributing to chilling effects is uncertainty and ambiguity in surveillance – being uncertain about whether you are being watched, by whom, and why. Modern surveillance, which is pervasive and ambiguous, takes advantage of this reality. As David Lyon observes, it aims to "generate regimes of self-discipline through uncertainty."[28] This discussion has not aimed to be exhaustive; the point is simply to show how uncertainty is central to social conformity and compliance, and is thus also a critical factor in chilling effects.

3 *Personalization*

Personalization is another central factor. It encompasses scenarios where a person is more personally targeted – they are singled out in some way from the broader population or group. Personalization can take many forms, from more personal or targeted threats to more tailored or personalized interventions from authorities. Put simply, the more targeted, tailored, or personalized the threat, intervention, or scenario, the greater the chilling effect. Once again, social psychology and conformity theory help us understand why.

Personal threats – like threats of harm or violence – are among the more potent forms of personalization and lead to among the most powerful kinds of chilling effects. Indeed, the notion of self-censorship in the face of coercive personal threats is centuries old, even ancient.[29] Classical Greek poets and dramatists like Aristophanes and Eupolis, for example, often engaged in self-censorship in their work to protect themselves from prosecution or reprisal.[30] In medieval times, people testifying before the Catholic Inquisitions, chilled by threats of execution or torture for heresy, regularly self-censored.[31] Today, journalists are regularly chilled in their work due to threats to their personal safety,[32] while experts in privacy and online abuse like Citron, Mary Anne Franks, Alice Marwick, and many others have highlighted how targeted harassment and online abuse can have devastating chilling effects on victims and their own speech, sharing, and engagement online.[33]

We can understand these chilling effects on a visceral level – a person would be easily chilled into silence, or change their speech or behavior, to conform to more acceptable norms, to avoid harm to their personal safety. However, conformity, and not just self-censorship, is essential to understanding these chilling effects too. An abundance of evidence demonstrates that people have an especially strong tendency to engage in social conformity and compliance when personally threatened or feeling individually vulnerable.[34] In such cases, people conform both to majority opinion as well as group values and norms.[35] There is cross-cultural evidence of this as well. Cultures that disproportionally encourage conformity compared with others tend to develop in regions historically characterized by persistent existential threats, like a greater prevalence of pathogenic diseases.[36] In contexts where one is under threat, dissenting from the group or creating division by violating social norms makes much needed – even life-saving – social support far less likely.

However, personalization need not *only* involve threats to personal safety to cause chilling and conforming effects. Other kinds of personal threats – including personal legal threats or targeted surveillance – as well as other forms of personalization can do so too. Social conformity theory helps us understand why. To begin with, when a person is targeted or singled out in a group or population by authorities and they are aware of it, they know their behavior has been monitored up to that point, and is then in the "spotlight" of surveillance, and therefore may be subject to continued targeted surveillance going forward. This increases the possibility their behavior may be met with social disapproval and sanction if found to have violated norms or broken with social consensus, causing chilling effects. This "singling out" chill is clear from the famous Hawthorne experiments – the workers that were singled out for the study all changed their behavior, conforming more closely with the expected norms of their employer, thus working harder, taking fewer breaks, and ending up being more productive. When people know they are being personally targeted for monitoring, then such surveillance chill and conforming effects result.

Furthermore, an intervention that is more personalized – one that is, for example, communicated directly to them and concerns their behavior – likewise can have greater chilling and conforming effects. Such information can provide compelling "feedback" as to the person's compliance or conformity with the group or pertinent social norms. When social or group norms are made salient – that is, brought to the attention of a person this way – then a person who may have departed from those norms, or violated them, experiences far more pressure to change their behavior and conform.[37] In public policy, social influence and social norm approaches are increasingly seen as a potentially powerful and cost-effective way of addressing social harms – like policies aimed at reducing harmful and destructive behavior in society like alcoholism, smoking, drug use, and gambling.[38] The most promising among them are approaches that employ forms of personalization, what social psychologists call "personalized normative feedback" (PNF) interventions.[39] As the name suggests, PNF interventions provide personalized and tailored information, usually delivered via computer or digital means, to a person on their own behavior; "social proof" as to expected behavior or social norms in the context, and how they may fall short of that norm. Though more study needs to be done, the evidence suggests that the reason these interventions are more effective is that they are targeted and personalized. Being singled out personally and receiving information that their behavior may be deviant or falls short of social expectations greatly increases a person's risk of social disapproval if the bad behavior continues. To avoid it, they conform.

For these same reasons, personalization is a key factor in chilling effects. When a person feels personally threatened due to a personal legal threat or forms of harassment or abuse, chilling and conforming effects result. When someone is singled out as they would when it comes to targeted legal enforcement, then this also increases awareness for the person that they may have violated a law – a serious breach of social norms while raising awareness as to personal legal risks – magnifying chilling and conforming effects. Again, this is not meant to be an exhaustive discussion of personalization and chilling effects, the point is to understand it as a key factor, to be employed as a way of understanding and predicting chilling effects in a variety of contexts.

4 *Power and Authority*

Conformity is central to understanding chilling effects, but the closely related concept of *compliance* is also important, as chilling effects often concern actors with power and authority in society – governments, law enforcement, big business, for instance. This power and authority is another chilling effect primary factor. That is, people are much more likely to engage in conformity and compliance in contexts involving a figure or entity with power and authority; which is to say, someone with the capacity to exercise power over them.[40] In fact, there is an extensive body of social science exploring obedience, compliance, and conformity in response to figures with power and authority.[41]

Much of this research has built on one of the most famous experiments in social psychology, conducted by Stanley Milgram. In those experiments, participants were ordered by a presumptive figure of authority to deliver increasingly powerful electric shocks to patients and most participants did so despite the "victim" patients seemingly crying out in pain (the patients were confederates in the experiment and were only pretending to feel pain, but participants did not know it).[42] Milgram's findings have been reproduced in other contexts, with the key insight being that people tend to defer to and comply with figures or actors with perceived authority. In Milgram's experiment, authority was derived from expertise – a researcher in a white lab coat – but of course authority in this context includes other more traditional forms too – like political leaders, business leaders, members of government, and police.[43] The literature on social psychology typically treats conformity on the one hand and obedience and compliance with power and authority on the other as related but distinct phenomena. But evolutionary psychologists see commonalities underlying each.[44] That's because a tendency to engage in conformity or defer to figures of power and authority likely provided evolutionary fitness benefits – it helped people survive in the past.[45] I'll say more about the evolutionary reasons for conformity (and thus chilling effects) later, but Milgram himself offered conformity as a possible explanation for his findings.[46] Indeed, it is not surprising that people often self-censor and refuse to "break the silence" even on issues of major societal importance.[47] This is often when figures or entities with power and authority are involved as this magnifies conformity and compliance effects, leading more people to remain silent or conform to the norm preferred by the authority.

Milgram understood the magnitude of his findings. His studies were originally inspired by the Holocaust and the unspeakable atrocities carried out by countless officers and average citizens in Nazi Germany during the Second World War – who complied and obeyed blindly.[48] In fact, he began the experiments themselves against the backdrop of the trials of Adolf Eichmann, the Nazi war criminal, whose routine work as a bureaucrat contributed to the deaths of millions of Jews during the Holocaust, famously described by Arendt as the "banality of evil."[49] That description resonated for Milgram when analyzing his findings: "After witnessing hundreds of ordinary people submit to the authority in our own experiments, I must conclude that Arendt's conception of the banality of evil comes closer to the truth than one might imagine."[50] Whether he and Arendt were right or wrong about Eichmann, the importance of Milgram's findings remains clear.[51]

Chilling effects will thus in many cases involve conformity and compliance – through self-censorship, conformity, and other chilling effects – in response to commands, threats, requirements, and processes of entities with power and authority. Chilling effects are thus conforming *and* compliance effects.

WHY ARE CHILLING EFFECTS SO POWERFUL?

Why are we so chilled by these threats? The answer lies in why we engage in social conformity, and its deeper psychological foundations. People conform for many reasons, depending on context. But when it comes to chilling effects – the most powerful form of conformity and compliance effects caused by overreaching surveillance and targeted forms of legal enforcement by powerful entities like police, government, and corporations – threat perception is key: People conform out of fear and anxiety due to perceived threats to them, the group they identify with, and things they care about; and conformity provides a sense of security, support, and protection. There is safety in numbers. This tendency to conform in situations involving threats to us or our families and communities is likely explained best by evolutionary psychology – it has helped us survive and thrive in the past. But to understand this point, we need to understand the benefits of conformity.

First, conformity helps us get things right. When unsure how to act, people seek out what Robert Cialdini calls "social proof" in the behavior of others, especially those we perceive to be "similar" to us.[52] When uncertain, people are influenced by what others *do* in the same situation. They are also influenced by what people *say* is the right thing to do in the same situation. Social norms performed or expressed by legitimate authorities also have particularly influential impact in these circumstances. Research suggests that people look for consensus, so the more people who appear to follow a norm, the more influential it will be in conforming behavior.[53] This makes sense. If one is uncertain about how to act and others around you have already done so, they may have more information or experience than you, so following their lead increases the likelihood your choice is the right one. Those odds increase when greater numbers of people are similarly following the norm or when someone with genuine expertise or authority likewise adheres to the norm. These reasons explain Sherif's findings perfectly. People were uncertain about the right answer – they were attempting to measure what was actually an optical illusion – and therefore conformed to the social norm of the group because the consensus suggested the answer was more likely right.

Second, people engage in conformity and compliance to avoid social sanction or ostracism – like negative judgments from others – if they behave contrary to broader social norms. Ostracism and social sanction can cause people "emotional distress, feeling alone, hurt, angry, and lacking in self-esteem."[54] Sociologists likewise have documented various mechanisms of social influence, with research showing the importance of social norms and social sanctions in shaping behavior.[55] Also driving these conforming effects is the related concern for "affiliation" – humans are fundamentally motivated to create and maintain meaningful social relationships, and so look to social norms and behavioral cues of others, for affiliation, reciprocity, and approval. Again, by following the behavior of others there is a higher likelihood the decision will be approved by others leading to reciprocity and affiliation while avoiding social sanction and, over time, a self-image of being different, deviant, or intransigent.[56] These reasons explain Asch's experimental findings. Even though participants were more certain about the right answer, over a third of the time they still conformed to the norm of the group, likely due to social pressure – not wanting to go against the judgment of the group, and face social disapproval.

These same reasons also explain why simple observation by other people leads to conformity. If we are aware that someone or something is watching us, we may be under threat – they could be an enemy or a predator that wishes to harm us. Observational chill here is responsive to a kind of personal threat. There is a social dimension here too. If we are being watched, then there is also a greater likelihood our behavior, if inappropriate or norm-violating, is going to be observed by others, leading to social sanction and potential ostracism. This is clear from studies on both the "watching eye" and the Hawthorne effects, where people when aware they are being watched behave in ways that conform to typical or expected norms. Awareness that they are being watched heightens the possibility they may face social sanction or alienation for violating social norms – their actions are being watched and possibly tracked, so if they act against social norms, they are more likely to face social consequences.

So, the chilling effect of observation involves perceived threats – social alienation and ostracism – and social benefits of conformity – support, reciprocity, and affiliation. Hence, awareness of others present and watching us causes chilling and conforming effects – people not only self-censor, they are also more likely to behave in accordance with expected social norms – like behaving in more honest and trustworthy ways. Ellickson also relied on conformity theory to understand his case study on Shasta County ranchers. Ranchers conformed to neighborly norms to avoid threats to reputation, person, or property, through negative gossip or violent retaliation for norm breaking. In a close-knit community, people were easily watched and under social surveillance, so norm following was even more strict and regular.

Given the benefits, it is easy to understand how conformity – and chilling effects – has a deeper psychological foundation for evolutionary reasons.[57] Indeed, social conformity is a "highly rewarding process" that is known to "activate reward systems in the brain."[58] By contrast, social rejection and ostracism have been found to trigger parts of the brain normally associated with physical pain.[59] Evolutionary psychologists see commonalities and similar impacts across all forms of social influence usually treated as distinct – conformity, compliance, obedience, for instance.[60]

From an evolutionary perspective, behaving like others helped one to survive, thrive, and prosper throughout history. A tendency to conform when facing threats likely led to "fitness-enhancing decisions," thus selecting for imitation, mimicry, and other forms of social conformity over time. For example, these types of psychological strategies are less likely to lead to social sanction and ostracism, which would impact on survival.[61] Furthermore, as earlier noted, the "watching eye" research and other surveillance and observational studies confirm the psychological basis for surveillance chilling effects. Being under surveillance immediately increases anxiety, nervousness, and distress, leading to chilling and conforming effects. People in these studies also engage in privacy-protective behaviors like turning away from the "watching eyes" or raising a book to cover their own face, which are also forms of chilling effects that likewise suggest deeper psychological impacts and a wish to avoid surveillance that, for example, may scrutinize behavior.

These deeper psychological foundations also explain why we often find forms of observation or surveillance "creepy." Most of us have experienced this. You're walking alone on a dark street one night and suddenly you get an anxious, nervous, and creepy feeling like you're being watched. Or you are standing in a crowded room and notice that someone across the room is staring at you, and you freeze, feeling creepy and uncertain. In fact, as Neil Richards documents in his important book *Why Privacy Matters,* "creepiness" is also our most common reaction to new privacy threats like increasingly invasive observation, tracking, and surveillance.[62] Richards documents countless cases, from day-to-day life to academia, politics, journalism, technology, and beyond wherein "creepy talk" dominates our discussions about, and responses to, privacy and surveillance threats. Even many leading privacy theories, he argues, often draw on creepiness as a means of assessing the seriousness of a privacy violation. Richards ultimately argues that "creepiness" is a bad metric from which to advocate or measure privacy. He's surely right. For our purposes in understanding the chill of observation, I'm interested in *why* we feel "creeped out" due to being watched – a reaction that Richards says is so common it is almost a "natural reaction."[63]

Until recently, this "creepy" feeling has not been well understood and received little empirical study. But several recent studies provide critical new insights. That creepy feeling, it turns out, is all about the psychology of threat perception.[64] Our brains are wired to perceive threats, and being watched or observed by other people or things can constitute a threat – as noted earlier, they could be an enemy or a predator. So actually being watched or being reminded of the possibility of it triggers these deeper psychological states of anxiety, distress, discomfort, and yes – creepiness – part of a natural response we have to threats. But with observation, there is often ambiguity too. There is uncertainty about the watcher and their motivations and intentions. There is also ambiguity about the context of observation – maybe it is hard to know if you are *actually* being watched. And in situations of uncertainty of surveillance, creepiness is especially amplified. That's why we often feel more creepy about possibly being watched on a dark street or while alone – there is more ambiguity and fewer visual cues for our brains to process potential threats or the absence thereof. We feel creepy about being watched because we are nervous and uncomfortable about possible threats. Our natural response to these threats is not just to feel anxious or creepy – we also conform, which provides important benefits for survival when threatened.

These evolutionary psychological foundations also help explain why personal threats, especially those expressing or implying violence or physical harms, are such a powerful force for conformity – and thus chilling effects. If conformity enhances fitness for survival, a behavioral tendency to conform to the norms of the group or community that you belong to makes sense as an innate survival strategy – there is safety, support, and protection within the group and conformity is more likely to attract social approval, solidarity, and reciprocity. Others in the group may also possess information or strategies that enhance self-protection, so conforming when threatened increases the chances of choosing the "correct" strategy to survive or avoid harm. Personal threats also cause uncertainty – about our safety and belonging.[65] This, too, enhances conformity effects.

And they help explain why people are more likely to engage in conformity and compliance in relation to entities or actors with authority. As evolutionary psychologist Steven Neuberg and his colleagues observe, historically, social structures of hierarchy and authority likely offered groups competitive advantages for survival.[66] Thus, it is reasonable to expect that behavioral and psychological tendencies for obedience and deference to authority, which leads to greater conformity, have an evolutionary basis.

These examples and these deeper psychological foundations all point to another reason chilling effects are so powerful: We are in many cases not even conscious of them. In his book *Thinking, Fast and Slow*, Daniel Kahneman, who won a Nobel Prize in Economics for his work on the psychology of decision-making, discusses decades of research showing how people operate by using two different systems of thought.[67] System 1 is quick, simple, and automatic with no deliberate or voluntary control – using an "intuitive" thought process.[68] We use System 1 for quick and easy tasks and decisions, like understanding the meaning of a simple sentence; recognizing emotions in a person's face; or doing easy math problems, like simple addition. By contrast, System 2 is slower, controlled, and deliberate, involves more complex tasks and decisions, and employs a thought process that is more conscious and reasoned.[69] When we think about our persona, including identity, preferences, and attitudes, and how we think and make decisions, we are thinking about System 2 – our conscious and reasoning self. But the reality is, most of our decision-making on a day-to-day basis is done on autopilot via System 1's automatic processes while System 2 runs on "low effort" or idle mode, until difficulties arise, like being confronted by a surprising event or complex task or problem.[70] At that point, System 2 is activated and its more detailed and specific thought process employed.

Chilling – and thus conforming – effects occur under both System 1 or System 2 thought processes. Obviously, there will be times when chilling effects are a product of a conscious deliberative process – like where we learn we are being targeted by government for prosecution or surveillance, for example, and decide to stay silent or conform so as not to attract unwanted attention or be caught violating either a law or some other social expectation, leading to other negative ramifications. In such cases, chilling effects would be a product of System 2 – a conscious and deliberative process. But given their deeper psychological basis, it is clear chilling effects are not always a product of a conscious or deliberative process. In many cases, possibly even most, they involve a more automatic thought process – System 1. Hence, the tendency for people to feel anxiety and reactively conform when under simple observation, an effect that occurs even when people know, for a fact, the observation is artificial. Or our natural tendency to remain silent immediately when personally threatened, especially with threats of violence. That is a System 1 chill. The widely studied phenomenon of "primitive automaticity" is another example. When experiencing heightened uncertainty and threat, people sometimes ignore most information available to them and simply use the "single-piece-of-good-evidence" approach to decision-making.[71] Often that one good piece of evidence is the behavior of others.[72] Other subconscious factors also drive conformity and chilling effects like behavioral mimicry, which involves people subconsciously matching posture, expression, and mannerisms.[73] In each of these cases, our automatic System 1 processes drive us to chilling and conforming effects in response to the threat. All this is to say: We are, at a very fundamental level, wired to be chilled. And those chilling effects have profound impacts on us.

ADDITIVE EFFECTS: ANOTHER WAY POWER MATTERS

One final reason why chilling and conforming effects are so powerful is what Jennifer Nadler calls their "additive effects."[74] These additive dimensions mean that chilling effects can be caused not only by a single entity or factor but a number of causes or factors that are compounding or additive. In other words, the more contributing factors you add, the greater the chilling effect. Similarly, when factors themselves are magnified or more powerful or significant, the greater the chilling effect.

Chilling effects work this way because that's also how conformity works, with multiple factors or threats compounding impact. For instance, when perceptions about social threats like alienation and ostracism are added to uncertainty, it has an additive or compounding impact on social conformity – it increases the magnitude of the conformity.[75] And social factors that contribute to "groupthink" – how social groups tend to conform in their thoughts and attitudes – are likewise additive; the more that are present, the stronger the groupthink.[76] The magnitude of each factor also matters. This dynamic is apparent throughout social influence. For instance, with informational influences on conformity, the stronger the apparent consensus about a social norm, the more influential it will be in causing people to conform.[77] So, a person who is being watched by a crowd is going to be more likely to conform than someone who is being watched by a single person. A person who is more uncertain about what to do is going to be chilled more than someone who struggles with more minimal uncertainty.[78] Milgram also demonstrated these additive dimensions. After his original experiment showing how people are more likely to engage in obedience, conformity, and compliance in relation to figures of power and authority, Milgram conducted a series of variations on that experiment to explore different conditions or factors that impacted the level of obedience or compliance. Among his additional insights, he showed that obedience or compliance was greatest when the power of the authority figure in question was maximized – and was reduced as the status and authority of the figure was also reduced.[79] Put simply, the greater the power and authority, the greater the level of obedience and conformity.

On this understanding, a situation involving a greater number of these chilling effects factors – uncertainty, surveillance, personalization, and power/authority will likewise have much stronger and impactful chilling effects. For example, as Kaminski and Shane Witnov note, those who are more uncertain about what to say or do in a given context are more affected by surveillance, and more likely to conform as a result.[80] That means, a situation involving uncertainty about law enforcement action combined with awareness of surveillance where the person is personally targeted – like a personal legal threat – will have greater chilling effects than a scenario involving only legal uncertainty. The addition of each factor increases or compounds the resulting chilling effect. Furthermore, just as circumstances with a greater number of the chilling effect factors lead to more powerful chilling effects, contexts where there are more substantial or significant forms of these factors – like more pervasive and invasive surveillance; or large-scale data collection and retention over longer periods of time; or actors with more unconstrained or absolute power and authority, like an authoritarian state unconstrained by laws – will lead to greater chilling effects.

How chilling effects are magnified this way shows why power, and the actors that wield it like government and big business, matters in a conformity theory of chilling effects. These actors can cause the *most* powerful and pervasive forms of chilling effects, on both individuals and societies. That is because they have far greater capacity for such "additive effects" via coordinated action carried out by law, surveillance, data collection, and targeted legal or regulatory threats. This is also what makes chilling effects *different* from your average day-to-day social conformity. Rather, they are a uniquely powerful behavioral effect as they tend to involve more powerful or multifaceted threats to safety magnified by the power and authority of government, law enforcement, and well- resourced commercial enterprise. Milgram himself was so deeply disturbed by his own findings about the level of compliance that people showed in relation to a single person with status and authority, that he worried what a government, with vast powers and authority, could unleash:

> The results are to this author disturbing. They raise the possibility that human nature, or more specifically, the kind of character produced in American democratic society, cannot be counted on to insulate its citizens from brutality and inhumane treatment at the direction of malevolent authority .... If in this study an anonymous experimenter could successfully command adults to subdue a

fifty-year-old man, and force on him painful electric shocks against his protests, one can only wonder what government, with its vastly greater authority and prestige, can command of its subjects. There is, of course, the extremely important question of whether malevolent political institutions could or would arise in American society.[81]

In Chapter 7, I explain how chilling effects can be weaponized as a tool of power and repression – both the power of the state and the forces of surveillance capitalism. These additive dimensions are a key reason why.

A CONFORMITY THEORY

Social and behavioral science tells us how people respond to contexts involving uncertainty, observation, personalization, and power/authority – they are far more likely to conform their behavior. These very same contexts also lead to chilling effects. This is because uncertainty, observation, personalization, and power/ authority are all forms of threats that, as noted earlier, have traditionally been associated with chilling effects – they arise in these very contexts in response to these same factors. Thus, Karen Sharvit notes that self-censorship tends to also accompany other forms of conformity and compliance.[82] My theory of chilling effects demonstrates why – they are largely the same behavioral response: Self-censorship is chilling effects and chilling effects are conformity and compliance effects, and these key conformity and compliance factors – uncertainty, observation, personalization, and power/authority – are all in fact "chilling effect factors" that also cause and contribute to chilling effects. However, one important difference is that chilling effect scenarios tend to involve more powerful forms of conforming and compliance effects because they involve actions or powers – like law, surveillance, and targeted legal threats – typically exercised by governments, police, security agencies, and big business. That is, the entities with the most power and authority in society. Thus, chilling effects are not identical to conformity effects to this extent: They are usually qualitatively and quantitatively far greater in magnitude and scope.[83]

This makes sense when we recall the deeper psychological foundations of conformity and chilling effects. Conformity has many benefits and people do so for many reasons, but threat perception is the key factor when it comes to the chilling and conforming effects of government, law, police or corporate surveillance, and similar actions of powerful entities: We conform out of fear and anxiety in response to threats and conformity provides safety, protection, and support. Our tendency to do so is likely a product of evolution, as people who showed greater group conformity in response to the threats throughout history were more "fit" for survival, and so were their children. The power, authority, and additive effect capacity of government and big business compounds the scale and scope of the threat, hence increasing the scale and scope of conformity and thus chilling effects.

With these empirical and theoretical foundations set down, in Chapter 5 I elaborate more clearly my new theory via a taxonomy of both conventional and more contemporary forms of chilling effects and related scenarios, including those associated with statutes and regulations, government and corporate surveillance and data mining, online bullying and abuse, disinformation, and beyond.

5

A Taxonomy of Chilling Effects

Conventional theories of chilling effects were too narrow and could only explain chilling effects in limited situations with legal and privacy harms. We saw this in Chapters 1 and 2. One of the great benefits of a conformity theory of chilling effects, by contrast, is its explanatory power – it can explain chilling effects in a far wider range of contexts. In this chapter, I elaborate this new theory further by applying it to explain a range of different scenarios involving chilling effects – a taxonomy of chilling effects. This taxonomy includes more common examples and scenarios typically associated with chilling effect claims and concerns – like regulatory or surveillance chill – but it also introduces ones less often analyzed or socially recognized, like the phenomenon I describe later as "disinformation chill," which concerns the impact of false information online.

My aim here is threefold: first, to demonstrate the explanatory power of this new theory relying on the four chilling effect factors set out in Chapter 4 – observation, uncertainty, personalization, and power/authority – as key guiding measures; second, to illustrate a broader range of different forms of chilling effects that may affect us, and a scale of the problem beyond simply government surveillance or over-reaching laws – the predominant focus of conventional theories; and third, to foster a better understanding of chilling effects across a broader range of contexts and circumstances so that researchers can better investigate, courts and legal scholars can develop better law, and policymakers can forge better solutions, to address, mitigate, and resist chilling effects and in the long term resolve their corrosive impact on rights and democracy. In the end, I hope this exercise provides a more comprehensive and pluralistic understanding both of my new theory of chilling effects and the behavioral phenomenon of chilling effects itself.[1]

The taxonomy is organized in three parts. The first part discusses types of chilling effects that are associated with information, data, and its analysis – a focus of conventional privacy theories – including surveillance chill, data breach chill, and the chill of data analytics, profiling, and prediction. The second part addresses chilling effects associated with law – including statutory, regulatory, and targeted legal enforcement chill. I show how my theory can explain each far better than predominant legal

67

theories of chilling effects. The third part addresses broader societal or infrastructure forms of chilling effects including what I call "system" or "institutional" chill; disinformation chill; and the chill of online abuse. For each case in the taxonomy, I identify or explain the scenario or type, how or why it has been associated with chilling effects, and explain how a conformity theory allows us to best understand any chilling effects involved. While the taxonomy focuses on activities and scenarios that can and do cause chilling effects, in applying the theory, I will also show how some concerns about chilling effects – like those due to surveillance, personal threats, targeted enforcement, and data breach chill – are more justified and well-founded than others – like general statutory or regulatory chill.

INFORMATION AND DATA-RELATED FORMS

1 *Surveillance and Data Collection Chill*

When people are aware they are being observed by others or are aware of the possibility of it, they are chilled from freely speaking and acting. This book has already recounted many high-profile and widely covered stories about overreaching government and corporate surveillance: the Snowden revelations about mass government surveillance; Clearview AI and its work with law enforcement and militaries in North America and abroad; and the Cambridge Analytica scandal involving social media data collection and analysis done for political purposes. This has led to increasing concerns about chilling effects – and rightly so.

Take the Cambridge Analytica scandal, whose chilling effects on people's behavior online has been well documented. How can we understand or explain these impacts? The Cambridge Analytica scandal has different layers. One is that the scandal involves large-scale data breach – arguably the most widely publicized and consequential data breach to date.[2] But it is not *only* that, and not a typical data breach example at that. It was not a single hack or data breach. Rather, it involved a large- scale surveillance, data collection, and data-mining operation spanning multiple years – data was stolen not once, or twice, but continually through a flaw in Facebook's interface. The scandal thus involves surveillance and data tracking – without it, the operation would not be possible. But it also involved data mining – powered by algorithms and data-driven analytics. The firm stole data about nearly 100 million people and with an aim to use it to target and manipulate those people, and others like them, on critical matters of public importance. Algorithmic data mining enabled these disturbing aims, providing the means to analyze the stolen data and understand hidden relationships and insights in it necessary to influence and manipulate.

A conformity theory offers a powerful framework to explain and understand each of these layers, and more. Indeed, chilling effects associated with state or corporate surveillance and data collection – like those in the Cambridge Analytica scandal – would have a more significant conforming and chilling effect, with all chilling effect factors present – observation; uncertainty; personalization; and authority/power. Start with the first chilling effect factor – observation. If very simple forms of observation – like being watched by a peer or stranger alone – can have these chilling effects as in Hawthorne and "watching eye" studies – it is easy to understand how *surveillance* can have profound chilling effects. It is, after all, observation that is systematic, planned, purposive, and persistent, and carried out by powerful actors like police, national security agencies, and commercial enterprise, and enhanced by technology and big data.

There are different ways of defining surveillance. One simple definition is that surveillance is "systematic observation" – which is how the US military defines it, as do security experts like Bruce Schneier.[3] Sociologist David Lyon expands on this understanding, defining surveillance as "the focused, systematic and routine attention to personal details for purposes of influence, management, protection or direction."[4] Neil Richards adopts Lyon's definition but expands it further still, adding that surveillance also "transcends the public-private divide."[5] All of these definitions offer important insights, but they have the same central point in common: Surveillance involves observation that is intentional, methodical, organized, planned, and pursued with a purpose – essentially, a more powerful version of observation.

Expansive data collection is central to modern surveillance, rendering it a more systematic and powerful form of observation than most other forms of surveillance. The concept dataveillance, coined by Roger Clarke in the late 1980s and developed extensively in the surveillance studies field since, speaks to this very point.[6] Clarke originally employed the term as shorthand for "data surveillance" to highlight the then emerging practice of collecting and analyzing personal data to systematically monitor, track, or investigate individuals or populations.[7] He argued that dataveillance would render obsolete the "two way" ubiquitous mass video surveillance envisioned by Orwell in *Nineteen Eighty-Four* – the "telescreen" Big Brother installed in every home to keep everyone under fear of surveillance around the clock.[8] Even though the technology for the telescreen was likely available it would never be deployed, Clarke surmised, because dataveillance, as a means of population sorting, manipulation, and control for government and corporations, was technically and economically superior.[9] Traditional forms of surveillance, like physical observation, have always been expensive. Even when enhanced by technology, they are labor intensive and require centralization.[10] Big Brother required a massive and cumbersome centralized bureaucracy to carry out its surveillance operations.[11] Dataveillance, by contrast, is quiet, decentralized, far less visible, and more easily scaled up. It could also be automated by computers and then, all it required was a network of personal data systems and a uniform system of identification to track people across different contexts.[12] But most importantly, it was also technically superior: How you could monitor and observe a person and what you could know and learn about them by analyzing their personal data would also be far greater than what you could learn through other forms of surveillance. The cost-effective, automated, and systematic observation and control made possible through data surveillance would supplant, not supplement, other forms of surveillance.

He was right. Today, the Snowden revelations demonstrate that Western governments, security agencies, and law enforcement all engage in sophisticated forms of mass and targeted data surveillance, collection, and tracking. The Cambridge Analytica scandal demonstrates that surveillance and collection is also a major industry. The business models of the biggest and most innovative companies today are predicated on mass collection and exploitation of people's personal information and data, which are used to target, track, observe, and manipulate consumers, and serve other commercial and corporate interests.[13] We are living in an era of what Shoshana Zuboff calls "surveillance capitalism."[14]

Yet, the chill of surveillance's systematic and enhanced observation is compounded by the uncertainty and ambiguity of modern surveillance practices. One of the key insights from the surveillance studies field – a subfield of sociology but one that also cuts across other social science fields and disciplines like privacy, communications, criminology, and cultural studies – is that surveillance is inherently ambiguous and uncertain. The "panoptic urge" of modern surveillance and data collection, Lyon has written, is to "generate regimes of self-discipline through uncertainty."[15] Surveillance studies theorists have taken this point even further, theorizing a broader surveillance culture that is pervasive and participatory. Everyone – armed with their own smartphones, Apple Watches, GoPro cameras, and other ubiquitous personal recording and computing devices – and everything – think always on, always listening smart appliances in our homes and places of work – is involved, making surveillance malleable and ambiguous in its scope, reach, and purposes.[16] Zygmunt Bauman and David Lyon's concept of "liquid surveillance" speaks to these attributes, in how surveillance permeates all aspects of modern life, fostering uncertainty and constantly shifting.[17]

This ambiguity and uncertainty in modern surveillance extends to the broader set of related data and information practices that drive and empower it.[18] Indeed, privacy scholars have long highlighted the uncertainty and ambiguity in the collection, retention, sharing, and use of data. Paul Schwartz noted decades ago, for instance, that people "know little or nothing about the circumstances under which their personal data are captured, sold, or processed."[19] And Solove spoke to the "fear and uncertainty" about the myriad of possible future uses for information collected about us.[20]

Fear and uncertainty about such abuses now and in the future are only compounded by the new realities of ubiquitous computing, social media, and digitization. Greater sums of data are collected and retained in massive permanent databases in a form that never degrades nor ever becomes scarce because countless new digital copies can be made at almost no cost. "The internet never forgets," as

Eben Moglen, my former Columbia law professor, once said to us in class. The same can now be said of social media and almost any platform or device that generates and retains data and information about our activities today. Though people inevitably face different levels of scrutiny and surveillance – a fact apparent from the FBI's race-infused history of spying on black activists – the permanence of data today arguably makes it not just possible but *probable* that our information will at some point be leaked, shared, stolen, hacked, or disclosed either publicly or to unauthorized third parties or used for purposes we would never agree with. As a reflection of this fact, there is today a small but growing cottage industry of websites like HaveIBeenPWNED.com or DeHashed.com that allow you to search for your email, phone number, IP address, or other personal data or information in large databases of literally billions of compromised, hacked, and leaked accounts to see if you have been a victim.[21] Often, it is not even hackers or cybercriminals we need to worry about most, but companies like Cambridge Analytica that may have authorized access to some Facebook data, but have commercial incentives to exploit that access to collect far more data in order to monetize it.

The chilling effect factors discussed so far – observation and uncertainty – apply to mass forms of surveillance and data collection and retention, affecting large groups, even entire communities or populations – like concerns about mass governmental surveillance or data collection activities after the Snowden revelations. Simply having an awareness of such surveillance has a chilling effect, even without knowing if specific information or data has, in fact, been collected about you or your activities.

But personalization is another relevant factor. Surveillance and data collection need not just be large scale and indiscriminate; they can also be targeted and highly personalized. As Richards documents, there are countless historical examples of targeted surveillance being used and abused to blackmail critics; discredit dissidents and opponents; discriminate against marginalized populations; and manipulate the public.[22] Perhaps the most infamous example of such abuse was the FBI's surveillance of Martin Luther King Jr., under COINTELPRO – a covert federal surveillance program during the Cold War that first targeted communists in the 1950s but by the 1960s expanded to target civil rights activists.[23] Despite years of surveillance, including wiretaps, covert hotel room recordings, and paid informants, neither the FBI nor the NSA found evidence that King had communist sympathies or was under the influence of foreign agents, as FBI Director J. Edgar Hoover had baselessly surmised, but did find evidence of extramarital affairs that the FBI nevertheless used to blackmail and threaten him. The FBI even sent King an anonymous "suicide letter" that threatened to expose his extramarital affairs unless he committed suicide.[24] The benefit of targeting Dr. King, was not only that it would chill the activities of the most important and charismatic civil rights leader at the time – but it would also have a chilling effect on other civil rights leaders and activists in the broader movement.

Today, surveillance technology offers even more capabilities for personalized and targeted monitoring, tracking, and information collection. There is a growing and profitable global commercial spyware industry that markets its technologies and services to governments, security agencies, and commercial enterprise around the world.[25] Those technologies and services – spyware, malware, and other malicious technology-enabled surveillance tools – are now increasingly being used to systematically target human rights activists, journalists, and civil society organizations.[26]

Lastly, power and authority are critical to understanding these chilling effects. And modern surveillance and related data practices are a perfect example of this. Surveillance has long been employed as a tool of authority by government, law enforcement, and wealthy and powerful commercial interests, and is viewed that way by the general public. Concerns about overreaching government surveillance and its threat to privacy and freedom pervaded public imagination during the Cold War years, with the looming threat of communist and authoritarian regimes in the East.[27] Emblematic of these public sentiments is Orwell's "Big Brother," the all-seeing and all-knowing totalitarian regime in *Nineteen Eighty-Four*, which is by far the most famous and pervasive fictional exploration and the key metaphor for surveillance in the West.[28] Surveillance studies scholars, building on Foucault's work on panopticism, have explored how surveillance is a tool of population "social control" and "sorting" pursued via governmental, social, and institutional apparatus and processes.[29] Surveillance and government authority are closely linked.

Yet, modern surveillance and data-mining practices are also constitutive of corporate and commercial power and authority. Consumer surveillance, writes Kirstie Ball, is an "enactment of corporate power" that seeks to align people's preferences with "corporate goals."[30] This authority and power has manifested itself in the digital age in at least two ways. First, is the emergence of the surveillance–industrial complex – the confluence of political, economic, and social relationships that mediate and incentivize powerful public and private sector partnerships in developing surveillance systems specifically for security and law enforcement purposes.[31] Second, is through the transformational and political–economic influence of information and surveillance capitalism. The work of Zuboff, noted earlier, is relevant here, as is that of Julie Cohen and Sarah Myers West, among others, who have linked commercial surveillance and other data extractive practices with new forms of capitalism and corporate coercion.[32] The internet's "primary business model," Schneier has flatly observed, "is built on mass surveillance."[33] Corporate power, Joseph Turow argues, is a "reality" at the "very heart of the digital age."[34] And surveillance is a central tool of that power and authority.

A conformity theory thus helps us understand the chill from the Cambridge Analytica scandal, and so much more. Observation and surveillance alone have chilling and conforming effects, especially when conducted by actors with considerable power and authority like government, police, and big business. This is especially so, when state or state-affiliated actors and powerful private sector entities forge partnerships to develop and carry out such surveillance and data mining – Cambridge Analytica. On top of that, the uncertainty, ambiguity, and "liquidity" of modern surveillance and data collection and retention, especially targeted and personalized forms, amplify and compound these effects.

All of these additive dimensions – with all four chilling effect factors at play – magnify the scope and scale of impact by increasing the threat that surveillance and expansive data collection pose, both in perception and reality. For those aware, and especially for those with reason to believe they may be targeted, this in turn triggers deeper psychological mental states – fear, anxiety, distress – that drive more powerful forms of conformity and chill.

2 *Data Breach Chill*

A data breach can have substantial chilling effects for similar reasons as surveillance and data mining. A data breach involves the loss, theft, or unauthorized disclosure of data, which usually includes both sensitive and personal information.[35] Large-scale data breaches are increasingly common. Every sector is affected,[36] and the range of data implicated is vast, including: consumer data; government data; business records; information about voting rolls; patient records and healthcare provider information; scientific data; trade secrets and other intellectual property.[37] Essentially, almost anything that is electronic or digitized is at risk.[38] In 2021, the number of data breaches reached record heights, jumping 68 percent.[39] The data breaches affected 294 million people.[40] In the words of Daniel Solove and Danielle Citron, data breaches have become an "epic problem."[41]

One reason is how victims of a data breach are impacted. Many scholars have argued that data breaches like this have significant chilling effects. For instance, Solove and Citron rely on the concept of risk. That is, a data breach involving personal, sensitive, and financial information renders victims at a greater risk of identity theft, fraud, and harms to reputation. Once aware, they argue, a victim may be "chilled" from engaging in activities that depend on good credit – like taking out a loan, purchasing a new home, or looking for a new job.[42] A person may not bother taking these expensive and time-consuming steps when issues with credit reports, due to the data breach, may undercut those efforts. Data breaches effectively chill a person's ability to "engage in life's important activities."[43]

Solove and Citron are right that a data breach has a chilling effect, but the increased risk of identity theft, fraud, and reputational harm is only part of the story. A conformity theory of chilling effects points to other factors as well. First, victims of a data breach suffer from a surveillance chill. Having their sensitive information or data leaked or stolen, potentially for malicious or illegal reasons, creates a similar feeling of being watched, tracked, and monitored both by the malicious actor involved in the misappropriation and any number of additional third parties that may gain access to that same data. And that data and information can be potentially used to identify the victim and place them under surveillance in other ways, now and in the future. Calo notes this surveillance effect of data breaches:

> When a consumer receives a notice in the mail telling her that her personal information has leaked out into the open, she experiences the exact sort of apprehension and feeling of vulnerability the first category of privacy harm is concerned about. That is, she believes that there has been or could be unwanted sensing of her private information.[44]

When a data breach involves publicly leaked data, then the surveillance effect is magnified even further, with not just malicious third parties potentially watching, but any member of the public that has seen or has accessed the leaked data.

Second, in addition to this surveillance effect, a data breach creates countless uncertainties for victims. Earlier, I noted that Solove argued that data collection on its own creates "fear and uncertainty" as to the "future uses" of information gathered and retained.[45] Chilling effects, as Kiel Brennan-Marquez and Helen Nissenbaum have both observed, stem not just "exclusively" from the initial surveillance and collection, but also "stem from anxiety about where sensitive information, once collected, might flow."[46] Those fears, anxieties, and uncertainties are even greater when it comes to data breaches, as the perpetrator that has stolen the victim's data likely has criminal or malicious aims, and is therefore more likely to use or abuse the stolen data in damaging or harmful ways. Here, it is the uncertainty created by the data breach, rather than increased risk of future harms like identity theft, fraud, or reputational harms, that causes the chill. Furthermore, in cases of a targeted hack, where there is evidence that a victim was specifically targeted by hackers or malicious third parties in a data breach, then both the surveillance and uncertainty – and any resulting conforming and chilling effects – impacts are even further heightened.

These chilling effect factors – surveillance, uncertainty, and personalization – are central to understanding data breach chill, as a first order. However, this analysis can then be complemented and synthesized with the additive effects of increased risk that Solove and Citron write about. This, in turn, would magnify chilling effects of a data breach, depending on the scope and nature of the data, and the future risks.

An experimental study by behavioral economists Yoan Hermstrüwer and Stephan Dickert provides some illustration of these dynamics.[47] In their study, participants played a "dictator game," which is a standard game often employed in experimental psychology that gives participants an opportunity to behave generously or selfishly in relation to other players.[48] They found that when participants were told that data and information about how they played the game would be published online later – including how selfishly or generously they acted – they behaved much more generously and less selfishly than those who were not. The chilling effect was strong enough not only to deter very selfish behavior, but caused overall improvement in the social behavior of participants.[49] In other words, the awareness that data about their activities would be publicized and accessible to others online – comparable to a data breach or leak online – significantly chilled participants leading them to behave in conformity with social norms of generosity.[50] This is entirely consistent with a conformity theory of data breach chilling effects.

3 *Data Processing, Profiling, and Prediction Chill*

A lot has changed in the fifteen years since Daniel Solove wrote about information processing in his influential article *A Taxonomy of Privacy*.[51] Data processing, analytics, and mining – which I use here to refer to using, combining, manipulating, and analyzing information – is now far more sophisticated. It has to be, to tackle the challenges of big data – massive data sets generated from billions of daily online transactions that are larger, more varied – relating to every aspect of our lives – and more complex than at any other time in history.[52] Today we are surely living in what Solove and his colleague Hideyuki Matsumi call a "prediction society," wherein data mining, algorithmic profiling, and predictive technologies are pervasive.[53] Ironically, in his original taxonomy, Solove maintained that the harms of information processing and data mining were more bureaucratic in nature – a sense of powerlessness and vulnerability – and not chilling effects – "inhibited behavior."[54]

In fact, Solove has since changed his mind on this count, at least with respect to certain kinds of data-processing applications today like predictive analytics. Here is how Solove and Matsumi describe the chilling effects resulting from algorithmic big data mining and predictive analytics today:

> In addition to being constantly watched, people's every action, every click, and every twitch is being recorded and analyzed for patterns and then resulting in fortune or ruin. The Panopticon chills outliers; it aims to induce them to conform. The Predicticon casts outliers out of consideration. It doesn't care if they conform. Even worse, the Predicticon usurps people's stories and writes a clichéd ending. Instead of a grand Borgesian library with an infinitude of tales, the imaginatively-stultified Predicticon allows only the same predictable stories. The Predicticon is a prison of predictions, where our future paths are closed off, where we live in a cell that continually constricts.[55]

Clearly, the power and reach of modern algorithmic data processing has led Solove to change his mind about its capacity for chilling effects. He was right to do so. Indeed, privacy, surveillance, and communications scholars now increasingly argue that new forms of pervasive and automated data processing, profiling, and analytics have substantial chilling effects on people's speech and behavior, especially online.[56] And how these practices foster new forms of systematic observation, uncertainty, personalization, and power for state and corporate interests – and powerlessness for the rest of us – are all key factors in these chilling effects.

But Solove's explanation for the change of heart isn't entirely clear. This passage alludes to Foucault's "Panopticon," wherein persistent surveillance creates chilling effects. Clearly, Solove sees parallels between data-driven predictions and surveillance and I agree and a theory of chilling effects as conformity provides a full explanation as to how and why data processing, profiling, and predictive analytics have powerful chilling effects – like the kind Solove describes.

Let us begin with the first chilling effect factor: observation. Today, data processing, profiling, and predictive analytics *do* involve systematic observation and surveillance and they *do* require surveillance and information collection to provide the data that is analyzed and mined, and which, as we have seen, causes substantial chill. But not only that. The most popular applications of big data analytics and mining today – prediction of human behavior – themselves constitute a powerful and unprecedented form of surveillance and observation that can be just as chilling. Advanced new data-mining techniques, powered by algorithms and enhanced by emerging technologies like machine learning and AI, have been developed to analyze and excavate massive data sets for useful information, intelligence, and hidden patterns and other insights, especially about people's personalities and behaviors, to advance both state and corporate interests.[57] A central assumption of these new analytical techniques is that they can explain and predict human behavior.[58] And not just in the consumer context, but *in any domain*, from business, politics, medicine, finance, employment, housing, law and crime, and beyond.[59] Big data analytics and mining work by employing algorithms to uncover preferences, values, and other factors that underlie and influence people's decision-making and behavior.[60] They aspire to perfectly predict how people will behave in any given context. These powerful forms of predictive data analytics are arguably today's most powerful forms of surveillance and observation.

Stephen Spielberg's 2002 science fiction film *Minority Report* is a compelling illustration of this point. The story takes place in the year 2054 and centers on Washington DC's new "pre-crime" policing division, which has effectively eliminated murder in the city by tapping into the minds of three psychics – "precogs" – whose dreams predict murders before they happen.[61] These dreams, or predictions of the future, give police a head start, so that people are arrested before they even have the chance to commit the crime.[62] John Anderton, the movie's main character, is another pre-crime officer and deeply committed to the work of the division. That is, until the day the precogs predict *he* will commit murder in thirty-six hours, which puts him on the run in a desperate bid to prove his innocence and the fallibility of the supposedly perfect pre-crime law enforcement system to which his work was devoted.[63] *Minority Report* is ostensibly about clairvoyance and metaphysical psychic predictions, but it is really about a dystopia plagued by total surveillance and bereft of privacy.[64] Central to Spielberg's vision for the film, from its earliest conception, is a future where privacy is "a thing of the past" and we are constantly under total surveillance – eyes being scanned, identity assessed, location logged.[65] But in the film, those forms of routine and granular surveillance are largely driven by market forces – "Welcome back to the Gap," Anderton is greeted by a holographic image while entering a futuristic version of the clothing retailer, "[h]ow did those assorted new tank tops work out for you?"[66] But in *Minority Report*, the state and law enforcement need not bother with these forms of simple and routine daily surveillance. Why? They had something far more powerful – the power of prediction. You don't need to watch or track everyone all the time if you already know what they're going to do even before they do it. A system with access to perfect behavioral prediction capacity is also the perfect surveillance system.

Even though clairvoyant predictions like those fictionalized in *Minority Report* are not yet possible, we are nevertheless living in a brave new world of powerful predictive capacity.[67] Whether we like it or not, many companies are confident they can predict our futures.[68] And there are many examples suggesting they can. An oft discussed one, chronicled by *New York Times* reporter Charles Duhigg, involved retailer Target using a large-scale data-mining operation to successfully predict which of their customers was pregnant, and when she was most likely to give birth, based on shopping habits, in order to provide them with tailored advertisements and promotions.[69] When the father of a teenage girl saw coupons for baby products that Target had sent her, he complained to the store that this was inappropriate only to learn later that his daughter was in fact pregnant.[70] Target's data science team, using customer profiling and analyzing purchasing patterns, had discovered the man's daughter was pregnant before he did. Like consumers, employees are also increasingly the targets of data-mining operations and predictive analytics by employers. For instance, starting in 2013, Hewlett-Packard (HP), which then and still today employs over 300,000 people, began using data mining and predictive analytics to predict when each of its workers would most likely quit their job.[71] HP called these predictive assessments the "Flight Risk" score, which was delivered to managers.[72] Imagine your boss knowing when you would quit your job even before you did.

But darker and more reminiscent of *Minority Report* is the story of Robert McDaniel, a resident of Austin, a neighborhood in Chicago with a very high murder rate.[73] In 2020, Austin saw seventy-two homicides – nearly 10 percent of Chicago's overall total in an area with only 3 percent of the city's population.[74] Despite having no record of violence, a Chicago Police Department (CPD) predictive policing program, based on algorithmic data mining and analytics, determined in 2013 that McDaniel would be involved in a shooting – literally "a party to violence."[75] That is, based on his proximity to and relationships with known shooters as well as victims of shootings and other factors, the CPD's predictive algorithm found that McDaniel was more likely than 99.9 percent of Chicago's population to either be a shooter or a victim of a shooting. The algorithm could not conclusively predict precisely which one, but McDaniel was nevertheless found to be a danger. With this algorithmic prediction, Chicago police officers placed McDaniel on their "heat list," a kind of "person of interest" list, and kept him under surveillance – and even notified him in person that they would be watching him – despite him not being under suspicion for any crime.[76]

He was, like Anderton in *Minority Report*, essentially accused of pre-crime. But since the surveillance that the prediction triggered was overt and apparent, including visits from police officers and social workers among others, people in his neighborhood came to believe he may be a police informant. This not only damaged McDaniel's reputation in the community, but it also put a target on his back. Since being added to the "heat list," McDaniel has been the victim of two shootings – one in 2017 and another in 2020. Both, he believes, were a result of people thinking he was a snitch. "In McDaniel's view," wrote journalist Matt Stroud who reported on the story for *The Verge*, "the heat list caused the harm its creators hoped to avoid: It predicted a shooting that wouldn't have happened if it hadn't predicted the shooting."[77] So, the prediction turned out to be right, twice over, but in a darkly ironic twist, only because it was a self-fulfilling prophecy.

Each of these stories demonstrates not only the unique challenges that arise as predictive technologies proliferate in society, but also how these technologies involve an unprecedented form of systematic observation – modern data processing and analytics, powered by algorithms and machine learning, can discover surprising and deeply intimate insights about people and their life and behavior, and future – like when they may quit their job; when they are expecting a baby; and whether they may commit or be victimized by serious crimes – and do so by only analyzing data and information that would appear to most of us as fairly prosaic and benign, like a user's "likes" or "clicks" on a social media platform.[78]

This capacity to infer sensitive information or insights from non-sensitive data, impacts every personal trait or attribute – our age, gender, ethnicity, education, income, location, political and sexual orientations, health, and social class, can all be, and have been in countless studies, inferred from more benign non-sensitive data and information.[79] Now, every click, like, website visited, article viewed, and product purchase, when analyzed through algorithms and machine learning processes, may reveal far more about us than we would ever want to disclose. It is a kind of systematic observation and surveillance into us and our lives that even Big Brother's terrifying "telescreen" could never hope to match. Yet, applications of big data processing and analytics are now apparent across every sector – government, industry, and civil society.[80] Some of these changes have a long history – like finance, insurance, and credit scoring – wherein data has long been used and analyzed for decades to predict how investors, borrowers, or the insured will behave in the future. But others, like big data and predictive analytics employed in criminal justice, employment, and education, are more recent.[81] As Matsumi and Solove observed, predictive tech has impacts comparable to surveillance chill, but arguably even more invasive and powerful.[82]

But these stories also illustrate other factors at play – like personalization and uncertainty. Central to each of these stories is algorithmic profiling – the use of algorithms to process personal data to evaluate or track different attributes of specific individuals.[83] Algorithmic profiling is also a perfect example of personalization that amplifies chilling effects. Algorithmic processes are automated and continuous, and can be done for many purposes, but they are often highly targeted – literally by definition, as they involve creating unique data profiles for each person or user, both to analyze and discover patterns and correlations in the broader data set, and to then apply those inferences and predictive models to individuals or groups. Take the Target example. Each customer was assigned a unique Guest ID number. All information and data the customer provided – like personal and demographic information – age, location, gender, employment history, and so on – was automatically linked to the Guest ID, as was everything the customer bought or did with Target, online and offline, from buying a product or visiting the website to using a coupon, or opening or clicking a link on a Target email. In other words, Guest ID became an algorithmically created and analyzed profile for each customer. These profiles made it possible to analyze the vast amount of customer data and discover patterns, including what pregnant women were more likely to purchase at different times of their pregnancy. They combined these insights into a "pregnancy prediction" score for each Guest ID, which allowed them to predict with astounding accuracy not only which customers were pregnant, but when they would likely be expecting their babies to arrive.[84]

In the case of McDaniel, the specifics as to how the CPD made predictions about who belonged on the "heat list" are much less known, but algorithmic profiling and analytics is almost surely central to the story. When the *Chicago Tribune* first reported on the CPD's crime data operations in 2013, the story only hinted at algorithmic processes with a nod to "mathematical analysis" but Stroud, reporting years later, would learn that it was indeed an algorithm "built" by the CPD that had made the prediction.[85] That algorithm developed profiles for residents based on a range of data points including criminal record; parole or warrant status; weapons or drug arrests; and friends and acquaintances – including their own arrest records and whether they were themselves victims of shootings and similar violent crimes. No doubt McDaniel's high-crime neighborhood, multiple arrests for more minor non-violent offences, and close personal relationship to a recent shooting victim – his best friend since childhood was shot and killed the previous year – were key factors that led the CPD algorithm to profile him as a serious risk worthy of the "heat list."[86] In each of these cases, algorithmic data collection, mining, and analytics were used to make mass forms of data collection and processing more personalized: by creating a unique profile for each consumer, employee, or city resident that was in turn used to generate highly personalized individual forecasts and behavioral predictions. In the McDaniel case, the program was also highly personalized in how it was implemented and enforced. It was Chicago Police Commander Barbara West herself who personally visited McDaniel to deliver the notice of targeted operations: "Don't commit any more crimes or face the consequences."[87] City social workers also came knocking, offering McDaniel help. Awareness of such a highly personalized algorithmic profiling and police surveillance operation would substantially amplify chilling effects. McDaniel's own words reflect this reality: "[I]f you're watching me," he said when first interviewed by the *Tribune*, "then you can obviously see I'm not doing anything."[88]

At the same time, data processing, profiling, and analytics, much like surveillance and data collection, also foster fear and uncertainty, especially when conducted at mass scale by algorithmic processes. There is uncertainty about the nature and purpose of these data processes. A central feature of algorithmic data collection and processing is that it is often automated, pervasive, and deployed at mass scale in its operation at the same time that it allows the constant creation and refinement of profiles tied to individuals and their behavior that are, or will be, employed for more specific or targeted purposes at some undefined future time.[89] It is thus inherently uncertain and ambiguous in its purpose and about its targets – those profiled intentionally or indiscriminately. It also fosters fear and uncertainty that intimate personal preferences, habits, or behavioral patterns might be unearthed by powerful data mining and analytics techniques, or by combining existing data with new information and data accessed in the future. And with the fields of AI and machine learning advancing so quickly, the reach and capability of algorithmic data analytics and mining is itself uncertain. And when predictions about future behavior are made and communicated, fear and uncertainty are also likely to be heightened.

In the McDaniel case, his main response to being added to the "heat list" was confusion, mystery, and uncertainty. He had been notified that he was 99.9 percent likely to be a party to serious life-threatening violence, a shooting, but neither he nor police had any idea whether he would be the one pulling the trigger or suffering the harm. Having not committed any crimes or acts of violence beyond minor misdemeanor offences, he could not understand how he attracted additional police attention or what to do about it. He's the perfect modern personification of Joseph K., the main character in Franz Kafka's *The Trial*, who embarks on a frustrating quest for exoneration for crimes despite not knowing the illegalities for which he is accused. This includes attempting to determine the contents of the secretive "dossier" that has allegedly been created about him, leaving him feeling "powerless, uncertain, and uneasy."[90] The CPD have likewise created a secretive dossier on McDaniel – an algorithmic profile that has flagged him as dangerous or in danger – but he has no means to exonerate himself for crimes he has not yet committed, and likely never will. Data processing, profiling, and predictive analytics are themselves uncertain and ambiguous, and create fear and uncertainty about what is known or can be known about people's past, present, and future, which magnifies chilling effects.[91]

Lastly, power/authority is also a key chilling effect factor here. In his seminal work *The Black Box Society: The Secret Algorithms That Control Money and Information*, Frank Pasquale argues that algorithms have altered the traditional sources of power and authority in modern society.[92] "Authority," he observes, "is increasingly expressed algorithmically."[93] That is easily apparent in cases like McDaniel, where powerful entities and institutions of authority like police, government, and security agencies employ algorithmic data processing and predictive analytics fueled to extend and advance their power, reach, and effectiveness in carrying out traditional state practices like targeted surveillance, law enforcement, and the protection of national security. And algorithms themselves, a product of science, machine learning, and other complex and highly sophisticated technology, are also a source of authority to which people tend to defer, and thus conform with, as they would to more traditional forms of authority.[94] Danielle Citron calls this "automation bias" – the tendency of human workers to defer to algorithmically produced decisions.[95] Even professionals have been shown to defer to algorithms in their own fields of expertise.[96]

But there is also a newer form of algorithmic authority and power being employed here as well, to use Pasquale's terms. Target's marketing strategies, enabled by algorithmic data processing, profiling, and predictive analytics, are called "behavioral advertising."[97] Such practices are controversial for many reasons,[98] but a central one is that they allow businesses to manipulate and influence people's behavior over the long term, a subtle but unmistakable form of power and control.[99] Now, imagine this kind of power being deployed beyond business and at greater scale – by governments, foreign and domestic, criminal enterprise, even political parties and operatives. Indeed, at the center of the Cambridge Analytica scandal, and no doubt its chilling effects, was behavioral influence and manipulation driven by big data and algorithmic profiling that allowed it to "model" the personality of every American, some 230 million people, in order to influence, manipulate, and control them.[100]

In the end, all four key chilling effect factors – observation, uncertainty, personalization, and power/authority – are present, meaning data processing, profiling, and predictive analytics have powerful chilling effects. Indeed, a society of increasingly powerful algorithmic data processing, profiling, prediction, and inference, as *Minority Report* teaches us, is one where we are placed under a new and powerful form of observation – systematic surveillance of not just what we did in the past, but what we will do in our future, long before we experience or know it ourselves.

The chill of such highly personalized algorithmic profiling and prediction is clear from the McDaniel story. The impact on his life was profound and long lasting. He was not only chilled from engaging in any further criminal or antisocial behavior, but also disengaged from police protection and broader government services – he refused to report his second shooting to police and also persistently rejected help from the many city social workers and community organizers who visited him offering help.[101] These chilling effects were no doubt the product not only of being subject to a targeted surveillance and tracking operation fueled by big data processing and predictive analytics, backed by the power and authority of police, but also the immense fear and uncertainty about the risks of social sanction, alienation, and threats to both his reputation and personal safety in his community – he could not be seen to be cooperating with police, a profound violation of social norms in his neighborhood.

Yet, there are significant chilling effects even in cases involving more seemingly benign corporate forms of algorithmic processing and profiling, as is clear from the Target example. Female customers who realized Target had somehow figured out that they were pregnant – likely a deeply personal intimate fact for many – were likewise deeply chilled. Women were reportedly "spooked," "queasy," and "uncomfortable," and not only declined the personalized behavioral promotions, but started avoiding Target altogether.[102] The chilling effect was so serious that Target began to camouflage its targeted behavioral ads so women would not be tipped off that they were being "spied on." These reactions match broader studies exploring public perceptions of targeted and behavioral advertising, describing such practices as creating a "feeling of being watched" – observation – and the possibility of "inferences" about private or intimate facts from big data analytics "creepy," leading to chilling effects and loss of trust.[103]

LAW-RELATED FORMS

1 *Statutory and Regulatory Chill*

Statutory and regulatory chilling effects are the predominant focus of legal and judicial considerations of chilling effects. A conformity theory of chilling effects has no difficulties explaining these impacts too. This seems like a counterintuitive idea – complying with the legal command or requirement would seem to involve acquiescing to that legal command, to avoid the repercussions, not *conforming* to social norms. Yet, that is precisely how legal chilling effects work in most cases. An uncertain law is a personal threat – if a person is uncertain whether they might break the law and face legal punishment for it – and when faced with a personal threat, people engage in conformity to resolve the uncertainty but also for safety and security.

A vast social science literature over the last few decades shows that most people comply with the law because they believe it is moral and legitimate. This, in a sense, is a social norm – people obey legitimate laws and legal rules. Chilling effects arise due to moments of situational uncertainty about the law's requirements – a person thinks their conduct is legal, but they are unsure. In those moments, the social science tells us that people look to social norms and other "social proofs" for guidance as to how to act. And the widely accepted social norm of following the law will have a powerful conforming impact on the person – leading them to avoid the action, or to change their behavior, to ensure they comply with the law. However, on this theory, and research supporting it, there is also reason to believe that chilling effects arising due to a typical statute or regulation will be less common, and if it happens, will be among the weaker and least impactful forms of chilling effects.

A central factor in my theory is uncertainty. Uncertainty is a threat that leads people to conformity – to seek out social norms to resolve the uncertainty, and for safety and security, which in turn causes self-censorship, conformity, and other forms of chilling effects, despite believing their behavior or speech was lawful. A law or regulation could, of course, create such uncertainty as legal rules are inherently uncertain.[104] That uncertainty can arise as a result of unclear, vague, or ambiguous legal terms or statutory language, as well as uncertainty about the likelihood of enforcement of a given law or legal rule.[105] Legal uncertainty was an important element of Schauer's chilling effects theory. He emphasized uncertainty in the legal process, including its interplay of fallible humans, people-made rules, and unpredictability.[106] And a standard tenet of behavioral law and economics research has held that when laws are uncertain, people are likely to over comply with the law – chilling lawful and even desirous behavior – due to being risk averse.[107]

Indeed, there is empirical legal research, consistent with findings in social psychology, that when faced with legal uncertainty, people are also more likely to rely on social norms to make a decision about their law-related behavior. Early research on legal ambiguity and organizations by Lauren Edelman found that uncertainty in the law invites responses that engage broader societal norms and interests.[108] Similarly, experimental research by Yuval Feldman and Alon Harel demonstrated, among other findings, that when facing legal ambiguity, people rely primarily on social norms to decide how to behave, and that the level of ambiguity is an important factor in that reliance.[109] That is, the greater the uncertainty or ambiguity, the more heavy reliance a person will place on social norms to decide how to act.[110] In another study, Feldman and Doron Teichman also found strong reliance on social norms in contexts of legal uncertainty, but also found that if the law is too unclear or vague, it might undercut the law's capacity to guide behavior.[111]

So, there is situational uncertainty in the law that could lead a person to seek guidance in the norms of others, which can lead to chilling and conforming effects – following others in how they speak or act in the circumstances. Furthermore, this tendency will be informed by social norms around legal compliance in society. If we understand social norms as behaviors that are seen as desirable or legitimate in broader society and whose violation thus may at least lead to social sanction or "informal disapproval," then certainly legal obedience is a widely accepted social norm in society.[112] Richard McAdams and Eric Rasmusen refer to this social norm as the "norm of legal compliance" while Amir Licht calls it the "rule of law" social norm, arguing that it serves a critical interface between informal social norms and formal laws and legal requirements in society.[113] Whether this rule-of-law social norm is a product of other norms concerning following rules that are moral and fair, or socialization processes, this norm would have a powerful conforming effect on a person uncertain about the legality of their course of action.[114]

Of course, there will be cases where the law creates more traditional forms of legal chilling effects, such as where a person is aware of the law, its requirements, and potential punishments – civil or criminal – and especially believes the law will be enforced against them if they violate it. This is particularly the case when a person or group is targeted or singled out. In such cases, the law can certainly have chilling effects where a person is uncertain about how the law applies to their conduct, leading them to likely comply even where they believe they would be acting legally. But as discussed in Chapter 1, those conditions are rarely met in practice. What about other cases where people may be generally aware of the law, but not its requirements or punishments; have no idea if it would be enforced; or are simply uncertain about the legality of their course of conduct? As I have argued here, at least as a threshold matter, legal and regulatory uncertainty and ambiguities can lead people to engage in the same process that leads to conformity in other contexts – resolving ambiguity by looking to the social norms of others. And, absent some other norms suggesting rampant noncompliance, a conformity theory of chilling effects can explain how the prevalence and power of such rule-of-law social norms can chill someone from speaking or doing, even if they might believe their action was both legal and even desirable. They were simply uncertain and instead were chilled and conformed their behavior to avoid legal and social sanction and other social repercussions. So, Schauer was right about the uncertainty in the law being a key part of chilling effects, but wrong about *how* and *why*, in the end, a person may be chilled. That said, there are countervailing factors that suggest such legal and regulatory chilling effects are far less common than other forms, and when they do occur, are weak. In Chapter 9, I elaborate more fully.

2 *Targeted Legal Enforcement Chill*

Though general statutes may ultimately have weaker chilling effects, if legal rules and their enforcement become more targeted there is good reason to believe then associated chilling effects would be far more substantial. One very simple or common example of targeted enforcement would be regular law enforcement action or prosecution. That is, a person is made aware that they are the focus of criminal or civil investigation and may be soon targeted for prosecution or some other personal legal threat or action. Being aware that you are the target of a government intervention or prosecution is a paradigmatic chilling effects case.[115] In fact, being faced with a "credible fear of prosecution" has been recognized by countless courts as a legitimate basis for a chilling effects claim.[116]

Yet, there are few, if any, works explaining precisely why targeted enforcement or personalized law might have chilling effects, beyond the usual conventional accounts relying on legal threats alone. Nor is there any explanation as to whether those chilling effects might be greater than those caused by other kinds of threats. A conformity theory of chilling effects does so, showing why such concerns are well founded and why these kinds of chilling effects are powerful. First, power and authority are both key factors. Targeted legal enforcement is often wielded by government, law enforcement, or powerful commercial entities and this will magnify any chilling effects due to the legal threat. Second, when an individual is notified that they are a target of law enforcement action, it also triggers a surveillance or observation effect. It says: We have been watching you and will continue to watch you. Third, any legal enforcement would, if acted upon, be pursued and decided in the criminal or civil justice system. But the legal process itself is inherently uncertain – a point that Schauer argued at length about in his account. Such uncertainty adds to any chilling effect. Fourth, targeted legal enforcement amounts to a personal threat. Social psychology tells us that conformity and related chilling effects are significantly amplified when threats are more personal and specific.

Moreover, synthesizing social influence theory with insights from other theoretical accounts similarly suggests powerful chilling effects in this context. Targeted legal enforcement brings deterrence theory into play. A personally received legal threat increases awareness of the law's requirements – and its potential uncertainty – and the probability of legal punishment, especially instances with more sophisticated forms of technology-enabled targeted enforcement like personalized law.[117] That will also magnify compliance effects, and thus chill. Similarly, social norm behavior suggests that a norm that is activated or brought into focus, and made more salient, has more impact on behavior. A specific legal directive could be interested in or understood as bringing into focus a key legal norm or a social norm it reflects.

Given all of these chilling effect factors, such targeted legal enforcement, especially if personalized, would likely be among the most potent and powerful forms of chilling effects. In fact, we saw the profound chilling effects of something very analogous to targeted legal enforcement in the McDaniel case, once he was notified that he was on the "heat list." He was chilled not only from any activities that he believed would create risks of *legal* sanction by police who were watching him closely, but also from anything that would cause *social* sanction from people in his community. That led him to not only disengage from police protection but also from any social service or government institution that was seeking to help him – a form of system or institutional chill.

Beyond this case, there is empirical research demonstrating the chill of such targeted legal threats and personalized enforcement. For example, a number of empirical legal studies in the 1980s and 1990s have examined "libel chill" in more traditional media settings.[118] These studies documented how libel threats – a threat to launch a lawsuit against the target for publishing damaging false statements – chilled the work of journalists and media organizations, including chilling certain journalistic practices, media publishing, and content coverage. These chilling effects also have disparate impacts, with smaller independently owned media organizations with fewer resources more likely to be chilled by libel threats than others.[119] Empirical studies of targeted enforcement strategies that focus on specific individuals and groups, like "focused deterrence," provide additional evidence as to the substantial chill of targeted and personalized enforcement.[120] Those studies find that unlike more general enforcement and deterrence approaches, focused deterrence is far more effective at securing legal compliance by targeted individuals.[121] Chilling effects are likewise more powerful when legal enforcement is targeted and personal.

SOCIETAL/INFRASTRUCTURE-RELATED FORMS

1 *System/Institutional Chill*

The earlier recounted McDaniel story also hints at another kind of chilling effect – a kind of system chill or avoidance, where the victim disengages from social and government institutions due to their connection to surveillance operations. The spread of surveillance practices, technologies, and infrastructure in society has included institutions of health, education, finance, and government administration.[122] These institutional "surveillance assemblages," as Kevin Haggerty and Richard Ericson call them, can also cause a kind of system chilling effects – wherein people are chilled from participating in or engaging with these institutions due to the formal records that they may collect and retain about them.[123] Sociologist Sarah Brayne has empirically documented this form of chill, which she calls "system avoidance."[124] Using quantitative analysis of data drawn from the large and nationally representative National Longitudinal Study of Adolescent Health and National Longitudinal Survey of Youth in the United States, she found people with previous experience with the criminal justice system – those who have been stopped by police, arrested, prosecuted, and imprisoned – were more likely to avoid "surveilling institutions," that is, institutions like hospitals, banks, schools, and employers that may keep formal records about them, that is, put them "in the system."[125] Yet, these same "justice-involved" people did not avoid non-record-keeping institutions like religious groups or volunteer associations.[126] Brayne concluded that these "chilling effects" were the result of people "deliberately and systematically" avoiding the record-keeping institutions so as to evade heightened police surveillance.[127] This is precisely what happened with McDaniel when he rejected help from social workers and other city public servants who came to him to help – they had only come because they, like police, were notified that he had been included on the so-called heat list. From his angle of view, they were all a part of the same targeted surveillance and data-profiling apparatus and so he avoided them, undercutting the mandate of these same social and government services designed to help residents like him.

Others have documented comparable forms of system chilling effects. Sociologist Sarah Lageson has documented a similar chilling effect in her work on the digitization and proliferation of criminal justice records and data online.[128] She has found that the availability of such records online can lead such justice-involved people to avoid not just institutions but any situations that might lead to discovery of such records about them, like avoiding volunteering for their child's school as this may lead to others doing an internet search for their name. Even some whose only criminal justice experience was getting a mugshot taken without charges were chilled this way. Similarly, privacy scholar and social scientist Karen Levy in her ethnographic study of long-haul truck drivers and technology found that truckers were chilled by "electronic logging devices" (ELDs) required by federal law to be installed in their trucks, which truckers believed could create data logs of their activities that could be shared in real time with police and other third parties in order to spy on them.[129] In her important book *Data Driven: Truckers, Technology, and the Workplace Surveillance*, she documents how the ELDs impacted trucker behavior, with some leaving the industry entirely due to increased surveillance, with others adopting various avoidance activities.[130]

However, Levy also raises an important challenge for thinking about these chilling effects in terms of conformity. Citing my prior work, she argues that while her ELD-resisting truckers and Brayne's system avoiders are no doubt chilled, the outcome is not necessarily more conformity, but nonconforming behavior: These people are avoiding technologies, activities, places, and institutions that would otherwise be the norm for them to engage with and in some cases build enduring attachments with in order to live a full and stable life.[131] This, she concludes, is "in tension" with a theory of chilling effects as conformity, and thus calls for further research on the point to better understand what is produced by these chilling effects. This is a compelling observation and I do agree that on one angle of view, it appears as if the truckers and system avoiders are chilled into *departing* from typical social norms, which is evidence of nonconformity not conformity. I also agree with her that more research on the point is needed to better understand this phenomenon. That said, I still believe conformity and compliance provides the best lens to view their actions.

A central reason people conform is to avoid social disapproval, shame, and ostracism for engaging in activities that violate social norms. For Brayne's and Lageson's "justice-involved" avoiders, all of these things could happen if records of their involvement in the criminal justice system were discovered while being put "in the system" at institutions with access or at places inclined to do background checks and other online searches. This discovery could, in turn, lead to additional targeted surveillance and scrutiny of their activities, with the records and other collected data shared, copied, and retained in other databases, or disclosed to other institutions, law enforcement, people in the community – even their present employers. People could lose their jobs or have their professional or personal lives turned upside down. Indeed, here is how one participant in Lageson's study explains her avoidance of employers who may discover her records via background checks:

> I applied for two jobs over Christmas and then they said they were gonna do a criminal background check, and that means they hire a company to look up your record. Then they find it and then it's permanently in databases even if you get it expunged later … it will go around the Internet. It could go anywhere.[132]

The initial act of participating in an institution or place of work likely to discover the digitized criminal records creates the risk that the records end up in a permanent database or shared "around the internet," going literally "anywhere," creating endless future possibilities for social disapproval, ostracism, and other related reputational harms, and affecting their life forever. The concern is obviously about far more than police surveillance – it is about "fitting in"; preserving their personal and professional reputation in their communities and broader society. The records put all of that at risk.

So, instead of participating in these institutions or putting themselves in a situation that risks social sanction and disapproval, they instead avoid it – they detach and disengage. In so doing, they are engaging in socially conforming behavior by taking steps to avoid discovery of their past very serious nonconforming behavior, which would likely lead to social disapproval, sanction, and ostracism today. Sometimes the best way to avoid such negative social consequences is to say nothing and do nothing and just remain silent. These are also questionably forms of chilling effects, and they can be explained by the same motivation not to attract unwanted attention and social disapproval. This is essentially what Brayne's and Lageson's "justice-involved" avoiders are doing – maintaining an appearance of normality and conformity by avoiding situations that may reveal their past nonconformity. The same can be said of Levy's truckers. They fear that the ELD data could lead to more scrutiny of their activities, and sharing with other unknown entities, too, leading to chilling effects.

Moreover, other factors help elucidate these chilling effects even further: surveillance; ambiguity and uncertainty; personalization; and authority. Indeed, Levy's explanation of her findings speaks to *each* of these factors:

> In both the truckers' case and the case of system avoidance explored by Brayne, it is crucial to recognize that the source of chill is the ambiguity around what information is being tracked, by whom, and when. The beliefs held by truckers and the justice-involved, even if mistaken, are not unreasonable – they are rooted in real experiences, the emergence of public/private surveillance partnerships, and sometimes misleading or inflated messaging about the capabilities of a technology. The result is a generalized feeling of being watched by powerful entities, leading to a concomitantly generalized anxiety. And this anxiety, in turn, affects and constrains behavior: as constitutional scholar Frank Askin wrote, "anxious men are rarely free men."[33]

Here, quite clearly, is the chill of surveillance alone – the constrained behavior and anxiety due to being watched – and the importance of power and authority: It is "powerful entities" doing the watching; possibly police, government, and business, in a "public/private surveillance partnership." On top of that, there is uncertainty and ambiguity in the information gathering – what, when, and by whom – compounding the chilling effect. Lastly, there is an element of personalization here – those chilled are those with previous experience in the criminal justice system. Not unreasonably, they believe that they may be personally targeted and their records more closely monitored and shared, with more negative consequences. All of these chilling effect factors lead to a kind of system chill – disengagement and avoidance in order to maintain conformity and avoid social sanction and related consequences.

2 *The Chill of Online Abuse*

At the outset of the book, I talked about the story of novelist Stephanie Feldman, who was chilled by a large-scale campaign of targeted harassment and abuse. Her story is far from unique. Online abuse is a problem that is growing in both scope and intensity. A 2021 Pew Research Center survey of over 10,000 US adults found roughly four in ten had experienced some form of online abuse.[134] The study also found that more severe forms of such abuse – like physical threats, stalking, and persistent harassment, including sexual harassment – are increasingly common.[135] Other recent studies have found that online abuse also surged during the COVID-19 pandemic, particularly abuse targeting women and minorities, as more people spent more time online.[136] Such online abuse can have "devastating" and "totalizing" impacts on victims.[137] Not surprisingly, as experts like Citron, Franks, and Marwick have exhaustively documented, such online abuse can have powerful chilling effects.[138]

This is easy to understand. For many of the same reasons that targeted or personalized legal enforcement have more significant chilling effects, online abuse – like targeting an individual persistently with threats of violence, sexist and racist epithets, defamation, and sexual and racist abuse and harassment – has greater impacts. First, such targeted online abuse almost always involves personal threats. Those personal threats involve either explicit threats of violence and personal injury or such abuse implies such threats. Such personal threats, especially those involving violence and physical harm, are a powerful force for self-censorship and chilling effects.[139] Such threats trigger deep psychological states of fear, anxiety, and severe emotional distress that in turn amplify conformity and thus chilling effects. Second, the chill of personal threats is compounded by surveillance effects. That's because ongoing online threats, harassment, and abuse, also suggests to the victim that they are being monitored, tracked, and possibly stalked by perpetrators, creating fear and uncertainty about repeated abuse in the future. New surveillance technologies employed by abusers, like spyware and malware to stalk and track victims in newly sophisticated ways, compound these chilling effects even further.[140]

Lastly, online abuse campaigns can be directed and promoted by perpetrators with authority, adding an additional chilling effect factor. For example, President Donald Trump's behavior towards women, including repeated attacks and verbal abuse on social media, likely promoted an increase in online abuse directed towards women.[141] The devastating chilling effects of this kind of personal abuse and threats, both online and offline, can be more fully understood with a conformity theory.

3 *The Chill of Disinformation*

Disinformation also has chilling effects, and a conformity theory of chilling effects helps us understand why. As we saw in Chapter 3, social conformity shapes behavior online just as it does offline. Disinformation online actors, often with malicious intent, spread disinformation, gossip, rumor, and "fake news," as well as trolling and other polarizing behavior, in order to create chilling effects on democratic engagement and collective action. Sociologist Zeynep Tufekci, for instance, has written about viral harassment campaigns and how governments have deployed "troll armies" and automated processes like "botnets" in order to sow what she calls "censorship by disinformation," that is, the digital public sphere is flooded with information, much of it distorted and false, with an aim to simply "confuse and overwhelm" the public.[142] Tim Wu has called these tactics "flooding strategies," a kind of "reverse" censorship in that rather than censoring speech directly, it seeks to drown it out.[143]

A theory of chilling effects as conformity and compliance helps us understand how these strategies work. The spread of disinformation, misinformation, rumors, and gossip creates immense uncertainty and ambiguity, leading people to seek out information in social norms about online speech and engagement. But in an environment of troll armies, fake news, inauthentic amplified messaging, viral harassment campaigns, and polarization around divisive issues like race, many people, consistent with the "spiral of silence" effect, are chilled into silence and disengagement.

If people are unsure about what is true and false and what information or news they can trust, like whether certain political scandals or allegations are true when trying to decide how they will vote while being bombarded by countless examples of fake news, conspiracies, and manipulated media (like deep fakes), then that uncertainty can have a powerful chilling effect – causing people to disengage from politics, or the democratic process entirely, exhausted by the pervasive disinformation but unable to resolve it. This itself is an act of conformity as speaking or acting in such an environment creates risks – for example, supporting the wrong platform or candidate, and risking social embarrassment, disapproval, or alienation. While others at the same time end up engaging in more antisocial norms like trolling and sharing false news and disinformation – either because they are a norm of a community with which they self-identify, or they are mistaken about the norm – which in turn contributes to a broader environment that is more polarized, abusive, and chilling. Indeed, such abusive behavior, in turn, can also lead to chilling effects on targets of such online hate, harassment, trolling, and abuse. The result is a corrosive chilling effect on collective action and democratic understanding, due to confusion and mistrust, and a downward spiral of conformity, division, and silence.

PART III

Implications

In our post-Snowden, Cambridge Analytica, and Clearview AI world, concerns about chilling effects have taken hold in daily discourse. So, the need to develop an accurate theoretical and empirical understanding of the phenomenon has itself taken on greater public importance. As discussed in Part I, both the legal and wider public understanding of chilling effects has largely been shaped by conventional accounts that take us only so far. Conventional theories are singular – focused on legal harms or privacy harms – and have critical theoretical, empirical, and normative limitations. They made assumptions with little empirical support; were unable to explain chilling effects in a variety of contexts; and normatively, offered no means to distinguish between different kinds of chill – good or bad, for example.

A conformity theory of chilling effects does so, better explaining and illustrating *what* chilling effects are, to clarify discourse and improve understanding about chilling effects and their impact. Without an accurate understanding we cannot hope to respond effectively. Furthermore, it complements and supports privacy and legal strategies aimed at guarding against the corrosive impact of chilling effects while also providing a sounder normative, theoretical, and empirical foundation to unpack, understand, and resist the processes and impact of broader societal shifts like the current surveillance and information capitalism paradigm. Lastly, a conformity theory speaks powerfully to what chilling effects *produce* and the implications of this, moving us beyond the narrow framing of conventional theories focused predominantly on self-censorship to bigger questions about their implications for human rights, autonomy, identity, and democracy. In this part of the book, I further elaborate these theoretical, empirical, legal, and normative advantages, both today and tomorrow.

6

The Dangers of Chilling Effects

There are two dimensions to the dangers of chilling effects: repression and production. What does this mean? Surveillance studies theorists have long written about the repressive and productive dimensions of surveillance and power. Foucault was among the first to do so. A central insight of his work was that power had both repressive and productive qualities. The repressive dimensions of power primarily concerned the state and its capacity to repress individuals, their rights, and their speech.[1] Repressive power is conceived entirely in a "negative" sense: Its central aim is to stop or prevent activities through command or force of a law with a threat of punishment. That is to say, the object is to repress and suppress activities and "reduce to silence."[2] Repressive power echoes the central focus of conventional understanding of chilling effects – it is predominantly concerned with the state and its capacity to promote self-restraint and self-censorship.

On a conventional understanding, the central impact of chilling effects is self-censorship – deterrence leading to an *absence* or loss of speech or doing, which *is* a harm and implicates rights and freedoms. In other words, conventional understanding focuses almost exclusively on the repressive dimensions of chilling effects. Foucault would say that this is not surprising. He traced the intellectual origins of repressive power to the monarchy and notions of sovereignty, law, and prohibition that have been deeply embedded in Western systems of government since the Middle Ages.[3] We are conditioned to think about power – and the law – this way. And while they're no doubt important, focusing *only* on these repressive aspects of chilling effects, you will miss the real extent of their impacts – and dangers.

What's missing is the dangers caused by the productive dimensions of chilling effects. Here is how Foucault explained "disciplinary power" – which was not predominantly repressive, but productive:

> We must cease once and for all to describe the effects of power in negative terms: it "excludes", it "represses", it "censors", it "abstracts", it "masks", it "conceals". In fact power produces; it produces reality; it produces domains of objects and rituals of truth. The individual and the knowledge that may be gained of him belong to this production.[4]

This new form of power was not only different from repressive power, but in his view more important and salient in modern society. It operated not by repressing behavior – like how a law chills behavior or speech – but by *producing* new individuals, objects, fields of knowledge, and social rituals, and through these productions, entirely new social and cultural realities. Chilling effects, properly understood, create new social and cultural realities too.

Indeed, conventional understanding neglects a critical insight from a range of social science fields about how chilling effects involve not just an absence – a lack of speaking or doing – but they also shape behavior: people speaking, acting, or doing, just in a way that conforms to, or is in compliance with, a perceived social norm. Chilling effects thus also have *productive* dimensions. They not only involve the silencing of speech, or repression, but also the production of socially conforming speech and behavior. Our new understanding of chilling effects, based on a conformity theory, offers a critical change in perspective. This theory focuses not just on *why* people are chilled but also *how* people are chilled – as a predictive matter – and *what* these chilling effects produce and their broader implications.

Those broader impacts are not just self-censorship, but social conformity through both speech and behavior that is conforming to, or compliant with, broader social, economic, and political norms, structures, power, and hierarchies. In neglecting these productive dimensions, conventional theories have helped foster skepticism and misconceptions about chilling effects and their impact. Even worse, it has weakened our understanding of the true impacts of chilling effects and the dangers they pose to people, our rights and freedoms, and democratic society. In this chapter, I show how a conformity theory of chilling effects avoids both of these problems.

DANGERS TO INDIVIDUALS

Despite their flaws, conventional theories nevertheless offered important insights on the repressive dangers of chilling effects. What they got right is that chilling effects *do* involve deterrence leading to self-censorship and self-restraint. Sometimes chilling effects lead only to silence or inaction, for example. Just as often, however, chilling effects involve socially conforming speech and behavior. But even here, when a person is chilled and speaks or acts in conformity with expected norms of speech and behavior due, for instance, to surveillance or a personal legal threat, they are deterred from speaking or acting in the way they otherwise would have but for the threat. There is both deterrence and self-censorship here too, it is just more subtle.

1 *Repressing Rights, Freedoms, and Autonomy*

The *repressive* dimensions of chilling effects – the speech and action they chill, deter, and silence – highlight how chilling effects clearly reduce basic rights and fundamental freedoms. This has traditionally been explored by legal scholars in the context of legal rights that people are chilled from exercising freely, especially constitutional rights. A repressive law targeting the speech or activities of a specific minority group, for example, can easily chill full enjoyment of constitutional rights by members of that group. This idea is at the core of First Amendment jurisprudence on chilling effects from which the concept itself first gained prominence in the postwar jurisprudence of the US Supreme Court. Recall the key rationales for concerns about chilling effects in Chapter 1 on conventional understanding – they each tracked First Amendment rationales, including the value of speech providing a truth-identification function in society and underpinning self-government. As we have seen, scholars like Daniel Solove, Julie Cohen, Neil Richards, and Daniel Citron have each demonstrated that other forms of personal threats – threats to privacy or threats to the person in the form of online harassment and abuse – likewise create powerful chilling effects that endanger these same critical First Amendment interests, and have advocated for greater judicial and public policy recognition of that reality. These same concerns also apply in nonconstitutional contexts. A chilling effect due to the unlawful actions of a private actor, like misappropriation of personal information in a data breach, can similarly chill, and therefore repress, the full enjoyment of certain private law rights and interests. Chilling effects thus reduce our access and enjoyment of all rights, constitutional and otherwise.

However, conventional theories and jurisprudence on chilling effects recognized impacts beyond legal rights. A chilling effect leading to self-censorship or loss of speech is more than just a legal harm, but a personal harm as well. People in a free society value the ability to freely speak and express themselves, and to live freely, without interference from the actions of governments or private actors that chill people into silence. Jonathan Siegel has similarly argued that a "chill" on free speech – beyond any legal or constitutional rights – is a profound personal injury as it violates at a fundamental level a core American value – the ability to speak out on public issues in a debate in a way that is "uninhibited, robust, and wide-open."[5] Yet, the personal harm is not just for loss of speech or legal rights. Chilling effects also undercut our basic liberties to live freely and shape our own lives – what philosophers call personal autonomy. That is, when surveillance, overreaching laws, targeted threats, and other chilling effect threats, chill us into self-censorship, silence, and restraint, this undercuts our self-determination and autonomy – it interferes with our right to determine for ourselves want we want to do, what we want to say. That's because when chilled, we are inhibited from acting as we normally would choose but for the law or surveillance that has chilled us into silence or into more conforming behavior. And when we lose self-determination, we also lose our personal autonomy – when we cannot act or decide freely, we also lose control over our lives and who we are. The "ruling idea behind the ideal of personal autonomy," legal philosopher Joseph Raz writes, "is that people should make their own lives."[6] Chilling effects make that impossible.

2 *Undermining Identity and Personal Development*

If we lose our autonomy and self-determination, we are harmed not only because
we lose our ability to make fundamental decisions for ourselves, but also the right
to shape our own individuality and identity, rendering us more docile and easily
controlled. That's another central danger of chilling effects due to its repressive
dimensions. But how? The work of Cohen and Richards is critical in this context.
Both are privacy scholars, attentive to established and emerging technologies,
whose works also draw insights from both surveillance studies and the behavioral
sciences. Cohen, for instance, rejects the traditional liberal conceptualization
of the individual or self as rational, autonomous, and pre-cultural assumed by
conventional understanding.[7] It does not exist, she argues, nor could it, given
the constitutive power of social practices.[8] Her work instead embraces what she
calls the "emergent and relational character of subjectivity,"[9] which is to say,
the reality that people's identity and selfhood is entirely socially shaped and
constructed.[10]

   This conceptualization of identity, personality, and self is grounded in the social,
cognitive, and behavioral sciences, in particular sociology.[11] The social and devel-
opmental theories of George Herbert Mead and Erving Goffman, both influential figures in the symbolic interactionist school of sociology, are illustrative. These
theories emphasize how identity and personality are continuously being developed
and constituted through social interaction.[12] Here, our identity and personalities
emerge out of ongoing ritualistic processes of self-presentation and performances
before evaluative others.[13] Goffman, arguably the most influential writer in this
symbolic interactionist tradition, viewed identity and personality as emerging from
social interactions in a continual and ongoing process.[14] He used the metaphor of
theater to explain identity and personality – the self emerges from performances
via different characters we present to different audiences – much as an actor por-
trays patterns of behavior appropriate to the role they have taken on before an audience that appraises and responds.[15] Similarly for Mead, the "complete self" emerges
from a process of socially interacting, responding to social situations, and reflecting
thoughtfully.[16] In short, by speaking and acting in social contexts, we cultivate what
Goffman calls our "expressive order" – an image that we express and present to
others, that they in turn, reflect and confirm by showing us deference and respect,
where and when it is due.[17]

   If chilling effects are conforming effects, as I have argued, it is easy to see how
they would impact on identity and personality. Since our personality and identity are continually developing, it means that they are also always at risk, because
these social interactions – this "chain of ceremony" in Goffman's terms – can
always be disrupted, preventing the development of a "complete" identity, personality, or self.[18] When overreaching laws, surveillance, personal threats, and

other public or private sector actions chill us into conformity, they are leading us to act and speak *differently* than how we would normally act, depending on our personality or preferences. Chilled individuals are thus *changed* individuals – they say and do things differently than they otherwise would, both alone and especially when engaging with others – chilled into conformity rather than acting as they believed was right or preferable. In this case, chilled individuals are no longer authors of their story; no longer the actor in charge of the performance, to use Goffman's metaphor.

But it's not just that individuals are displaced as the authors of their own identity and development by coercing them to act differently, but that chilling effects coerce people in the same normative direction – toward conformity. Cohen, speaking more to pervasive and data-driven surveillance today, describes its chilling and conforming effects, and how that detrimentally impacts the social construction of our identity and personality. Critical here is her notion of the "play of everyday practice," which speaks to how we form our identity through social interaction.[19] This idea speaks to personal experimentation and how people find unique and creative ways to define and express themselves in response to "different institutional, cultural, and material constraints in broader society."[20] The pervasive chill of surveillance and data-driven tracking and processing entirely undermines this process, Cohen writes, pushing us "toward the bland and the mainstream."[21] By limiting the range of acceptable beliefs and behavior, chilling effects undercut the play of everyday practice, ushering in a "subtle yet fundamental shift in the content of our character," including a "blunting and blurring of rough edges and sharp lines."[22]

Richards' theory of intellectual privacy also helps us understand how chilling effects impact on identity and personality in this context. Intellectual privacy involves protection for critical intellectual freedoms like the freedom to read, think, and communicate privately.[23] Our identities are complex, varied, creative, serious, and playful all at the same time or at different times – sometimes conforming to broader culture and sometimes not.[24] For Richards, intellectual privacy allows us to develop our personalities and identities in private spaces – whether our bedrooms, dinner tables, libraries, personal confessionals – or online.[25] And in the sociological theories of Mead and Goffman, you can see the importance of having space to think and reflect. Richards himself notes that Goffman, in explicating his theater metaphor, speaks to a "backstage," wherein the performances and impression management are less intense, even paused, allowing for more experimentation and freedom.[26] But Mead also speaks to the importance of personal reflection on our social interactions – he describes this cognitive process as the "essence" of the self, from which it emerges. It is impossible to do so under the conforming gaze of observation and surveillance or the invasive informational foresight of algorithmic data analytics.[27] Instead, we are chilled into conformity, losing our individuality, diversity, and eccentricities.[28]

DANGERS TO DEMOCRATIC CULTURE

1 *Repression and Conformity at Societal Scale*

So the repressive dimensions of chilling effects are a dangerous threat to basic rights, freedom, autonomy, and identity. But chilling effects are not only repressive, they are also productive. Chilling effects, understood as conformity and compliance effects, have this same productive dimension – it produces more conforming and compliant behavior. But I also want to make a point about the scale of the problem: the productive impact of chilling effects producing repression and conformity at mass scale. This poses great danger to progress in society and a healthy democratic culture.

My own study on Wikipedia chilling effects, discussed at the outset of the book, offers a stark example. What the findings showed was a clear chilling effect – and one that implicated some very fundamental and basic rights and freedoms. Here, literally millions of people were chilled from exercising their freedom to seek out and inform themselves with information. And this freedom wasn't necessarily a freedom exercised in public spaces that might be more scrutinized, although it could be, but one that many would likely exercise often in the privacy and intimacy of their own home, connecting via personal laptops or smartphones. Even here, people did not feel free to do so but instead avoided sensitive and controversial content. The right or ability to seek, receive, and impart information is not just a trivial interest – it is foundational to all other rights and freedoms – because you need information to know about your rights and to exercise them fully, and to impart the information to others, so they can exercise their rights too. It's why the right – to seek out and receive information freely – has been recognized internationally in some of the world's most famous human rights documents that date back decades to the founding of the United Nations after the Second World War – like the Universal Declaration of Human Rights.[29]

But it is not *just* a right to seek out information that is chilled here, but those other critical rights – the freedom to read and think free of interference and fear of exposure – that is, the other intellectual privacy interests Richards and Cohen talk about. None of the Wikipedia users felt free enough or safe enough to read freely and inform themselves, and then think about the information, process it, and form beliefs about it – including thinking critically about the broader and important public policy issues at stake. There were also surely people who were chilled from accessing information on certain minority religious groups or faiths that have sometimes been associated with terrorism or acts of extremism. So, freedom of thought, belief, and even religion are also implicated here. And we can also surmise other chilling effects based on what the study documented here. If people online are chilled from accessing information on controversial but important topics due to surveillance threats, then you can be sure they are chilled from doing other things online too – they are likely chilled from speaking freely about it; chilled from associating with groups or individuals implicated in these controversies; perhaps even chilled from voting for candidates in elections who run on a platform to address a controversial topic or public policy issue.

Beyond impacting each of these fundamental rights and freedoms, my findings also offer a powerful illustration of the *scale* and *scope* of chilling effects – population-wide, though possibly even greater than that. The chilling effects caused by the NSA surveillance – or awareness as to the possibility of it – were substantial. First, in terms of the severity of the chill – the large drop off and complete trend reversal in overall article views. Second, in their longevity – the chilling effects were apparent over a year after the Snowden revelations in June 2013. Lastly, their sheer scale – tens of millions of people are represented in the Wikipedia article data in this study, with total article views in the study nearing 80 million. And this is just one group of Wikipedia articles, one website – albeit an immensely popular one in America and around the world – and one activity: seeking out information and knowledge online. And the study involved just a small sample of Wikipedia articles – tens of millions, maybe hundreds of millions more, are likely affected. Chilling effects impact *all* behavior, so people's willingness to visit other websites and seek, receive, and impart information; engage in lawful and socially beneficial activities online and offline; and the exercise of countless other fundamental rights and freedoms were no doubt also chilled.

My study has not been an outlier. It has since been backed up by countless other studies. My findings were consistent with an earlier MIT study I discussed in Chapter 1, which found evidence of chilling effects in Google searches for privacy-sensitive terms after the Snowden revelation. It was also consistent with a series of surveys and polls of Americans published by Pew Research and PEN America after the Snowden disclosures finding people reporting that they were chilled in a range of online activities due to their awareness of government surveillance programs after June 2013. One Pew Internet survey, taken in the months following the Snowden revelations, found most Americans were unwilling to speak about Snowden and the NSA surveillance programs online.[30] A Harris Poll from early 2014 found nearly half of Americans had changed their behavior online due to government surveillance.[31] The findings have also been corroborated by a range of additional empirical research in recent years, including one study finding awareness about possible NSA surveillance online chilled the contributions of Wikipedia editors, and another finding evidence of chilling effects in what search engines people used after June 2013 – avoiding ones more easily monitored and tracked by government.[32]

And keep in mind that my study is only *one* measure of the chilling effects of *one* set of surveillance practices, albeit very large and sophisticated and supported by other studies of those same practices. This is not even to mention the broader range of studies that have documented chilling effects in contexts beyond simply government surveillance and similar activities – from corporate surveillance and data mining to online trolling and abuse – and impacting activities beyond just accessing and reading information online, but also impacting online expression, including political, search, sharing, social media engagement, and connectivity, to name a few.[33]

For instance, Elizabeth Stoycheff has done important experimental research on chilling effects, with a special focus on social media contexts. For instance, her Facebook-based experimental study, published in 2016, found that exposing participants to "terms of agreement" – which reminded participants that their online activities could be "monitored" led to a significant chilling effect, whereby participants who believed their political opinions were outside the mainstream were chilled from expressing them.[34] In a follow-up study, she found that participants made aware about possibly being subject to internet surveillance via similar terms of service were significantly chilled in their behavioral intentions to engage in "illegal online behavior" the following week, and were also chilled from political engagement online, including sharing political opinions, searching for information about conspiracy theories, criticizing government or government policy, and searching for information about the 2016 US presidential candidates.[35] In my own study conducted following the Wikipedia research, I similarly found that awareness of both government and corporate surveillance online had significant chilling effects on people's willingness to speak or express themselves online; search for certain content online; share personally created content; and engage in social media and online more generally.[36] Given the prevalence of both government and corporate surveillance, data collection, and tracking, all of these findings suggest critical rights and freedoms are chilled and repressed at mass, even societal scale.

But chilling effects also produce socially conforming speech and behavior at this mass scale as well. This is where the scale and scope of private sector and commercial practices are of import, spurred on by the powerful and extractive forces of surveillance and information capitalism. You don't need direct suppression of core rights or civil liberties for chilling effects to endanger the social and cultural dimensions of democratic societies.

That is an insight from research on the chill of private sector and algorithmically driven data collection and processing practices so prevalent across every commercial sector today. Those chilling effects are subtle – like those Target customers spooked and then chilled by their targeted personal ads – but substantial from a societal perspective, especially over the long term. One often-cited study published in 2010, found a substantial majority of participants (64 percent) indicated the idea of online behavioral advertising, driven by personalized data collection and analysis, was "invasive," with 40 percent indicating they would change their online behavior if advertisers were collecting data.[37] More recently, Joanna Strycharz and Claire M. Segijn found personalized targeted advertising also chilled consumers, with personal factors, like attitudes about privacy, personalization, and the need for positive self-presentation, all impacting the scope of the chill.[38] And Kiran Kappeler, Noemi

Festic and Michael Latzer, in a qualitative study, found participant responses evidenced chilling effects not just on willingness to express opinions or search for certain content online, but on a broader range of more mundane and ordinary daily activities, like being chilled from using online dating sites or purchasing certain products online.[39] Responses also indicated that the source of the chilling effect – the awareness of the data collection, analysis, and targeting – was varied, ranging from more high-profile news reports on data breaches or scandals like Snowden or Cambridge Analytica, as well as more personal experiences with invasive corporate data practices. In other words, people's awareness of being watched, tracked, and processed increases over time, through both high-profile events that might be said to more directly impact or implicate privacy and democratic politics and through personal experiences with routine corporate data tracking and surveillance – like those Target customers.[40] The new chilled way of speaking and doing becomes the new baseline that never recovers to the original. And, over time, people and society are increasingly chilled into more substantial levels of conformity. In other words, chilling effects caused by, and affecting, ordinary consumer activities can cause or contribute to overall behavioral chill and conformity.

Such mass and societal-scale production of conformity and compliance poses many social and cultural dangers in democratic societies. First, it undermines eccentric individuality, creativity, diversity, and experimentation – things that we should embrace and cultivate in a free and democratic society.[41] A truly free and open society should tolerate and accommodate dissent and unpopular views and celebrate not only mainstream culture, expression, and behavior but also more eccentric, diverse, and deviant culture and expression as well. Even if most people naturally identify as "normal" or "average" and prefer mainstream tastes, a society that is open to unpopular and dissident ideas, alternative tastes, and a greater range of cultures and subcultures, will be inherently richer, more diverse, and robust.[42] "Freedom," writes Richards, "must mean more than just the freedom to be like everybody else."[43]

Second, it undermines progress. It is corrosive to advances in science, knowledge, and innovation. That's because the mass-scale conformity spread by chilling effects suppresses new ideas, information, and ways of knowing or doing things in the world. Though largely neglected by legal scholars, deterrence theorists, and economists examining chilling effects in other contexts – like statutory and regulatory chill – privacy scholars and theorists have long raised such concerns about the impact of surveillance. If chilling effects produce docile, muted, bland, and increasingly conforming individuals and populations, they will be less creative, dynamic, and innovative. When engaged in social conformity, people rely only on existing ideas, information, and ways of doing things and knowing things that everyone else is already using. No one brings new ideas or information. No new methods or knowledge are offered or considered. No one experiments. Everyone is content to go along with the group. This is a problem not just for science, knowledge, and innovation in society – as no one is challenging existing ways of knowing or doing.

Third, it corrupts social meaning. Mead's notion of a "complete self," noted earlier, helps explain how the conformity and compliance that chilling effects produce constitute another social and cultural danger. It's not just that surveillance and other threats chill us and therefore interfere with our ability to think, experiment, reflect, make choices, and develop our self but by promoting conformity on a broader societal scale, they can also rob social value and meaning from the choices we make.

The work of Charles Taylor, one of the leading contemporary philosophers, is foundational here. Among Taylor's contributions is a powerful genealogy on the origins of modern identity.[44] Like Goffman and Mead, Taylor recognized that our identities are socially shaped – they are "fundamentally dialogic in character."[45] That is, we continually develop our identities throughout our lives in dialogue with others who matter most to us – those who sociologist Harry Stack Sullivan called "significant others" – our friends, romantic partners, family – those people most influential in informing our beliefs, attitudes, and personality and recognizing us and our identity.[46] But key to our dialogic identities, and the struggle for recognition from others, are broader moral and social contexts – what Taylor called "horizons of meaning" – that give meaning and significance to our choices, including how we dialogue, respond, and struggle against and with our significant others. These horizons are inescapable, Taylor argues, and are critical to us developing our authentic selves. And without these horizons of meaning, our personal development, and our lives themselves, collapse into meaningless solipsism or narcissistic hedonism.

But meaningless conformity and compliance are just as problematic. And here is where chilling effects – and conformity – are again so corrosive. By fomenting conformity on a broader societal scale, chilling effects disrupt, even corrupt, the broader social and moral contexts – horizons of meaning – that give significance and meaning to the choices we make in defining ourselves. It's not just that individuals are displaced as the authors of their own identity and development by being coerced and influenced to act differently by chilling effects and the conformity they produce – as I argued earlier – but that coercive force always pushes people in the same normative direction – toward conformity. This not only makes our "complete" or authentic self impossible, it also makes personal and social interactions and development far less meaningful. That's because both the social interactions we internalize and reflect on and the broader social and cultural contexts against which those interactions have meaning are weakened and corrupted by increasing levels of societal conformity and compliance, fomented by various chilling effect threats in modern society – like surveillance, data collection, legal and personal threats, and beyond.

With our horizons of meaning all increasingly horizons of conformity and compliance, how can there be value and authenticity in our personal and social lives? In a world of chilling effects, we may not emerge as "complete" and if we do, our lives and choices may be far less meaningful.

2 *Fomenting a Spiral of Polarization, Extremism, and Abuse*

Polarization and political extremism is on the rise and the internet and social media are a big part of the problem.[47] But so are chilling effects. Indeed, chilling and conforming effects need not only produce silence or self-censorship. They can also produce greater polarization, extremism, and abuse. Typically, we associate conformity with forms of self-censorship and restraint, with a person being more restrained, polite, respectful, and perhaps at the same time less original, dynamic, or individualistic. Hence the concerns of privacy scholars and surveillance theorists noted earlier about how surveillance, data tracking, and other causes of chilling effects incline us towards the "bland," "boring," and "mainstream." It does that, to be sure, as more mainstream, common, or popular views or behavior, when speaking about popular culture or broader society, will inevitably feel more familiar, typical, and unoriginal to us. We've seen it all before. Hence, it will also feel restrained, boring, and bland. So, if surveillance and other threats chill us into conforming with the norms of broader society, it can lead to a broader society that is increasingly this way – restrained, boring, and bland, with implications for dissent and democracy, as we've seen.

But conformity can also mean conforming with more problematic, even destructive, behavioral norms as well. "Conformity also makes atrocities possible," legal scholar Cass Sunstein has observed. "The Holocaust was many things, but it was emphatically a tribute to the immense power of conformity."[48] He's right. Social norms are not universal behavioral norms or practices, but often tied to specific social and cultural contexts, so social norms will vary across cultures and contexts.[49] Conformity will lead to different sorts of behavior depending on the context, like the norms of the community or group and whether the person identifies more with the group than the norms of broader society. In Shasta County, the norm that developed among ranchers was to behave neighborly, though there were also "self-help" norms that developed around enforcing neighborliness – people would gossip and potentially threaten violence and physical retaliation. Those norms were different than those you would find in other parts of California but the ranchers that lived in this county disregarded them – they were a part of this close-knit community and adhered to its local norms.

These same dynamics play out online. Where, for example, a social media user faces uncertainty about surveillance or some other chilling threat within certain online communities, social media groups, or with certain online audiences, they may turn to norms typical to that group – or one of those groups or audiences – and conform and comply with them. That is especially the case where the user strongly identifies with that particular online group and its values.[50] And where that group's norms are more polarized, extremist, or antisocial, then chilling and conforming effects will lead more people to engage in extremist or antisocial behavior, be it hate, bullying, trolling, abuse, and even violence. Just as conformity has played a role in atrocities and hate throughout history, multiple studies have documented its role in fostering or promoting online abuse and similar antisocial behavior on the internet.[51]

Sunstein has written extensively on polarization and extremism, especially in online contexts.[52] The tendency for members of a deliberating group to end up with more extreme views over time is a well-documented social phenomenon known as group polarization.[53] There are different factors that contribute to group polarization, but conformity is a key part of the story.[54] And the way we interact and consume information online, and on social media especially, is central to polarization both within certain groups and in broader society.[55] The internet, Sunstein argues, is a "breeding ground" for extremism.[56] For instance, he talks about "filter bubbles" – how it's very easy to filter out information or differing and dissenting views – customized newsfeeds, algorithmically filtered content, based on what we specify or what the algorithm predicts we would like, are central to social media today.[57] Such personalized content is a key factor in polarizing people into extremes.[58] He also talks about how these platforms are designed to promote polarization and extremism – once you've found a group that matches your politics or worldview, the way social media platforms are designed incentivizes polarization – likes on Facebook, reposts on X (formerly Twitter), view counts on YouTube, karma on Reddit all encourage group members to express or show support for the cause in stronger, possibly even extreme terms, to attract favor with other members who express support via these features. All of these aspects of the internet and social media accelerate a process that Sunstein calls "cyberpolarization."[59]

But an important factor Sunstein does not mention in any of his works on polarization and extremism, but should, are the different public and private sector practices that cause or contribute to chilling effects – and conformity – like surveillance, and the many other threats discussed in Chapter 5. It is often assumed, thanks to conventional understanding, that surveillance would likely deter extremism – chilling people out of extremist or abusive activities out of fear of legal punishment or law enforcement action;[60] or, at the very least, chilling people away from the extreme towards the bland, boring, and mainstream.

But what if it actually encouraged extremism? In some contexts, it surely does. And as we have seen, online surveillance, data collection, processing, and analysis – including by social media platforms themselves – all cause and contribute to chilling effects – among the most powerful forms of conforming effects. We know the informational influences that encourage conformity, and thus polarization, are triggered when people are most uncertain – think of Sherif's experiment, where participants resolved their uncertainty by conforming to what they believed was the norm. As I argued in Chapter 5, online surveillance, data collection, and processing all foment uncertainty and ambiguity. And we know informational influences are most impactful when people are aware of actual surveillance or the possibility of it – the surveillance chills, and people conform to the norm of the group – thus the influence of information from the group is greater.[61] And as groups become more polarized and extreme, so does the behavior. Thus, a 2017 study found that awareness of government surveillance online actually increased participants' tendency to rumors – two of the three rumors studied involved unverified conspiracies about government cover-ups.[62] The authors noted the paradoxical nature of the findings – surveillance, it was surmised, should decrease such behavior – and interpreted the findings as a product of mistrust in government caused by the surveillance. But another way of interpreting the results is that the surveillance awareness chilled the participants into greater conformity and in this case, the group norm was to share conspiratorial anti-government rumors and related information. Chilling effects accelerate cyberpolarization, leading to extremism, and a conformity theory of chilling effects tells us how and why.

SOCIETAL/DEMOCRACY DANGERS

1 *(Re)Producing and Entrenching Inequalities*

One critical societal danger of chilling effects, and what they produce, is a world that is less equal and less fair. First, the typical *causes* of chilling effects – surveillance; targeted law enforcement activities; corporate data mining; legal threats; personal harassment and abuse – are not uniformly deployed in society. They are disproportionately visited upon minorities and marginalized communities, both historically and today.[63] From the FBI's COINTELPRO program – employed to chill black activism in the Civil Rights Era – to national security agencies targeting Muslim communities for surveillance after 9/11 to police tracking and investigating Black Lives Matter activists today, surveillance and law enforcement have persistently targeted racial minorities and other disadvantaged groups.[64] Leftwing political movements, especially those within these same racial and minority communities, have also been targeted and victimized.[65] In Canada, the Royal Canadian Mounted Police likewise have a history of targeting black and Indigenous populations,[66] and more recently, along with Canadian intelligence services, have targeted Indigenous and environment activists opposed to corporate energy projects.[67] Technologies of surveillance and control – including new predictive policing and automation technologies powered by big data and machine learning algorithms – are more often employed by government, police, and corporate actors against these same communities.[68] Scholars like Ruha Benjamin, Safiya Noble, Simone Brown, and Ngozi Okidegbe have critiqued such technologies as helping entrench structural social inequalities.[69] As Scott Skinner-Thompson has persuasively shown, legal protections from these disparities in surveillance and policing are often not as accessible to these same communities, and when they are, they are far less effective.[70]

Second, the *impacts* of chilling effects are also not equally suffered.[71] Not surprisingly, already disadvantaged groups and marginalized communities – like racial, religious, and sexual minorities – are also chilled more by surveillance, targeted law enforcement threats, and personal harassment and abuse. For instance, the report *Mapping Muslims: NYPD Spying and Its Impact on American Muslims* amassed countless testimonials as to how Muslim American communities, already a smaller religious minority facing bigotry and discrimination in society, have suffered "horrifying" chilling effects due to targeted police surveillance and ethnic profiling in the years since 9/11.[72] Black and Latino communities have likewise suffered substantial chilling effects due to targeted policing and ethnic profiling over the years, like New York City's infamous "Stop and Frisk" policy that annually ensnared hundreds of thousands of innocent black and Latino people.[73] When it comes to online harassment, bullying, and abuse, again, it is women and minority groups who are more often targeted and ultimately suffer greater chilling effects as a result.[74] This is a point that Danielle Citron has argued forcefully, observing that women and minority groups disproportionately suffer the worst and most chilling forms of abuse.[75] In my own empirical research on chilling effects, I have likewise found similar disparate impacts, finding young people more chilled by surveillance and women more chilled by personal threats than other groups.[76] And at an organizational level, studies have also found that smaller independent organizations and associations, with fewer resources, are chilled more by targeted legal threats.[77] Chilling effects thus compound existing social inequalities and disparities.

Third, chilling effects and conformity magnify and entrench inequalities in other ways as well. As we saw, it can make speaking up against inequalities or resisting them far more difficult and dangerous through spirals of silence and conformity. Those same processes also feed polarization and extremism that can lead to conflict and violence – with minority and marginalized groups disproportionately impacted. On top of that, as forms of targeted surveillance and data collection and processing spread from police and security agencies to other institutions in society, you can have forms of system or institutional chilling effects that we talked about in Chapter 5 and as evident in the McDaniel case. Minority groups and marginalized communities that are disproportionately targeted by overreaching security and law enforcement activities are chilled from seeking help from the very social services and other civic institutions designed to help people in their circumstances, to recover and rebuild their lives after being victimized. The most in need are chilled again, perpetuating their disenfranchisement and marginalization while feeding racist norms, prejudices, and stereotypes about these same groups. And problematic social norms, including ones that people do not necessarily even believe or accept as proper or moral, can nevertheless be difficult to change once entrenched, with some having influence across multiple generations, through inter-generational transmission and social learning.[78]

This entrenching process is fed by chilling effects as conformity breeds silence, and it also helps entrench speech, views, or norms that may not reflect those of the broader democratic majority. The result? The damaging impact of chilling effects on disadvantaged groups and marginalized communities do not dissipate quickly but persist for years, even generations. In her book *Dark Matters: On Surveillance of Blackness,* Simone Brown offers a compelling account of how black bodies have been historically targeted and subjugated with surveillance technologies throughout history, leaving black communities, already disadvantaged and marginalized, still suffering a greater share of the resulting harms today.[79]

2 Corrosive to Democracy

The mass-scale repression of rights and freedoms, disparate impacts, and production of increasing levels of conformity in daily activities – where chilling effects and conformity are subtle but compounding over longer periods of time – has serious implications for the health and functioning of democracy and democratic societies.

First, it is corrosive to democratic deliberation. The dominant theories of pluralistic democracy today are deliberative and participatory.[80] Participatory democracy envisions "active citizenship" with robust popular participation in democratic processes, like policy formation and decision-making.[81] Deliberative democracy is even more demanding – it envisions not just popular participation, but citizens engaged in public reason – directly involved in open, public, and contested debate and deliberation over key matters of public interest, including democracy itself.[82] It is common today to speak of a "deliberative turn" in democratic theory, and today people increasingly recognize that constitutional democracies entail deliberation in some fundamental way.[83] Even famed liberal philosopher John Rawls joined the "turn" in 1999, declaring a concern for deliberation in constitutional democracies.[84] At the core of all theories of deliberative democracy is a reason-giving requirement: Citizens and their representatives must justify laws and give reasons for decision-making and other claims, and they must respond to the reasons of others.[85] Though different theories envision reason-giving differently, the key point here is that for democracy to be healthy and successful over the long term, citizens must be active, engaged, participatory, and deliberative. And to do so, they must be free to speak, engage, express, and associate, among other fundamental rights and freedoms, but they must also be free to think, read, and gather information to inform themselves about matters of public interest.[86]

However, if people are chilled from doing so, like being chilled from informing themselves about breaking news stories and other important news events, or from researching matters of law, security, and public policy related to "terrorism" online, or other matters of public importance, then any full citizen participation or deliberation is impossible. If people do not feel free to engage politically, including expressing political opinions, due to the chill of possible government or corporate surveillance as I or Stoycheff found, then people cannot engage in public reason, nor can they scrutinize or assess the deliberative explanations of their representatives. With people potentially chilled from such basic acts of information gathering or engagement, this means a less informed and engaged citizenry over the long term significantly weakening broader processes of democratic deliberation. Chilling effects, caused not just by the studies in government surveillance but all the other forms of chilling effects discussed in Chapter 5's taxonomy, clearly undermine deliberative and participatory democracy.

This is what Richards means when he says intellectual privacy is foundational to democratic self-government – by guaranteeing each of us the space and freedom to read, think, and communicate privately.[87] Such intellectual privacy and freedom make the acts of thinking, communicating, and decision-making in politics and beyond not only possible but meaningful. Schauer argued that the loss of speech due to chilling effects is a "general societal loss" and thus worthy of protection under the First Amendment.[88] But society loses far more than just speech when chilling effects are pervasive – we lose new acts of politics; new political views; new social movements; new ways of associating and assembling together; and new ways to hold governments and corporations accountable. Chilling effects threaten all of this. As such, it is easy to see how chilling effects are corrosive to a healthy and vibrant democracy, both in the near term and especially in the long term.

Second, it undermines eccentric individuality, creativity, diversity, and experimentation – something that endangers not only democratic culture, as I argued earlier, but democracy itself. The healthiest and most vibrant liberal democracies are also pluralistic – enriched by a diversity of opinion, cultures, and perspectives, including dissent. Exposure to a diversity of opinions and perspectives fosters tolerance for difference – what democratic theorists call pluralistic conditioning – that in turn promotes greater social cohesion and peace over the long term.[89] This is what Nobel Laureate Amartya Sen calls the "civil path to peace" – promoting respect and mutual understanding of difference and diversity is critical to mitigating grievance, isolation, and misunderstanding that feed division, polarization, extremism, and conflict.[90] His argument applies not only to democracies in the West, but anywhere.

Third, it undermines social progress – a concern related but different to the point I made earlier about conformity endangering knowledge, science, and innovation. Dissent and deviation from social consensus and norms are essential to democracy.[91] Democracy needs new ideas and information; and not just new ideas and information about law and politics, but literally all facets of life – art, science, culture, business, what it means to live a good life – even new ideas about democracy itself. It needs them to function properly as a healthy democracy that is both participatory and deliberative and dialogue about ideas, old and new, is central to these core democratic processes. But democracy also needs new ideas and information to progress. Without them, we will never see positive social change either in any of these specific domains or in society as a whole.[92] If people always engaged in social conformity and just complied with the law or just followed the expected or typical norm – never dissenting, asking questions, protesting, or challenging unjust laws or norms – then positive social change would be impossible. Bad laws would never be repealed; wrong and harmful social norms – like racism and bigotry – would remain; and injustices would endure.

Fourth, the conformity that chilling effects promote makes dissent not only difficult but dangerous. In Chapter 3, I spoke about the "spiral of silence," a body of research focused on a social phenomenon whereby dissenting voices are increasingly silenced or chilled in the group due to social conformity. The spiral of silence, cultivated and accelerated by the chilling effects, makes dissent more difficult and dangerous when it is already difficult and dangerous enough. New ideas can be controversial. As Richards points out, many of our most cherished freedoms and ideals today – race, gender, and sexual orientation equality; state neutrality; political and religious freedom; even democracy itself – were once deeply controversial ideas, even considered dangerous by many.[93] Dissenters and dissidents who refuse to conform open themselves up to the most powerful forms of social sanction and punishment as we discussed in Chapter 4. They may be publicly ridiculed and scorned. They may be alienated and ostracized in their communities; losing friends, partners, and social status no doubt upending their personal lives. They may lose their jobs and have their professional reputations ruined. When it comes to new ideas that challenge more entrenched social, political, and economic norms and interests, the stakes can be even higher with dissidents, social movements, and their ideas suppressed through repressive laws, abusive police, angry mobs, threats of violence, and actual acts of violence and reprisal.[94]

Chilling effects thus raise the stakes for *every* act of dissent and deviation. Over time, a society where chilling effects and the conformity they produce are widespread becomes even more conforming and compliant; and those in the majority more sure of their righteousness; more extreme in their resistance to change and reform; and more strengthened in their resolve to punish and sanction those who would challenge the majority's consensus. Inevitably, increasingly hardline and extreme forms of social sanction and repression are almost sure to follow dissent, and the spiraling effect continues onward, making progress and democratic deliberation impossible. On this count, the McCarthy Era, a period of widespread social conformity and chilling effects in American society, offers a compelling case study:

> Yet the developments brought on by the countervailing force of national security put considerable pressure on American privacy rights and, in the process, facilitated a widespread chilling effect on social and political expression. One of the better interpretations of McCarthy's legacy comes from historian Ellen Schrecker, who suggests that perhaps the damage is best appraised by examining "what did not happen" because of this hysteria. That by crippling the far-left, the nation lost a political network that created a space where serious alternatives to the capitalist model could be entertained. Also, any opposition to the Cold War was so quickly associated with communism that it was essentially impossible to challenge the foundations of America's foreign policy without inviting at least some accusations of disloyalty. On cultural matters, anti-subversive rhetoric contributed to the reluctance of publishers, television producers, and filmmakers to take on controversial social and political subjects.[95]

The chill of McCarthy Era measures – repressive laws, surveillance, public investigations, personal threats and persecution – also significantly chilled dissent and social and political progress on a number of fronts. As in Hans Christian Anderson's famous parable, if the emperor is not wearing any clothes, we need *someone* to dissent from the crowd and tell the truth, so society can correct course. Otherwise, everyone, even the emperor – naked as he is – will be worse off. Chilling effects makes such critical acts of dissent more difficult and dangerous – for everyone.

A PROFOUND AND URGENT THREAT TO DEMOCRACY AND FREEDOM

With these impacts it is easy to see how chilling effects are also a clear and present danger to democracy both in the near term and long term. Chilling effects can suppress at mass scale fundamental rights and basic freedoms that are critical to the function and health of democracies: freedom of speech; freedom of expression; freedom to seek, receive, and impart information; as well as intellectual privacy – freedom to read, discuss, and reflect in private and intimate contexts. They chill the diversity of opinion and perspective, creativity, and individualism that are necessary for vibrancy, creativity, and innovation in democracies and foster tolerance and understanding necessary for social cohesion and peace. They create spirals of silence and conformity that over time make dissent dangerous. They feed polarization and extremism that in turn foments division, conflict, abuse, and violence. And they help increase and entrench inequalities, impacting women and minority groups disproportionately, encouraging cycles of generational marginalization and neglect.

7

What Chilling Effects Theory Is for

In September 2021, the state of Texas enacted Senate Bill 8 (SB 8), also known as the Texas Heartbeat Act,[1] which effectively banned abortions in the state after six weeks of pregnancy.[2] Based on prior data, the ban would cover nearly all abortions in the state.[3] The statute was a blatant violation of women's privacy and – then – constitutionally protected right to abortion recognized in the US Supreme Court's famous decision in *Roe v. Wade*.[4] Of course, the Supreme Court has since overturned *Roe* and eviscerated women's constitutional right to choose in its highly contentious 2022 decision in *Dobbs v. Jackson Women's Health Organization*.[5] Nevertheless, how the Supreme Court decided a legal challenge to SB 8 offers a compelling illustration of how chilling effects are weaponized to completely annihilate rights, even constitutionally protected ones, with chilling effects theory showing how.

In Chapter 6, we talked about the dangers of chilling effects, which we can understand far better with a conformity theory of chilling effects. This chapter builds on those arguments, offering a fuller explanation of the different functions and purposes of chilling effects theory and research, though the discussion is certainly not exhaustive. I argue that chilling effects theory can help us to better understand how chilling effects are weaponized, both on an individual level and on a societal level; to demonstrate the limits of conventional thinking and dispel skepticism and myths about the harms of chill; and to better understand both privacy and the law.

SB 8: CHILLING EFFECTS AS POWER

Perhaps the most important purpose of chilling effects theory, what it is "for," is to understand chilling effects as an instrument of power and control. That is, to use chilling effects theory and research to better understand cases like SB 8: *how* repressive governments, commercial enterprise, and other powerful interests weaponize chilling effects and *why* chilling effects are so powerful and effective at repression, manipulation, and control.

SB 8 was controversial not just for its explicit attack on women's then constitutional rights, but for another reason as well – its unusual enforcement mechanism.[6]

Rather than having Texas state officials or agencies enforce it, SB 8's complex scheme outsourced enforcement to private parties. Under SB 8, any member of the public can bring a lawsuit against those who violate the ban or assist others in doing so. The law encourages such legal vigilantism by offering anyone successful in their lawsuit cash bounties starting at $10,000, while also covering legal fees and costs.[7] And they can do so without showing injury, stake, or any personal connection to any abortion. As US Supreme Court Justice Sonia Sotomayor would later note, the law had effectively "deputized" all state citizens as "bounty hunters," offering them "cash prizes for civilly prosecuting their neighbors' medical procedures."[8] The law, at least on its face, thus employed *legal* chilling effects – the looming threat of countless lawsuits for doctors, nurses, clinics, and anyone else helping a woman obtain an abortion – to chill women from exercising their constitutional rights.

And the chilling effect was profound. By the time a lawsuit brought by Texas abortion clinics challenging the constitutionality of SB 8 had wound its way through the lower courts and arrived at the Supreme Court in late 2021, the "chilling effect" of SB 8 was "near total" – as Justice Sotomayor would later describe it – depriving women of "virtually all" opportunity to seek abortion in Texas after six weeks.[9] In other words, SB 8's enactment had entirely obliterated women's access to abortion within the state, and their constitutional rights, through these powerful state-wide chilling effects.

Not surprisingly, these chilling effects were a central issue in a "pre-enforcement" lawsuit that challenged the legality of SB 8, a challenge the Supreme Court heard and ultimately rejected in its decision *Whole Woman's Health et al., v. Jackson et al.*[10] In *Jackson*, Justice Neil Gorsuch, writing for the conservative majority, ultimately refused to issue an order blocking SB 8's operation. In doing so, he rejected the argument that SB 8 had a chilling effect on abortion access. Since no SB 8 lawsuit had yet been filed at this pre-enforcement stage, nor even threatened specifically, Gorsuch found that any such chilling effect would simply be due to the law being "on the books," which did not meet the high burden required for the court to intervene.[11] So, the majority rejected the pre-enforcement challenge, and SB 8 went into effect.

SB 8 offers a compelling demonstration of how chilling effects can be weaponized as a powerful tool of repression and control. Its chilling effect on abortion access – at the time, a constitutionally protected activity – was near total. But therein lies a puzzle. How had the law's chilling effects been so powerful and far-reaching that it had effectively wiped out access to abortion in Texas before it was even in force? That is, before even a *single* lawsuit being filed or even threatened to be filed – a fact that the majority in *Jackson* relied on heavily to reject claims that the law had a chilling effect, thus refusing to block it before it was even "enforced" by anyone – state officials or private citizens. How and why had SB 8 created such a powerful chilling effect? If you were to simply read the *Jackson* decision, you would never find your answer because the court was singularly focused on legal chill. Instead, we need to look at the broader context of SB 8 and draw on our new understanding of chilling effects to solve the puzzle.

Perhaps the most important purpose of chilling effects theory, what it is "for," is to understand chilling effects as an instrument of power and control. That is, to use chilling effects theory and research to better understand cases like SB8: *how* repressive governments, commercial enterprise, and other powerful interests weaponize chilling effects and *why* chilling effects are so powerful and effective at repression, manipulation, and control. The puzzle of SB 8 was how it caused profound chilling effects on women and abortion provision in Texas despite we need to look at the broader context of SB 8 and draw on our new understanding of chilling effects to solve the puzzle.

We already know one way that power and authority matter to chilling effects – it is one of the key chilling effect factors. When people are faced with actors that possess power or authority in concrete ways, especially power or authority that can be used to dominate and command others, as in the Milgram experiments, chilling effects are amplified. But that is not the *only* way that power matters to chilling effects. It also matters via the additive dimensions of chilling effects, which I talked about in Chapters 4 and 5. This means that chill can be caused not only by a single cause or factor but a number of causes or factors that are compounding or additive. As you multiply the threats, and especially if you make them more personal and targeted, the scale, magnitude, and scope of the chilling effects likewise increase. So, when a greater number of these chilling effect factors are present – uncertainty, surveillance, personalization, and power/authority – chilling effects are more powerful. The same goes for when the factors – or threats – are themselves more powerful or significant. Cases involving more invasive and targeted surveillance; or large-scale data processing with more powerful analytics; threats of violence; or actors with more power and authority – like powerful corporate entities or authoritarian governments – will magnify chilling effects. These additive effects are a product of the psychological foundations of chill as both conformity and compliance work this way too.

Governments also have the power to shape norms. They shape behavior not just by passing laws that deter, but also how those laws send a message to society. This is known as law's expressive function. That is, law can deter conduct but also plays a symbolic or expressive role, sending a strong societal message as to what conduct is approved and what is disapproved, which also shapes behavior and societal norms.[12] As I noted in Chapter 4, the social norm of legal compliance or "rule of law" norm, expressed by governments through law and policy-making can have a powerful impact on someone who is uncertain about the legality of a course of action, leading them to instead engage in far safer and less risky behavior that conforms with widely accepted behavior.[13] But that expressive function can also be used to promote other antisocial and harmful behavior and norms – where the law, like SB 8, essentially sends a message to society that certain people or groups should be targeted and victimized. Here, the law, backed by state enforcement capacities, can be a powerful instrument of chilling effects with far-reaching impact and scope.

Governments can also martial the vast resources and technologies of law enforcement and the appendages of state national security apparatus to conduct surveillance on people at mass scale, with potential chilling effects beyond the more simple instances of social observation. And they have the resources to target people personally, through targeted surveillance or law enforcement action. Big business and other powerful private actors, for their part, can similarly leverage control over popular consumer sectors, technology, and social media platforms to employ sophisticated technologies to track, monitor, and influence us for commercial gain, and deploy resources to target people individually with legal and regulatory threats. And with legal schemes like SB 8, their capacity to weaponize laws to chill behavior, even constitutionally protected activities, in order to advance their interests is even greater today. Lastly, when it comes to online platforms, corporate actors also have immense power to shape norms of behavior through terms of service, platform design, and content moderation in ways comparable to the expressive function of laws.[14]

All this is to say, more powerful actors, like government and big business, have greater resources, formal powers and authority, and thus capability to multiply threats or more powerful forms of such chilling effect threats – like more persistent surveillance, more threatening legal penalties, access to more sophisticated data analytics or more sensitive types of information. Power, and the ability to exercise it, allows one to weaponize chilling effects more effectively.

These insights help us understand the true impact of SB 8. While the Court debated SB 8's possible legal chilling effects, none of the justices, liberal or conservative, spoke about the *other* chilling effects of SB 8. Not only does the law with its abortion ban violate women's privacy and constitutional rights, but it empowers and encourages *everyone else* to do so too. Not just by lawsuits encouraged through cash bounties and special rules that make it difficult for those sued to defend themselves and recover their costs in doing so, but encouraging *extralegal* forms of surveillance, harassment, and intimidation as well. Justice Pitman, who heard one of the legal challenges to SB 8 in the District Court for Western Texas, described in his findings a "relentless" campaign of harassment, intimidation, surveillance, and similar forms of abuse.[15] Since SB 8 was enacted, he observed, clinics endured violent threats to doctors, patients, and staff; trespassing; destruction of property and vandalism; roadblocks; illegal sound amplification directed at clinics; surreptitious recording inside clinics; and video recording of people, vehicles, and license plates outside, with activists attempting to track and follow staff home.[16] One clinic reported that at night, antiabortion activists "flooded the areas" around the clinic with light, "shining flashlights into the cars of patients as they entered and exited the parking lots."[17] Later, activists "brought in giant lights and shined them at the clinic, illuminating the parking lot and the building" to track "every move" of staff and patients.[18] Another clinic reported that staff were "plagued by fear and instability" not just due to the threat of SB 8 lawsuits, but such "state-directed harassment."[19] The internet, social media, and other technologies magnified the scope, reach, and impact of these chilling effects. Shortly after SB 8 came into force, the Texas Right to Life group set up a "whistleblower" website (prolifewhistleblower.com) that invited people to help "enforce" the law, including litigating, acting as plaintiffs, or collecting data about violators.[20] On Reddit, a thread was created around the same time where countless individuals discussed how they could become "bounty hunters" under SB 8 and "turn doctors into the police."[21]

The law had not just created an army of legal vigilantes or "bounty hunters," to use Justice Sotomayor's term. It had called forth *actual* vigilantes. It had created a massive surveillance apparatus of all private citizens, with neighbors spying on and informing on neighbors, targeting women's privacy, health, and fundamental rights. It unleashed a state-directed tribalist mob to threaten and intimidate. These things, altogether, created powerful chilling effects that eviscerated not just abortion rights, but speech, privacy, and security for women and anyone helping them vindicate their rights, including doctors, nurses, clinical workers, staff, family, and friends.

So when Justice Sotomayor wrote that SB 8's intended chilling effects had succeeded – they were "near total" in depriving women in Texas access to an abortion after six weeks – it was not *just* due to the threat of lawsuits, but this state-directed campaign of targeted surveillance, harassment, and intimidation as well. And when Justice Gorsuch held that the *only* chilling effect caused by SB 8 was the fact that it is a law "on the books," he was ignoring the stark reality on the ground. In fact, the Court in the past has cited such chilling effects intending to "harass" and "discourage" the exercise of constitutional rights to justify halting state legal proceedings, as the Court did in its famous 1965 "chilling effects" decision *Dowbrowski* discussed in Chapter 1. The difference here, of course, is that the harassment and legal threats are not coming directly from state actors, but private individuals. But that was by design. With SB 8, Texas outsourced not just the enforcement of its abortion ban, but its accompanying state-directed campaign of fear, harassment, and intimidation.

All of these legal and extralegal chilling effects were intentional. The *legal* chilling effects of SB 8 – via threats of countless lawsuits from legally empowered vigilantes and bounty hunters – were clearly intentional. "[B]y design," Chief Justice Roberts held in his dissenting opinion, "the mere threat of even unsuccessful suits brought under S. B. 8 chills constitutionally protected conduct."[22] But the *extralegal* chilling effects – the state-enabled campaign of surveillance, stalking, harassment, and abuse – were *also* by design. Jonathan Mitchell, a conservative lawyer and activist and former Texas Solicitor General, was the chief architect of SB 8, which represented the culmination of years of effort to use and abuse laws, legal processes, surveillance, stalking, and harassment to chill women's access to abortion, and thus reproductive freedom, and to punish anyone helping them protect and defend their freedoms.[23] For instance, at a public hearing in the town in New Mexico where local politicians were considering an abortion ban modeled on SB 8, a local resident raised a concern about how the proposed law turns "neighbor against neighbor."[24] Mitchell's response was telling: This was necessary to ensure an "effective prohibition" on abortion.[25] In other words, turning neighbors on neighbors and citizens on citizens via state-sanctioned surveillance, stalking, harassment, and personal threats – legal and otherwise – was fully intended by SB 8's passage to create multifaceted chilling effects on activities that were, at the time, entirely legal and constitutionally protected.

In light of this, it is no coincidence that the Texas Right To Life group, a well-funded and resourced antiabortion lobbying organization, had its abortion ban surveillance and stalking "whistleblower" website ready to go online immediately as SB 8 was passed, because it had worked very closely with Mitchell and Texas government officials designing and enacting SB 8.[26] It knew that SB 8's private enforcement scheme created new opportunities to foment powerful chilling effects on abortion rights through new forms of digital surveillance and stalking, sourced from the mob, targeting women who were simply seeking to exercise their rights. And it could do so without limit or accountability – state officials, in fact, supported its efforts while judges would likely be powerless to stop them, as SB 8 was also specifically designed to avoid judicial review, a reality confirmed by the Supreme Court, which refused to intervene.[27] The result is a "campaign of terror" with profound chilling effects on women seeking abortion and their loved ones.[28]

With the help of chilling effects theory, the SB 8 puzzle is solved. We understand better both what caused SB 8's powerful chilling effects and *how* the Texas Government was able to create and magnify them to totally eviscerate women's right to abortion access as effectively and substantially as possible. This was not a case where a law simply sitting "on the books" had caused such sweeping chilling effects, although the likelihood of lawsuits and similar legal threats later on were no doubt still a factor. Rather, this was a case where the state integrated all four chilling effect factors in its SB 8 chilling effects schema – surveillance, uncertainty, personalization, and power/authority – and then used its lawmaking powers, powers of coordination, communication, and norm-shaping to weaponize an angry mob to magnify the threats in a state-directed "campaign of terror," empowered through technology like online crowdsourcing and surveillance, that spread the chill far and wide.

DEMONSTRATING THE LIMITS OF CONVENTIONAL THINKING

Beyond demonstrating how chilling effects are a tool of power and repression, SB 8 and the Supreme Court's related decision in *Jackson* are also compelling illustrations of the limits of conventional understanding of chilling effects that is so predominant among lawyers and judges. How had *all* the justices of the Supreme Court missed the *real* chilling effects of SB 8? It was not only Justice Gorsuch and the conservative judges in the majority that missed them, whom critics might charge are inclined to disregard such extralegal impacts. No, it was the dissenting liberal justices as well, like Justice Sotomayor, who commands a powerful grasp of the law and its broader context as evident from her fiery dissent in this decision. She mentioned nothing about surveillance, nothing about threats and intimidation, and the only harassment she spoke to in her opinion, was harassment due to threatened and actual lawsuits that would be filed by private citizens under the law. How to explain how *she* had missed them too?

Both the conservatives in the majority and the liberals in dissent evince a conventional understanding of chilling effects – they all agreed that chilling effects caused directly by the law are the only chilling effects that matter. The only real disagreement between them was whether SB 8 causes a chill even if lawsuits have yet to be filed. Justice Gorsuch thought not. Justice Sotomayor thought so. They are all, as conventional understanding dictates, focused only on the law and its direct impact on constitutional rights. And while the law is not irrelevant, the chilling effects in the case are almost surely the result of other *extralegal* factors – a government-supported, mob-led, digitally empowered campaign of targeted surveillance, harassment, stalking, threats, and abuse. All ignored by the judges.

This is not uncommon. The US Supreme Court decision in *Counterman v. Colorado* is another great example.[29] At issue there, was a criminal conviction under a Colorado anti-stalking law challenged on First Amendment grounds by the accused as having a chilling effect on speech.[30] Ultimately, the Supreme Court found the Colorado anti-stalking law's objective standard for intent – that required the state only to prove a reasonable person would have viewed his messages to the victim as threatening not that he subjectively intended them to be – was inconsistent with the First Amendment as it would likely chill protected speech.[31] Writing for the majority, Justice Elena Kagan wrote that a recklessness mental requirement was required for the anti-stalking law to avoid such chill.[32] But in doing so, as critics like my colleagues Danielle Citron and Mary Anne Franks argue, the Court wholly ignored the *other* chilling effects in the case: how the accused's stalking and harassment had a powerful chilling effect on his victim – Coles Whalen, a singer-songwriter based in Denver – whose life was turned upside down by the stalking and threats, leading her to cancel performances and ultimately abandon her music career as a result.[33] Again, entirely ignored both by the justices writing in the majority and in dissent.

This is why conventional understanding of chilling effects is not sustainable – legalistic and narrow, it creates glaring blind spots to the reality of chilling effects. Naturally, a theory of chilling effects focused primarily on laws, statutes, and regulations cannot explain impacts due to threats beyond the law, like the targeted harassment, abuse, and surveillance unleashed by SB 8 or the deeply chilling stalking in *Counterman*. This is a serious problem for understanding chilling effects, and their impact and implications. But another likely consequence is that this legalistic conventional focus has perpetuated persistent skepticism about such chilling effects beyond the law – like those due to personal threats in the SB 8 case and *Counterman* – or due to privacy threats – like mass or targeted government surveillance, data collection, and processing as seen in cases like *Laird* and *Clapper*, two Supreme Court decisions that expressed skepticism about chilling effects while denying standing for claims based on them.[34]

DISPELLING SKEPTICISM AND DEBUNKING MYTHS

But conventional thinking also leads to misconceptions and myths about chilling effects, which in turn likewise feeds skepticism. In the days following the explosive Snowden revelations about the NSA's mass surveillance programs published in the *Guardian* and the *Washington Post*, the *New York Times* convened a panel of experts to debate whether such government surveillance was a "threat" to democracy.[35] The main experts debating were Jameel Jaffer, then Deputy Legal Director of the American Civil Liberties Union (ACLU), and Eric Posner, a widely cited legal scholar and professor at University of Chicago School of Law and son of Richard Posner, the influential law and economics scholar and jurist noted earlier in the book for his skepticism about the value of social theory. The title the *Times* chose for the debate – "Is the N.S.A. Surveillance Threat Real or Imagined?" – itself reflected a skepticism common among journalists and lawyers concerning negative impacts due to government surveillance like chilling effects.

The ACLU's Jaffer, not surprisingly, played the role of government critic, while Posner defended the government surveillance programs. Jaffer offered a number of pointed criticisms but his central concern centered on what he considered to be the "greater threat" to democracy posed by surveillance: chilling effects. If people know the government is watching them or might be, he argued, they become "reluctant to exercise democratic freedoms" like avoiding visiting controversial websites, joining unpopular political groups, or publicly protesting or criticizing government policy.[36] These chilling effects undermine democracy as they make "our public debates narrower and more inhibited and our democracy less vital."[37]

Posner, in response, dismissed these concerns. Echoing the skepticism of the debate title – and his father's skepticism of social theory – Posner argued that chilling effects are more imagined than real premised on a misconception about the nature of chilling effects and how they manifest in society:

> This brings me to another valuable point you made, which is that when people believe that the government exercises surveillance, they become reluctant to exercise democratic freedoms. This is a textbook objection to surveillance, I agree, but it also is another objection that I would place under "theoretical" rather than real. Is there any evidence that over the 12 years, during the flowering of the so-called surveillance state, Americans have become less politically active? More worried about government suppression of dissent? Less willing to listen to opposing voices? All the evidence points in the opposite direction.
>
> Views from the extreme ends of the political spectrum are far more accessible today than they were in the past. It is infinitely easier to get the Al Qaeda

perspective today – one just does a Google search – than it was to learn the Soviet perspective 40 years ago, which would have required one to travel to one of the very small number of communist bookstores around the country. It is hard to think of another period so full of robust political debate since the late 1960s – another era of government surveillance.[38]

For Posner, the very fact people are still politically active; there is "robust" debate in society; and views from the "extreme" ends of the political spectrum are more easily accessed today than decades ago – a Google search away online – is strong evidence that surveillance chilling effects are mythical or simply trivial.

This type of thinking is common. David Sklansky, a law professor at Stanford Law School, has similarly argued there is evidence "all around us" contradicting the idea that surveillance would "chill independent thought, robust debate, personal growth, and intimate friendship."[39] He cites as evidence against any such chilling effects the widespread sharing of personal information online; how employer email monitoring has not deterred employee emailing; how freedom of information laws have not deterred intragovernmental communications; and how young people share and engage online more than previous generations. Like Posner, Sklansky claims the fact that people persist in such activities, despite large-scale surveillance programs like those disclosed by Snowden or reported on in media, is compelling evidence that chilling effects either do not exist, or if they do exist, they are not worth the worry.[40]

Posner explains this lack of apparent chilling effects in society with another misconception. In addition to arguing that the presence of robust debate proves chilling effects are likely more imagined than real, he also argues that because data and information collection, mining, monitoring, and retention are already so common and prevalent in society, their impacts would be trivial and not chilling. We already provide the government and corporations with an "enormous" amount of information about our lives such that we are now "used to the idea" that they know everything about us – the tax authorities know our finances; health authorities and insurers know our medical history; telecommunications companies know where we are and who we speak to daily; social media companies know what we read, follow, purchase, and with whom we interact online.[41] The data and information the NSA was vacuuming up was no different from what is already known to government bureaucrats and internet companies – and anyways, was carried out by automated programs and algorithms, not human beings who might have a motive to misuse the data.

This is again another common trope among lawyers, judges, and social theorists skeptical of chilling effects.[42] Such skepticism is a product of what Anupam Chander and Uyen Le call the "diffuseness" of chilling effects and what Evan Selinger and Judy Rhee call "unexceptional habituation" surveillance normalization – the idea that as surveillance becomes so routine in daily life people will come to see it as acceptable and unremarkable and, in turn, will become numb to it, reducing its impacts.[43] That numbness means chilling effects are unlikely, Posner concludes, especially given the little evidence of any risks of individual privacy harms, which is more proof chilling effects are a fantasy.

Of course, there is little suspense in the broader debate here. We already know that Jaffer is right and Posner, Sklansky, and other skeptics are wrong – chilling effects are not only real, they are a profound threat to democracy. However, the debate serves another important purpose – it helps demonstrate the flaws in how Posner, Sklansky, and other skeptics reason about the nature of chilling effects.

For skeptics like Posner and Sklansky, since "robust" debate, dissent, sharing, and expression persist in society, any chilling effects are likely either imagined or too trivial to care about. Elsewhere, I have argued these misconceptions can be attributed, in part, to dystopian depictions of mass surveillance – and related chilling effects – in popular culture like Orwell's *Nineteen Eighty-Four* or Aldous Huxley's *Brave New World*, wherein totalitarian regimes use mass surveillance, propaganda, and violence to chill not only all societal debate or dissenting opinion but independent thought.[44] But these popular depictions are compounded by the real culprit: conventional theories of chilling effects, which Posner, Sklansky, and similar skeptics exemplify. Conventional theories are singularly focused on the repressive dimensions of chilling effects – deterrence, self-censorship, and an absence of speech or action – to the exclusion of its productive dimensions. If that is your focus, then it makes perfect sense, as Posner, Sklansky, and other skeptics do, to believe that if you see debate, discussion, and sharing throughout society, then there are no chilling effects. Or if there are, they are too trivial to worry about.

A conformity theory of chilling effects – which highlights what chilling effects produce and not just what they deter – helps debunk these myths and misconceptions. Simply because social and political discussion or debate appears today in democratic societies does not mean there are no such chilling effects or that they are trivial. Yes, this can mean being deterred or discouraged from speaking or doing entirely, but more often chilling effects still involve speech and activities, just more socially conforming and compliant ones. This is the productive dimension of chilling effects. It means that there can be plenty of debate, discussion, and sharing in society and yet there are chilling effects even at mass scale as several studies have documented. And this outcome is no less corrosive to freedom and democracy.

To begin with, chilling effects need not be so obvious and society wide – like the chill of the totalitarian Big Brother regime. As discussed in Chapter 6, people can be chilled in more subtle ways, including by just routine commercial practices that produce individual conforming behavior that at a societal level and over the long term becomes a serious problem. Recent research on the chill of widespread commercial data collection and processing – usually driven by algorithms and big data analytics that I talked about in Chapter 6 – speaks to these dynamics. That research shows how people's awareness of being watched and tracked and processed increases over time, not only due to high-profile events like the Snowden disclosures and Cambridge Analytica but also through personal experiences with prosaic forms of data tracking and surveillance usually in a commercial context.[45] These experiences and events increase our awareness over time, compounding the chilling and conforming effects creating a new baseline to which we never return. In short, seemingly benign commercial practices can cause subtle chills that spill over from consumer behavior to behaviors and practices we associate with healthy democracies – freedom of speech, association, and democratic deliberation.

Now, to be clear, there *is* evidence of surveillance normalization and Selinger and other theorists have done an excellent job exploring it. But the process I just described itself is a kind of normalization but it does not mean that chilling effects are not real or likely or that we become more numb to surveillance or other threats that cause chilling effects – rather, chilling effects are more subtle, but just as problematic in aggregate and over the long term. In fact, a lot of research on the impact of surveillance or data tracking finds some elements of normalization co-present with chilling effects. That is, people can feel helpless and resigned to the realities and ubiquity of surveillance and data collection today, but are still inhibited or chilled in certain contexts when their awareness is more heightened or the perceived threat is greater – as when dealing with more sensitive activities or information that might be targeted or tracked. An example of this is work by Lina Dencik, Jonathan Cable, and others on "surveillance realism," where activists and journalists post-Snowden felt helpless and resigned to the pervasiveness of surveillance in society but nevertheless reported being chilled and changing their behavior as a result, especially when dealing with confidential communications.[46] This makes a lot of sense, given that chilling effects on a conformity theory should be understood not just as repressive but productive of conforming behavior, which is another way of saying that people alter their behavior – consciously or subconsciously – in response to chilling effect threats like surveillance, but those changes can be fluid and contextual, depending on threat perception. If you only expect widespread societal chill as Posner, Sklansky, and others do, you miss these realities.

This raises another reason why this line of thinking about chilling effects is wrong. Now that we know that chilling effects are conforming and compliance effects, we also know – as I argued in Chapter 6 – that all of the things that cause chilling effects – surveillance, targeted legal threats, personal threats, abuse – can lead not just to silence or benign behavior but in some cases more tribalist and extremist speech and behavior – if that kind of speech is the group or expected norm. And through the spiral of silence, and group polarization, that speech and behavior will only get increasingly extremist and polarized over time. Once again, that means that the presence of radical speech or access to extremist content in society – as Posner notes – is not at all evidence against chilling effects; but entirely consistent with its impacts.

This is not to say that Orwell and other popular depictions of mass surveillance and chilling effects are necessarily wrong. For instance, if a government adopted Big Brother's totalitarian tactics from *Nineteen Eighty-Four* – and there are certainly ones that have arguably done so today and in the past[47] – including sophisticated mass surveillance, propaganda, torture, arbitrary arrest, imprisonment, and targeted

political violence and assassinations ("vaporizations" as Winston Smith called it) –
then society-wide chilling effects and suppression of democratic debate and dissent
would almost certainly be an outcome. Such a regime would check all the boxes for
the most powerful kind of chilling effects on a conformity theory. The point, rather,
is that while mass surveillance and other forms of governmental repression *can* lead
to widespread chilling effects where all debate and dissent are nonexistent or rare,
that does not have to be the case, nor is it often so.

UNDERSTANDING LAW

Another function of chilling effects theory is to better understand the law and its
impact. The debate as to why people generally follow the law has predominantly
involved two theories – deterrence and legitimacy.[48] Deterrence theorists, as we
have seen, argue that it is the law's coercive force, including social and penal costs,
and probability of punishment, which guarantee compliance.[49] Law and economics
scholars fall into this camp. As do legal theorists like Schauer. His book *The Force
of Law* made the case about how the law, independent of other factors, coerces
behavior, something consistent with his conventional theory of chilling effects.[50]
Legitimacy theorists like social scientist Tom Tyler argue that people obey the law
because they see it as legitimate and worthy of compliance.[51] But this long-running
and entrenched debate has arguably neglected other factors in the force of law and
its impact.[52]

Indeed, these theories appear as inadequate to understanding the true impact of
SB 8, and its chilling effects, as the US Supreme Court's reasoning. To understand
the *true* force of law – and how it might unleash profound chilling and compliance
effects like SB 8 – you have to look at its broader context, beyond the law, deterrence, and even people's perceptions of its morality and legitimacy. You also need to
consider each of the chilling effect factors discussed here – uncertainty, observation,
personalization, and power/authority – as each can help understand people's behavior in response to the law, and legal threats, how the law itself can be weaponized
to chill and repress.

Indeed, as this book has recounted, there is a long history of chilling effects being
weaponized as a tool of repression and control, like those anti-communist laws
enacted during the McCarthy Era discussed in Chapter 1 that were later repurposed to repress the civil rights movement. Similar tactics laid the foundations for
overreaching national security laws and surveillance post-9/11, and continue to be
used today to chill political activists and anti-government sentiment, and repress
disfavored and disempowered groups and communities.[53] The point is that in every
era, malevolent actors – in the public and private sector – have weaponized chill for
repression and control and to extend their power. But as SB 8 and many other examples in the book demonstrate, they are getting increasingly sophisticated at it too, by
magnifying chill by every tactic and lever available, including weaponizing mobs

and vigilantes and using digital platforms and emerging technologies to increase scope and reach. Fortunately, with our new understanding, we can see these trends, identify the factors, and respond.

UNDERSTANDING PRIVACY

Chilling effects theory is also essential to understanding privacy. More than any other body of research, it helps connect the dots between privacy and key values and concepts at the heart of leading privacy theories like autonomy, identity, and trust, personhood, and intimacy. Some already do – like Cohen, Richards, Solove, Nissenbaum, and Citron among others – but many do not. Take autonomy. The idea that lack of privacy threatens our right of "self-determination" or "autonomy" is pervasive in privacy scholarship.[54] These ideas underpin theories of privacy as a "right to be left alone," as Samuel Warren and Louis Brandeis defined it in their famous law review article "The Right to Privacy" published in 1890, which has been so influential in shaping American conceptions of privacy.[55] Thus, autonomy and self-determination – making fundamental decisions without interference by government – also explain conceptions of privacy in US constitutional law, including famous cases like *Katz v. United States*, *Roe v. Wade*, and *Griswold v. Connecticut*, albeit a narrow conception of privacy that the Court has in any case largely abandoned in recent decisions.[56] Autonomy is also regularly invoked to explain why privacy is so important to democracy. Privacy scholar Paul Schwartz, for instance, in a well-known and widely cited article made the case that privacy is essential to freedom and democracy because it creates the necessary conditions for self-determination and autonomy – the capacity for each individual to think for themselves, formulate their own conceptions of the good, and make decisions for themselves and their society, something essential to deliberative democracy.[57] Other leading privacy scholars like Ruth Gavison, Cohen, and Richards have all argued similarly.[58] Citron and Solove thus recently named "autonomy harms" as among the critical privacy injuries that impact both individuals and broader society in their comprehensive topology.[59]

In Chapter 6, I explained how chilling effects endanger fundamental freedoms and democratic societies and undermine many of these very values – including autonomy, identity, and personal development – and I won't repeat those arguments here. The point is that privacy theorists and scholars can now draw on chilling effects theory and research to better elaborate these core privacy values and interests. For instance, Schwartz argues that surveillance, "perfected" with endless data trails online, and the Orwellian "Cyber Thought Police" that it enables, undermines autonomy and self-determination.[60] The threat of persistent surveillance operates as a "coercive influence" and essentially "takes over, or colonizes, a person's thinking processes."[61] But how exactly does surveillance "colonize" our thinking processes? It is not entirely clear on his account. Gavison, for her part, references privacy as important to avoiding the "inhibitive effect" of both observation and the threat of social disapproval, which all undermine "moral autonomy," but does not explain precisely how these impacts occur, nor how they undermine our capacity for "reflective and critical acceptance of social norms."[62] On this point, she readily confesses: We "do not know."[63]

But now we do. A conformity theory of chilling effects provides an explanation for these impacts. These chilling effects, as I have argued, have deeper psychological foundations, likely an instinctual behavioral response to perceived threats that is now hardwired into our brains because it helps us survive, which is why we can be chilled both consciously and subconsciously. We are chilled and conform when under simple observation by other people – an effect that Gavison talks about – even when we know the observation surveillance threat isn't real. And we are chilled even more so when facing persistent targeted surveillance entities with power and authority like law enforcement or government, which is what Schwartz is worried about. *This* is how our "thinking process" is hijacked by surveillance and other chilling effect threats, and how it undermines our capacity to make decisions for ourselves (Schwartz) and critically evaluate norms before accepting or rejecting them (Gavison). Schwartz and Gavison were both correct, but chilling effects theory, especially a conformity theory, helps to more clearly and explicitly connect the dots.

Yet chilling effects theory also demonstrates how privacy threats – like surveillance or large-scale data collection, retention, and processing – can have both coercive and manipulative impacts, which in turn helps us better understand personhood theories of privacy. These theories posit privacy as protective of key elements of the self, like unique individuality and dignity.[64] These theories of privacy link Warren and Brandeis' concept of "inviolate personality" to more contemporary notions of human dignity.[65] We associate human dignity with self-integrity and self-worth.[66] Dignity, like identity, is an inherently social, relational, and ritualistic concept, and develops through social interactions.[67] It is, as Jeremy Waldron has observed, a form of *status* or standing among others in social life.[68] To be treated with dignity, is to be respected and treated with equal worth by others. On these theories, privacy has a relational quality – they speak to not just a right to be left alone to decide for ourselves, but also a right to be treated a certain way by others.[69] Privacy, on this view, is important because it protects against what Edward Bloustein called "demeaning" conduct that is an "affront to personal dignity."[70]

We know, as discussed in Chapter 6, that the chilling effects of privacy threats undermine our identity formation and personal development – by silencing us, and making us more dull, mute, and bland; undermining what Goffman called our "expressive order." But chilling effects also coerce us and manipulate us, because these threats not only prevent us from speaking or acting as we prefer, but also cause us to speak and behave *differently* – often in ways *others*, those who have the power to threaten and chill us, would prefer instead. We become mouthpieces of the group and its expected norms, which themselves can undermine human dignity and respect – like racist, bigoted, violent, and antisocial norms. We are chilled into becoming an instrument of power and oppression.

That sometimes subtle manipulation, sometimes more direct and intentional coercive impact of chilling – and conforming – effects strikes at the heart of dignity and personhood. Chilling effects due to threats – like coercive threats of violence – are the easy case. Philosophers like Lon Fuller have long argued that coercion is contrary to dignity.[71] That's because coercion entirely removes our agency and free will to choose. The coercer's choice becomes the only choice for the victim, obliterating the victim's autonomy, self-determination, and dignity.[72] But manipulation does so as well, just through different means.[73] Manipulations make us an instrument of another's will by undermining our decision-making process – we think we are making our own decision, to speak or act, but we are manipulated into again adopting someone else's preferences or choice as our own.[74] Chilling effects operate like this too, especially when the privacy threat that causes the chill – like targeted surveillance – is designed not to track for law enforcement or security purposes, but to manipulate the target into conformity and compliance – an enduring form of power and control, especially where the new values are eventually internalized.

These insights also help convey the full spectrum of harms caused by chilling effects. In defining "autonomy harms," Citron and Solove explicate multiple categories – coercion, manipulation, limiting information, thwarting expectations, and undermining data control – but list "chilling effects" as one mere subcategory.[75] But chilling effects properly understood implicate each of these harms – they coerce and manipulate; chill information access and data choices; and thwart our expectations by chilling our thinking and decision-making.

Lastly, a conformity theory of chilling effects highlights the social dimensions of privacy itself, and thus the value in its social protection.[76] In recent years, there has been a social and relational "turn" in privacy, like theories of privacy focused on trust, intimacy, and contextual integrity, which all emphasize privacy's social value.[77] That said, privacy is not just an individual right or interest, there is collective and societal value in protecting it. So, when privacy is threatened or lost, there are social harms beyond mere individual interests, like personal or economic harms. A conformity theory, which links chilling effects caused by privacy threats to forms of social influence, compliance and conformity, highlights these social foundations of privacy. For instance, it helps us better understand how threats to privacy erode trust and intimacy. As Richards and Woodrow Hartzog note, trust is critical to "healthy relationships and societies," including social relations, expression, and commerce.[78] It is, in Ari Waldman's terms, a "natural" almost "designed-in" aspect of "social life"[79] and, as Citron has pointed out, is essential to forging relationships.[80] Such relationships, including both casual and intimate, develop through a process of social interactions, involving presentation of the self in social settings, sharing, and disclosure.[81] Chilling effects undermine all of these things. By undercutting both consciously and subconsciously how we present ourselves, like fostering silence or conformity when we would normally act otherwise, chilling effects undermine our expressive control and ordering, creating inconsistencies, gaps, and confusion about our social interactions, identities, and our personal expression. This, in turn, undermines the trust and intimacy necessary to maintain existing relationships or forge new ones. Chilling effects impact us, and our essential connections with others.

But chilling effects can also promote informational norms that in turn weaken privacy and its social value. This point is clear from Helen Nissenbaum's widely influential theory of privacy as "contextual integrity." This theory also treats privacy as a social value, and relies on what Nissenbaum calls "context-relative informational norms," as a heuristic to determine privacy violations.[82] But those informational norms are simply social norms, which are highly contextual and evolve over time due to a range of different historical, cultural, and even geographic factors.[83] But as is clear on a conformity theory, the threats that chill can similarly entrench problematic informational norms, shift them, or even produce harmful or abusive behavior that flouts or violates other informational norms. Indeed, chilling effects can also promote antisocial norms and behavior, including online hate, trolling, bullying, and abuse, leading to more division, polarization, and tribalism. These are destructive to not only personal relationships and trust, but also the broader social fabric, including privacy norms. Often, as Ignacio Cofone has argued in his noteworthy book *The Privacy Fallacy*, privacy law and policy tend to commit a "privacy fallacy" by neglecting that value in practice.[84] Chilling effects theory and research can help us better understand privacy, and the true societal import of privacy threats, to better avoid that fallacy.

In summary, if privacy is concerned with fostering social conditions for autonomy, trust, personal development, and intellectual freedom, then privacy theorists must consult and understand chilling effects theory. This is because chilling effects foster competing social conditions – self-censorship, conformity, and compliance – that frustrate and undermine these very things. A conformity theory of chilling effects helps explain how these contrary social conditions are promoted via privacy and other similar threats, thus helping expose them, and their long-term impact. Only with better understanding via chilling effects theory can these challenges be effectively addressed through privacy law and policy.

CHILLING EFFECTS BY DESIGN AND SYSTEMS OF POWER

Lastly, chilling effects theory helps us better understand the tools and systems of power. SB 8, for instance, was intentionally crafted and implemented to enable profound chilling effects, magnify them, and insulate them from scrutiny, accountability, and legal challenge. With chilling effects theory, we can fully understand such insidious and sophisticated *chilling effects by design*. In his essential book on privacy design, Woodrow Hartzog talks about this very point: how products can be designed in ways that expose us and our information, causing chilling effects.[85] In other words, chilling effect factors can be weaponized through the design of systems and products in the same way they can be through laws like SB 8. This is another purpose of chilling effects theory and research – to understand chilling effects as a design principle, whether we are talking about laws, technologies like social media platforms designed to expose us, or broader social and political institutions and systems. Chilling effects can be weaponized to repress and control disfavored people and groups, and to extend state and corporate power through such means. But there is an additional design layer here – because chilling effects *produce* conformity and compliance, they have implications for broader social, political, and economic shifts too. Chilling effects thus help perpetuate and sustain broader systems of power and control in this way.

Foucault understood this point well. In fact, our new theory allows us to see with fresh eyes both the brilliance in Bentham's famous "Panopticon" prison design, and Foucault's own work analyzing it. It was a new technology – a prison technology – employing chilling effects by design. Though many privacy and surveillance scholars tend to minimize the relevance of panopticism for understanding surveillance and related challenges today,[86] a theory of chilling effects as conformity helps illustrate not only that its design reflects a sophisticated understanding of human behavior and chilling effects, but that it is more relevant than ever. Here is how Foucault described the prison design:

> We know the principle on which it was based: at the periphery, an annular building; at the centre, a tower; this tower is pierced with wide windows that open onto the inner side of the ring; the peripheric building is divided into cells, each of which extends the whole width of the building; they have two windows, one on the inside, corresponding to the windows of the tower; the other, on the outside, allows the light to cross the cell from one end to the other. All that is needed, then, is to place a supervisor in a central tower and to shut up in each cell a madman, a patient, a condemned man, a worker or a schoolboy. By the effect of backlighting, one can observe from the tower, standing out precisely against the light, the small captive shadows in the cells of the periphery.[87]

In using this design as a way of understanding the chilling and self-disciplining effect of modern surveillance technologies and practices, Foucault emphasized two key features of the design. Each was essential to understand how surveillance chills and disciplines: First, unverifiability – the prison was designed to ensure that prisoners were always in a state of uncertainty as to whether they were being watched. In Foucault's words, the prisoner "must never know whether he is being looked at at any one moment; but he must be sure that he may always be so."[88] Uncertainty was thus key to the prison's surveillance structure. It is this feature that commentators often focus on, as Foucault theorized that surveillance in modern society operates precisely this way – people conforming their behavior out of the *possibility* they are being monitored at all times.

But to ensure this chilling effect, there needs to be a constant reminder of that possible-but-unverifiable surveillance. Thus, the second key feature of the prison – visibility – is just as important. The prison was designed such that each prisoner would "constantly have before his eyes the tall outline of the central tower from which he is spied upon."[89] The central tower remained a powerful and ubiquitous reminder to all prisoners of the possibility of surveillance. It was always there, always visible to prisoners. The central tower is the trigger for the chilling and self-disciplining effects caused by the Panopticon design. Without the central tower as an inescapable reminder of possible surveillance, prisoners may very well forget they are under watch, and thus the chilling and normalizing effects of the design dissipate. In a sense, the central tower in the Panopticon serves a similar function to the sets of artificial eyes in the "watching eye" studies. The artificial eyes are a reminder of the *possibility* of surveillance by others, which triggers chilling effects among the participants, leading them to engage in more conforming or compliant behavior. With these factors, a conformity theory also allows us to better understand technologies, systems, and other infrastructures that are designed to cause or contribute to chilling effects.

For Foucault, Bentham's "Panopticon" was not just a prison design, but a perfect metaphor for the operation of disciplining power in modern society – producing "docile" subjects via the disciplining power of surveillance.[90] He thus interrogated prisons, schools, hospitals, and other systems of the modern administrative state that emerged in the eighteenth century, that also employed forms of systematic observation and surveillance modeled on the prison system to discipline people into conformity.[91] Foucault was thus interested in *institutions* and *systems* that incorporated chilling effects by design, and studied it as an exercise in power and how that power was maintained and sustained. That is, not just in a single law like SB 8, weaponized by one or even several governments, but in broader social institutions and political and economic systems.

Today, we live in an era of surveillance capitalism. Shoshana Zuboff, in her widely cited and highly influential book, has argued that this is an age wherein commercial interests claim human activity and experience as "free raw material for translation into behavioral data," to analyze and process that data to "anticipate what you will do now, soon, and later."[92] Powerful social media platforms like Facebook, X, and Google now wield the capability to harvest vast amounts of data and use it to "shape our behavior at scale."[93] Surveillance capitalism is thus extractive: People are not customers or users, but objects from which raw material – data about us and our activities – is extracted and used to develop behavioral technologies – what Zuboff calls "prediction factories" – that are commercialized and monetized.[94] Those technologies do not only predict behavior but also manipulate and shape it, such that the profits of surveillance capitalism are not only predictable, but almost certain. In her landmark book *Between Truth and Power*, Julie Cohen similarly makes a powerful case that we are amid a transformative shift in political economy from an industrial capitalist paradigm to an informational one.[95] A sweeping and comprehensive account, Cohen's book also offers a clearer explication of how law has played a role in enabling and "constituting" this shift.[96]

However, as Amy Kapczynski has noted, Zuboff mostly *declares*, but does not soundly defend, the proposition that mass behavioral influence and manipulation through surveillance and data analytics is the core tenet of this new capitalism paradigm.[97] In fact, the evidence on whether behavioral advertising can impact and influence the way that Zuboff claims has yet to be established.[98] Kapczynski is correct that dismissing Zuboff's warning would be "foolish" despite the lack of empirical support, but a fuller explanation is still lacking. It is puzzling that Zuboff cites *some* research on chilling effects – noting only aspects of social media chilling effects[99] – but draws no other connections, neglecting other important work relating to the chill of corporate surveillance and the kind of data-driven profiling she warns about.

Chilling effects theory can help fill in some of these gaps. The key is looking to what they produce. When people are chilled from speaking or from engaging in activities they would otherwise pursue, then there is more opportunity for their attention to be hijacked or their activities influenced and manipulated for informational or surveillance capitalist purposes. Indeed, a conformity theory, which points to deeper psychological foundations for chilling effects, helps us understand how platforms can more easily manipulate us with surveillance, platform designs that expose us, and content moderation that seeks to polarize for engagement and monetization. From this angle of view, we can see how large-scale data collection, retention, and analysis by platforms not only advance the commercial interests of platforms, but they also promote chilling and conforming effects, where people are more likely to follow the norm, which online can often mean increasingly polarized and abusive behavior, which in turn leads to more clicks and engagement and more time spent on the platforms, thus greater profits. Platforms and other surveillance capitalists understand and exploit these behavioral tendencies to bypass our critical faculties to chill us and manipulate us for their own benefits. Chilling effects by design thus can have an influence, manipulation, and profiting effect. Precisely *who* is doing the manipulation and *why* are key insights of Zuboff and Cohen on surveillance and information capitalism, and a conformity theory of chilling effects helps us understand more of the *how*.

Moreover, since chilling effects produce conforming and compliance effects, they also help explain how these new capitalist paradigms can be entrenched over time. Chilling effects involve following, and not challenging, social norms that would themselves be shaped and in some cases engineered by capitalist forces. In short, chilling effects help perpetuate and entrench this new capitalist paradigm. More conformity means more surveillance and informational capitalism, and vice versa. Interestingly, Zuboff even dismisses the relevance of conformity as it suggests a possibility of "escape," suggesting near the end of the book that there may be "no exit."[100] But as noted earlier, this is not what social science tells us about social norms. They are not static, and they can be shaped, impacted, and changed, not just by dissenters, authority figures, or broader economic and cultural shifts, but they can also be shaped by laws, and not just through regulation but also through their expressive effects. By not investigating conformity more in depth, Zuboff also misses these possible exits. Understanding how chilling effects, and the threats that cause them, help perpetuate systems of power, control, and exploitation is also what chilling effects theory is for.

8

A Framework for Hard Cases

Some cases of chilling effects are easy – like blatantly repressive laws that are designed to target and persecute vulnerable people with the aim of chilling all aspects of their lives. Or cases of overreaching targeted surveillance by governments that aim to chill and repress the political speech and other activities of innocent citizens, or activists, eroding democracy and freedom. These are easy cases where that should lead to a law and policy response. But chilling effects can also involve hard cases. That is, where the public and private sector practices that cause chilling effects, be it surveillance, laws, online hate and abuse, or other personal threats, are often justified on the basis of other competing interests or values – like safety, security, and freedom of speech. Or, alternatively, legal protections – like privacy laws – that may reduce or mitigate chilling effects are often legally challenged on the basis that they restrict or impact competing rights or interests, like free speech. This chapter sets out a framework to deal with hard cases, where chilling effects claims must be predicted, evaluated, or balanced against competing interests.

Why do prediction, evaluation, and balancing matter, both to our broader understanding of chilling effects and hard cases? Chilling effect arguments and claims are often predictive – they predict that a chilling effect will occur as a result of some public or private sector action or practice.[1] So, being able to *predict* chilling effects is a critical function for any chilling effects theory. And on that count, a conformity theory has predictive power. That is, combining this new understanding of chilling effects, key factors that magnify or mitigate chilling effects, and how the theory can be synthesized with other complementary theories – privacy, legal, and social – in some contexts for better understanding, the theory offers a framework to both predict and evaluate chilling effects. By predict, I mean estimate, based on various factors, when chilling effects are likely to be present and whether they would be stronger or weaker in a given context. But this understanding of chilling effects provides a means to evaluate chilling effects as well. By evaluate, I mean be able to assess, compare, balance, and scrutinize chilling effect claims, like if a case or controversy involves competing chilling effect claims, assess which claim should be given priority or how best to balance and navigate such claims.

131

PREDICTING PRESENCE AND MAGNITUDE

What would a framework for predicting and evaluating chilling effects look like? Helen Nissenbaum's influential work on privacy as contextual integrity provides some helpful theoretical and normative guidance, as she also sets out an ambitious framework that relies heavily on social norms – around information practices – and seeks to not just determine when new practices have breached those norms, but when those new practices should be welcomed or resisted.[2] Nissenbaum sets out a framework for a "decision heuristic" with a series of "evaluative factors" and I will do the same here.

Also as with her heuristic, any framework to predict or evaluate chilling effects will necessarily rely on prior work in privacy, expression, and other relevant areas of research,[3] as well as moral and political thought.[4] Indeed, chilling effects are complex and no single theory, including a conformity theory, can explain them or their impact in all circumstances alone. Other theories like legal deterrence and privacy are necessary to understand some dimensions of chilling effects like how they can be magnified or predicted in certain circumstances.

1 *Apply the Four Chilling Effect Factors*

The first step in predicting the magnitude and scope of chilling effects will involve the four key chilling effect factors – observation; uncertainty; personalization; and power/authority:

Observation: When people are aware they are being watched and observed by others or are aware of the possibility of it, they are chilled from freely speaking and acting. This is amplified when the observation is more systematic, as with data tracking and surveillance.

Uncertainty: The more uncertain we are about a situation or choice the more likely we are to be chilled and conform. A very simple example is an uncertain law that is likely to be enforced against a person or group, causing chilling effects.

Personalization: The more personal or targeted the threat, intervention, or activity – when a person is "singled out" and targeted – the greater the chilling effect. Personalization can take many forms, from more personal threats of violence to targeted surveillance.

Power and authority: People are much more likely to be chilled into conformity and compliance when the threat, intervention, or activity allegedly causing the chilling effect is being carried out by or for an entity with power and authority.

These factors provide the central heuristic in determining whether chilling effects are likely to be present in any given context, and also their magnitude or scope. When assessing the likelihood of chilling effects in a given context, you ask whether each factor is present, and the level of awareness of the claimant – keeping in mind that chilling effects can be conscious – the product of a deliberative process – but are just as likely to be the product of more subconscious or automatic thinking/processing. In the latter case, someone might actually be aware of a chilling effect factor but do not necessarily process it consciously or deliberately. Contexts where all four factors, or a majority of the factors, are present would suggest that a chilling effect is highly likely. However, you do not need all four factors present to have a chilling effect nor even a majority. For example, a personal threat (factor #3) or surveillance (factor #1) alone can have a chilling effect if the person is aware of the threat or surveillance.

On observation, the central issue is whether the claimant is being watched, tracked, monitored, or analyzed. On this count, some other relevant questions and issues: Is the observation systematic, as in, planned, purposive, and persistent? And if so, is the claimant aware of the observation, whether systematic or otherwise? Affirmative answers to each of these questions would be suggestive of a chilling effect. Observation need not only be carried out in traditional visual forms. As I argued in Chapter 5, observation can be pursued through other means as well. Analyzing someone or their personal information can be a form of observation and surveillance as it can provide means of tracking and prediction even more powerful than more traditional forms of observation and surveillance – hence the term dataveillance coined by Clarke. The same goes for processing or mining someone's data to predict what they might do in the future or to infer additional undisclosed, private, or intimate facts about them. These are all forms of systematic observation and surveillance that can cause chilling effects. If one or more forms are present, that suggests a likely chilling effect.

The key question on the second factor, uncertainty, is whether the claimant finds themselves in a context involving uncertainty or ambiguity – usually that uncertainty will be about some decision, like whether to speak out or engage in some activity – that can cause chilling and conforming effects. The classic such instance would be someone unsure whether to act or speak after being made aware that their actions may violate a statute that provides serious legal penalties for violations, but that statute is vague and ambiguous. However, the chilling uncertainty need not only concern a decision; it can be more generalized as well, like the uncertainty and ambiguity of mass surveillance. On this factor, some pertinent questions would be: Is there a vague or ambiguous law that could apply to the conduct of the claimant and are they aware of the law itself? Is the claimant subject to a kind of surveillance that is uncertain or ambiguous, like the possibility that their personal data was collected by a pervasive and indiscriminate algorithmic data collection operation, the purpose or reasons for which are unknown? Is there a possibility that sensitive information about the claimant may be disclosed without authorization at some unknown time in the future, as in a case where a claimant is the victim of a large-scale data breach? Each of these scenarios raises significant uncertainties and if present would suggest a chilling effect is likely.

On the third factor, personalization, the key issue is whether the target is personally targeted or singled out in some way by the public or private sector action that is claimed to cause or will cause a chilling effect. Personalization can come in many forms, from personally received threats to forms of personalized law or regulatory enforcement. Here, some important questions to explore include: Has the claimant received personal threats – whether legal, physical, or otherwise? Has the claimant or the group to which the claimant belongs been "singled out" or targeted in some way, as in targeted surveillance, and are they aware of that targeting? Has a statute or regulation been designed specifically to target and prosecute the claimant or their group and are they aware of these personalized regulatory efforts? Has the claimant received personal notice of targeted legal action, like a notice of impending lawsuit from a private party or from state actors – like government prosecutors or regulatory agencies providing notice of impending law enforcement action? A "target letter" like the ones received by President Donald J. Trump from Special Counsel Jack Smith, informing him of impending federal indictments, would be one such example.[5] Each of these scenarios would involve forms of targeting and personalization so affirmative answers to any of these questions would similarly be suggestive of a likely chilling effect, and one that is substantial.

On power and authority, the fourth factor, the key issue is whether the problematic conduct – the action or threat that is alleged to cause the chilling effect – is being carried out by or for a person, group, organization, or entity with power and authority. The power or authority in question can be formal – like the legal powers or authority that governments or law enforcement exercise in carrying out their functions. But it can also be informal – in Milgram's experiment, the authority figure was a researcher in a white lab coat giving the participants commands. The person held no formal legal authority or power over participants. Instead, it was informal authority – the perceived expertise of the researcher – that amplified compliance and chill in this context. On this factor, some relevant questions would include: Is the action being carried out by a state actor or commercial actor with either formal or informal power and authority? What is the nature of the power/authority and is the claimant aware of the exercise? Is the entity with the power/authority physically present in some way in relation to the chilling intervention, action, or scenario? Again, affirmative answers to these questions will suggest a chilling effect.

2 Assess Additive Effects

The next step is to determine additive effects. The central issue is how many factors are present and what is the magnitude and significance of each. As discussed in Chapter 4, the additive dimensions of chilling effects mean they can be caused not only by a single action or factor but a number of causes or factors that are compounding or additive. That means the greater the number of chilling effect factors present, the greater the chilling effect. So, contexts where all four factors are present would suggest that a chilling effect is not only highly likely, but it is much more powerful in scope and magnitude. We have discussed many examples so far in the book. In Chapter 5, for instance, both state and corporate surveillance or data processing and analytics typically involve all four factors and therefore lead to more substantial chilling effects.

Additive effects also concern the magnitude of each factor. That is, a more powerful or significant version of each factor would lead to a greater chilling effect. For instance, if the observation is more pervasive and systematic surveillance – where greater amounts of data are collected, analyzed, and retained for longer periods of time – that would be a more significant version, and thus lead to more chill. Similarly, a scenario with greater levels of uncertainty – perhaps a relevant statute or law is even more vague and overreaching, creating immense uncertainty; more specific or targeted kinds of personalization – like personal legal threats or more violent and credible personal threats, as you would see in forms of online abuse; or a scenario involving an entity with more power and authority – like government or police – would all lead to greater chilling effects. When you have all four factors present, and the instantiation of each factor is greater, that would point to among the most substantial chilling effects.

3 *Synthesis*

A chilling effect is best understood as a conformity or compliance effect. However, as noted earlier, a conformity theory should also be synthesized with insights from other social, legal, and privacy theories for a fuller understanding of the scope and magnitude of chilling effects where appropriate.

There is also empirical support for this. One comprehensive meta-analysis of empirical studies of legal deterrence, for instance, found that the impact of deterrence factors on law-related behavior was "at best weak," and in more rigorous studies, often reduced to zero.[6] By contrast, the "threat of non-legal sanctions," which were described as more personalized threats – fear of damage to personal reputation and substantial social alienation and ostracism for being caught acting illegally – were among the "most robust" predictors of deterrence and legal compliance.[7] Another meta-analysis similarly found that "extra-legal" risk perceptions were far more powerful deterrents of illegal behavior than legal risk perceptions.[8] In other words, it was other chilling effect factors like personalized threats and observation, and not threats of legal harm, that chilled people to comply with the law's requirements.

However, both studies also found interaction effects, that is, as both legal and extra-legal or social factors did interact to impact behavior there was a greater impact on participants. Thus, authors of both studies spoke to the benefits of synthesizing theories of extra-legal sanctions with legal ones to understand law-related behavior more fully.[9] That's because legal compliance is a complex social phenomenon, and no single theory can explain law-related behavior in all contexts. The same can be said of chilling effects. Though a social influence theory is the best way to understand chilling effects, synthesizing the theory with insights from other theories like deterrence and privacy can help us understand chilling effects and their impact more comprehensively – like how chilling effects are magnified. Thus, an important step in predicting chilling effects is synthesizing the conformity theory of chilling effects with insights from other relevant theories – privacy and deterrence theories among others – where appropriate for a complete picture.

For example, as we saw in Chapter 1, empirical research on deterrence theory shows that for laws to deter behavior a very specific set of conditions must be present – conditions that are not often present day-to-day, like awareness about the law and its requirements along with rational decision-making before speaking or doing. However, in cases where a person receives a personal legal threat, the recipient is no longer ignorant of the law's requirements and has a heightened awareness as to the personal threat posed – damage to reputation and social sanction if accused of acting contrary to laws, which themselves reflect social norms; but also the possibility of legal punishment for illegal behavior. On top of that, a person may nevertheless still be uncertain about how to act and may feel that they are under surveillance, given the person who sent the legal threat must have been tracking or monitoring them, leading to the legal threat. In these circumstances, chilling effect factors like observation, uncertainty, personalization, and power/authority combine with elements of legal deterrence theory to better understand the greater threat perception causing more powerful chilling and conforming effects.

Privacy theory also provides critical insights that can be synthesized with social influence theory. For example, where a person is made aware of more invasive forms of surveillance and monitoring that invade our most private and intimate spheres, undercutting our ability to think and read privately or engage in intimate sharing and disclosure with our partners, Richards earlier-discussed work on intellectual privacy[10] and Citron's work on intimate and sexual privacy[11] offer compelling explanations for why this kind of surveillance will likely have even greater chilling effects. Or in cases where data is collected about us and then leaked or disclosed in ways that substantially violate entrenched social norms of how that data is typically shared, Nissenbaum's work on contextual integrity helps us understand why that kind of leaking or disclosure can have greater chilling effects.[12]

Insights from other fields like communications and surveillance studies are also important. For instance, studies applying Goffman's theories, discussed in Chapter 6, show how people rely on self-censorship, disengagement, and other forms of self-restraint to cope with multiple audiences and norm expectations online.[13] Other forms of social surveillance online, especially in social media contexts, can likewise magnify the chilling effects. It is not just the social media platforms themselves conducting surveillance on users, collecting and analyzing data at mass scale for commercial reasons, but also every user is engaged in surveillance of other users.

Lyon's notion of "surveillance culture" speaks to this dynamic – surveillance today is pervasive and participatory.[14] When speaking to social media, only when you synthesize a conformity theory of chilling effects with these insights, with that of Goffman's theories of self-presentation, and the realities of both government and corporate surveillance and data collection online, will the true nature and scope of the chilling effects emerge. Of course, this discussion is not exhaustive. The point is that through synthesizing different privacy, legal, and social theories with social influence, our understanding of chilling effects is strengthened. As well, synthesis highlights the importance of taking into account any relevant empirical research on chilling effects and related phenomena that may also impact estimated scale and scope.

THE CHILLING EFFECTS CURVE

So far, our discussion has assumed the relative equal importance of the four chilling effect factors in predicting the presence and scope of chilling effects, and that would be the correct approach. You need to examine each and explore their additive effects for accurate chilling effect predictions and estimations. However, given the deeper psychological foundations of conformity – and thus chilling effects – discussed in Chapter 4, it is likely that some factors will have greater chilling effects than others. Since our tendency to conform is strongly tied to threat perception for evolutionary reasons – doing so helped us survive threats in the past – it would not be surprising that personalization, especially personal threats, would have the greatest chilling effect among the different factors. A study conducted in 2017 provided some insights on that hypothesis – and how to compare the impact of the different factors more generally. That published and peer-reviewed study involved over 1,200 online participants and tested multiple "chilling effect scenarios" with the same repeated measures – that were designed to measure chilling effects – to explore the relevant impact or chill of each scenario.[15] Each scenario involved a different kind of chilling effect factor. One scenario concerned a vague new statute applying to some types of online speech (uncertainty). A second involved online surveillance conducted by government (observation by a powerful authority) and another involved the very same surveillance online only conducted by an internet company (observation by an entity with less formal authority). A fourth scenario involved a personal legal threat sent by a corporate third party (personalization/personal threat).

The findings demonstrated the chilling effects of all the factors, but comparatively, it was the scenario involving personalization and personal threats that had the greatest chill. The scenario with the uncertain statute had the least chilling effects. In this scenario, there was no information that participants were targeted with enforcement, so no personalization or personalized threat. Next, were scenarios with government and corporate surveillance – each with substantial evidence of chilling effects. In these scenarios, participants were made aware that their online

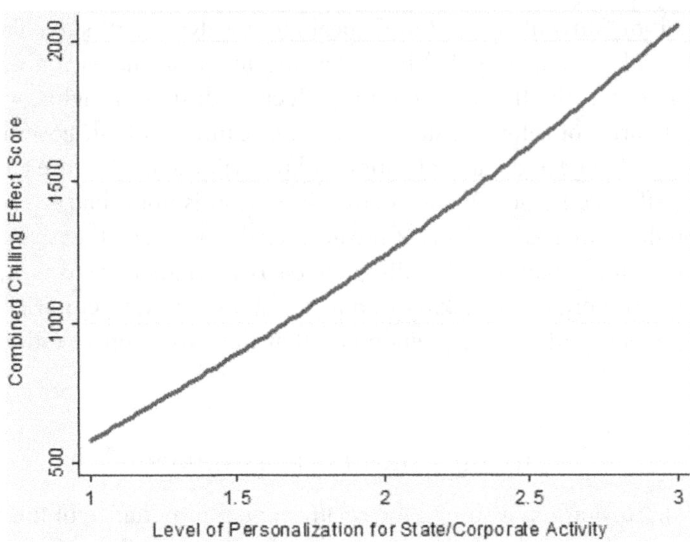

FIGURE 8.1 The chilling effects curve.
The greater the level of personalization in the scenario, the greater the chilling effect.

activities may be monitored either by the government or an internet company. So there was *some* level of personalization. Finally, the most chilling was the scenario with the personalized and personally received legal direct threat. This, obviously, had the most personalization. Aggregating the data, I created what I call the chilling effects curve (Figure 8.1).

This graph illustrates a simple regression analysis – created by plotting a quadratic line-of-best-fit for two variables, one that combines all participant responses indicating a chilling effect from the four primary scenarios in the study and another based on the level of personalization for each scenario (e.g., a general internet statute being the least personalized, surveillance being more personalized, and a personally received legal threat being the most personalized). The curved trend line shows that as the level of personalization (or personal threat) increases for the different state or corporate activities, the associated chilling effect also increases; with the curve of the line showing the chill increases even more for the most personalized threats. This "chilling effects curve," and the relationship it represents, can be used to predict the magnitude of chilling effects in other contexts. Moving from corporate or governmental actions that are more general and not targeted (statutory) to more personalized (surveillance, algorithmic profiling, micro-targeting, and targeted legal enforcement) increases the scope and magnitude of chilling effects. While obviously there will be exceptions and nuances, and more work needs to be done to document this finding in other contexts, this relationship should hold in more general terms. In short, the more personalized the chilling effect factor, the greater the chilling effect – even compared to other chilling effect factors. The point is not that personalization "trumps" or takes precedent over all the other factors, but it provides a compelling decision heuristic, to use Nissenbaum's term, for predicting chilling effects – and evaluating them, as I will argue in the next section.

DEALING WITH HARD CASES: EVALUATING AND BALANCING

Conventional theories of chilling effects offered no way to navigate cases of competing chilling effects. The example I discussed in Chapter 2 would be a privacy statute enacted to reduce or mitigate surveillance chilling effects, but that might be challenged with a Volokhian argument that this statute would have an improper (and unconstitutional) chilling effect on speech. The statute might be argued to prevent privacy chill, but in this case is being attacked by a claimed chill on speech. Conventional understanding offers no wait to determine what claim takes precedent. A theory of chilling effects as conformity provides a means to navigate and better resolve such competing chilling effect concerns, and evaluate chilling effects more generally. For example, if the theory predicts – and existing empirical research supports – that privacy- and surveillance-related chilling effects would be greater than statutory chilling effects of a given privacy statute, then the scope and magnitude of chilling effects could be used as an evaluative metric to resolve the conflict in favor of the privacy statute. This same impact metric also provides a foundation to discriminate between desirable and undesirable forms of chilling effects. This book has approached chilling effects as typically involving lawful activities. But not all lawful activities are necessarily desirable, which raises the question – how to determine whether a chilling effect is desirable or not? Though a fully theorized normative framework for determining "good" and "bad" chill goes far beyond the scope of this chapter – it could probably form the basis of its own book! – I will at least lay a foundation here.

IMPACT, NATURE, SOURCE, AND EFFECTIVENESS

One core preeminent factor in a framework to evaluate chilling effects would be *impact*, which can be predicted using the earlier-set-out framework. Here, the greater the impact on the individual, and broader society, the less desirable the chilling effect. So, as a first order, an analysis following the earlier predictive scheme would be appropriate: application of the four factors; assessing additive effects; and synthesis; taking also into account the comparative impacts of the different factors (the chilling effects curve) and any relevant empirical research that provides further insight. To be clear, impact concerns not just individuals but also impacts on broader society. A theory of chilling effects as conformity, by definition and understanding, also speaks to broader social concerns. It speaks to the influence of social norms on people's behavior, and those social norms are steeped in broader social, cultural, political, and economic forces and currents. This is one of the lessons of the productive dimensions of chilling effects. The true impact of chilling effects is not only that it chills or deters certain speech and activities, but also in doing so, helps foster the production of more conforming speech and activities, which will almost always be more consistent with, and conforming to, existing power structures in society. So, how the chilling effect relates to broader relations of power in society. For instance, if a chilling effect impacts the voices or engagement of marginalized individuals or groups, this would indicate a far less desirable chilling effect.

Another evaluative factor would be the *nature* of the chilling effect itself or the nature of the threat causing it. For instance, this speaks to the speech or behavior that is or is likely to be chilled. If more socially beneficial behavior is being chilled – like voting or creative expression – then that would be a much less desirable chilling effect. The more benign the activity chilled, the more tolerable the chilling effect will be. Also relevant is how the chilling effect relates to broader relations of power in society. For instance, if a chilling effect creates new inequalities or exacerbates existing ones, like chilling voices or engagement of marginalized individuals or groups, such a chilling effect would be less tolerable. However, if the behavior that is being chilled is more antisocial or problematic – like forms of online abuse and harassment or is analogous to that kind of behavior – then that would be a much more desirable chilling effect.

There would also need to be evaluation of the *source* of the chilling effect itself. If the source of the chilling effect is a democratically enacted law, then it would be a more desirable chilling effect – due to its democratic legitimacy – than where a source is an unaccountable corporate actor or an authoritarian state. Both of these "sources" would color the chilling effect as less desirable. Also, if the source of the chilling effect has mass application – like mass surveillance – then it would be less desirable as it affects more people. This is like a utilitarian argument, but it is not absolute. More tailored activities causing chilling effect threats affecting fewer people, depending on the context, may be more desirable, though this of course could have more significant chilling effect on the targeted individual or group. Balancing these interests is important.

Finally, *effectiveness* is also a consideration, where relevant. This factor, in ways, speaks to impact, but a different kind of impact from just the scale or scope of the chilling effect. Rather, it speaks to how effective a measure may be in either addressing claimed chilling effects – like a new social media policy or privacy statute aimed at mitigating privacy chill – or in the case of a law that may itself have chilling effects, achieving its other aims or objectives. The key question here, is how effective is the measure in mitigating chilling effects or achieving its objectives compared or balanced against the chill it may be causing. As with Nissenbaum's decision heuristic on contextual integrity violations, an assessment of the desirability of chilling effects will necessarily require engagement with broader moral, ethical, and political theory in some contexts, and of course, empirical research specific to chilling effects as well. As above, the point here has not been to set out a comprehensive framework for evaluation in all cases, but to set out some markers as to how my theory of chilling effects, and its application, can provide stronger normative guidance on evaluating and reasoning about chilling effect claims.

I offer three hard cases to illustrate how one might employ this predictive and evaluative framework in practice.

CASE ONE: PRIVACY/DATA REGULATIONS (THE RIGHT TO BE FORGOTTEN)

As noted earlier, privacy and data protection laws are regularly attacked on First Amendment free speech grounds by corporations which use chilling effects arguments to launch those challenges. Such claims are neither coincidental nor isolated. In Chapter 1, I talked about how legal scholars have documented how corporations have systematically employed the First Amendment, and chilling effect claims, like this in support of a deregulatory agenda. The broader context of these claims is a story both Cohen and Zuboff tell about surveillance and information capitalism – how powerful companies are able to use the law to insulate their activities from democratic control. Part of the challenge is that this kind of weaponization of chilling effects often involves competing chilling effect concerns. Laws *can* chill speech, but they can also enable it by protecting privacy. How can we resolve these competing concerns? My evaluative framework set out above, offers a way to do so.

Consistent with this deregulatory agenda, there is little doubt that if comprehensive data protection regulations – like Europe's General Data Protection Regulation (GDPR) – were enacted in the US, they would eventually be challenged by companies based on First Amendment grounds.[16] A key target would be the GDPR's "right to be forgotten" (RTBF), which is largely a European innovation. First recognized by the Court of Justice of the European Union (CJEU) as a right under EU law in its well-known decision in *Google Spain*,[17] it has since been codified in Article 17 of the GDPR and embraces both the right to forget (erasure) but also to be forgotten ("right to oblivion").[18] The GDPR right is actually broader than the one recognized by the CJEU as requests can include deletion by "every data controller" and the deletion or erasure is retroactive.[19] The right, in short, essentially provides for "retro-active" erasure or deletion of previously collected personal data.[20] The RTBF comes in different forms – the GDPR's is among the broadest and strongest versions – but nearly all involve the right for people to seek deletion, delisting, or deprioritization of certain information about them in online contexts, like in search engine results.[21] These laws aim to ameliorate the chilling effects of privacy invasions posed by the unrestricted collection, retention, and circulation of personal information online,[22] but are regularly criticized and opposed as having improper chilling effects on speech.[23]

Despite those criticisms, public support is widespread with surveys consistently finding a strong majority of Americans supporting such a right – from 74 percent up to 88 percent.[24] And the RTBF has recently taken on greater importance and urgency with the development of sophisticated AI systems, like large language models, with the capacity to retain vast amounts of data and information in perpetuity, but offering new compliance challenges.[25] US states have also begun experimenting with versions of the RTBF, with California and Virginia recently enacting a "right of deletion" – allowing consumers to compel businesses to delete from their data stores personal data that they have collected from them.[26] Canada has tabled proposed data protection reforms that include a version of the European RTBF and Australia, too, is contemplating such a law.[27] Other thoughtful proposals have been offered to operationalize the RTBF in ways consistent with US law, particularly the First Amendment, such as narrowing the right in relation to private persons, public figures, and public officials.[28] However, the success of any transatlantic version of the RTBF will depend upon addressing competing chilling effect concerns – privacy and speech. And on this count, our predictive and evaluative framework, based on a theory of chilling effects as conformity, can provide guidance.

I will direct my analysis toward the stronger version of the right – the GDPR's Article 17 – because if that version can be defended on chilling effect grounds, the same analysis would surely apply to weaker versions. Following our framework discussed earlier, a central consideration would be the comparative *impact* of the competing chilling effect claims. That requires applying the four chilling effect factors, with an eye to additive effects, synthesis, and the chilling effects curve. The aim of Article 17 is to allay privacy-related chilling effects due to the reality that personal data and information – that may be collected, retained, and stored by businesses – is rarely ever deleted.[29] The RTBF in Article 17 seeks to address this issue by providing individuals with a right of deletion or erasure. In other words, the RTBF attempts to mitigate the chill of modern-day data collection and processing practices that can have substantial chilling effects – as discussed extensively in Chapter 5. All four chilling effect factors are relevant here – observation (through data collection, processing, and retention); uncertainty (possible retention of data in perpetuity); power and authority (these businesses wield substantial power today through capacity to collect and extract large-scale amounts of data about us, retain it with little costs, and employ it to manipulate us and predict our behavior); and last but not least, there is also personalization. That is, retention of data for long periods of time creates risks of significant personal threats – fears and risks of future reputational harms, social sanction, and alienation due to intentional or unintentional disclosure, creating longer-term chilling effects. However, the chill addressed by Article 17 can also be very targeted and immediate in some cases – like a user seeking deletion of embarrassing sensitive personal information that has been shared online without authorization causing immediate personal harms.

By contrast, the competing "chilling effect" claims advanced by Jeffrey Rosen and other First Amendment critics are far weaker. These critics argue that the RTBF's serious penalties for violations would incentivize platforms like Facebook or Google to opt for data deletion in ambiguous cases, creating a broader chilling effect on internet expression.[30] Applying our four factors, a legal requirement that platforms delete personal or sensitive information about an individual in response to their personal request raises no observation or surveillance chill; nor are there issues concerning personalization or power/authority. Rather, the argument is best understood as a more conventional chilling effects claim centered on more general regulatory and legal uncertainty – fear of legal harms combined with uncertainty in the RTBF's application, which would have a chilling effect on social media platforms and other service providers out of hosting certain kinds of information in ambiguous cases, which would indirectly affect online expression in some cases. I have argued at length about the weakness of such conventional chilling effect claims – and provide even further reasons in Chapter 9 – but even putting those points aside, using our predictive and evaluative framework it is easy to see how these general chilling effect claims are weaker – only one factor is at play, with the other factors falling in favor of the chill being addressed by the RTBF. On grounds of *impact*, the privacy chill claim should take priority.

The same would apply in terms of the *nature* and *source* of the competing chilling effect claims. The chilling effects that the RTBF attempts to mitigate are mass scale – the large-scale data collection, processing, and retention in society today – and thus cause chilling effects on any number of activities; and the same goes for instances where more sensitive information is available about a person, as on a search engine (nature). And it would do so via legally and democratically enacted legislation, at least if done so in the US (source). By contrast, the nature of the activity that is claimed to be chilled by the RTBF would be platforms hosting user-generated content – though indirectly, it would affect forms of speech, content, and other information. These are obviously important and desirable activities, but still what is chilled likely involves a narrower range of affected behavior compared to the broader impacts of data collection by commercial enterprise across society. Further, the nature of the speech/hosting chill on platforms is not mass scale – the RTBF must be exercised by individual users; it does not require mass automatic deletion, even though that is what Rosen claims would happen, at least in theory. Finally, *effectiveness* is more difficult to assess. At least one experimental study – discussed more expansively in Chapter 5 – found that a version of a RTBF may not necessarily mitigate certain kinds of chilling effects,[31] but more research needs to be done. This factor is thus far from determinative.

In sum, applying our predictive and evaluative framework, the important privacy-related chilling effect concerns that the RTBF in Article 17 aims to address should trump the competing speech/hosting chill claimed by critics. The point would be even stronger with reconceptualized versions of the RTBF, where information is not deleted, but merely sees reduced emphasis in search returns and in other indexes. Though the US Supreme Court has increasingly rejected this kind of "balancing methodology" in recent First Amendment cases – where different rights, interests, values, and harms are balanced against one another to resolve constitutional issues – in favor of a more historical approach; similar forms of balancing remain in both First and Fourth Amendment jurisprudence.[32] Thus, as doctrine on chilling effects itself evolves, this exercise aims to provide a compelling argument to defend privacy statutes against similar kinds of chilling-effect-based First Amendment attacks, and on how to balance competing interests and chilling effect claims. Now, when it comes specifically to the RTBF, there may be good *policy* reasons for not enacting one, based on its impact on costs or innovation or even just the difficulties in implementing it.[33] But at least on the question of the First Amendment and any related chilling effects it may cause – that's not a good reason against pursuing the right. Lastly, but just as important: This analysis provides a framework to evaluate and effectively counter corporate chilling effect claims weaponized for deregulatory purposes.

CASE TWO: ANTI-ABUSE LAWS

Another category of laws regularly attacked as having a chilling effect are statutes aimed at addressing forms of abuse both online and off, like anti-stalking, anti-harassment, and revenge porn laws. Such laws attempt to address forms of persistent targeted abuse and personal threats, including defamation, privacy invasions, hateful speech intending to cause emotional distress, and threats to personal safety and violence.[34] Since these laws often directly or indirectly cover forms of speech and expression – oral and written threats, harassing and hateful speech, unauthorized sharing of intimate images, and so on – they have been criticized as having a chilling effect on First Amendment protected speech,[35] and have also faced legal challenges on those grounds as well.[36] The *Counterman v. Colorado* decision, discussed in Chapter 7, is a great example of this. There, the accused successfully convinced the Supreme Court to throw out his criminal conviction under a Colorado anti-stalking law on the basis that it had been obtained based on an overly broad interpretation of the law that the Court predicted would have chilling effects on First Amendment protected speech. It did so by ignoring the profound chilling effects that the stalking itself had on the victim – singer-songwriter Coles Whalen.

But imagine for a moment if the Court had not ignored those chilling effects – that it had acknowledged them. How should it have evaluated those chilling effect concerns and balanced them against the speech chill that it did recognize? These are the questions the framework set out in this chapter attempts to address. Following that framework, again, a central factor is the comparative *impact* of the competing chilling effect concerns – on the one hand, the chill of the stalking, harassment, and abuse that the law attempts to mitigate and that is evidenced on the facts of the case itself; and on the other hand, the potential chill that the anti-stalking law has on speech and expression, which was the basis for the Supreme Court's actual decision to quash the accused's conviction under the Colorado anti-stalking law.

Let us examine the former concern first. As elaborated in Chapter 5's taxonomy of different forms of chilling effects, forms of harassment, stalking, and abuse typically involve all four chilling effect factors, and that is also the case here – Whalen was victimized by highly personalized stalking, harassment, and threats, as well as a persistent threat of observation and surveillance. Not only that, but using the chilling effects curve as a decision heuristic, the highly personalized nature of this kind of abuse often renders it far more chilling than other forms by comparison. That is very likely true of the stalking detailed in *Counterman*. Over the course of two years, from 2014 to 2016, the accused Billy Counterman sent Whalen thousands of Facebook messages.[37] They had never met in person and she blocked him multiple times, but each time he would create a new account and continue sending her messages.[38] Though some of the personal messages were merely "weird" and "creepy,"[39] many were angry and threatened her life and safety, including wishing she would "fuck off permanently," "die," and that not meeting with him in real life would "kill" her.[40] Importantly, many messages suggested the victim was under surveillance in her daily life, with messages asking "[w]as that you in the white Jeep?"; referring to "physical sightings" over a five-year period; or referencing the victim making a "fine display" with her "partner," and that he was watching her doing "things that [she did] out and about."[41] The messages also threatened other forms of surveillance – that her phone would be "tapped."[42] Another factor was *uncertainty*. There was a lot of uncertainty and ambiguity for the victim not only about the possibility of being watched all the time, but uncertainty about what her stalker could do at any moment – harming her or even killing her. For instance, messages suggested he was psychologically unstable and capable of anything; that he was "currently unsupervised" and the "possibilities" of what he could do were "endless."[43] All of these threats were magnified when Whalen learned that her stalker was on probation for a federal criminal offence.[44] This meant his threats were thus not harmless or empty – he had committed crimes before, and could do it again.

Lastly, *power* is also a factor but not in a traditional sense. Counterman was not a figure of authority – but as a stalker, he used the threats, harassment, and stalking as a way to exercise power over Whalen. This is a typical motive for stalkers who resent being rejected by their victims and use stalking and threats to reassert power and control over the victim.[45] That was certainly true here, with Counterman evading all of his victim's attempts to escape his threats and surveillance by blocking his Facebook accounts and even cancelling her musical performances, and who always found a way to continue to send her messages. And those messages often expressed anger and resentment over her rejection of him and refusal to reply to any message, and hinted at potential violence or death. There was thus a power imbalance here between stalker and victim magnified by the asymmetry between Whalen being a public figure who always had a public presence online and offline – she was always easy for Counterman to find and track – and the realities of social media, which make stalking, harassment, threats, and other kinds of personal abuse easy to do at scale and often anonymously, and very difficult to deter or stop – as Whalen learned; simply blocking or ignoring the messages did nothing to stop Counterman.

Whalen, in short, endured a relentless multi-year campaign of targeted and highly personalized harassment, stalking, and threats, including threats to her life and personal safety. That personalized abuse was magnified by uncertainty about how the stalker might be watching her, and how and when he might harm her, with messages saying he was capable of anything. There was also a power imbalance typical between a stalker and their victim here compounded by social media that made threats, harassment, and surveillance easy for the stalker, and difficult to stop. The resulting chilling effects were powerful. Whalen was put in a constant state of "fear" that "upended her daily existence" as she believed he was threatening her life and constantly watching her.[46] She lost sleep, suffered severe anxiety, stopped walking alone, withdrew from social relations, and even began canceling her musical performances.[47] The chill was so overwhelming, it forced her to even abandon her lifelong dream – a music career – due to the fear of the stalking and threats.[48]

The competing chilling effect claims that Counterman himself advanced to challenge the constitutionality of the Colorado anti-stalking law, and that ultimately persuaded the Supreme Court to overturn his conviction, are pale and feeble by comparison. It is, again, just a conventional chilling effects claim based on legal uncertainty – fear of criminal liability based on First Amendment protected speech that may be captured by the scope of the anti-stalking law, combined with uncertainty in the legal system. Given that criminal laws are at stake, both uncertainty and power/authority are relevant factors, but neither personalization nor surveillance come into play. Furthermore, as argued at length earlier in the book, empirical evidence for these kinds of generalized chilling effects based on uncertainty is very weak. In fact, Mary Anne Franks has observed that the Supreme Court in *Counterman v. Colorado*, despite relying on these chilling effect claims, cited no evidence to justify them.[49] There is simply no evidence in the record of any actual or even potential chill, beyond speculative hypothesizing. On *impact*, then, the chill of the stalking, harassment, and abuse that the anti-stalking law itself targets far outweighs the conventional speech claims raised by the Supreme Court.

Another key evaluative factor here would be the *nature* of the chill – what is being chilled, and is it normatively desirable. Assuming for the sake of argument that there would be a chilling effect on speech caused by the anti-stalking law like the one at issue in *Counterman* – despite the lack of theoretical or empirical bases for such a claim – any such chilled speech would likely not be very socially desirable or beneficial. That's because such speech would be very close to the line dividing protected speech from speech that crosses over into true threats, which are not legal or constitutionally protected. Justice Kagan, for the majority, acknowledged this point in justifying a recklessness standard as constitutionally satisfactory. The reason a more stringent standard was not required, she wrote, is that the speech on the "other side of the true-threats boundary line" – speech that may be chilled by Colorado's anti-stalking law – is unlikely to be either political or democratically important speech, so it is neither central to the "theory" of the First Amendment nor typically vulnerable to government prosecution.[50] In other words, the speech would not be valuable or important speech – it would almost surely be very threatening and harassing speech, but just not quite bad enough to criminalize. It would be lawful but awful speech. So if *some* lawful but awful speech is chilled, it is not the end of the world.

Two other evaluative factors also point in the same direction – both the *source* – what is causing the chill – and *effectiveness* – does that "source" achieve its other objectives balanced against any chill? The *source* of the chilling effect here is less problematic. Like the RTBF, the source is a legally valid and democratically enacted state statute that has been vetted by both policymakers and political actors. And those actors could be held accountable later, at least in theory, via the electoral process. Again, *effectiveness* of this Colorado law is difficult to assess here as there are no empirical studies as to its impact or effectiveness in deterring or curtailing stalking – other than the *Counterman* prosecution itself. However, we *do* know that studies have demonstrated how other kinds of anti-abuse laws closely related to anti-stalking laws – cyber-harassment laws – can actually encourage speech and engagement of women who are disproportionately the victims of such abuse.[51] That reality adds an additional dimension to the evaluative exercise – anti-stalking laws can lead to *more* speech, and not less. That is also something the Supreme Court ignored.

In sum, applying our predictive and evaluative framework, chilling effects of the stalking, harassment, surveillance, and personal threats that Whalen suffered should, in any legal analysis, outweigh competing concerns based on mere general statutory chill due to legal uncertainty, like those that were determinative in *Counterman v. Colorado*. But what does that mean in practical terms? In my view, it means that if the Supreme Court were to both acknowledge the chilling effects on Whalen and integrate this evaluative analysis into its decision-making, the case should have been decided differently. That means, both reasoned differently – that would be inevitable – but the outcome should also be different. In its actual decision the Court's majority engaged in a kind of balancing analysis, settling on a recklessness standard as a kind of compromise that avoids some chill on protected speech while not entirely "sacrificing" all the benefits of ensuring such stalking was prosecuted.[52] But the Court acknowledged that as with "any balance," something is lost on both sides of the compromise: The recklessness standard was "neither the most speech-protective" nor was it "the most sensitive to the dangers of true threats."[53] This evaluative analysis and balancing of the competing chilling effect concerns would dictate a different balancing and intent standard: the original objective standard used to convict Counterman at trial, which would be more sensitive to the dangerous chilling effects of stalking and other threats, especially when balanced against the weakness and negligible foundations for the legal chill concerns raised by the Court, and the little value that any speech that was chilled would ultimately have. Thus, both the objective standard, and Counterman's conviction, should have been affirmed.

CASE THREE: NATIONAL SECURITY SURVEILLANCE

A final category of cases where chilling effects are often balanced or evaluated against other important competing public interests is in the context of national security surveillance. Often invasive and large-scale state surveillance and data collection practices are justified by public officials as necessary to protect against threats to national security like terrorism, while state secrecy privileges and laws insulate those practices from legal accountability or public scrutiny.[54] Policymakers, judges, and lawyers all acknowledge that these issues require balancing individual rights and transparency with national security but all too often the balance struck heavily favors national security and its secrecy.[55] David Gray, for instance, has criticized Fourth Amendment cases on this basis.[56] Robert Chesney has argued for the same in state secrets doctrine cases, as courts tend to heavily favor national security even over constitutional rights and democratic accountability.[57] This is precisely what happened in *Wikimedia Foundation v. NSA*, the case I was personally involved with as an expert witness on behalf of the plaintiff Wikimedia Foundation.[58]

In that case, the Wikimedia Foundation and ACLU brought a lawsuit that challenged the constitutionality of the NSA's "Upstream" surveillance program on First and Fourth Amendment grounds. Upstream involved the NSA tapping into the internet's backbone – its network of high-capacity cables, switches, and routers – and collecting, retaining, and analyzing the communications data of Americans at mass scale.[59] The Wikimedia Foundation alleged First and Fourth Amendment claims. First, that the NSA had "seized" without warrant its communications data via Upstream thus violating the Fourth Amendment right against unreasonable search and seizure. Second, that being subject to Upstream surveillance had a substantial chilling effect on the Wikimedia Foundation and its users as demonstrated by my research discussed in Chapter 2.[60] Though the Fourth Circuit demonstrated the kind of skepticism all too common among federal courts when it comes to chilling effect claims concerning national security surveillance – the court cited *Clapper* to suggest the Wikimedia Foundation's chilling effect claims were too speculative for standing[61] – ultimately the lawsuit was dismissed not on the basis of standing but state secrets doctrine. That is, the court held that the litigation could not proceed because the lawsuit would require the government to disclose state secrets – information about intelligence sources and methods – and doing so threatened national security.[62] Under the doctrine, the US Government may prevent disclosure of information in a judicial proceeding if there is a "reasonable danger" that the disclosure would expose intelligence or military matters and thus threaten national security.[63] As Chesney has observed, the doctrine strikes a "harsh" balance heavily in favor of national security over individual rights and democratic accountability.[64] That's precisely what both the District Court and Fourth Circuit did in this case – both courts, in dismissing the case based on state secrets doctrine, favored national security and secrecy over core constitutional rights that the surveillance was harming with substantial chilling effects.

Yet this result was not inevitable. In the past, courts have limited the state secrets doctrine and created exceptions, like allowing whole trials to be conducted *in camera* (in private) rather than dismissing the action or by refusing to allow the government to invoke the doctrine where the secrets in question had become public or there was evidence of government misconduct.[65] Courts have also held that the doctrine can be displaced through legislation.[66] Though courts today predominantly uphold the doctrine and its slanted balancing between rights and national security, the evaluative framework set out here provides a means for both courts to strike a different balance in cases like *Wikimedia Foundation v. NSA* and policymakers to do so through Congressional legislation.[67]

Applying the framework, a central factor would again be the *impact* of the chilling effect claimed. This requires taking into account the four chilling effect factors along with additive effects, synthesis, and the chilling effects curve. There is no need to repeat discussion from Chapter 5: When it comes to government surveillance, especially national security forms, all four factors would be present here. The Upstream surveillance and its large-scale data collection and retention, all shrouded in secrecy, implicate both observation and uncertainty. And when the surveillance is being conducted by a powerful intelligence agency like the NSA, backed by the US Government and broad national security laws and privileges, both power and authority are clearly present. Lastly, while personalization in this context may seem less relevant – the Upstream surveillance appeared to be broad and in many ways very indiscriminate – it is also publicly known, thanks to top secret NSA documents leaked by Snowden, that the NSA has specifically targeted Wikipedia in its surveillance programs.[68] So Wikimedia Foundation had good reason to believe that Wikipedia and its users were being targeted here as well.

This is an important factor in this evaluation and balancing. The publicly available evidence acknowledged by the Fourth Circuit suggested that Upstream involved the NSA capturing *all* internet communications data traveling through a specific internet node – not just for Wikipedia or whatever national security subject the agency may or may not have targeted, but data concerning every internet user, site, and activity was, in ways, caught up in this sweeping dragnet surveillance program. In other words, the scale of this surveillance program was not just "large" but exponentially so, and in ways unimaginable – such that the Court agreed that it was likely that *some* of Wikipedia's communications data would have been captured regardless of whether the site was targeted or not. But coupled with that you also had public evidence that Wikipedia was being targeted by NSA surveillance programs, which provides good reason to believe that was happening with Upstream as well. If you are capturing all communications traffic indiscriminately, you are capturing both benign data but also highly sensitive data as well for an untold number of people. But the Wikimedia Foundation also may have been specifically targeted on top of that.

This combination of mass arguably global population-scale surveillance along with the credible threat of personalization via targeting, creates a uniquely powerful chilling effect threat, and thus *impact*. The other factors in the evaluative framework like *source* and *nature* likewise strongly suggest a less desirable or tolerable chilling effect. With such a mass-scale surveillance program, then the range of activities chilled will include both benign activities but also fundamental ones – like speech and privacy raised by the Wikimedia Foundation in the litigation itself (nature). And the *source* here, while an agency of the US Government that is in theory democratically accountable, and level of secrecy around the NSA generally and the Upstream program specifically likewise suggest a less tolerable chilling effect. Lastly is the *effectiveness* factor. That is hard to assess here, given the secrecy surrounding Upstream. Perhaps the program has allowed the NSA to stop or disrupt activities that were genuine national security threats. But maybe not. In fact, Schneier has made a compelling argument that data mining and the mass surveillance and data collection required to feed it like the Upstream program are simply not effective tools for identifying and tracking national security threats like dedicated criminals and terrorists, despite clear signs and warnings often identified after the fact.[69] That's why the government was unable to "connect the dots" and prevent any number of terrorist threats and plots from 9/11; to the Boston Marathon attacks; to the Fort Hood shooter, and beyond.[70]

The point here is not to argue that all larger-scale national security surveillance programs are ineffective and their secrecy should give way to other concerns around chilling effects on rights and public accountability. Rather, my argument is that in certain contexts like the set of facts in *Wikimedia Foundation v. NSA*, a different balance should be struck. And it is not necessarily an all or nothing decision either – dismiss or expose. As noted earlier, some courts in the past have been willing to place limits on state secrets doctrine or how it is operationalized in practice. The court could conduct sensitive parts of the trial *in camera* to protect state secrets as much as possible while also vindicating the interests of victims whose rights have been chilled. The government's argument that both the District Court and Fourth Circuit accepted was that allowing the litigation to proceed would risk exposing state secrets about Upstream, which would in turn put national security at risk and perhaps chill the government from engaging in similar such surveillance and data collection, which may also put national security at risk. Certainly, those are important concerns, and one can imagine other circumstances – perhaps ones that would cover most cases where national security surveillance is challenged in court – where those concerns should win out. Like, for instance, where you have a mass surveillance program but no credible evidence the plaintiff was targeted or had been targeted – like Wikipedia had been here. Or another set of facts where you had a more targeted surveillance operation that only impacted the plaintiff, their organization, or a smaller cross section of people; but did not impact or potentially chill so many others – like Upstream would. In those cases, dismissal based on state secrets doctrine perhaps would be justified – or better justified, at least. But in this case, all of the factors here point to a uniquely powerful chilling effect on core constitutional rights that is hard to tolerate and justify, even based on national security grounds. The case should have been decided differently, and the evaluative framework here helps demonstrate why.

In Chapter 9, I elaborate how our new understanding of chilling effects has concrete implications for existing chilling effects law and doctrine.

9

Transforming Chilling Effects Doctrine

I have argued that chilling effects are an urgent threat to fundamental rights and freedom and democratic societies. We must respond, with key law and policy change in the near term and long term. While I advocate for broader reforms – comprehensive and structural – in Chapter 10, I talk about some of the necessary near-term legal and doctrinal changes in this chapter.[1] Specifically, I argue that the existing law of chilling effects – often referred to as "chilling effects doctrine" – must be improved and explain how: by making it easier for victims of chilling effects – especially those chilled by privacy or personal threats – to vindicate their rights in court, while also extricating it from conventional thinking, which privileges legalistic chill claims that have often been hijacked by surveillance capitalists and other corporate interests.

Today, chilling effects doctrine is neither settled nor clear. And as we saw in Chapter 1, because the law is based mainly on the predominant conventional theory of chilling effects – chilling effects as fear of legal harm – it also suffers from a number of afflictions I identified with that conventional account. The law often assumes a legal deterrence model, for example, which requires a very specific set of conditions that are not often present, like knowledge and awareness of the law and rational decision-making before speaking or doing.[2] And the law is narrow and focused primarily on a limited set of legal harms, namely, statutory and regulatory chilling effects involving self-censorship of constitutionally protected speech. So the courts have essentially privileged chilling effect claims that are based on legal harms – like criminal or regulatory penalties. At the same time, they have largely discounted nearly all other forms of chilling effect and the injuries they might cause. The courts show both a deep-seated skepticism for chilling effects claims based on privacy threats – like government surveillance or data breaches – and they regularly ignore other kinds of chilling effects – like how personal threats – physical, legal, and otherwise – harassment, and abuse all have profound impacts. So skeptical are courts of these sorts of chilling effect claims, they have often created special legal rules and doctrines – like standing doctrine in US law – that make it exceedingly difficult to go to court to vindicate your rights if you are the victim of chilling effects beyond conventional examples based on law, like overly broad statutes or regulations.

You might assume these observations apply only to US law – the origins of the modern concept of chilling effect – and courts. They do not. The same can be said of laws relating to chilling effects and how courts approach them in many jurisdictions around the world, for as discussed in Chapter 1, nearly every jurisdiction that has recognized or adopted the chilling effects concept has likewise adopted the American conventional view, with all of its limitations, including accompanying skepticism for chilling effects beyond legal harms. That includes courts in some jurisdictions fashioning doctrinal rules that act as legal barriers to chilling effect claims based on less conventional threats, like privacy or personal threats.

Our new understanding of chilling effects, based on a conformity theory and extensive findings from the social and behavioral sciences, should change much of chilling effects doctrine, and these problems. First, I challenge the skepticism that courts have shown for chilling effect claims based on privacy and other kinds of threats. Not only are the reasons for this skepticism baseless, but it has led to messy and nearly incomprehensible doctrine. Second, working largely within the constraints of existing standing law and chilling effects doctrine, I set out an approach, informed by a conformity theory, for determining standing for chilling effect claims. Third, moving beyond standing, I argue for both changes in other elements of chilling effects doctrine – vagueness and overbreadth doctrines – both modest changes in the near term, but also more significant changes that would require more sweeping reforms.

THE NARROW AND MESSY LAW OF CHILLING EFFECTS

Existing law of chilling effects is shaped largely by the narrow focus of conventional legalistic theories – self-censorship caused by legal harms and penalties. Not surprisingly, the only area of law where courts have consistently recognized and enforced chilling effect claims has been in constitutional law – cases involving First Amendment challenges to statutes or regulations that chill protected speech. Chilling effect claims have also been raised in Fourth Amendment cases where privacy interests are at stake – as in cases involving warrantless government or police surveillance. The Fourth Amendment's protection against unreasonable searches and seizures by government and law enforcement should, at least in theory, make it critical to addressing chilling effects but due to a variety of factors, the Fourth Amendment has proven largely ill-suited to the task. Since Fourth Amendment cases typically involve only a specific instance of problematic executive action – a single unreasonable search or seizure – it is less useful in addressing collective or societal impacts of chilling effects.[3] And the often criticized *Katz* test – the central analytical framework for Fourth Amendment challenges – centers on reasonable expectation of privacy in the place or thing searched, which means that societal expectations based on existing conditions become the measure of how much privacy – and by extension, how much chilling effects – people should expect.[4] That means that *more* surveillance and data collection in society, as we are seeing today, necessarily means courts will extend fewer protections based on the finding that it's reasonable that people should expect less privacy and by extension *more* chilling effects as well.[5] The Fourth Amendment is thus "increasingly useless" for privacy in the internet age and the same can be said about it concerning chilling effects unless there are significant changes in how courts theorize and apply it.[6]

Chilling effect claims have also been raised in tort law, but consistent with conventional understanding, only in the form of speech chill, and usually only as a competing interest or value that must be balanced with the aims of any given tort. For instance, courts and scholars have long debated "libel chill" – concern that tort claims concerning libelous or defamatory speech may chill lawful and socially desirable expression, especially freedom of the press.[7] Those debates are less salient today since the Supreme Court's famous decision in *New York Times v. Sullivan* – discussed in Chapter 1 – which cited these very First Amendment chilling effect concerns in order to limit defamation claims to those that were intentional and malicious, a much more stringent standard.[8] Courts have similarly limited the scope and application of privacy torts also based on First Amendment speech chill concerns.[9] One could certainly argue that the privacy torts – like Prosser's tort for intrusion upon seclusion – help guard against certain kinds of chilling effects, but again, chilling effect claims are not an express aspect of the tort analysis; they are mainly implicit – raised as a justification for the torts themselves.[10] Furthermore, the privacy torts have not evolved in decades, rendering their very narrow and specific focus of limited use and application to modern forms of surveillance and data collection, and thus chilling effects.[11] Beyond that, there is a patchwork of statutes that relate to chilling effect claims and concerns – mostly privacy related – like the Fair Credit Reporting Act and the Electronic Communications Privacy Act of 1986, but again, only incidentally as violations of aspects of these statutes might be said to cause chilling effects in some contexts, though courts again have been hesitant to recognize that fact.[12]

In sum, if there is a "law of chilling effects" today it is largely chilling effects doctrine found in US constitutional law jurisprudence. Chilling effects are now a well- established First Amendment injury that courts regularly invoke to strike down or invalidate statutes and regulations on that basis – that the statutes are vague and overreaching and thus lead to self-censorship, chilling constitutionally protected speech – also known as the void-for-vagueness doctrine.[13] The US Supreme Court has even developed special standing rules – "the overbreadth doctrine" – to allow plaintiffs to challenge regulations for chilling effects based not on their speech, but the hypothetical speech of third parties that are not even before the court.[14] Standing rules are rules that courts use to determine who has the legal right to go to court to seek redress for their injuries. Courts have essentially made it easier for plaintiffs to go to court and get statutes or regulations invalidated for violations of the First

Amendment based on claims that the statute or regulation has a chilling effect on speech due to vagueness or uncertainty in its application or scope.

But even with this narrow focus, the law is messy, complex, and uneven. For example, though courts approach chilling effects as deterrence-based injuries[15] they do not always describe them that way, at times calling them "fear-based" injuries,[16] or "risk-based" injuries,[17] using the terms interchangeably and without clear explanation if there are differences. Courts also have developed a range of standards to determine how proximate government action must be in order for a legitimate chilling effects claim to arise – requiring that government action must be "certainly impending";[18] or where there is a "substantial risk"[19] thereof; or, different still, a "credible threat" of government action.[20] Courts have also shifted on the temporal dimensions of chilling effects, sometimes treating them as present harms, other times as future harms,[21] and elsewhere as anticipatory harms.[22] One commentator has remarked that chilling effects have "polluted" the law,[23] while another has observed, accurately, that courts have treated chilling effects "haphazardly, even sloppily."[24]

Furthermore, when it comes to *other* kinds of chilling effects, beyond legal or regulatory forms, they are either ignored or approached skeptically. The US Supreme Court's decisions in the SB 8 challenge and in *Counterman*, discussed in Chapters 7 and 8, provide a stark illustration of how conventional thinking can lead courts to ignore the realities of chilling effects both inside and outside the courtroom. And when such chilling effects concerns are raised in court and not entirely ignored, like those associated with privacy threats like surveillance or data breaches, they are treated far more skeptically.[25] Often that skepticism has been expressed via rigid application of rules concerning who has "standing" or a legal right to go to court and sue to vindicate their rights.[26] Courts have relied on these "standing" rules to erect barriers to chilling effect claims, especially those due to privacy threats like surveillance or data breaches.[27] In the 1972 Supreme Court case *Laird v. Tatum*, the plaintiffs challenged the constitutionality of the US Army's surveillance of civil rights groups, after the assassination of Martin Luther King Jr., arguing that the existence of the Army surveillance program had a chilling effect on their First Amendment speech.[28] The Court rejected the claim for lack of standing, finding that such "subjective" chilling effect allegations did not constitute an "objective harm or a threat of specific future harm."[29] The more recent decision in *Clapper*, mentioned earlier in the book, in many ways took the same skeptical approach as the court did decades earlier in *Laird*. In *Clapper*, the complainants – lawyers, journalists, and activists – challenged the constitutionality of NSA surveillance under Section 702 of the Foreign Intelligence Surveillance Act on the basis that they were likely being surveilled by the NSA, which was having a chilling effect on their communications. Citing *Laird*, the Court dismissed the lawsuit, again for lack of standing, finding the chilling effects were "self-inflicted injuries" that were "too speculative" and based only on "subjective fear."[30] But *Laird* and *Clapper* not only expressed skepticism, they also created significant barriers to future chilling effect claims based on privacy and surveillance threats, in finding that chilling effects were merely "self-inflicted" and thus not injuries sufficient for standing purposes.

As noted earlier, these problems are not unique to US law and courts. Just as the conventional theory of chilling effects has been adopted in countless other countries – nearly anywhere where the concept has been recognized in law – so have these same problems. Again, my home country of Canada is a good example of this. Canadian courts, including the Supreme Court of Canada, have remained deeply skeptical about chilling effects due to privacy threats, like the chill of police or national security surveillance, often ignoring or downplaying these impacts. And, like the US Supreme Court, it has created legal and evidential hurdles to such chilling effect claims. Typical is the Supreme Court of Canada's decision in *R. v. Tessling*, a case about police surveillance technology wherein concerns about any potential chilling effects caused by the surveillance were entirely ignored.[31] In *Tessling*, police used an airplane equipped with a Forward Looking Infra-Red ("FLIR") camera to take pictures of the accused's properties from the sky, and then used those infrared images – which showed heat emanating from the properties – to obtain a warrant to search them.[32] The accused argued that police using the FLIR without a warrant was an unreasonable search contrary to Section 8 of Canada's Charter of Rights and Freedoms, but the Supreme Court disagreed.[33] While the Court paid lip service to privacy concerns – citing George Orwell's *Nineteen Eighty-Four* in its reasons – it found the FLIR camera to be "non-intrusive" and "mundane" in the information it provided via infrared images.[34] In doing so, the Court entirely neglected the possible chilling effects that widespread adoption of such surveillance technologies by police and state actors might have on society, especially if this "mundane" data were combined and analyzed with other presumed mundane data to disclose far more personal and sensitive information.

When chilling effect concerns are not entirely ignored, courts have been dismissive. In *Carey v. Ontario*, the Supreme Court of Canada was skeptical of chilling effects caused by the threat or actual disclosure of private communications, remarking that it is "very easy to exaggerate [the] importance" of those impacts.[35] Some lower courts, both in the past and more recently, have even taken the view, citing US First Amendment cases, that chilling effects demonstrated through testimony of victims targeted by the surveillance being challenged are too "subjective" to adjudicate.[36] In *R v. Khawaja*, a case involving anti-terrorism measures enacted after 9/11, both the Ontario Court of Appeal and Supreme Court of Canada were dismissive of the trial judge's finding it was "inevitable" that overreaching police anti-terrorism investigations and national security surveillance would have a chilling effect on the expression, thought, and religion of members of the country's Muslim community, who would be disproportionately targeted.[37] The Ontario Court of Appeal rejected that finding as based "entirely on speculation," including both the very "existence" of such chilling effects and "their source," implying, as the US Supreme Court did in *Laird* and *Clapper*, that any chilling effect may be self-inflicted, "if indeed one exists," the Court stated almost ruefully.[38] On appeal, the Supreme Court of Canada was equally skeptical, likewise stating that courts should not infer or take judicial notice of chilling effects due to improper or over-reaching police or government surveillance without direct evidence.[39] However, the Court did say that judges could take judicial notice of chilling effects in other contexts – based only on "known facts and experience" – and gave the example that a law that created liability for the press in reporting on political figures would "probably" chill the speech of the press.[40] Such skepticism of privacy chill and privileging of legal and regulatory chill – as seen in *Khawaja* – is entirely consistent with conventional approaches.[41]

MESSY UNDERSTANDING, MESSY LAW

Why the mess? There are plenty of reasons. First, this body of law is based on the predominant conventional approach to chilling effects – which is narrow and legalistic – and as I have argued at length in this book, suffers from legal, theoretical, and empirical problems. Not surprisingly, courts have struggled with these limitations, creating a variety of related tests, standards, and conceptualizations, with limited success, to compensate. Much like Professors Posner and Sklansky discussed in Chapter 7, most courts, lawyers, and legal scholars have also not sufficiently engaged with social theory and a lot of the empirical work that has helped to substantiate chilling effects, and as a result, have long questioned the existence and impact of chilling effects, especially in relation to privacy-related chilling effects.[42] That persistent skepticism doubtlessly influenced the crabbed and narrow approach to chilling effects seen in these cases.

Second, chilling effects is a complex yet largely under-theorized phenomenon that is also not well understood empirically. This is compounded by the reality that chilling effects can be understood both as a *legal* concept as well as a *social* fact. The concept came to prominence in the legal context – in First Amendment cases – but it is also a social phenomenon that describes concrete factual things in reality best understood through social theory, which lawyers have largely failed to engage. This dual nature can confound and confuse courts and scholars alike, and it has. Moreover, as theoretical and empirical understanding of chilling effects improves, this will also create new complexities as courts struggle with legal doctrine based on narrow and limited conventional accounts.

Lastly, on top of all these factors, there are no doubt ideological factors driving this uneasiness and skepticism. For instance, the US Supreme Court under the influence of conservative judges like Justice Antonin Scalia and Chief Justice John Roberts, has proven far less willing to entertain challenges based on chilling effects of government surveillance programs, but has readily employed the concept in other contexts, like invalidating statute and regulations based on chilling effects claims, when those statutes don't align with those judges' political preferences.[43]

MAKING CHILLING EFFECTS DOCTRINE EVIDENCE BASED

A conformity theory of chilling effects is an evidence-based theory that would require substantial changes to chilling effects doctrine. One change is that skepticism and subjectivism must be rejected. As I argued in Chapter 7, skepticism about the existence of chilling effects among lawyers and judges is no longer sustainable, either in theory or practice, and must be abandoned. As this book has recounted, there is now a growing body of chilling effects empirical research that has clearly documented not only the existence of chilling effects, but their vast scope in impact and shaping people and their behavior. Not only that, but our new understanding of chilling effects as conformity connects the phenomenon to an even broader body of social and behavioral science that spans countless fields as well as decades of theory and research. Chilling effects are *real*, and they have profound and destructive impacts on democracy, civil society, and fundamental rights and freedoms. Courts cannot stick their collective heads in the sand, ignore these realities, and continue muddling along with bad law based on bad theory and understanding. Enough.

Claims that chilling effects are too "subjective" and are "self-inflicted" injuries fare no better when subjected even to a modest level of critical scrutiny. To begin with, both on a basic theoretical and empirical level, it makes no sense to say chilling effects are merely subjective and self-inflicted. The chill of a vague and over-reaching law is caused by the vague and overreaching law. The powerful chilling effect of corporate or state surveillance is caused by the surveillance. The corrosive silencing effect of online abuse and harassment is caused by the abuse and harassment. A conformity theory of chilling effects helps us understand this reality far better than conventional theories of chill. Unlike those accounts, which have been discredited by empirical research, a conformity theory is deeply grounded in social theory and behavioral science. In particular, the four chilling effect factors, and their additive effects, help us understand the scope and impact of chilling effects in a variety of contexts, and how law, power, and social factors interact to create even more powerful and far-reaching chilling effects in some contexts. Yes, there is a psychological foundation to chilling effects – which explains our tendencies to conform in the face of observation, personal threats, uncertainty, and authority – but the sources of the surveillance, threats, uncertainty, and authority that activate those tendencies are not subjective, but come from other people and entities, especially those actors who hold power and authority in society – government, law enforcement, and big business.

Not only does the charge not make sense on a theoretical level, but it also makes no sense logically. If the point is that the behavior of a claimant in some way contributed to the injury or harm in question – hence self-inflicted – then the same can be said of countless other injuries that the court has recognized as sufficiently "objective" and "concrete" for standing and adjudication. For instance, the US Supreme Court in *TransUnion* cited the 1987 decision *Meese v. Keene* as an example of a case involving an intangible injury – reputational harm – that was sufficiently concrete for standing and therefore not subjective and self-inflicted.[44] But the reputational harm in that case would be self-inflicted in the same sense the Court has claimed about chilling effects – at least the kind due to privacy threats. In *Meese*, a California state senator named Barry Keene challenged the Department of Justice's designation as "political propaganda" three Canadian films that he wanted to screen – dealing with acid rain and nuclear war.[45] He also commissioned an opinion poll showing people would be less likely to vote for someone who showed a film that was designated "political propaganda" by the federal government.[46] He argued that the government's action chilled his First Amendment speech. The Court accepted that he had a sufficiently concrete injury for standing not based on a chilling effect – bizarrely – but based on the reputational injury that the designation threatened – both the risk itself, and affirmative steps he'd take to avoid the harm in light of that increased risk.[47] Yet, these injuries would be entirely self-inflicted too. That's because in order to suffer the reputational injury in question, Keene would have to acquire the films, screen or exhibit them, and then ensure the screening was sufficiently publicized such that his reputation would be harmed by the screening that he himself had organized. There is no difference between Keene's injuries and many chilling effect injuries, at least on this count – both are a product of the claimant's own actions. Of course, it is absurd to dismiss either claim on this basis – Keene's complaint was about being chilled by the government's "propaganda" designations – the survey he offered was simply evidence to support his claim of a chilling effect on his speech. Similarly, in *Laird* and *Clapper* the plaintiffs were chilled by government surveillance that they reasonably believed would target them. If the point is that chilling effects are still different in that they are entirely "self-imposed" – the claim seems to be chilling effects are wholly due to self-restraint and self-censorship – it still doesn't make sense because, as already noted, chilling effect injuries are widely recognized and adjudicated in First Amendment cases. This means that in every single case wherein courts have granted standing and struck down a statute for its potential chilling effects on First Amendment speech, what the court had in actuality done was vindicated a claim – a chill on speech – that was also too subjective and self-inflicted. But they weren't. And neither are other forms of chilling effects. It's a baseless argument.

STOP PRIVILEGING LEGAL/REGULATORY CHILL

A conformity theory would dictate other changes to chilling effects doctrine. One necessary corollary of rejecting skepticism about privacy or abuse-related chilling effects, is that chilling effects doctrine should also no longer privilege legal or regulatory forms of chilling effects claims that impact speech over others. While courts have been deeply suspicious of chilling effects associated with privacy and other threats beyond the law, they regularly grant standing for chilling effect claims involving supposed vague or overly broad laws, statutes, or regulations, and frequently invalidate them on the basis of two famous "chill-based" doctrines: the void-for-vagueness doctrine and the overbreadth doctrine.[48] The void-for-vagueness doctrine is a classic and conventional chilling effects application in US law: Courts invalidate a statute or regulation that is imprecise or vague in its language or scope and concerns about chilling effects are a key justification for doing so. The uncertainty created by the vagueness creates a chilling effect whereby people "steer far wider of the unlawful zone" to avoid liability than they would if the statute or regulation were clearer.[49] Though the void-for-vagueness doctrine is said to have due process origins, it is applied more strictly in First Amendment cases. The overbreadth doctrine is another example of that privileging, allowing a party to challenge a law based not on their own speech or injuries but on the hypothetical speech and activities of third parties not even before the court.[50] An overbreadth challenge is, as noted earlier, based on an assumption that an overly broad law is chilling the speech of a substantial number of third parties who never end up in court because the law chilled them into silence, so no prosecution even happens. By contrast, there are no equivalent doctrines that assume or operationalize the application of other forms of chilling effects – like those due to privacy or personal threats. Rather, as we've seen, such claims face persistent skepticism and increasing legal barriers. And as Leslie Kendrick has noted, while chilling effects arise in other areas of the law, the Supreme Court tends to treat chill caused by statutory and regulatory uncertainties with far more sympathy than uncertainties caused by other factors.[51] Chilling effects doctrine thus privileges claims of legal and regulatory chill.

But this privileging is no longer sustainable.[52] These conventional forms of chilling effects, while most entrenched in legal doctrine, have the weakest empirical and theoretical foundation. First, the narrow and legalistic conventional understanding of chilling effects, which underpins this privileging, is largely based on deterrence theory. And as I noted earlier in my critiques of deterrence theory, people are rarely sufficiently aware of the legal or regulatory requirements or related punishments such that they would be uncertain about the legality of their course of conduct and the risks of legal harms or penalties.[53] They would simply act or speak, ignorant of any law applying to their conduct. In other words, there would not be a single chilling effect factor present. No observation or surveillance. No personalization. No power/authority because the law is not even being exercised, it's just sitting on the books. And there would be no uncertainty either, because the person is just not aware of the law and its requirements, uncertainty or otherwise. Second, even when people are to some extent informed about statutory or legal requirements and possible liabilities, legal uncertainties do not necessarily lead to chilling effects. In empirical studies by Feldman and Harel, in addition to finding that people often rely on norms to decide how to act when the law is uncertain, they also found that general, vague, and uncertain laws – those that Schauer's conventional account associated with speech chill – open the door to self-interested motivations, where people or entities like corporations interpret the law or perceived legal obligations narrowly out of self-interest, to justify noncompliance.[54] So even with *some* awareness and *some* uncertainty, people are not necessarily chilled but find reasons to act. Finally, those studies also found the greater the uncertainty or ambiguity in the law, the more the expressive power or effects of the law are undercut, which would similarly dictate against overcompliance and chilling effects.[55] Law can have an expressive impact that also shapes behavior, leading to chilling effects in some cases. But if the law is not clear, then any message about appropriate behavior may be frustrated. In short, even a person who is at least to some extent informed, does not necessarily end up getting chilled either due to legal uncertainties alone. That changes, of course, where there is an actual or a credible threat of legal enforcement against a person or specific group – that increases the personalization – making it a personal threat, increasing the awareness, fear, and risk of punishment, exposure, and social sanction, that in turn creates a real and powerful chilling effect. But in cases of a general legal, statutory, or regulatory chilling effect – where a statute is simply on the books and there is only uncertainty about the law's application to possible behavior or conduct at stake – chilling effects are far less likely, or if they even occur, they are often negligible.

For these reasons, though legal and regulatory chilling effects in response to a typical regulation or statute can certainly happen, and can be powerful if enacted to target specific groups, they are far less common and weaker in general – in many cases negligible – compared to other forms of chilling effects, like those associated with surveillance or personal threats. In fact, in my own empirical legal study published in 2017, this was precisely my finding – the scenario involving a statute that was enacted to regulate harassing speech online had the *least* chilling effect on speech, sharing, and other activities online, compared to other scenarios.[56] The chill was negligible, as many participants reported a salutary effect in response to the statute. More recently, in a series of empirical studies conducted with my colleagues Danielle Citron and Alexis Shore Ingber, we found similarly: A law designed to protect intimate privacy – restricting the nonconsensual sharing of intimate imagery – had no chilling effect on speech or expression of participants.[57]

However, the point is not to say such statutory and regulatory chilling effects may not occur, just that there are important countervailing forces, and that the theoretical and empirical case for other kinds of chilling effects – due to privacy or personal threats – is far more compelling. This means courts should treat such chilling effect claims with deep suspicion rather than assuming or privileging these claims as void-for-vagueness, overbreadth, and other doctrines in the law of chilling effects do today, especially where those claims do not have some other chilling effect factor present like surveillance, targeted enforcement, or personal threats, or some other compelling evidence or proof that would substantiate the legal and regulatory chilling effect claim. In short, an evidence-based approach to chilling effects, dictated by a conformity theory, would require discarding these doctrines, or at least requiring far stricter standards of evidence before applying them.

FIXING CHILLING EFFECTS STANDING

Standing doctrine must also change as it largely operates as a substantial barrier to real victims of chilling effects going to court to vindicate their rights. The doctrine of standing is based on the US Constitution's Article III's grant of jurisdiction to the federal judiciary to hear and decide "Cases" and "Controversies."[58] The standard is that a plaintiff must show an "injury-in-fact," that is, "an invasion of a legally protected interest" that is "actual or imminent, not conjectural or hypothetical."[59] Sounds simple enough, but the way courts have applied this standard in practice has created immense uncertainty and complexity. Standing doctrine itself has been criticized as "incoherent, inconsistent, and unprincipled,"[60] "subjective,"[61] and simply a "meaningless litany" of rules that disguise the court's political preferences.[62]

This is especially so concerning chilling effect claims. Indeed, on top of *Laird* and *Clapper*, which suggest chilling effect claims based on privacy threats could never be sufficient injuries for standing purposes, the Supreme Court recently introduced additional formalistic harm requirements for standing in its *Spokeo* and *TransUnion* decisions. In *Spokeo*, the Supreme Court held that cognizable injury must be *both* "particularized" *and* "concrete."[63] And after *TransUnion*, you likely have to prove a harm or "injury-in-fact" even in cases where Congress has indicated otherwise.[64] Though both *Spokeo* and *TransUnion* emphasized concrete tangible harms, they did say that intangible harms could also be sufficiently concrete for standing, but such an intangible injury would have to have historical pedigree – bearing a "close relationship" to a harm that has "traditionally been regarded as providing a basis for a lawsuit in English or American courts."[65] So, standing doctrine is not just an overly technical, confused, and incoherent morass, but also inexplicably requires injuries and harms to be ancient or at least resemble the kinds of harms people have sued over for centuries.

Needless to say, even putting aside *Laird* and *Clapper*, chilling effect claims do not fit well with these complex and formalistic requirements. Chilling effects, as a behavioral phenomenon, are in some ways intangible and abstract but as I have argued in this book, also very concrete and tangible in their impacts. Further, many of the most serious threats to privacy and the person that may cause chilling effects today are due to new and emerging technologies – like AI, facial recognition technology, big data collection and analytics – and so have little historical connectedness to traditional English and American legal claims. Chilling effects are very ill suited for standing law. It was not always this way. Early on, chilling effects standing was simple: A chilling effect on a legal right – like a constitutional right – was an injury sufficient for standing.[66] In the 1965 decision *Lamont v. Postmaster General*, for example, the plaintiffs claimed their First Amendment rights were chilled by government provisions labeling certain mail "communist political propaganda."[67] Justice Brennan, who in his separate opinion directly addressed standing, accepted this chilling effect as sufficient injury and ultimately found that "inhibition as well as prohibition against the exercise of precious First Amendment rights is a power denied to government."[68] Very simply: A chill that denies full enjoyment and exercise of a legal right is a violation of that right and a cognizable injury for standing.

However, the doctrine of standing shifted in the late 1960s and 1970s from an earlier focus based primarily on legal interests for standing to today's standard focused on "pre-legal" factual injuries or harms.[69] This shift created needless complexity and fragmentation in standing law overall,[70] but has caused particular problems for chilling effects, given its dual nature as a legal concept based on the far less understood social and psychological phenomenon. *Laird* was decided in 1972 and, in my view, exemplifies this shift, wherein the court struggles to reconcile earlier cases where claims of chilling effects on legal interests sufficed for standing, with its denial of standing for similar threats to First Amendment interests based on privacy and surveillance.

One simple solution to the problem of standing and chilling effects is for the Court to return to this earlier, simpler, and more flexible approach – where standing is granted where any chilling effect deters or inhibits the free exercise of a legal right or any activity that one has a legal right to partake in. However, a lot has changed in standing law and a critic might say that courts are very unlikely to return to this earlier approach. So, if turning back the clock is not realistic, another straightforward solution is to expand the exception to technical standing rules for lawsuits alleging chilling effect claims that the overbreadth doctrine creates. Earlier, I argued that overbreadth, like void-for-vagueness, should be abandoned for its flawed theoretical and empirical assumptions, and privileging of legal and regulatory chill. On the other hand, the overbreadth doctrine also plays a worthwhile prudential role in chilling effects adjudication, relaxing the overly technical standing requirements so that various chilling effects claims can be addressed on the merits. This is something that Justice Antonin Scalia, a fierce skeptic of chilling effect claims, did get right – he made the point that it is inherently contradictory to require a plaintiff to demonstrate chilling effects as an injury for standing because, by definition, they have not been chilled enough to avoid retaining counsel and suing as they have ended up in court; not chilled into inaction.[71] But that point is true for the victim of most kinds of chilling effects, including those due to privacy or personal threats, certainly not just a chill on speech due to a vague law that Justice Scalia was happy to privilege while ignoring other kinds of chilling effects.

So, perhaps the better option is not necessarily to discard overbreadth in total, but to expand its pragmatic relaxation of standing rules for other kinds of chilling effect claims. The rationale for the doctrine is that the very *existence* of a statute would chill the speech of third parties not before the court, so they would never actually speak or act, just self-censor, and therefore never have an opportunity to challenge the statute on First Amendment grounds or otherwise.[72] But as I have argued, that is a flawed assumption – those third parties are more likely to be acting in ignorance of the law and the reason they are not before the court is that they have not been chilled. In fact, on a conformity theory of chilling effects, that reasoning applies more appropriately to surveillance chilling effects. The very *existence* of observation, or a reasonable threat of government surveillance, has chilling and conforming effects. Those impacts occur even when the observed person is aware that the surveillance is artificial; just the awareness of being watched, and not even targeted, can lead to chill. So, we don't need an overbreadth doctrine, but chilling effects standing doctrine, that relaxes technical standing rules so these claims can be adjudicated on the merits. In practice, courts should nevertheless treat legal and regulatory chilling effect claims more suspiciously and skeptically, while that would certainly make it easier for legitimate victims to vindicate their rights in court.

REASONABLE CHILLING EFFECT CLAIMS

But expanding the overbreadth exception to standing requirements to allow a broader range of chilling effect claims to reach decision on the merits in court is not enough – as proving chilling effects remains very difficult and in some cases impossible to prove; this remains true despite a growing body of empirical research documenting this behavioral phenomenon. As we have seen, chilling effects and their impacts can be obvious and profound but in other cases subtle, impacting us in ways that are difficult to understand and appreciate consciously. And often those with the data to prove a chilling effect – big business or big government – are the ones perpetrating it, and would not be willing to disclose that data to help victims. So, even when victims get to court, and get past standing requirements, they still face difficult evidentiary standards to prove their claims and vindicate their rights.

But we now have a far better understanding of chilling effects, what they are, how they operate, and what factors contribute to their having greater impacts. And the law should reflect that new understanding. One simple way to do so in chilling effects doctrine itself is for courts to grant standing for, and enforce, chilling effect claims that are reasonable. What does that mean? There are two parts to this. First, courts should simply look for a credible threat, or a credible risk thereof, that *reasonably causes or contributes to a chilling effect*, in light of what we now know about them, and any additional theoretical or empirical evidence offered by claimants. The second part is *what* is being chilled. To avoid the criticism that chilling effects in some circumstances are intentional – you want to chill illegal and undesirable behavior – then it would make sense for courts to enforce a chill on either a legal right – including common law, statutory, constitutional, or otherwise – or any activity the claimant has a legal right to engage in. And yes, that could include basic freedoms in our day-to-day lives. This needs elaboration. Allowing standing for, and then enforcing, reasonable chilling effect claims implies those claims must have an objective empirical and theoretical foundation. Hence, they are *reasonable*. That accords with a conformity theory of chilling effect, which is evidence-based and deeply grounded in social and behavioral theory and science. To make out a claim, claimants could draw on the framework set out in Chapter 8: draw on the four chilling effect factors – observation, uncertainty, personalization, and power/ authority – to make a theoretical case for a chilling effect in a given context, combined with any empirical evidence to support the claim. An emphasis on "targeted threats" also makes sense as it reflects the theoretical and empirical realities of chilling effects – reflected in the chilling effects curve discussed in Chapter 8 – that more *personalized* and *targeted* threats lead to greater chilling effects.

Recognizing and enforcing reasonable chilling effect claims is essentially the approach the Supreme Court has taken in cases like *Meese* and *Laidlaw*. In *Meese*, as noted earlier, the plaintiff Keene essentially alleged a personal threat – to his reputation – that chilled him from screening the films because the Department had labeled them "political propaganda." The Court found he had standing and contrasted his claim with *Laird*, where the plaintiffs offered nothing but a "subjective chill" claim. Keene, instead, had provided evidence via a commissioned survey to show the threat of reputational harm due to the government action reasonably caused a chilling effect on his First Amendment right.[73] If argued using our framework and chilling effect factors, Keene would argue his case involved *personalization* or a clear personal threat, in this case to his reputation and chances of reelection (thus impacting his economic interests and livelihood) due to the government labeling him a propagandist, which could also lead to ostracism and other social repercussions. He could argue that if he went ahead with the screening, he faced both additional threats of government *surveillance* and *uncertainty* about it, and any future targeted criminal or civil legal action by the Department of Justice. And he could raise the point that the chilling action is carried out by a powerful entity with authority – something especially intimidating and chilling in the context. So, the government labeling was a concrete threat that *reasonably caused or contributed to a chilling effect* on his First Amendment protected activities. That's essentially what the Supreme Court found in that case.

The plaintiffs in *Laidlaw* similarly alleged a personal threat to safety – and provided affidavit evidence to that effect – that pollution in a nearby river caused by the defendants had a chilling effect on the plaintiffs' legal right to use and enjoy the river where they would normally "fish, camp, swim, and picnic."[74] The Court granted standing for the lawsuit, finding the plaintiffs being chilled from engaging in their "recreational," "aesthetic," and "economic" activities due to concerns about how the pollution threatened their health and safety was "reasonable."[75] If argued using our framework and chilling effect factors, the plaintiffs would argue both *personalization* or a clear personal threat to health and safety from the apparent river pollution and *uncertainty*, due to the uncertainty of how the pollution might impact the plaintiffs if they engaged in recreational activities near the river. The apparent pollution was a credible threat that *reasonably caused or contributed to a chilling effect* on their recreational use of the river – an activity they had a right to engage in. Though *Laidlaw* was a standing case, it could also be an approach that applies on the merits – reasonable chilling effects.

This approach would also accord with case law recognizing chilling effects should have some objective empirical reality or reasonable foundation to succeed. Indeed, a different way to read *Laird* is that the court did not find chilling effect as inherently subjective, just that any chilling effect claim must be *reasonable*, that is, based on a "specific and objective threat" to the plaintiffs.[76] Consistent with this reading, there was no specific threat against the plaintiffs alleged in *Laird*. Rather, the chilling effect claims arose simply due to their awareness as to the existence of the Army surveillance program. Their chilling effect injury was thus based on a more general grievance – shared by any member of the public that *could* be subject to surveillance – and was not specific to *them*. So, it was not a reasonable chilling effect, but a chill based on a subjective fear, because there was no objective evidence to support the existence of a "specific threat" to the plaintiffs causing or contributing to any chilling effects. This reading is further supported by the fact that the Court acknowledged that chilling effects *could* be a cognizable injury for standing, and cited earlier First Amendment cases to that effect.

Importantly, however, this approach – reasonable chilling effects – must also be evidence based in practice. That is, it should not privilege legal and regulatory chilling effect claims, but as I argued earlier, it should treat these claims with more suspicion and require more strict evidence. Furthermore, a reasonable chilling effects approach could easily be adopted in other jurisdictions afflicted by the limits of conventional understanding. In Canada, for instance, though courts have been too skeptical of chilling effects due to privacy threats, they have often simply required objective evidence of such impacts before judicially recognizing and enforcing them. That, in a sense, is one way to read *Khawaja* – that courts should not take judicial notice of chilling effects without an evidential foundation. The same can be said for *Vice Media Canada*, wherein the court while refusing to presume chilling effects, simply required objective evidence. Certainly, reasonable chilling effects, with a theoretical and empirical foundation, would meet that standard.

TODAY AND TOMORROW

The law of chilling effects, otherwise known as chilling effects doctrine, would be significantly improved were each of these changes implemented. In particular, rejecting the chilling effect skepticism and subjectivism among lawyers and judges, relaxing technical standing rules, and enforcing reasonable chilling effect claims would make it far easier for victims to vindicate their rights and interests in court. That's important today and tomorrow. And over the long term, ending conventional privileging of legal and regulatory chilling effect claims – now baked into chilling effects doctrine – would also have broader political, economic, and societal implications as well. As I argued in Chapter 7, corporate actors have long employed legal and regulatory chilling effect arguments for self-interested commercial and neoliberal ends – successfully bringing legal challenges to court to invalidate government regulation and human rights laws across a variety of sectors on the basis that they chill First Amendment speech – often with very little evidence to substantiate any chilling effects and where they show no injury as basis for standing thanks to the void-for-vagueness and overbreadth doctrines. Yet, these changes to doctrine are not enough. Broader more comprehensive reforms are also needed. I talk about those next.

10

The Future of Chilling Effects and How to Stop It

Imagine a future in which computer systems, powered by AI, automatically interpret and enforce the law.[1] And not just any law, all laws. In this future, you constantly receive highly personalized instructions for how to comply with the law in real time. These directives are sent to you personally by a system operated by your government or local law enforcement agencies. You receive these legal directives for every situation with legal implications – how and when you should cross the street; how fast you drive on the way to work; or what you might say or do online. Not only that, but the AI system interpreting laws and sending these personal legal directives at societal scale is so sophisticated and complex that no one can explain how it reasons or works, not even its designers. Yet, if you ignore one of these personal legal directives, the system will know and it'll be exhibit "A" in any enforcement or prosecutorial action that is sure to follow.[2]

Legal scholars Anthony Casey and Anthony Niblett have written about AI-driven mass surveillance and automated enforcement systems just like this, highlighting those personally received legal directives, which they call "microdirectives."[3] Made possible by advances in surveillance, communications technologies, and big-data analytics, microdirectives will be a new and predominant form of law shaped largely by machines. They are "micro" because they are not impersonal general rules or standards, but tailored to one specific circumstance. And they are "directives" because they prescribe action or inaction required by law. Casey and Niblett predict that computationally personalized law and its automated enforcement like this is the future of law. They are not alone. Many legal scholars, computer scientists, communications scholars, data scientists, and machine learning scientists agree.[4]

THE EMERGENCE OF SUPERVEILLANCE

An AI-driven "microdirectives" system like this is an example of what I call "superveillance." Superveillance systems are mass surveillance and automated enforcement systems that combine a few different core features: first, large scale physical and data surveillance operationalized via identification and tracking technology – like today's facial and bodily recognition technology; second, powerful AI and machine learning capabilities to analyze massive amounts of data in real time; and third, automated targeted enforcement, which is large scale and highly personalized. Superveillance systems can enforce legal rules and norms, but they can also enforce social norms and rules as well. China, as I will discuss later, is developing these kinds of superveillance systems already. Roger Clarke famously argued in the late 1980s that then emerging forms of data surveillance – what he coined as "dataveillance," that is, tracking people using data trails – were technically and economically superior to the video-focused conceptions of surveillance that were predominant before that time and reflected in pop cultural classics like Orwell's *Nineteen Eighty-Four*. Similarly, superveillance will likewise supersede data surveillance, which is predominant today, because superveillance systems not only track you with data, they also track you physically, and provide personalized enforcement for near perfect efficiency and compliance.

Sound like science fiction? In fact, AI-driven superveillance is likely not far off. Automated law enforcement is not fantasy but a reality.[5] Speeding and red-light traffic cameras have been around for years, which detect lawbreaking and then deliver personalized notices of violations to the car owner based on their license plate, along with accompanying punishments – like a speeding fine or traffic violation citations.[6] There are already statutes like the Digital Millennium Copyright Act, enacted in 1998 to police digital copyright issues online,[7] which are today largely enforced algorithmically.[8] Robot cops and dogs, designed to conduct surveillance, patrol, and help enforce laws, are being deployed by police departments internationally.[9] Big tech – companies like Google, Microsoft, and Amazon – is investing billions in AI legal tech like "law bots" and *WIRED* magazine reports that AI robots are likely soon to be seen in courtrooms across the country.[10] In New York, Boston, and other cities, AI systems equipped with facial recognition technology (FRT) are being used by businesses to identify shoplifters.[11] Similar AI systems, supported by government, are being used by retailers in the United Kingdom and Europe to identify shoplifters and provide real-time tailored alerts to employees or security personnel.[12] And companies like Clearview AI, the serial mass privacy violator I introduced at the outset of the book, are providing sophisticated AI-powered facial recognition capabilities to law enforcement, national security agencies, and militaries not just in North America, but around the world.[13]

And let's not forget China. The Chinese government has been experimenting with superveillance systems for years. Those systems almost always include very powerful and centralized AI-driven mass surveillance and automated legal enforcement, which attempt to predict crime and social disruption before they happen. With these superveillance systems, if three people with criminal records check into the same hotel, the system flags that as suspicious activity and authorities are notified.[14] The same thing happens if someone with a history of political protest boards a train heading to a city where Chinese leaders are meeting.[15] Or if someone who is diagnosed with pandemic virus – like COVID-19 – is captured on AI surveillance leaving their home without permission.[16] But China's most sophisticated superveillance systems enforce not only laws but social norms. China's "social credit score" system, an AI- and data-driven system that aims to monitor, assess, and shape the behavior of all citizens and businesses, is an example of this.[17] Here, mass facial and bodily recognition technology is combined with big data and AI analytics to enforce not only laws automatically and individually, but also social norms about good or bad behavior. People worry about criminal records hurting their reputation permanently. With China's "social credit score" system, it's not just criminal behavior that is tracked, but any antisocial behavior – behavior that violates expected social or behavioral norms as defined by authorities. Any such antisocial behavior is tracked and permanently linked to your identity and reputation via a "social credit score."[18] And social repercussions are immediate. Take the example of Lao Duan, a Chinese citizen who worked in the coal industry and who was "blacklisted" after the coal industry collapsed – due to changes in Chinese energy policy – leaving him unable to pay back a number of loans.[19] Duan's banking and credit card accounts were automatically frozen; others received automated warnings on their phones before dialing his number; and when visiting Beijing, where FRT is ubiquitous in public, his face, name, and citizen ID number were displayed on a large electronic billboard at a major intersection with a message saying he was an untrustworthy person.[20] And if that sounds far-fetched, like a bad episode of *Black Mirror*, it really is happening and is practiced in smaller cities now too, like Luoyang – a historically important city in East-Central China that was the capital of the Northern Wei dynasty (494–534 CE) and one of the first cities on the Silk Road.[21] With a population of a little over 7 million, it is today among China's smaller cities. During a recent visit to the city, a former student of mine took a photo and sent it to me, immediately recognizing its implications for privacy and surveillance – topics we covered in class (Figure 10.1).

The photo shows a superveillance system in action – a digital billboard at an intersection in Luoyang displaying information about a citizen caught violating a traffic law by the system, including his name, citizen ID number, and location of the traffic law violation, in this case jaywalking, along with a photo of the person – both a picture of their face taken when they committed the offense and their official photo retained in government databases. Clearly, the system employed FRT combined with AI-driven social and legal infraction tracking: The system spotted the offense, recorded it, identified the perpetrator by matching their face with official state facial photos, and broadcast it as a means of deterring and socially shaming both the person identified, and other citizens who would consider doing the same or worse. This is China's nightmarish "social credit" superveillance system – a massive chilling effects machine on a societal scale.

This is the future of chilling effects. But in many ways, the future is now. How do we stop it? The same way we stop the many chilling effect threats, outlined in this book, that are already an urgent problem for democracy and society *today*. First, we need a

FIGURE 10.1 Superveillance in action. Photo taken by a former student of the author shows superveillance in action in the city of Luoyang, China – a digital billboard at an intersection displays the name, citizen ID number, official profile picture, and other photos of a person captured by the system committing a traffic law violation, along with the location where the violation took place. (Photo credit: Yi (Kevin) Li.)

better understanding of the threat, what is at stake. Second, we need to understand how chilling effects themselves can enable this deeply worrying future and render us more vulnerable to its harms. Third, we need to think and talk differently about chilling effects to better capture their dangers, and to be more creative thinking about the role of law in meeting the challenge. Fourth, we need granular changes but also comprehensive and multifaceted reforms – including shifts in legal rules and doctrine; prohibitions on certain technologies and practices; broader regulations; and more sweeping structural reforms – that address all of the chilling effect threats and factors: surveillance; uncertainty; personalization and personal threats; and power/authority. In fact, a conformity theory of chilling effects, advanced in this book, itself provides a clear roadmap and broader framework for law, policy, and broader structural reforms to address chilling effects. I set out these plans in the remainder of this chapter.

A NEW UNDERSTANDING

A central claim of this book is that conventional thinking about chilling effects is deeply flawed. As argued in Chapters 1 and 2, it is too narrow, focused mostly on legal and statutory chill or very narrow privacy claims, and cannot explain most forms of chilling effects. It is theoretically and empirically weak, with little support in empirical research or in behavioral theory and social science. And it is too individualistic, focused only on the rights or interests of individuals directly targeted and neglecting the broader societal implications of chill. To put this point another way, conventional thinking has focused almost exclusively on the *repressive* dimensions of chilling effects – how individual rights, especially speech rights, have been violated and repressed – and neglected their *productive* dimensions – how chilling effects also shape and produce behavior that is socially conforming or compliant.

This book has offered several reasons for this, but the main one is that legal scholars have simply not engaged sufficiently with social and behavioral theory and related social science. Some of that is due to lawyers just not being comfortable with some of the implications of social science for the tenets of classical liberalism, as Cohen has argued, but some of it can also be chalked up to the influence of law and economics on conventional understanding, which tended to ignore rather than embrace social science and social theory at least until the latter parts of the twentieth century. If you neglect social theory, you will easily miss how chilling effects are conformity and compliance effects – just with greater orders of magnitude given the far more significant threats that usually cause chilling effects. One final reason, not yet discussed, may have to do with a point Foucault made about different conceptualizations of power. To focus only on the repressive dimension of chilling effects is to focus only on their repressive power. In Chapter 6, I talked about how repressive power is the most common and familiar conceptualization of power, because it is associated with the state apparatus. Foucault even traced its intellectual origins to the monarchy and notions of sovereignty, law, and prohibition that are deeply embedded in Western systems of government since the Middle Ages.[22]

Whatever the precise reason, conventional thinking about chilling effects has led to a lot of theoretical, empirical, and legal problems. First, it often leads judges, lawyers, legal scholars, and policymakers to entirely miss or ignore *other* extralegal forms of chilling effects or foments skepticism about them, whether it is chilling effects due to privacy threats or personal threats. That is clear from cases like *Jackson, Counterman, Clapper, Laird,* and many other cases discussed throughout the book. Or it leads them to look for the *wrong* impacts of chilling effects – for instance, always expecting an Orwellian societal-level repression of speech and ideas. That *can* be what chilling effects look like, but not always. And if you're only looking for that, you're going to miss the actual impact, and dangers, of chilling effects. Conventional thinking thus makes chilling effects that much easier for malevolent state and corporate actors to weaponize in order to repress, control, and manipulate, as it renders them less visible; the impacts more unknowable or inexplicable; and the weaponization itself more immune to legal challenge or democratic accountability. This, in turn, allows for the expansion and entrenchment of state and corporate power coupled with norms that weaken democracy like inequality, hierarchy, and extremism.

It is thus clear that conventional theories, accounts, and thinking must be rejected, in favor of new ways of thinking about chilling effects and new discourse

to describe them and their impacts accurately. We need theories a
of chilling effects that better account for their impacts beyond in
to their impacts on society. So far, much of that work has not con
Amendment scholars; constitutional law scholars more generally; law a   ..om-
ics scholars; nor even technology law scholars – who to greater or lesser extents
remain mired in conventional thinking and approaches to chilling effects. Rather,
privacy scholars have largely led the way on this count, at least in respect of privacy threats, providing rich accounts of their societal impacts, including chilling
effects. As I have already recounted elsewhere in the book, Daniel Solove, Julie
Cohen, Neil Richards, Margot Kaminski, and Danielle Citron, among others, have
all made critical contributions on this count, highlighting the societal impacts of
privacy threats like surveillance or data collection, including their chilling and conforming effects. Moreover, they have often worked to ground their analyses in social
theory and behavioral science. Solove, Richards, and Cohen, for instance, all draw
on surveillance studies and social psychology theory and research to analyze the
chilling effects of surveillance. Similarly, recent work by European media and communication scholars like Michael Latzer, Mario Büchi, Joanna Strycharz, Claire
M. Segijn, and others likewise provides critical insights on the chill of dataveillance,
and is thoughtfully grounded in social psychology and behavioral theory.

The conformity theory advanced by this book builds on these contributions. My
only critique is that they are incomplete. Dataveillance theory is predominantly
focused on a "sense" of dataveillance, that is, a sense of surveillance and observation,
but neglects other central factors that likewise contribute to chilling effects, like
personalization, uncertainty, and power/authority. The same can be said of these
privacy contributions – critical to understanding privacy and the chill of privacy
threats, but incomplete in respect of chilling effects themselves. It's only part of the
story. That's where my conformity theory offers a far more complete explanation
of chilling effects, the factors and threats that cause and contribute to them, and
is grounded in both empirical studies and a vast range of social and behavioral science. Chilling effects *are* conforming effects, just at a greater magnitude and scale,
and in highlighting both the repressive and productive dimensions of chill, the theory helps us better understand the broader impacts on people and society.

Perhaps the most important thing needed to address chilling effects today and
tomorrow is a better understanding of them and their dangers and harms. Only *then*
can effective solutions be found. This has been a central aim of this book, which
has advanced a new understanding – a conformity theory – that is more empirically
and theoretically robust and grounded in behavioral science. This new theory, as I
have shown, can be used both to explain a broader range of chilling effects and the
factors that cause them. It helps us better understand how chilling effects have both
repressive and productive dimensions, and deeper psychological and evolutionary
foundations, and thus provides a far more accurate picture as to the urgent threat
they pose to freedom and democracy. It reveals how public and private sector actors

take advantage of those dimensions to weaponize chilling effects to control, manipulate, and repress. And it can be used to both predict the scale and scope of chill, and to navigate competing chilling effect threats and concerns, using the framework set out in Chapter 8.

That same framework can tell us how and why these emerging superveillance systems can be so deeply chilling if not properly regulated. Indeed, Casey and Niblett, who very thoughtful about the risks of such systems, themselves worried that the highly personalized machine-enforced law would raise serious privacy and autonomy concerns, despite great benefits like certainty and efficiency.[23] Many privacy and technology law scholars agree. Niva Elkin-Koren and Michal Gal, for example, have raised concerns about how personalized law and similar algorithmic, data-driven, and individual-focused legal and regulatory approaches can seriously chill civil liberties.[24] Ryan Calo, Lisa Shay, Woodrow Hartzog, and others have similarly raised privacy and chilling effect concerns about automated or robotic legal enforcement.[25] Yuval Feldman and Yotam Kaplan, after analyzing different forms of personalized legal enforcement, acknowledge similar concerns and the need to "minimize chilling effects" for these "enforcement mechanisms" to be used "successfully."[26]

With a theory of conformity of chilling effect, we can fully understand such concerns. Such a system would be based on persistent and unrelenting *surveillance* on both a societal scale but also on a personal level as well – such a system would no doubt employ forms of facial and bodily recognition technology to identify people in real time and at mass scale. Every decision with legal or possibly even social implications may be tracked, observed, recorded, and compiled to create a permanent persona or dossier that can be used against us indefinitely. We know from Chapter 5 how chilling that kind of invasive surveillance and data processing can and will be. Such a system would also involve immense *uncertainties* as well – not just the ambiguities inherent in societal-scale surveillance and data processing, but also uncertainty about how you may be affected in the future, and uncertainties about the security and impact of the system itself. Even today, the most powerful AI and machine learning systems are so complex that their processes, rationale for predictions, and determinations are inexplicable even to the scientists and experts who have designed those systems and operate them. This is the famed "black box" problem with AI and machine learning.[27] An AI that could power a societal-scale automated legal enforcement system like the one described above would require immense computing power and complexity, and would almost surely be entirely opaque; its legal reasoning and basis for recommendations similarly unexplainable and unknowable. This, in turn, creates even more uncertainty about whether people or groups will be treated fairly and with dignity by the system – given the biases and disparities inherent in AI systems and similar technologies – and uncertainty about whether anyone will ever know or find out, one way or the other.[28] Lastly, personalized superveillance directives would constitute a highly tailored *personal threat*: A specific legal direction about how to comply with the law or behavior expectation norm, would be among the most extreme forms of personalization, which would increase chill. And this highly personal targeted threat would be backed by the *power and authority* of the state, including the threat of criminal or civil penalty, and permanent personal reputational damage for noncompliance – retained forever in your "social credit" score. An ultimate form of what Frank Pasquale calls "algorithmic authority."[29]

If you received a directive from an AI superveillance system, would you feel like you had a choice? More than likely, you'd be chilled into conformity and compliance no matter how much you wanted to act and speak or how much you believed doing so was entirely legal and beneficial to you or society. This is just what Casey and Niblett were worried about, and they were right to be.

DARKNESS ON THE EDGE OF TOWN

There are dark times ahead.[30] The emergence of superveillance and similar forms of AI-driven mass tracking and automated law and norm enforcement systems is largely a product of surveillance capitalism – the predominant capitalist paradigm of our time. Many firms developing superveillance technologies could not have done so without data extracted and monetized by big tech firms at the heart of surveillance capitalism. Clearview AI, as we noted earlier in the book, trained its AI-driven facial recognition application on billions of facial images it illegally "scraped" from popular social media platforms. PimEyes, the similarly shady European AI facial recognition search engine, likewise illegally crawled the internet for images of people's faces to train its AI.[31] Later, it would be reported that the images PimEyes used were misappropriated from both social media platforms as well as family and ancestral sites – which often include pictures of people's faces, including deceased family members – and included sensitive images of children.[32] None of those "raw materials," to use Zuboff's term, would be available were it not for these social media companies extracting and retaining those images for their own commercial interests. And when it comes to AI itself, which is essential to power and operationalize these technologies both today and tomorrow, many of the most powerful AI firms are the same big tech firms – Meta, Apple, Microsoft, Google, Amazon, and so on.[33] Not surprisingly, a board member of Facebook's parent company, Meta, and early Facebook investor Peter Thiel, runs another surveillance firm called Palantir and was also an early investor in Clearview AI.[34] Surveillance capitalists, naturally, see value in superveillance.

The same can be said of China's AI-driven superveillance systems. Those systems are also only made possible with the active participation of China's own private sector surveillance technology industry. For instance, the Chinese firm Hikvision, which the *MIT Technology Review* called the "world's biggest surveillance company you've never heard of," owns video surveillance technologies that are deployed around the world and has been critical to China's efforts in developing superveillance policing systems.[35] In fact, the US State Department has sanctioned Hikvision since 2019 for its role in helping China build facial recognition and other superveillance technology in order to repress the country's Muslim minorities – mostly Uyghurs in the Xinjiang region.[36] Indeed, both Zuboff and Cohen have linked these developments in China to the logic of surveillance and information capitalism – comparable to the West, though with differing levels of entanglement with authoritarian state aims.[37] In China, superveillance is driven by authoritarian state designs for dominance and control, made possible by surveillance capitalist technologies. In America, and the West, it is AI superveillance firms like Clearview AI that are developing the tech and marketing it to government and law enforcement. At least, until now. Today, political economists and scholars of surveillance capitalism now speak of the next iteration of this paradigm – AI capitalism. AI capitalism still largely follows the logic of surveillance capitalism – it is data driven and extractive – but focuses on using AI to supercharge behavioral influence, manipulation, and control.[38] It is, in ways, an evolution of surveillance capitalism that is even more authoritarian, with Dyer-Witheford and his co-authors observing that AI has an "affinity" for "right wing populism" and is "fundamentally inhuman."[39] But again, perhaps China is the better example – both Cohen and Zuboff cite China as being a genuine global leader and innovator in combining AI with surveillance capitalist technologies to extend state power.[40] Perhaps it isn't AI capitalism that deserves our most focused attention, but what we might call AI *state capitalism*, with its unique mix of AI, surveillance capitalism, authoritarianism, and state power. Given their close ties with military, police, security agencies, and authoritarian designs, superveillance firms like Clearview AI, PimEyes, and Hikvision are the vanguard.

HOW CHILL ENABLES THIS FUTURE

And chilling effects enables all of it. In Chapter 7, I describe how chilling effects, especially their productive dimensions, preserve and maintain this kind of state and corporate power within broader social, political, and economic systems – today, that is surveillance and information capitalism. And in Chapter 5, I provided an extensive taxonomy of chilling effects, discussing a range of different government and corporate practices that cause them. Among those were practices most often associated with surveillance capitalism: large-scale digital and algorithmic surveillance, data collection, retention, and processing, including big data and predictive analytics, which are today algorithmic and driven by complex AI and machine learning systems. All of these same threats and their resulting chilling effects will likewise enable AI capitalism, and the superveillance technologies that it will produce.

But chilling effects will not only help usher in this new era of AI capitalism but magnify its impacts and facilitate its excesses too – by rendering us more visible, predictable, and legible to the machines and machinations of AI capitalism. That's because the "docile" and more conformist individuals and populations that chilling effects produce likewise double as objects that are more easily observed, analyzed, and predicted. That's because people who are more conformist are more predictable. This is true on a basic level – a kind of definitional truism. People who follow patterns of behavior – like a social norm – are almost by definition more predictable. In fact, one of the evolutionary explanations for people's tendency to conform in certain contexts is that it historically made life more predictable, stable, and safe – making it easier to coordinate and collaborate with others.[41] If people acted in bizarre and unpredictable ways all the time, life would be far more difficult, stressful, and dangerous. Yet the claim that more conformist populations are more predictable is also true as a matter of statistical analysis. Once you have a data set that is sufficiently large and randomly sampled from the general population, you can make predictions about the general population by statistically analyzing that data sample.[42] However, when the sample contains outliers – data points that are far different from the others and do not conform to the same patterns – the statistical probabilities are weakened, reducing the accuracy of predictions and even undercutting them entirely in some contexts.[43] A population that is more conformist will be more statistically predictable, as it will have fewer if any outliers, and the outliers it does have will not be as extreme.

This is particularly salient in a world of increasingly ubiquitous big data and predictive analytics. And most of these predictive technologies rely on forms of statistical analysis and are often supercharged by AI and machine learning. Chilling effects also supercharge these technologies, as conformity reduces population-level outliers and anomalies rendering prediction, based on statistical modeling and projections, more powerful and accurate. Chilling effects, then, produce populations that are more visible, transparent, quantifiable, and thus amenable to prediction and control via computational analytics. Not only that, but outliers also become more easy to identify – those that deviate from the norm. Once detected, they can be dealt with – labeled as social outcasts or deviants and targeted for normalization, or excluded and discarded. This is analogous to the sorting function of surveillance that sociologist Oscar Gandy and other surveillance studies theorists have explored – surveillance sorts and categorizes us and creates opportunities for disparate treatment according to the needs of commercial interests.[44] However, my argument is that such sorting is not only a product of surveillance, but of all the other public and private sector practices that contribute to chilling effects talked about in Chapter 5 and beyond.

Perhaps an even better way of understanding this outcome of chilling effects is political scientist James Scott's notion of legibility. In *Seeing Like a State: How Certain Schemes to Improve the Human Condition Have Failed*, Scott explores countless historical case studies of what he calls "high modernism" – attempts by states to regularize the social world in order to improve it.[45] To do so, the state needed ways to render the social world more governable – in the case of legibility, it meant making people, things, and even nature, more visible, simplified, and uniform. One central way to render something more legible was to create or impose a unit of measurement. No matter the state intervention, whether it was vaccinating a population, producing goods, mobilizing labor, taxing people and property, designing cities, conscripting soldiers, and so on, there had to be units of measurement – whether it was people, villages, trees, fields, depending on context. That's because the unit of measurement imposed both standardization and conformity onto the target population, which in turn made that population far more easily "identified, observed, recorded, counted, aggregated, and monitored."[46] In an age of information capitalism and AI, chilling effects operate the same way, producing individuals and populations that are more legible objects of study and control – more visible, measurable, and manageable. As Kate Crawford explains in her book *The Atlas of AI*, this is *precisely* what AI, and thus AI capitalism, requires of us to flourish:

> Along the way, we will see how AI is built on the very human efforts of (among other things) crowdwork, the privatization of time, and the seemingly never- ending reaching, lifting, and toiling of putting boxes into order. From the lineage of the mechanized factory, a model emerges that values increased conformity, standardization, and interoperability – for products, processes, and humans alike.[47]

Chilling effects thus produce individuals and populations that are more conforming, compliant, and easier to manage, organize, and sort into hierarchies – and, most importantly for the purposes of our discussion, easier for AI to analyze, predict, and subsume within the authoritarian dominion of AI capitalism, and the superveillance systems and other mass tracking and enforcement technologies that will follow.

HOW TO STOP IT

Beyond offering a new understanding of the dangers today and tomorrow, the theory advanced in this book also shows why chilling effects require a multifaceted and comprehensive law and policy response. A conformity theory emphatically demonstrates that focusing only on individual rights and freedoms that are violated or repressed by chilling effects while neglecting the dangers they pose for democracy and civil society will surely fail. It also shows that piecemeal approaches, that address only one chilling effect threat or factor – like law or surveillance alone – will obviously also not be enough, at least not in the long term. Nor will one approach to law and policy reform be adequate. For instance, advocating that courts should adopt better standing rules to accept a wider array of chilling effect claims – as I argued in Chapter 9 – while neglecting broader legal and regulatory changes and reforms that address other dimensions of chilling effects – like reforms to reduce uncertainty through transparency or to address power and authority in the public and private sector – will also fail to fully address the harms and dangers of chilling effects.

Take privacy and its protection as one example. Chilling effect law reforms that deal only with privacy threats will not be enough to protect privacy, nor the many other critical privacy interests discussed in Chapter 7, be it autonomy, dignity, intimacy, or trust, among others. That is, it's not only privacy threats that can cause chilling and conforming effects on individuals and society that endanger all of these interests, but also the broad range of threats discussed throughout the book, but especially in Chapter 5's taxonomy, including personal threats, regulatory threats, personal legal threats, disinformation, stalking, hate, harassment and other forms of abuse, as just a few different examples. Each of these threats can chill, to greater or lesser extents depending on the context, but none should be ignored, certainly not by privacy scholars or advocates. Cohen has argued that once one understands what privacy "is for" – as not just invaluable to individuals and their interests but also to broader society by supporting democracy, creativity, and innovation – then this necessitates structural requirements to preserve these values and institutions and reforms to ensure their protection. Privacy threats must be protected against in a systematic way in combination with more comprehensive reforms that also address these other threats. Privacy matters more than ever before,[48] but left on its own, it will not flourish or even survive.

The very same can be said about other kinds of threats that cause chilling effects. Dealing only with legal uncertainty is not enough. Dealing only with personal threats and abuse or power and authority is also insufficient. Rather, we need a multifaceted and comprehensive approach to chilling effects, drawing not just on law and policy, but other levers too. Our conformity theory of chilling effects, in fact, provides a framework for such a response. In the same way that we can use the four chilling effect factors to understand, explain, and predict chilling effects – surveillance; uncertainty; personalization; and power/authority – we can also use them as a guide to addressing chilling effects in a comprehensive way. Each must be addressed.

1 *Restricting and Regulating Surveillance*

Surveillance, persistent observation, and related practices – like data collection, retention, and processing, including AI and algorithmic-driven iterations – must be restricted and regulated. That can be accomplished via a range of different types of legal and regulatory responses. One necessary response, that privacy and technology lawyers are increasingly embracing,[49] would be outright *prohibitions* on the most chilling forms of surveillance technologies and related data practices. An example of this would be banning superveillance systems or, in the alternative, banning constituent technologies that form part of such systems – like banning FRT as proposed by Woodrow Hartzog, Evan Selinger, and others, and adopted by many cities and municipalities in the US.[50] It is also an approach European lawmakers have embraced in the European Union's new Artificial Intelligence Act (AI Act),[51] the first comprehensive AI regulatory scheme worldwide that is likely to become the global standard,[52] which prohibits certain AI uses or applications with "unacceptable risks" for people's health, safety, and fundamental rights.[53] Chilling effects put fundamental rights at risk, as I have argued at length, so they would be a consideration in any such prohibitions. In fact, the AI uses that the Act already prohibits read like a laundry list of technological applications and technical capabilities necessary to assemble an AI superveillance system, with automated legal and norm enforcement: facial recognition; "real-time" remote biometric identification; biometric categorization; social scoring; and risk assessments for criminal offenses.[54] Concerns about chilling effects caused by these AI applications were almost surely a central consideration in these prohibitions. Though such prohibitions are neither perfect[55] nor comprehensive, so long as they are carefully tailored, they offer a simple and straightforward way to avoid any and all chilling effects that would be caused by any corporate or state use of the proscribed surveillance technologies or practices.

Naturally, not every invasive surveillance technology or data practice can be prohibited, especially those used by government or private sector security vendors and defense contractors for national security purposes, like those NSA programs disclosed in the Snowden leaks. So, *regulation* of both state and corporate surveillance and data practices is also necessary to reduce or mitigate their chilling effects. One form would be targeted legislation, like data protection legislation that restricts the nature and scope of data surveillance, collection, and sharing like the European Union's influential General Data Protection Regulation (GDPR),[56] which has become the global standard.[57] However, such data protection laws must apply to both the public and private sector – to counter state and corporate power – and would need to be drafted with chilling effects theory and research in mind. Today, most are not. For instance, a key problem with the GDPR – and legislation based on it like the California Consumer Privacy Act or Canada's proposed Consumer Privacy Protection Act[58] – is that while the GDPR was designed to reduce chilling effects associated with data collection and processing by reducing uncertainty about the scope and invasiveness of such practices,[59] it also has features that likely exacerbate their chilling effects. First, the GDPR still relies heavily on individual data controls and consent, which require countless notices and notifications to users seeking approval or consent for various forms of data surveillance and tracking,[60] like those constant prompts from websites for users to "accept" cookies that effectively allow them to track you and your behavior all over the internet.[61] Not only can such consent be easily manipulated or circumvented by companies to allow for more surveillance and thus chilling effects, the constant notices and prompts themselves create a sense of persistent observation and surveillance, or a "sense" of dataveillance as Latzer, Büchi, and others call it, which in turn promotes chilling effects. Imagine the workers in the famous Hawthorn Effect experiments – who were chilled and conformed just after being notified *once* that they were under observation – were instead constantly reminded that they were being watched and observed through unrelenting and persistent notifications. Imagine the chilling effects they would have suffered *then*. Well, that is what the GDPR mandates for all of us online. Second, while reducing some uncertainty about the scope and nature of data practices by industry, the GDPR at the same time creates other ambiguities and uncertainties. The GDPR is itself highly complex, with many exceptions, allowances, and ambiguous requirements, and it leaves a lot of responsibility to the companies themselves, which can easily be obscured by opaque corporate and bureaucratic processes.[62] Such uncertainties promote chilling effects. Third, it also provides a clear legal and regulatory authority for data collection, retention, and processing, enhancing the power and authority of the corporate actors to engage in them; magnifying their impact even further.

In other words, the GDPR is a very flawed regulatory scheme if the aim is to reduce or obviate the chill of data surveillance and similar practices. It is no doubt better than nothing, but could be significantly improved. Data protection legislation designed based on our new understanding of chilling effects, for instance, would not be consent or approval based, with constant surveillance notices or reminders, but rules based, allowing for certainty and clarity. It would not leave the complexity and uncertainties of the scheme in the hands of either easily manipulated users or to the titans of surveillance capitalism, with their obscure corporate bureaucracies. It would reject needless complexity and ambiguity, like countless exceptions to data restrictions or allowances for shifting usage, where companies collect for one use, retain for long periods of time, and repurpose the data later, creating greater uncertainty about data use but also potential future risks and harms. It would mandate strict data minimization rules that are aggressively enforced. Data minimization rules usually only allow data to be collected for very specific and narrow purposes and only a very minimal amount of data sufficient to meet those purposes can be collected. The lesser the amount of data surveillance, collection, retention, and use happening in society, the lesser the chilling effects today and tomorrow.

But targeted privacy or data protection legislation would not be enough either. More general regulatory schemes that impose broader legal responsibilities and duties on entities and organizations engaged in surveillance, data collection, and similar practices would also be necessary, especially to rein in powerful social media platforms. Examples of such regulatory schemes include duties of "data loyalty" proposed by Richards and Hartzog[63] or platform duties of care or due diligence models like those enacted in the UK and currently being considered in the US, Canada, and Europe.[64] The central idea behind these legislated duties is that social media platforms and other technology companies should have special responsibilities concerning the data they collect about us, comparable to fiduciary responsibilities that doctors have with their patients or lawyers have with their clients. They are information fiduciaries, to use the concept coined by Jack Balkin.[65] A duty of data loyalty, for instance, would require such companies to act in the best interests of the people whose data they are collecting and using.[66] That requirement, Richards and Hartzog argue, would prohibit companies from collecting and using our data solely for their own commercial benefit or in ways that would be disloyal to people's interests or harm them.[67] Collecting and using data in a way that chills people's free exercise of fundamental rights would no doubt be disloyal and harmful, so a duty of data loyalty should, at least in theory, lead to restrictions on more invasive or larger-scale surveillance and excessive data collection, including algorithmic forms, which cause chilling effects. It would also create rebuttable presumptions that other forms of invasive data collection and processing are unlawful, placing the burden on companies to justify their data practices, rather than leaving that responsibility to people.[68] Legislated duties of care or due diligence for platforms and data collectors would likely also prohibit companies from collecting and using our data in ways that foreseeably cause harm or would be highly offensive to a reasonable user. Again, chilling effects should constitute such a foreseeable harm. Each of these measures would reduce chilling effects.

2 *Reducing Uncertainty*

Addressing surveillance and related forms of data collection is also not enough. Uncertainty and opacity in certain state and corporate activities must also be reduced in order to address the dangers and harms of chilling effects on an individual and societal scale. We have discussed many forms of uncertainty through this book that can cause or contribute to chilling effects. One example is the uncertainty and opacity in state and corporate surveillance and data collection and use, and similar activities. Legislation should be enacted to mandate both corporate and government transparency concerning surveillance and data collection and use, and similar activities that can cause or contribute to chilling effect threats. Such requirements reduce chilling effects on the theory that increasing transparency about how data is being used or shared may reduce uncertainty and with it, chilling and conforming effects.[69] Another form of uncertainty is the kind most often the subject of conventional theories and accounts of chilling effects – uncertainty in civil and criminal laws. Here, legal, regulatory, and statutory *design* and *drafting* also have a role to play, at least in the case of statutory or regulatory chilling effects. I have argued these kinds of chilling effects are likely much less common and significant than other forms, and their effects could be further mitigated and reduced with more carefully and narrowly tailored laws and statutes that would also reduce the uncertainty that contributes to chilling effects.

Yet, technologies and technical systems also need to be transparent otherwise they can also contribute to chilling effects. The "black box" problem of AI, machine learning, and similarly complex systems today creates many uncertainties and ambiguities for people subject to their processes. Superveillance systems are chilling for many reasons, but the AI systems that are driving them today and certainly in the future are so complex and opaque that they often cannot be explained or their results interpreted in intelligible ways. Again, that creates chilling ambiguities and uncertainties. But we need not be victims to a world of needlessly complex systems that decide questions of rights, interests, and even freedom. Laws can mandate interpretability and explainability for such systems to ensure everyone can understand and explain how the systems operate. Prohibitions on certain applications can be used here too; if a system is too complex to explain or understand, it shouldn't be deployed in legal contexts. Nor should such a system be making decisions that impact on people's fundamental rights.

Legislated duties for social media platforms, AI platforms, and other information fiduciaries could also help address uncertainties that cause or contribute to chill. For instance, legislated duties of care or due diligence models like those considered in Canada and Europe can be even broader than duties of data loyalty as they tend to focus on systemic risk, creating obligations on companies and platforms to identity potential risks of harm for their services and activities, to monitor those risks on an ongoing basis, and to take action to mitigate or reduce those risks.[70] A focus on risk would necessitate legal responsibilities for platforms and tech companies not just in relation to data collection and usage, but also responsibilities concerning transparency, accountability, content moderation, and use of algorithms, AI, and other technologies, which can be used to chill, manipulate, or influence users, for example.[71] Among those broader platform responsibilities would also be transparency. Platforms and other tech companies would be required by these duties of care and loyalty to provide more transparency about their activities, whether it is surveillance, data collection and use, or who they are sharing our information with and for what purposes. Broader legislated duties of care or due diligence would also include responsibilities to deal with harmful content being hosted and shared on these platforms, like fake news, conspiracies, and other forms of disinformation and misinformation. In Chapter 5, I talked about how the spread of disinformation and misinformation in democracies can be dangerous, causing broader societal chilling effects on democratic participation and activism. When people cannot discern what is true and what is false, then they are easily chilled from political participation or collective action to address public policy issues or concerns. Legislated duties of care and due diligence that focus on risks – including the risk of chilling effects on democratic activities – would require platforms to be more proactive in reducing the visibility, frequency, and spread of false stories and information. That would help reduce the chill of such disinformation, a concrete benefit for democratic societies in the near term and long term.

Of course, none of these proposals are flawless, and there is a possibility that broad and vague legislated duties of care and loyalty could themselves have chilling effects. This is especially so, as these duties would be implemented in multifaceted ways – via legislation; administrative action and regulations; the common law; and even through constitutional protections.[72] But as I have argued, chilling effects do require comprehensive measures like this, and so long as they are carefully designed and tailored – as Richards and Hartzog have helpfully elaborated – such legal chill can be avoided. And while more work needs to be done to flesh out the nature and scope of these duties, common law versions could offer flexibility to manage that process incrementally – they could be clarified over time and updated to respond to new technologies and threats that may cause chilling effects.[73]

3 *Curtailing Personalization and Personal Threats*

Among the most chilling state and corporate actions are forms of personalization and personal threats, backed by the power of criminal or civil penalty. This is another critical insight of chilling effects theory informed by social and behavioral science, with the chilling effects curve discussed in Chapter 8 illustrative of this reality. The more personal and personalized the threat, the greater the chilling effect. This is a big reason why superveillance systems would be so chilling because as I talked about earlier, their enforcement via microdirectives or similar mechanisms would constitute highly personalized and personally received legal threats. But other forms of personalization, like personalized law, and personal threats, like online stalking, harassment, threats of violence, and other forms of abuse, must also be addressed to reduce chilling effects.

As with restricting surveillance, a comprehensive legal and regulatory response would have to consider prohibitions on certain technology uses or applications. Bruce Schneier and I, for instance, have argued that one way to curtail the chilling impacts of AI-driven personalized legal enforcement – like superveillance – would be to simply prohibit the use of such technologies in the context of law enforcement.[74] Superveillance systems should never be deployed with the power of criminal law penalties – far too chilling. But the argument could also be made about other legal contexts as well, involving more significant, and thus chilling, civil law penalties and liabilities. But there are other forms of targeted legal enforcement beyond microdirectives and superveillance systems. Another example would be the "personalized law" that Cass Sunstein, Ariel Porat, and Lior Strahilevitz write about, where rules are personalized and tailored to each individual.[75] The legal personalization movement, driven by big data and predictive algorithms, is likewise the "wave of the future" argues Sunstein, as new forms of information computational capacity allow the law to be increasingly shaped to people's specific circumstances.[76] While there are obvious benefits to legal personalization – it could reduce legal and regulatory uncertainties – if implemented in heavy-handed ways such benefits would be easily outweighed by the privacy threats and resulting chilling effects. Both prohibitions on certain personalized law applications and uses should be considered – like, again, avoiding the criminal law context – as well as regulation, like the audits, transparency, accountability frameworks, and safety standards contemplated by the EU's AI Act.

However, personal threats due to forms of abuse, especially online versions, must also be addressed, as such threats are also among the most chilling both for the victims and for broader democratic societies. There are many reforms required to do so, especially on the legal responsibilities of social media platforms wherein campaigns of stalking, harassment, and cyber-mob abuse are carried out and amplified to terrorize and chill victims. On this count, as already discussed in Chapter 5 and elsewhere in the book, privacy and online abuse experts like Citron and Franks, and advocacy organizations like the Cyber Civil Rights Initiative, have been leading the way on this point for years: arguing for common sense law and policy reforms that would create serious criminal and civil penalties for these forms of online abuse like cyber-harassment, cyberstalking, online threats of violence and doxxing, intimate privacy violations like personalized spyware or nonconsensual sharing of intimate media (also known as revenge porn), among others. And they have advocated for incentives for more robust enforcement of these measures, by law enforcement and governments.[77] But targeted legislation is also not enough. Social media companies must have broader duties to deal with this abuse online, and if they do not, face significant penalties. Thus, Citron and Franks advocate for changes to Section 230 of the Communications Decency Act.[78] That famous and controversial provision enacted in 1996 essentially provides blanket immunity for social media companies and other service providers from liability for harmful content generated and spread on their platforms. For instance, in her important book *The Fight for Privacy*, Citron argues for due diligence reforms to section 230 that would require platforms to proactively monitor and manage certain types of harmful content and abuse activities.[79] Similar legal responsibilities could also be covered by broader legislated platform duties of care, loyalty, and due diligence, including those enacted in Europe and proposed in Canada.[80]

These reforms would all reduce the chill of personal threats and abuse not only by curtailing and reducing their incidence via targeted deterrence, but also would send a message to perpetrators about potential social and reputational risks of engaging in such conduct, and, most importantly to victims of such abuse that their speech, engagement, and protection matter. This is the expressive function of law that I talked about in Chapter 7, and there is growing evidence that such anti-abuse measures can help mitigate chilling effects more broadly, but also especially for victims. For example, Citron and I have elsewhere demonstrated how the expressive power of a cyber-harrassment law can have salutary effects on the speech, engagement, and sharing of women online – essentially reducing the chilling effects of online abuse for those most often victimized by it.[81] We have built on that research with forthcoming empirical studies, conducted with our colleague Alexis Shore Ingber, demonstrating how intimate privacy protections, implemented via both law or by platforms themselves, can also increase trust among women and minority groups, something critical to mitigating the chill of privacy threats and encouraging intimate expression and sharing in the long term.[82] In summary, all of these measures would help reduce and mitigate the chill of personal threats and abuse, especially for women, minority groups, and other marginalized groups and communities who are disproportionately targeted by such abuse, and thus disproportionately suffer greater chilling effects as a result.

4 *Constraining Power and Authority*

Lastly, state and corporate power – a defining factor in chilling effects today – must also be reined in. There are many forms of power and authority that can cause or contribute to chilling effects, and we have discussed many such types in this book. Some types are formal – like people or entities that exercise legal, statutory, or other governmental powers, like police or state agencies. Another is economic – power and authority due to one's access to greater sums of wealth and the immense advantages that this entails, whether it is access to advanced technologies that surveillance capitalists use to influence and predict our behavior or vast legal resources that can be used to threaten and chill critics. Indeed, perhaps the most important power today concerns power over data and information – the power to track us, collect our data, retain it, analyze it, and use its insights to manipulate and control us, including weaponizing chilling effects.[83] Other types of power and authority are more informal, like authority derived from expertise, knowledge, or information. An example would be social or cultural authority derived from social group membership, especially where that group has the capacity to threaten or exact reputational harms or other social sanctions on others. Colloquially we might call this the power of the crowd – or mob – depending on the situation; like those campaigns of stalking, harassment, and abuse discussed elsewhere in the book. Often, the kind of power and authority that contributes the most to chilling effects is the perception that a person or entity can credibly threaten the safety and security of others, whether through credible legal threats, threats of social sanction, or even physical threats, as is the case with personal threats of violence or harassment. To mitigate chilling effects, each of these sources of power and authority should be addressed.

But as we have seen in countless examples in this book, what's different about both state and corporate power is that each often combine nearly all of these types of authority – legal, economic, technological, informational, social, personal, and beyond. And sometimes state and corporate power even act in concert – as with the surveillance–industrial complex that Schneier talks about, or what Taylor Owen calls the "coming merger" of technology and state power, with Trump, Elon Musk, and Silicon Valley joining forces.[84] All of this significantly magnifies any resulting chill, adding to the urgency of addressing it. In fact, most of the proposals that I have already set out here are critical to doing so across a variety of domains – surveillance; data collection, retention, and processing; transparency; personal threats; personalization; and so on. For instance, privacy scholars like Lisa Austin, Neil Richards, and Carissa Véliz all argue that privacy is all about power.[85] That's because access and control over people's information without constraint would allow unbridled opportunities for the powerful to track, analyze, and manipulate whole populations and chilling effects are another means of manipulation and control – among the most sinister and powerful of all, as I have argued. And privacy and data protection laws reduce power imbalances between those subject to surveillance and data processing and the powerful state and corporate actors most often engaged in it. By restricting and in some cases prohibiting these practices, such laws mitigate the impacts of chilling effects and the capacity of these entities to weaponize them. If privacy is about power, so too are chilling effects. The same can be said about measures I have advocated for earlier concerning forms of online harassment, stalking, threats, and abuse – these laws would likewise reduce the chilling impacts of such abuse, which are disproportionately felt by women and other minority populations. To use Ari Waldman's terms, these proposals all reflect a new way of thinking about law and policy explicitly as counterweights to power, as wielded and possessed by actors in the public and private sector.[86]

Yet these proposals are not enough. We also need changes in laws and policy to further make powerful actors in government and society more easily accountable for their actions, especially those that may cause or contribute to chilling effects. A key such reform would include changes to standing doctrine, discussed at length in Chapter 9, which would make it easier for victims to go to court and vindicate their rights via claims concerning state and corporate chilling effects. I also advocated for changes to chilling effects doctrine to render it more evidence based and accommodating of a wider variety of chilling effect claims. Kiel Brennan-Marquez's proposal for a "void for breadth" doctrine to curtail authoritarian abuse of overly broad laws – which would certainly cause chilling effects – falls along similar lines.[87] But mere doctrinal changes are not enough, as they often are subject to slower more incremental change by courts. We also need legislative reforms on this count. In Chapter 7, I talked about SLAPP (Strategic Lawsuit Against Public Participation) lawsuits weaponized by companies to chill critics. In response, Anti-SLAPP laws have been enacted in the United States, Canada, and Europe, to address these very chilling effects and usually provide an expedited mechanism for defendants to dismiss frivolous lawsuits combined with a stay on costly and invasive litigation processes like discovery.[88] The aim of Anti-SLAPP laws is to mitigate the chill of corporate legal threats by making it easier for victims to challenge those lawsuits and for courts to dismiss such abusive claims at an early stage of the legal process, reducing uncertainty, legal costs, and their silencing effect. Recently, there have been calls for new Anti-SLAPP laws to protect the press from new threats from the US Government, with the Trump administration promising to target critics to chill and silence them.[89] The problem is that Anti-SLAPP laws only apply to legal threats; but do nothing to address other kinds of threats, like privacy, surveillance, and even forms of harassment or abuse of press reporters, that can lead to the same chilling effects on journalism and reporting.

However, these Anti-SLAPP laws could still be a model for more robust anti-chill laws today that not only address legal threats, but a wider array of threats causing chilling effects. Such anti-chill laws could, like Anti-SLAPP laws before them, provide ways for victims to more easily challenge both public and private sector threats and obtain relief. Such laws could provide standing and even statutory private causes of action for a wide variety of chilling effect claims affecting a broad range of rights, interests, and freedoms. It could also streamline litigation, providing for early discovery, injunctive relief, and forms of transparency to make discovering and investigating more abusive cases easier. Class action lawsuits, where large classes of victims are affected by chill – as in the case of surveillance or data breaches – could also be enabled by anti-chill laws.

Yet, reining in the powerful cannot be left solely to individual or even mass legal claims. An effective response must also include broader policy and structural reforms – not only to better address the many societal impacts of chilling effects, but to also undercut the chilling productions of surveillance and AI capitalism. A detailed discussion of such reforms would take us far beyond the scope of this chapter but I'll nevertheless offer a brief outline here. A more moderate approach – that balances concerns about chilling effects with legitimate government interests and public policy aims – like public safety, national security, and data monetization allowances to promote innovation – would, at minimum, propose law reforms to reduce power imbalances; strengthen accountability frameworks and regulators; and ensure public and private sector actors are more easily subject to democratic oversight and control.[90]

Far more sweeping changes would require reforms that would ultimately disrupt and undermine the business models of surveillance capitalism. For instance, new consumer protection laws, updated to deal with the challenges of data-driven public and private sector practices and emerging technologies, would be a critical reform. Such laws have historically helped reduce power imbalances between consumers and industry and undercut exploitative business practices and could do so again today. Richards has proposed new "information age" consumer protection laws focused on how companies use our data to manipulate and monetize us.[91] I have also previously advocated for new consumer protection laws focused on similar information economy issues like disinformation, misinformation, deception, and forms of online abuse, while reducing information and other power asymmetries between consumers and industry.[92] Naturally, antitrust and anti-competition law reforms would also be essential to reduce the abusive and exploitive industry practices based on new forms of market power – like data and information monopolies. For technologies like AI that similarly can further empower already powerful technology companies, specific regulations would also be warranted. The EU's AI Act, noted earlier, offers a useful framework for ensuring safe and trustworthy AI, though the Act entrusts too much responsibility to industry actors themselves, instead of independent third party organizations and regulators. Similarly in Canada, recently proposed AI regulations, based in part on the EU model, envision a new AI commissioner but without the independence, powers, and resources for adequate enforcement.[93] The same can be said for older regulators expected to enforce newly reformed anti-competition laws.[94] I'll have more to say on robust enforcement a bit later.

When it comes to state power, similar reforms would mean aforementioned privacy, data protection, and AI regulations that apply to government just as they apply to industry. It would also require ensuring more robust democratic oversight, to ensure accountability and constrain state power and its abuse. In the US, that would mean better oversight by Congress at the federal level and by legislative assemblies at the state level. It would also require strengthening access to information and weakening state secrecy laws – like state secrets doctrine discussed in Chapter 8 – that protect invasive national security surveillance and similar practices from legal accountability and public oversight. And it would mean empowering, funding, and supporting state and corporate watchdogs, both within government – like inspector generals – and in civil society. My colleagues at The Citizen Lab have contributed significantly to our understanding of how commercial spyware companies have enabled governments, often those with atrocious human rights records, to systematically target, threaten, and chill human rights activists, journalists, and civil society organizations.[95] Through its research and public reporting of these practices, the Lab has ensured greater state and corporate accountability.[96]

Lastly, my proposals here have talked about new prohibitions and both targeted and more general regulatory responses. That raises an important issue mentioned earlier – who or what will be enforcing those new measures? The most important enforcement requirement is that existing regulators or new ones must be independent from government and industry, transparent, well resourced, but also have the resources and legal powers to investigate, compel compliance, and impose significant criminal and civil penalties. Of course, this is not a new theme – an emboldened Federal Trade Commission (FTC), as envisioned by most privacy scholars, could fit that role. In the US, for instance, privacy and legal scholars like Cohen, Richards, Solove, and Hartzog have argued at length over the need for regulatory agencies like the FTC to be given more powers to pursue their regulatory mandates; to be more aggressive in pursuing violators and protecting consumers; and for the agency to act more independently of industry interests and self-interested policy framing to affect real change in corporate behavior.[97] Others like Ryan Calo have proposed new regulatory agencies or bodies to deal specifically with the challenges of emerging technologies with exceptional impacts, in his case, a federal AI/ Robotics commission.[98] The point is that regulatory agencies and actors need to be robust enough to counter the power and authority of state and corporate actors. Only then will law reform and regulations effectively deter chilling activities and disrupt the state activities and corporate business models that sustain them, whether it is mass privacy violations – like those committed by Clearview AI – or more granular level threats leading to chill, like corporate data breaches.

Conclusion

This book has been about documenting chilling effects and the threats and factors that cause and contribute to them today and tomorrow. In doing so, it has challenged conventional thinking about all of these things – something that has been predominant in law, public policy, and broader society. We must discard such thinking entirely. And since the public and private sector practices that cause chilling effects – whether surveillance, data collection, overreaching laws, or other personal threats – are often rationalized in reference to competing values and public interests, the book has also explained how to better predict and evaluate chilling effects claims and to balance them against other competing interests. Critically, the book has also been about better understanding the dangers of chilling effects; how they are an instrument of power and control and fundamentally threaten freedom and democracy. And about how best to respond: with multifaceted and comprehensive reforms.

Yet, advocating for such sweeping reforms, and ensuring their effectiveness and success over the long term, is not easy, and would require sustained and widespread public support. The issue is not merely theoretical. As I write, new authoritarian movements are on the rise around the world,[1] each promising to weaponize government, law enforcement, and emerging technologies to repress and victimize critics and political opponents in chilling new ways.[2] Newly elected President Trump is promising the same,[3] while likewise planning radical deregulation of AI and other technologies, making it easier to weaponize the forces of AI capitalism to promote and magnify chilling effects.[4] Indeed, Trump's election in many ways represents a new dawn of state, corporate, and technological power merged and wielded in unprecedented ways. Meanwhile, following the Supreme Court's decision in *Dobbs*, there are new forms of public and private sector surveillance of women's intimate activities and reproductive choices emerging to enforce and police the criminal abortion bans and restrictions automatically triggered by the decision or since passed across the US – all with powerful chilling effects.[5]

Put in Polanyian terms, how can a "protective" counter-movement in law and policy be sustained over the long term; one that addresses the dangers of chilling effects today and tomorrow?[6] Most importantly, we need what Ron Deibert calls a "reset"; a pause to collectively engage in a deeper rethinking of our broader communications and technological ecosystem,[7] including new ways of thinking and talking about chilling effects and the dangers and threats they pose. My new theory of chilling effects provides a foundation for doing so. Furthermore, chilling effects theory and research should no longer be considered simply a legal or privacy idea or doctrine; but a new and distinct field of study that will help us chart a path forward to address critical threats to freedom and democracy. And while there is a growing body of theoretical and empirical work in this new field, there is still plenty of work to be done. We still need new scholarship, research, and innovative research designs to explore chilling effects more fully and comprehensively, including factors that both contribute to and mitigate chill; how best to predict them and build resilience in groups and communities; and their implications for law and public policy. For instance, in a 2025 article, my co-authors Citron, Shore Ingber, and I published one of the first studies documenting the chilling effects of new abortion restrictions and intimate surveillance post-*Dobbs* on women's privacy and autonomy. Like the Snowden revelations, the *Dobbs* decision presents a unique opportunity to understand the impact of surveillance and overreaching abortion regulatory regimes before and after women's constitutional right to abortion was eviscerated. We also need far more research on how more discrete, insular, and marginalized populations are affected by chilling effects, and further research on the impact of chilling effects on civil liberties at larger scales – especially with the role of emerging technologies like AI and automation.[8]

Yet even that is not enough. We need, as Waldman has called for, new strategies that are expressly designed to counter power and to promote both equality and more robust democratic accountability and control.[9] I agree, and a conformity theory of chilling effects can help contribute to such a movement and broader projects for reform based on it. Indeed, power and authority are central to our new theory and understanding of chilling effects. They are one of the four central factors in chilling effects – with state and corporate actors with more power and authority having greater impact. You thus cannot theorize, predict, or analyze chilling effects without considering power. When it came to conventional theories, power and authority were more of an afterthought – and that is why such approaches helped perpetuate state and corporate power. For instance, conventional thinking often missed how chilling effects are weaponized to repress and control and how they produce conforming speech, behavior, and norms that sustain broader systems of political, social, and economic power. Not only that, but the predominant conventional theory of chilling effects, with its narrow and legalistic focus, has more often than not been misappropriated by corporate interests to legally and constitutionally challenge laws and regulations that constrain their activities – typically with claims being that such laws illegally chill expression or stifle innovation.[10] Such uses and abuses of chilling effects should be far more difficult under our new understanding.

A conformity theory can also help ensure democracy is more robust and resilient, by making clear the threats and dangers that chilling effects pose. It reveals how chilling effects have both repressive and productive dimensions, which when understood together, provide a far more accurate picture as to the urgent threat they pose to democratic societies, by undermining participatory and deliberative democracy; producing conformity and suppressing dissent at societal scale; and fomenting extremism and polarization. At the same time, chilling effects suppress and weaken practices and institutions of accountability, like activism and journalism. And the reforms that I have advanced all aim to increase democratic control and accountability, especially in the information economy. This new understanding of chilling effects also promotes equality by focusing on the experience of minority and marginalized groups, and harms they suffer, and how political and economic systems perpetuate inequalities by, for example, silencing and stigmatizing the voices of women, minority groups, and dissidents.[11] Certainly, a conformity theory would contribute here too. Chapter 7 discussed how chilling effects have been weaponized by state and corporate actors throughout history to repress, silence, and control disfavored (often minority) groups. And in Chapter 6, I talked about how chilling effects reproduce and sustain inequalities with disproportionate impacts on women, minority groups, and other marginalized communities; and by perpetuating and entrenching harmful behavioral and systemic norms, by producing conforming behavior that resists challenges to those inequalities. By foregrounding these insights about chilling effects, we better understand how systems, and their biases and inequalities, persist.

Lastly, we need to be creative about policy solutions that go beyond mere law and policy – to shaping broader behavioral, social, and cultural norms. Lawyers and legal scholars have arguably focused too heavily on these regulatory dimensions of law when it comes to privacy and chilling effects.[12] A conformity theory places norms at the center of our understanding of chilling effects, thus highlighting another powerful and important role for law here – its expressive function in shifting social norms over time. It can regulate and restrict surveillance and other data practices, but it can also impact social norms over time, leading to shifts in attitudes. Expressive law theorists argue that the law can shape legal behavior by impacting social norms and changing the social meaning of behavior. Social norms are not universal behavioral norms or practices, but often tied to specific social and cultural contexts, so social norms will vary across cultures. So, conformity to social norms will lead to different sorts of behavior – or chilling effects – depending on the broader social and cultural context. Furthermore, research shows that social norms, including ones that people do not necessarily even believe or accept as proper or moral, can nevertheless be difficult to change once entrenched, with some having influence across multiple generations, through inter-generational transmission and social learning. This entrenching process is fed by chilling effects, as clear from research on the "spiral of silence," as conformity breeds silence, it also helps entrench speech, views, or norms that may not reflect those of the broader democratic majority.

But social norms can and do shift over time, due to different cultural influences. In fact, among the most powerful sources for social norms change is the law, as it reflects widely accepted social norms that influence people's law-related behavior over time. As such, it can be a powerful and persuasive force for the development of more positive social norms. Law via this expressive function also impacts behavior. For example, Citron and I have previously demonstrated how the expressive power of anti-abuse laws – like a statute imposing serious penalties for cyber-harassment – can have salutary effects on victims – essentially reducing the chilling effects of online abuse.[13]

The point is this: Law has a multidimensional role in addressing chilling effects and mitigating their impacts over the long term. Beyond regulation and other more conventional applications – which are indispensable – law also can play a key role in shifting norms, helping break harmful inter-generational cultural practices that chilling effects help entrench. This is the path to a far less chilling and more promising future.

Notes

INTRODUCTION

1. Sarah Ellison, *Mahmoud Khalil's Arrest Violates First Amendment Protections, Lawyers Say*, WASHINGTON POST (Mar. 13, 2025), www.washingtonpost.com/politics/2025/03/13/khalil-columbia-trump-arrest-anti-semitism/.

2. April Rubin, *Marjorie Taylor Greene Calls for Probe into Tesla Attacks*, AXIOS (Mar. 12, 2025), www.axios.com/2025/03/12/tesla-attacks-elon-musk-marjorie-taylor-greene; Cristian Farias, *Elon Musk's Shadow Government Is on Shaky Legal Ground*, VANITY FAIR (Mar. 5, 2025), www.vanityfair.com/news/story/elon-musk-supreme-court-donald-trump.

3. Spencer S. Hsu & Patrick Marley, *US Attorney Hints at Prosecutions over "Targeting" of DOGE Employee*, WASHINGTON POST (Feb. 3, 2025), www.washingtonpost.com/dc-md-va/2025/02/03/martin-supports-for-musk-doge/; Ryan Bort, *DOGE Staffers Resign, Refusing to "Dismantle Critical Public Services,"* ROLLING STONE (Feb. 25, 2025), www.rollingstone.com/politics/politics-news/doge-staffers-resign-dismantle-critical-public-services-1235279584/.

4. Joseph Cox, *The 200+ Sites an ICE Surveillance Contractor Is Monitoring*, 404 MEDIA (Mar. 12, 2025), www.404media.co/the-200-sites-an-ice-surveillance-contractor-is-monitoring/.

5. Queenie Wong, *Social Media Platforms Engaged in "Vast Surveillance" and Failed to Protect Young People, FTC Finds*, LOS ANGELES TIMES (Sep. 19, 2024), www.latimes.com/business/story/2024-09-19/social-media-platforms-engaged-in-vast-surveillance-and-failed-to-protect-young-people-ftc-finds.

6. Shannon Bond & Bobby Allen, *2 Years In, Trump Surrogate Elon Musk Has Remade X as a Conservative Megaphone*, NATIONAL PUBLIC RADIO (Oct. 25, 2024), www.npr.org/2024/10/22/nx-s1-5156184/elon-musk-trump-election-x-twitter.

7. The chilling effect of each of these activities has been reported on: Lydia Polgreen, *Opinion: The Chilling Effect at Columbia Goes Far beyond One Student*, SALT LAKE TRIBUNE (Mar. 12, 2025), www.sltrib.com/opinion/commentary/2025/03/12/opinion-chilling-effect-columbia/; Ellison, *Mahmoud Khalil's Arrest Violates First Amendment Protections, Lawyers Say, supra*; Hsu & Marley, *US Attorney Hints at Prosecutions over "Targeting" of DOGE Employee, supra*; Lauren Egan, *Democrats Want to Break Elon Musk by Making Him Poorer*, THE BULWARK (Mar. 12, 2025), www.thebulwark.com/p/democrats-want-to-break-elon-by-making (noting the chill of Tesla protest prosecutions and Trump's plan to label them "domestic terrorism"); Joseph Cox, *Inside ShadowDragon, the Tool That Lets ICE Monitor Pregnancy Tracking Sites and Fortnite Players*, 404 MEDIA (Sep. 18, 2023), www.404media.co/inside-shadowdragon-ice-babycenter-pregnancy-fortnite-black-planet/ (speaking to the chilling effects of the US

Immigration and Customs Enforcement's surveillance activities); Brian Joseph, *Musk versus Media Matters: Free Speech on the Line*, Non-Profit Quarterly (Jan. 21, 2025), https://nonprofitquarterly.org/musk-versus-media-matters-free-speech-on-the-line/; James Evelegh, *The Chilling Effect of Online Abuse*, InPublishing (July 8, 2023), www.inpublishing.co.uk/articles/the-chilling-effect-of-online-abuse-22171.

8. In 1946, an intelligence-sharing alliance was formed between five English-speaking countries and their national security agencies: the US (NSA), the UK (Government Communications Headquarters), Australia (Australian Signals Directorate), Canada (Communications Security Establishment Canada), and New Zealand (Government Communications Security Bureau). These countries constitute the "Five Eyes" Alliance: Patrick Walsh & Seumas Miller, *Rethinking "Five Eyes" Security Intelligence Collection Policies and Practice Post Snowden*, 31(3) Intelligence and National Security 345 (2016); Julian Borger, *NSA Files: What's a Little Spying between Old Friends?*, Guardian (Dec. 2, 2013), www.theguardian.com/world/2013/dec/02/nsa-files-spying-allies-enemies-five-eyes-g8.

9. Barton Gellman & Laura Poitras, *US, British Intelligence Mining Data from Nine US Internet Companies in Broad Secret Program*, Washington Post (June 6, 2013), www.washingtonpost.com/investigations/us-intelligence-mining-data-from-nine-us-internet-companies-in-broad-secret-program/2013/06/06/3a0coda8-cebf-11e2-8845-d970ccb04497_story.html. See also Ronald J. Deibert, Reset: Reclaiming the Internet for Civil Society 38–39 (2020).

10. See Glenn Greenwald, *XKeyscore: NSA Tool Collects "Nearly Everything a User Does on the Internet,"* Guardian (July 31, 2013), www.theguardian.com/world/2013/jul/31/nsa-top-secret-program-online-data; Radhamely De Leon, *XKEYSCORE Spy Program Revealed by Snowden Still a Problem*, Vice (July 1, 2022), www.vice.com/en/article/xkeyscore-spy-program-revealed-by-snowden-is-still-a-problem-watchdog-says/.

11. See Nick Perry & Paisley Dodds, *Five Eyes Spying Alliance Will Survive Edward Snowden: Experts*, The Sydney Morning Herald (July 18, 2013); Corey Pfluke, *A History of the Five Eyes Alliance: Possibility for Reform and Additions*, 38(4) Comparative Strategy 302, 306–307 (2019).

12. George Orwell, Animal Fall, Burmese Days, A Clergyman's Daughter, Coming Up for Air, Keeping the Aspidistra Flying, Nineteen Eighty-Four (Complete and Unabridged) (1949).

13. Aldous Huxley, Brave New World (1932).

14. Deibert, Reset: Reclaiming the Internet for Civil Society, *supra*, at 39–40.

15. Jonathon W. Penney, *Chilling Effects: Online Surveillance and Wikipedia Use*, 31 Berkeley Tech. L. J. 117, 137–138, 149–150 (2016).

16. Penney, *Chilling Effects: Online Surveillance and Wikipedia Use, supra*.

17. The term "pro bono" is short for the Latin term *pro bono public* ("for the good of the public"). In this context, it means I did not receive any compensation for my work as an expert in the litigation.

18. Jimmy Wales & Lila Tretikov, Opinion, *Stop Spying on Wikipedia Users*, N.Y. Times (Mar. 10, 2015), www.nytimes.com/2015/03/10/opinion/stop-spying-on-wikipedia-users.html.

19. Carole Cadwalladr & Emma Graham-Harrison, *Revealed: 50 Million Facebook Profiles Harvested for Cambridge Analytica in Major Data Breach*, The Guardian (Mar. 17, 2018), www.theguardian.com/news/2018/mar/17/cambridge-analytica-facebook-influence-us-election; Cecilia Kang & Sheera Frenkel, *Facebook Says Cambridge Analytica Harvested Data of up to 87 Million Users*, N.Y. Times (Apr. 4, 2018), www.nytimes.com/2018/04/04/technology/mark-zuckerberg-testify-congress.html; Nathaniel Fruchter,

Michael Specter, & Ben Yuan, *Facebook/Cambridge Analytica: Privacy Lessons and a Way Forward*, MIT Internet Policy Research Initiative (Mar. 20, 2018), https://internetpolicy.mit.edu/blog-2018-fb-cambridgeanalytica/; Julie Beck, *People Are Changing the Way They Use Social Media*, The Atlantic (June 7, 2018), www .theatlantic.com/technology/archive/2018/06/did-cambridge-analytica-actually-change-facebook-users-behavior/562154/; Margaret Hu, *Cambridge Analytica's Blackbox*, 7(2) Big Data & Soc'y 1 (2020).

20. Beck, *People Are Changing the Way They Use Social Media, supra*.

21. Beck, *People Are Changing the Way They Use Social Media, supra*.

22. Kashmir Hill, *The Secretive Company That Might End Privacy as We Know It*, N.Y. Times (Jan. 18, 2020), www.nytimes.com/2020/01/18/technology/clearview-privacy-facial-recognition.html; Jonathan Zittrain & John Bowers, *A Start-Up Is Using Photos to ID You. Big Tech Can Stop It from Happening Again*, Washington Post (Apr. 14, 2020), www.washingtonpost.com/outlook/2020/04/14/tech-start-up-is-using-photos-id-you-big-tech-could-have-stopped-them/; see also generally: Kashmir Hill, Your Face Belongs to Us: A Secretive StartUp's Quest to End Privacy as We Know It (2023).

23. Kashmir Hill, *My Chilling Run-In with a Secretive Facial-Recognition App*, The Telegraph (Sep. 27, 2023), www.telegraph.co.uk/books/non-fiction/clearview-ai-facial-recognition-app-chilling/. See also generally: Hill, Your Face Belongs to Us: A Secretive StartUp's Quest to End Privacy as We Know It, *supra*, at xi–x.

24. Hill, *My Chilling Run-In with a Secretive Facial-Recognition App, supra*; Katherine Tangalakis-Lippert, *Clearview AI Scraped 30 Billion Images from Facebook and Other Social Media Sites and Gave Them to Cops: It Puts Everyone into a "Perpetual Police Line-Up"*, Business Insider (Apr. 3, 2023), www.businessinsider.com/clearview-scraped-30-billion-images-facebook-police-facial-recogntion-database-2023-4; Hill, Your Face Belongs to Us: A Secretive StartUp's Quest to End Privacy as We Know It, *supra*, at 130–139.

25. Hill, *My Chilling Run-In with a Secretive Facial-Recognition App, supra*.

26. Kashmir Hill, *Clearview AI Used Your Face. Now You May Get a Stake in the Company*, N. Y. Times (June 13, 2024), www.nytimes.com/2024/06/13/business/clearview-ai-facial-recognition-settlement.html.

27. Adrienne Greene, *The Room Where It Happened*, New York Magazine (May 21, 2021), https://nymag.com/intelligencer/2021/05/derrick-ingram-nypd-standoff.html; James Vincent, *NYPD Used Facial Recognition to Track Down Black Lives Matter Activist*, The Verge (Aug. 18, 2020), www.theverge.com/2020/8/18/21373316/nypd-facial-recognition-black-lives-matter-activist-derrick-ingram; Daniela Barreto & Serisha Iyar, *Facial Recognition and Police Protests*, Rights Back at You Amnesty International Podcast (Feb. 9, 2023), https://amnesty.ca/podcast-facial-recognition-and-policing-protesters/.

28. Greene, *The Room Where It Happened, supra*.

29. Vincent, *NYPD Used Facial Recognition to Track Down Black Lives Matter Activist, supra*.

30. Vincent, *NYPD Used Facial Recognition to Track Down Black Lives Matter Activist, supra*.

31. Vincent, *NYPD Used Facial Recognition to Track Down Black Lives Matter Activist, supra*.

32. Barreto & Iyar, *Facial Recognition and Police Protests, supra*.

33. Greene, *The Room Where It Happened, supra*.

34. Greene, *The Room Where It Happened, supra*.

35. Druv Mehrota & Jesse Marx, *The Age of the Drone Police Is Here*, WIRED (June 5, 2024), www.wired.com/story/the-age-of-the-drone-police-is-here/; Druv Mehrota & Jesse Marx, *Inside the City Policed by Machines*, WIRED (June 6, 2024), www.wired.com/story/inside-the-city-policed-by-machines/.

36. Mehrota & Marx, *The Age of the Drone Police Is Here*, supra; Mehrota & Marx, *Inside the City Policed by Machines*, supra.

37. Mehrota & Marx, *Inside the City Policed by Machines*, supra.

38. Mehrota & Marx, *Inside the City Policed by Machines*, supra.

39. Mehrota & Marx, *The Age of the Drone Police Is Here*, supra; Mehrota & Marx, *Inside the City Policed by Machines*, supra.

40. Mehrota & Marx, *The Age of the Drone Police Is Here*, supra; Mehrota & Marx, *Inside the City Policed by Machines*, supra.

41. Mehrota & Marx, *Inside the City Policed by Machines*, supra.

42. Danielle Keats Citron, The Fight for Privacy: Protecting Dignity, Identity, and Love in the Digital Age xvi (2022).

43. Laura Macomber, *Writers and Online Harassment: Evidence of a Chilling Effect*, Pen America (Apr. 20, 2018), https://pen.org/writers-and-online-harassment-evidence-of-a-chilling-effect/.

44. Macomber, *Writers and Online Harassment: Evidence of a Chilling Effect*, supra.

45. Macomber, *Writers and Online Harassment: Evidence of a Chilling Effect*, supra.

46. Macomber, *Writers and Online Harassment: Evidence of a Chilling Effect*, supra.

47. Macomber, *Writers and Online Harassment: Evidence of a Chilling Effect*, supra.

48. Charles W. Rhodes & Howard M. Wasserman, *Solving the Procedural Puzzles of the Texas Heartbeat Act and Its Imitators: The Potential for Defensive Litigation*, 75 SMU L. Rev. 187 (2022).

49. Patrick Petit, *"Everywhere Surveillance": Global Surveillance Regimes as Techno-Securitization*, 29(1) Sci. Cult. 30 (2020); Mark Scott, *Welcome to New Era of Global Digital Censorship: It's Dangerous to Ask Tech Companies to Decide What's Legitimate Free Speech*, Politico (Jan. 14, 2018), www.politico.eu/article/google-facebook-twitter-censorship-europe-commission-hate-speech-propaganda-terrorist/.

50. Volker Boehme-Neßler, *Privacy: A Matter of Democracy. Why Democracy Needs Privacy and Data Protection*, 6 International Data Privacy Law 222, 222 (2016); Christopher Kuner, Transborder Data Flow Regulation and Data Privacy Law 4ff (2013).

51. Seref Sagiroglu & Duygu Sinanc, *Big Data: A Review*, in 2013 International Conference on Collaboration Technologies and Systems (CTS) 42–47 (IEEE, 2013); Reihaneh H. Hariri, Erik M. Fredericks, & Kate M. Bowers, *Uncertainty in Big Data Analytics: Survey, Opportunities, and Challenges*, 6(1) J Big Data 1–16 (2019); Andrew McAfee & Erik Brynjolfsson, *Big Data: The Management Revolution*, Harv. Bus. Rev. 1 (Oct. 2012), https://hbr.org/2012/10/big-data-the-management-revolution.

52. Sagiroglu & Sinanc, *Big Data: A Review*, supra, at 42; Hariri et al., *Uncertainty in Big Data Analytics: Survey, Opportunities, and Challenges*, supra, at 1.

53. Sagiroglu & Sinanc, *Big Data: A Review*, supra, at 42; Hariri et al., *Uncertainty in Big Data Analytics: Survey, Opportunities, and Challenges*, supra, at 1.

54. Sagiroglu & Sinanc, *Big Data: A Review*, supra, at 45; Hariri et al., *Uncertainty in Big Data Analytics: Survey, Opportunities, and Challenges*, supra, at 8–13; Ike Kavas, *AI and Data Mining: Do You Have the Keys to the Castle?*, Forbes (July 26, 2022), www.forbes.com/sites/forbestechcouncil/2022/07/26/ai-and-data-mining-do-you-have-the-keys-to-the-castle/?sh=671af50f5cc5. See also Daniel T. Larose & Chantal D. Larose, Discovering Knowledge in Data: An Introduction to Data Mining (2014); David J. Hand, *Principles of Data Mining*, 30(7) Drug Saf. 621 (2007).

55. Damir Mujezinovic, *Google's AI and Deep Learning Researcher Warns about AI-Fueled "Mass Population Control*," INQUISITR (Mar. 22, 2019), www.inquisitr.com/opinion/4836851/googles-ai-and-deep-learning-researcher-warns-about-ai-fueled-mass-population-control/; Mind Matters, *AI Social Media Could Totally Manipulate You*, AI MIND MATTERS (Nov. 28, 2018), https://mindmatters.ai/2018/11/ai-social-media-could-totally-manipulate-you/; Darrell West & John Allen, *How Artificial Intelligence Is Transforming the World*, BROOKINGS INSTITUTE REPORT (Apr. 24, 2018), www.brookings.edu/research/how-artificial-intelligence-is-transforming-the-world/.

56. Woodrow Hartzog, Gregory Conti, John Nelson, & Lisa Shay, *Inefficiently Automated Law Enforcement*, MICH. ST. L. REV. 1763, 1763 (2015) ("[T]he automation of law enforcement is already here"); Frank Pasquale & Glyn Cashwell, *Four Futures of Legal Automation*, 63 UCLA L. REV. DISC. 26, 36, 39 (2015); Lisa Shay, Woodrow Hartzog, John Nelson, Dominic Larkin, & Gregory Conti, *Confronting Automated Law Enforcement, in* ROBOT LAW 235, 235 (Ryan Calo, Michael Froomkin, & Ian Kerr, eds., 2016).

57. SHOSHANA ZUBOFF, THE AGE OF SURVEILLANCE CAPITALISM: THE FIGHT FOR A HUMAN FUTURE AT THE NEW FRONTIER OF POWER (2019). See also JULIE COHEN, BETWEEN TRUTH AND POWER: THE LEGAL CONSTRUCTIONS OF INFORMATIONAL CAPITALISM (2019); Amy Kapczynski, *The Law of Information Capitalism*, 129 YALE L.J. 1276 (2020).

58. CITRON, THE FIGHT FOR PRIVACY: PROTECTING DIGNITY, IDENTITY, AND LOVE IN THE DIGITAL AGE, *supra*, at 1–23, 34–35, 54; Danielle Keats Citron, *Intimate Privacy in a Post-Roe World*, 75 FLA. L. REV. 1033, 1054–1058 (2023).

59. See for example: Richard Jones, *Visual Surveillance Technologies, in* THE ROUTLEDGE HANDBOOK OF TECHNOLOGY, CRIME, AND JUSTICE 436, 446–447 (Michael R. McGuire & Thomas J. Holt, eds., 2017) (discussing the potential "chilling effects" of new forms of visual surveillance technologies); Shay et al., *Confronting Automated Law Enforcement, supra*, at 30 (noting chilling effects likely caused by automated legal systems); Hartzog et al., *Inefficiently Automated Law Enforcement, supra*, at 1765.

60. Judith Townend, *Online Chilling Effects in England and Wales*, INTERNET POLICY (Apr. 3, 2014) at 1.

61. Robert Chesney, *COVID-19 Contact Tracing We Can Live With: A Roadmap and Recommendations*, LAWFARE BLOG (Apr. 14, 2020), www.lawfareblog.com/covid-19-contact-tracing-we-can-live-roadmap-and-recommendations; George Letsas & Virginia Mantouvalou, *COVID-19 and Free Speech: "Gagging" NHS Staff Is Not Proportionate and Lawful*, LSE BLOG (Apr. 14, 2020), https://blogs.lse.ac.uk/politicsandpolicy/covid-19-and-free-speech/. On concerns about the chilling effects of post-*Dobbs* privacy and legal threats, see: Jonathon W. Penney, Danielle Keats Citron, & Alexis Shore Ingber, *The Chilling Effects of Dobbs*, 77(2) FLORIDA L. REV. 357 (2025).

62. DEIBERT, RESET: RECLAIMING THE INTERNET FOR CIVIL SOCIETY, *supra*, at 136–172; RON DEIBERT, BLACK CODE: INSIDE THE BATTLE FOR CYBERSPACE 91, 96–98 (2013); Noura Al-Jizawi, Siena Antis, Sharly Chan, Adam Senft, & Ronald J. Deibert, *Digital transnational repression*, CITIZEN LAB REPORT (2020).

63. Pete Muselin, *The Steel Fist in a Pennsylvania Company Town, in* IT DID HAPPEN HERE: RECOLLECTIONS OF POLITICAL REPRESSION IN AMERICA 65, 65 (Bud Schultz & Ruth Schultz, eds., 1989); LAWRENCE CAPPELLO, NONE OF YOUR DAMN BUSINESS: PRIVACY IN THE UNITED STATES FROM THE GILDED AGE TO THE DIGITAL AGE 81–82 (2019).

64. CAPPELLO, NONE OF YOUR DAMN BUSINESS: PRIVACY IN THE UNITED STATES FROM THE GILDED AGE TO THE DIGITAL AGE, *supra*, at 110–111, 121. See also ELLEN SCHRECKER, THE AGE OF MCCARTHYISM: A BRIEF HISTORY WITH DOCUMENTS 83–84 (2nd ed., 2002).

65. Cappello, None of Your Damn Business: Privacy in the United States from the Gilded Age to the Digital Age, *supra*, at 121.

66. See generally Lawrence Soley, Censorship, Inc.: The Corporate Threat to Free Speech in the United States (2002). See also David L. Hudson Jr., *Anti-SLAPP Coverage and the First Amendment: Hurdles to Defamation Suits in Political Campaigns*, 69 Am. Univ. Law Rev. 1541 (2020); Laura Lee Prather, *SLAPP Suits: An Encroachment on Human Rights of a Global Proportion and What Can Be Done About It*, 22 NW. J. Hum. Rts. 49 (2023).

67. Hudson Jr., *Anti-SLAPP Coverage and the First Amendment: Hurdles to Defamation Suits in Political Campaigns*, *supra*, at 1542–1543; Prather, *SLAPP Suits: An Encroachment on Human Rights of a Global Proportion and What Can Be Done about It*, *supra*, at 53.

68. Prather, *SLAPP Suits: An Encroachment on Human Rights of a Global Proportion and What Can Be Done about It*, *supra*, at 49, 53–54; Rebecca Bonello Ghio et al., *Shutting Out Criticism: How SLAPPs Threaten European Democracy*, The Coalition against SLAPPS in Europe 2 (Mar. 2022), www.the-case.eu/wp-content/uploads/2023/04/CASEreportSLAPPsEurope.pdf; Business and Human Rights Resource Center, *SLAPPed but Not Silenced: Defending Human Rights in the Face of Legal Risks*, Business and Human Rights Resource Center Brief (June 2021), https://media.business-humanrights.org/media/documents/2021_SLAPPs_Briefing_EN_v657.pdf.

69. Selda Ulucanlar et al., *Corporate Political Activity: Taxonomies and Model of Corporate Influence on Public Policy*, 12 Int. J. Health Policy Manag. 1, 12 (2023).

70. Steve Morgan, Morris Barer, & Robert Evans, *Health Economists Meet the Fourth Tempter: Drug Dependency and Scientific Discourse*, 9(8) Health Econ. 659, 662 (2000).

71. Cappello, None of Your Damn Business: Privacy in the United States from the Gilded Age to the Digital Age, *supra*, at 121; Schrecker, The Age of McCarthyism: A Brief History with Documents, *supra*, at 106.

72. See generally Eleanor J. Bader, Patricia Baird-Windle, Targets of Hatred: Anti-Abortion Terrorism (2001); Meera Jagannathan, *"Companies Can No Longer Look the Other Way,"* MarketWatch (Feb. 23, 2022), www.marketwatch.com/story/companies-can-no-longer-look-the-other-way-is-it-time-for-corporate-america-to-throw-down-the-gauntlet-on-abortion-11645022034.

73. Bruce Schneier, Data and Goliath: The Hidden Battles to Collect Your Data and Control Your World 222 (2015).

74. Taylor Owen, *On the Coming Merger of Tech and State Power*, Tech Policy Press (Nov. 26, 2024), www.techpolicy.press/on-the-coming-merger-of-tech-and-state-power/.

75. Maggie Quinlan, *Architect of "Bounty-Hunter" Abortion Ban Wants List of Abortion Seekers*, The Austin Chronicle (Sep. 29, 2023), www.austinchronicle.com/daily/news/2023-09-29/architect-of-bounty-hunter-abortion-ban-wants-list-of-abortion-seekers/; Chrissy Stroop, *The US's Anti-drag Movement Is State-Sponsored LGBTIQ Persecution*, Open Democracy (Mar. 29, 2023), www.opendemocracy.net/en/5050/tennesse-drag-law-is-anti-lgbtq-people/; Priya Krishnakumar, *This Record-Breaking Year for Anti-transgender Legislation Would Affect Minors the Most*, CNN News (Apr. 15, 2021), https://edition.cnn.com/2021/04/15/politics/anti-transgender-legislation-2021/index.html; Silvia Blanco & Andrea Garcia-Baroja, *The Worldwide Offensive against the Rights of LGBTQ+ People*, El Pais (June 28, 2023), https://english.elpais.com/international/2023-06-28/the-worldwide-offensive-against-the-rights-of-lgbtq-people.html.

76. Nick Robins-Early, *Amazon and Google Fund Anti-abortion Lawmakers through Complex Shell Game*, THE GUARDIAN (June 3, 2023), www.theguardian.com/world/2023/jun/03/anti-abortion-lawmakers-donation-amazon-google-comcast.

77. Taylor Lorenz, *Meet the Woman behind Libs of TikTok, Secretly Fueling the Right's Outrage Machine*, WASHINGTON POST (Apr. 19, 2022), www.washingtonpost.com/technology/2022/04/19/libs-of-tiktok-right-wing-media/; Christopher Wiggins, *Libs of TikTok Mocks Pregnant Trans Man's Murder*, THE ADVOCATE (July 27, 2023), www.advocate.com/media/chaya-raichik-mocks-pregnant-death; Elad Nehorai, *Libs of TikTok is Fueling a Pogrom against Trans Youth*, FORWARD (Aug. 29, 2022), https://forward.com/opinion/515868/libs-of-tiktok-is-fueling-a-pogrom-against-trans-youth/. See also CITRON, THE FIGHT FOR PRIVACY: PROTECTING DIGNITY, IDENTITY, AND LOVE IN THE DIGITAL AGE, *supra*, at 54; Danielle Keats Citron, *Cyber Mobs, Disinformation, and Death Videos: The Internet as It Is (and as It Should Be)*, 118 MICH. L. REV. 1073, 1088–1090 (2020).

78. Jonathon W. Penney, *Understanding Chilling Effects*, 106 MINN. L. REV. 1451, 1459–1460 (2022); Penney, *Chilling Effects: Online Surveillance and Wikipedia Use*, *supra*, at 120–121, 125–126 (describing skepticism as to the impact of chilling effects). See also David Alan Sklansky, *Too Much Information: How Not to Think about Privacy and the Fourth Amendment*, 102 CAL. L. REV. 1069, 1094–1100 (2014) (finding little empirical support for surveillance chilling effects); Jeff De Mot & Michael Faure, *Public Authority Liability and the Chilling Effect*, 22 TORT. L. REV. 120, 121 (2014) ("the existence of chilling effects is not universally accepted … current empirical literature does not seem to pinpoint which side has the strongest case").

79. The US Supreme Court, for instance, has employed technical standing rules to dismiss chilling effect claims based on privacy threats. See: Penney, *Understanding Chilling Effects, supra*, at 1459–1460; Penney, *Chilling Effects: Online Surveillance and Wikipedia Use, supra*, at 120–121. See also Margot E. Kaminski & Shane Witnov, *The Conforming Effect: First Amendment Implications of Surveillance, beyond Chilling Speech*, 49 U. RICH. L. REV. 465, 482 (2015).

80. Clapper v. Amnesty Int'l, 133 S. Ct. 1138, 1152–1153 (2013).

81. 600 U.S. 66 (2023).

82. 600 U.S. 66 (2023); Danielle Keats Citron, *From Bad to Worse: Stalking, Threats, and Chilling Effects*, 2023(1) SUPREME COURT REV. 175–212 (2024); Penney et al., *The Chilling Effects of Dobbs, supra*.

83. 11 F.4th 276 (4th Cir. 2021) (hereinafter "Wikimedia 2021"). See also Wikimedia Found. v. Nat'l Sec. Agency/Cent. Sec. Serv., 857 F.3d 193, 200–07 (4th Cir. 2017) (hereinafter "Wikimedia 2017").

84. Penney, *Understanding Chilling Effects, supra*, at 1454–1455; Penney et al., *The Chilling Effects of Dobbs, supra*; Leslie Kendrick, *Speech, Intent, and the Chilling Effect*, 54 WM. MARY L. REV. 1633, 1649, n.74 (2013).

85. Penney, *Understanding Chilling Effects, supra*, at 1454–1455; Penney, *Chilling Effects: Online Surveillance and Wikipedia Use, supra*, at 120–121; Penney et al., *The Chilling Effects of Dobbs, supra*.

86. Schauer's 1978 article was the earliest in-depth discussion of chilling effects and the theory underlying it: Frederick Schauer, *Fear, Risk, and the First Amendment: Unraveling the Chilling Effect*, 58 B.U. L. REV. 685 (1978). See also Kendrick, *Speech, Intent, and the Chilling Effect, supra* (reviewing literature on chilling effects in relation to First Amendment doctrine). On its prominence, see for example: Julie Cohen, *A Right to Read Anonymously: A Closer Look at "Copyright Management" in Cyberspace*, 28

CONN. L. REV. 981, 1011 n.117 (1996) (suggesting Schauer's work was the "definitive treatment"); Penney, *Understanding Chilling Effects, supra,* at 1465–1468 (describing the conventional understanding of chilling effects in law and its influence among lawyers, judges, and legal scholars).

87. Margot E. Kaminski, *Standing after Snowden: Lessons on Privacy Harm from National Security Surveillance Litigation,* 66 DEPAUL L. REV. 413, 425 (2017).

88. Julie E. Cohen, *Studying Law Studying Surveillance,* 13 SURVEILLANCE & SOCIETY 91, 92 (2015); Julie E. Cohen, *Surveillance vs. Privacy: Effects and Implications, in* THE CAMBRIDGE HANDBOOK OF SURVEILLANCE LAW 455–469 (David Gray & Stephen E. Henderson, eds., 2017); Julie E. Cohen, *What Privacy Is for,* 126 HARV. L. REV. 1904, 1917 (2013) quoting: Mark Andrejevic, *Exploitation in the Data Mine, in* INTERNET AND SURVEILLANCE: THE CHALLENGES OF WEB 2.0 AND SOCIAL MEDIA I 71–73 (Christian Fuchs et al., eds., 2012). See also Julie E. Cohen, *Examined Lives: Informational Privacy and the Subject as Object,* 52 STAN. L. REV. 1373 (2000).

89. See for example: Jonathon W. Penney, *Internet Surveillance, Regulation, and Chilling Effects Online: A Comparative Case Study,* 6(2) INTERNET POLICY REV. 1 (2017) (empirical study finding chilling effects on a range of typical online activities due to both government as well as private sector online surveillance); Penney, *Chilling Effects: Online Surveillance and Wikipedia Use, supra* (finding chilling effects on Wikipedia use due to NSA surveillance); Alex Marthews & Catherine Tucker, *Government Surveillance and Internet Search Behavior, in* CAMBRIDGE UNIVERSITY HANDBOOK ON SURVEILLANCE LAW (David Gray et al., eds., 2017) (finding chilling effects on Google search users due to NSA surveillance); Elizabeth Stoycheff, *Under Surveillance: Examining Facebook's Spiral of Silence Effects in the Wake of NSA Internet Monitoring,* 93(2) JOURNAL. MASS COMMUN. 296 (2016) (experimental study finding chilling effects due to government surveillance on political speech and social media engagement); Elizabeth Stoycheff et al., *Privacy and the Panopticon: Online Mass Surveillance's Deterrence and Chilling Effects,* 21(3) NEW MEDIA SOC. 602 (2019) (experimental study finding an online government surveillance chilled behavioral intentions).

90. See for example: Penney, *Internet Surveillance, Regulation, and Chilling Effects Online: A Comparative Case Study, supra* (finding private sector internet surveillance chilling a range of internet user behavior); Nik Williams, David McMenemy, & Lauren Smith, *Scottish Chilling: Impact of Government and Corporate Surveillance on Writers,* SCOTTISH PEN REPORT (Dec. 6, 2018), https://strathprints.strath.ac.uk/66291/.

91. An innovative body of research has explored the chilling effects associated with "dataveillance," that is, data surveillance in communications scholarship, and algorithmic profiling. See for example: FREDERIK ZUIDERVEEN BORGESIUS, IMPROVING PRIVACY PROTECTION IN THE AREA OF BEHAVIOURAL TARGETING (2015) (arguing, among other things, that chilling effects is a central behavioral response to online data collection, tracking, and behavioral advertising); Moritz Büchi et al., *The Chilling Effects of Algorithmic Profiling: Mapping the Issues,* 36 COMPUT. LAW & SEC. REV. 1 (2020); Moritz Büchi, Noemi Festic, & Michael Latzer, *The Chilling Effects of Digital Dataveillance: A Theoretical Model and an Empirical Research Agenda,* 9 BIG DATA & SOC'Y 1 (2022); Rita Raley, *Dataveillance and Countervailance, in* "RAW DATA" IS AN OXYMORON 121, 123–124 (Lisa Gitelman, ed., 2013); Kiran Kappeler, Noemi Festic, & Michael Latzer, *Qualitative Evidence of Chilling Effects – How Users Imaginaries of Dataveillance Lead to Inhibited Digital Behavior,* THE 23RD ANNUAL CONFERENCE OF THE ASSOCIATION OF INTERNET RESEARCHERS (AOIR), Dublin, Ireland (Nov. 2–5, 2022); Joanna Strycharz & Claire M. Segijn, *The Future of Dataveillance in Advertising*

Theory and Practice, 51(5) J. ADVERT. 574 (2022); Joanna Strycharz & Claire M. Segijn, *Consumer Differences in Chilling Effects, in* ADVANCES IN ADVERTISING RESEARCH (VOL. XII) COMMUNICATING, DESIGNING AND CONSUMING AUTHENTICITY AND NARRATIVE (Alexandra Vignolles & Martin K. J. Waiguny, eds., 2023); Alexis Shore, Kelsey Prena, & James J. Cummings, *To Share or Not to Share: Extending Protection Motivation Theory to Understand Data Sharing with the Police*, 130 COMPUTS. IN HUM. BEHAV. 1 (2022); Alexis Shore & Kelsey Prena, *Platform Rules as Privacy Tools: The Influence of Screenshot Accountability and Trust on Privacy Management*, NEW MEDIA & SOC'Y (2023).

92. See for example: DANIELLE KEATS CITRON, HATE CRIMES IN CYBERSPACE 5–8 (2014); Mary Anne Franks, *Sexual Harassment 2.0*, 71 MD. L. REV. 655, 657–658 (2012); Danielle Keats Citron & Jonathon W. Penney, *When Law Frees Us to Speak*, 87 FORDHAM L. REV. 2317, 2319–2320 (2019). See also PEW RSCH. CTR., ONLINE HARASSMENT (2014).

93. Marthews & Tucker, *Government Surveillance and Internet Search Behavior, supra,* at 448.

94. Penney, *Understanding Chilling Effects, supra,* at 1459–1460; 1488–1503 (noting works of noted authors and linking chilling effects to a broader body of research on forms of conformity or *social* chilling effects); Penney, *Chilling Effects: Online Surveillance and Wikipedia Use, supra,* at 120–121.

95. Penney, *Understanding Chilling Effects, supra,* at 1499–1502.

96. Penney, *Understanding Chilling Effects, supra,* at 1500.

97. Penney, *Understanding Chilling Effects, supra,* at 1506–1507.

98. Penney, *Understanding Chilling Effects, supra,* at 1509–1513.

99. Penney, *Understanding Chilling Effects, supra,* at 1503–1513.

100. Penney, *Understanding Chilling Effects, supra,* at 1458–1459.

1 LAW'S FLAWED THEORY AND ITS MCCARTHY ERA ORIGINS

1. Schauer, *Fear, Risk, and the First Amendment: Unraveling the Chilling Effect, supra,* at 685, 687, 689 (noting legal uncertainty and deterrence as the "very essence" of chilling effects, with "fear" of legal punishment being central to that deterrent effect). See also Kendrick, *Speech, Intent, and the Chilling Effect, supra,* at 1649 ("The term 'chilling effect' refers to a claim that an otherwise legitimate regulation has the incidental effect of deterring-or chilling-benign activity, in this case protected expression"); Monica Youn, *The Chilling Effect and the Problem of Private Action*, 66 VAND. L. REV. 1473, 1481 (2013).

2. Schauer, *Fear, Risk, and the First Amendment: Unraveling the Chilling Effect, supra,* at 689.

3. Schauer, *Fear, Risk, and the First Amendment: Unraveling the Chilling Effect, supra,* at 689.

4. Schauer, *Fear, Risk, and the First Amendment: Unraveling the Chilling Effect, supra,* at 690, 698. It can certainly be said that there are some *good* and *bad* chilling effects. Later in this book, I provide a normative framework for helping determine which are which.

5. SCHRECKER, THE AGE OF MCCARTHYISM: A BRIEF HISTORY WITH DOCUMENTS, *supra,* at 1–3. See also DON E. CARLETON, RED SCARE! RIGHT-WING HYSTERIA, FIFTIES FANATICISM, AND THEIR LEGACY IN TEXAS (1985); MICHAEL J. HEALE, MCCARTHY'S AMERICANS: RED SCARE POLITICS IN STATE AND NATION, 1935–1965 (1998); DAVID

CAUTE, THE GREAT FEAR: THE ANTI-COMMUNIST PURGE UNDER TRUMAN AND EISENHOWER (1978); Seth F. Kreimer, *Sunlight, Secrets, and Scarlet Letters: The Tension between Privacy and Disclosure in Constitutional Law*, 140 U. PA. L. REV. 1 (1991).

6. SCHRECKER, THE AGE OF MCCARTHYISM: A BRIEF HISTORY WITH DOCUMENTS, *supra*, at 1–3; Youn, *The Chilling Effect and the Problem of Private Action, supra*, at 1487–1489; SAMUEL A. STOUFFER, COMMUNISM, CONFORMITY, AND CIVIL LIBERTIES 78–80 (1955).

7. For example, the 1940 Smith Act, the first peacetime sedition act in US history, criminalized both political speech and association, and aimed to effectively outlaw the Communist Party in America by making it illegal to advocate for the overthrow of the US Government or to associate with any group that did so: SCHRECKER, THE AGE OF MCCARTHYISM: A BRIEF HISTORY WITH DOCUMENTS, *id.*, at 18, 126, 279.

8. Kreimer, *Sunlight, Secrets, and Scarlet Letters: The Tension between Privacy and Disclosure in Constitutional Law, supra*, at 6.

9. SCHRECKER, THE AGE OF MCCARTHYISM: A BRIEF HISTORY WITH DOCUMENTS, *supra*, at 1–3, 5, 44, 86; STOUFFER, COMMUNISM, CONFORMITY, AND CIVIL LIBERTIES, *supra*, at 78–80; Kreimer, *Sunlight, Secrets, and Scarlet Letters: The Tension between Privacy and Disclosure in Constitutional Law, supra*, at 21; Youn, *The Chilling Effect and the Problem of Private Action, supra*, at 1487–1486.

10. SCHRECKER, THE AGE OF MCCARTHYISM: A BRIEF HISTORY WITH DOCUMENTS, *supra*, at 5, 44, 86; HEALE, MCCARTHY'S AMERICANS: RED SCARE POLITICS IN STATE AND NATION, *supra*, at 167.

11. STOUFFER, COMMUNISM, CONFORMITY, AND CIVIL LIBERTIES, *supra*, at 20 ("The McCarthy apparatus did not touch everyone, but for those who ran afoul of it the impact was brutal. Even citizens who were not called before loyalty boards or investigating committees felt what would later be called a 'chilling effect'").

12. Youn, *The Chilling Effect and the Problem of Private Action, supra*, at 1487; Leslie Kendrick, *Disclosure and Its Discontents*, 27 J.L. & POL. 575, 575 (2012).

13. See for example: David H. Souter et al., *In Memoriam: William J. Brennan*, 111 HARV. L. REV. 23, 27–28 (1997) (Horwitz noting that Brennan employed the "chilling effects" doctrine to shape First Amendment law, showing a "deep understanding" of American society in the McCarthy era, and the dangers it "posed to democracy").

14. CAPPELLO, NONE OF YOUR DAMN BUSINESS: PRIVACY IN THE UNITED STATES FROM THE GILDED AGE TO THE DIGITAL AGE, *supra*, at 121; SCHRECKER, THE AGE OF MCCARTHYISM: A BRIEF HISTORY WITH DOCUMENTS, *supra*, at 83–84. See also MICHAEL J. KLARMAN, FROM JIM CROW TO CIVIL RIGHTS: THE SUPREME COURT AND THE STRUGGLE FOR RACIAL EQUALITY 191 (2006); Robbie Lieberman & Clarence Lang, *Introduction, in* ANTICOMMUNISM AND THE AFRICAN AMERICAN FREEDOM MOVEMENT 2 (Robbie Lieberman & Clarence Lang, eds., 2009); JEFF R. WOODS, Black Struggle, RED SCARE: SEGREGATION AND ANTI-COMMUNISM IN THE SOUTH, 1948–1968 49 (2004).

15. 347 U.S. 483 (1954).

16. SCHRECKER, THE AGE OF MCCARTHYISM: A BRIEF HISTORY WITH DOCUMENTS, *supra*, at 83–84. Kendrick, *Disclosure and Its Discontents, supra*, at 578.

17. Vincent Blasi, *The Pathological Perspective and the First Amendment*, 85 COLUM. L. REV. 449, 482 (1985). See for example: New York Times Co. v. Sullivan, 376 U.S. 254 (1964); Bates v. City of Little Rock, 361 U.S. 516 (1960); NAACP v. Alabama, 357 U.S. 449 (1958).

18. Kendrick, *Speech, Intent, and the Chilling Effect, supra* at 1649 (citing Schauer and similarly defining chilling effects as a regulatory deterrent effect on benign activities).

See also Youn, *The Chilling Effect and the Problem of Private Action, supra*, at 1481; Wendy Seltzer, *Free Speech Unmoored in Copyright's Safe Harbor: Chilling Effects of the DMCA on the First Amendment*, 24 HARV. J.L. & TECH. 171 (2010).

19. Law and economics scholars have long examined regulatory chilling effects, employing a rational choice model. See for example: Isaac Ehrlich & Richard A. Posner, *An Economic Analysis of Legal Rulemaking*, 3 J. LEGAL STUD. 257, 263 (Jan., 1974); Louis Kaplow, *Optimal Proof Burdens, Deterrence, and the Chilling of Desirable Behavior*, 101 AMERICAN ECONOMIC REVIEW: PAPERS AND PROCEEDINGS 277 (2011); John E. Calfee & Richard Craswell, *Some Effects of Uncertainty on Compliance with Legal Standards*, 70 VA. L. REV. 965, (1984) Dru Stevenson, *Toward a New Theory of Notice and Deterrence*, 26 CARDOZO L. REV. 1535, 1547–1548 (2005); Russell B. Korobkin, *Behavioral Analysis and Legal Form: Rules vs. Standards Revisited*, 79 OR. L. REV. 23, 46 (2000); Amitai Aviram, *Allocating Regulatory Resources*, 37 J. CORP. L. 739, 750 (2012).

20. Youn, *The Chilling Effect and the Problem of Private Action, supra*, at 1481.

21. Chilling effects are now a well-established First Amendment injury, with courts regularly invalidating statutes on this basis: Kaminski, *Standing after Snowden: Lessons on Privacy Harm from National Security Surveillance Litigation, supra*, at 257.

22. See generally: Schauer, *Fear, Risk, and the First Amendment: Unraveling the Chilling Effect, supra*.

23. Harold Koh, *America's Jekyll-and-Hyde Exceptionalism, in* AMERICAN EXCEPTIONALISM AND HUMAN RIGHTS 112 (M. Ignatieff, ed., 2005) (noting America's "canonical commitments to liberty, equality, individualism, populism, and laissez-faire"). See also Frederick Schauer, *The Exceptional First Amendment, in* AMERICAN EXCEPTIONALISM AND HUMAN RIGHTS 45–49 (M. Ignatieff, ed., 2005); Phillip Bobbitt, *Is Law Politics?* 41 STAN. L. REV. 1233, 1284 (1989) ("The fundamental American Constitutional ethos is the idea of limited government"); PHILLIP BOBBITT, CONSTITUTIONAL FATE: A THEORY OF THE CONSTITUTION 101 (1983).

24. Michel Foucault, the foremost modern theorist of surveillance and power, wrote of the "repressive" dimensions of power that he linked to early concepts of monarchy, sovereignty, and the law. I discuss this further in Chapter 6. See MICHAEL FOUCAULT, POWER/KNOWLEDGE: SELECTED INTERVIEWS AND OTHER WRITINGS 1972–1977 118–121 (Colin Gordon, ed., Colin Gordon et al., trans., 1980).

25. Much of the judicial attention and academic discussion outside the US has been largely conventional, with debates centered on the issue addressed by the US Supreme Court in *New York Times v. Sullivan*: how laws like libel and defamation may chill speech and how the law should be changed or reformed to limit such self-censorship, with varying degrees of skepticism, reception, and balancing of competing interests. See generally: Adrienne Stone & George Williams, *Freedom of Speech and Defamation: Developments in the Common Law World*, 26 MONASH U. L. REV. 362 (2000). For European discussion of chilling effects conceptualizations in law and scholarship, see: Pierluigi Perri & David Thaw, *Ancient Worries and Modern Fears: Different Roots and Common Effects of U.S. and E.U. Privacy Regulation*, 49 CONN. L. REV. 1621, 1633 (2017); Bart van der Sloot, *The Individual in the Big Data Era: Moving Towards an Agent-Based Privacy Paradigm, in* EXPLORING THE BOUNDARIES OF BIG DATA 190 (Bart van der Sloot, Dennis Broeders & Erik Schrijvers, eds., 2016). For a discussion of the English, Australian, and New Zealand experience with this chilling effect debate, see: Jelena Gligorijevic, *Taming the "Chilling Effect" of Defamation Law: English Experience and Implications for Australia*, 50(2) FEDERAL LAW REV. 221 (2022); Stone & Williams, *Freedom of Speech and Defamation: Developments in the Common Law World, supra*.

26. See Stone & Williams, *Freedom of Speech and Defamation: Developments in the Common Law World, supra*. For additional discussion of chilling effects in Canadian law, see for example: David M. Lepofsky, *Making Sense of the Libel Chill Debate: Do Libel Laws "Chill" the Exercise of Freedom of Expression?*, 4 N.J.C.L. 169 (1994); Bob Tarantino, *Chasing Reputation: The Argument for Differential Treatment of Public Figures in Canadian Defamation Law*, 48(3) O.H.L.J 4 (2010); Hilary Young, *Rethinking Canadian Defamation Law as Applied to Corporate Plaintiffs*, 46 U.B.C. L. Rev. 529 (2013); André Schutten & Richard Haigh, *Whatcott and Hate Speech: Re-thinking Freedom of Expression in the Charter Age*, 34(1) Nat'l J. of Const. L. 1 (2015); Camden Hutchison, *Freedom of Expression: Values and Harms* 60 Alta. L. Rev. 687 (2022). In the Canadian context, chilling effects have also been raised in the privacy context, but often dismissed by courts or treated skeptically: John L. Savarese, *Warming up the Chilling Effect: A Comment on the Motive Clause Discussions in R V Khawaja (2010) and R V Khawaja (2013)*, 30 Windsor Y.B. Access Just. 199 (2012). This will be discussed in Chapter 9. There are of course exceptions: Kristen Thomasen, Beyond airspace safety: a feminist perspective on drone privacy regulation, 16(2) CJLT 307, 318–319 (2016); Kristen Thomasen & Suzie Dunn, Reasonable Expectations of Privacy in an Era of Drones and Deepfakes: Expanding the Supreme Court of Canada's Decision in R v Jarvis, In The Emerald International Handbook of Technology-Facilitated Violence and Abuse 555 (2021).
27. See for example: Grant v. Torstar Corp., 2009 SCC 61 (citing a "chilling effect" on speech as a reason to reform defamation law, and include a new "responsible publishing" defense).
28. Saskatchewan (Human Rights Commission) v. Whatcott, 2013 SCC 11 (finding hate speech prohibitions in the Canadian Human Rights Act prohibiting as too vague, imprecise, and overly broad, and thus causing unconstitutional chilling effects on Charter protected expression – very much akin to American First Amendment reasoning).
29. See generally Stone & Williams, *Freedom of Speech and Defamation: Developments in the Common Law World, supra*; Andrew Kenyon, *Investigating Chilling Effects: News Media and Public Speech in Malaysia, Singapore, and Australia*, 4 Int'l J. Comm. 440 (2010) (speaking to chilling effects in Malaysia, Singapore, and Australia, including American influence therein, and emergence of chilling effects in domestic commentary within the broader ASEAN region [Indonesia, Malaysia, the Philippines, Singapore, Thailand, Brunei, Cambodia, Lao People's Democratic Republic, Myanmar, and Vietnam]); Gligorijevic, *Taming the "Chilling Effect" of Defamation Law: English Experience and Implications for Australia, supra*.
30. Paul Freund, *The Supreme Court and Civil Liberties*, 4 Vand. L. Rev. 533, 539 (1950–1951). In fact, the term "chilling effects" pre-dates the twentieth century with usage consistent with more modern understanding as early as the late 18th Century: Jonathon W. Penney, *Chilling Effects Theory and Research as a Field of Study*, in Legal and Ethical Issues of Chilling Effects (forthcoming 2025).
31. Freund, *The Supreme Court and Civil Liberties, supra*, at 540.
32. Freund, *The Supreme Court and Civil Liberties, supra*, at 539–540.
33. Heale, McCarthy's Americans: Red Scare Politics in State and Nation, *supra*, at 122, 146 ("By 1950 the United States was succumbing to its second Big Red Scare. In that year Senator Joseph McCarthy began brandishing his lists of communists in the State Department, the Internal Security Act was passed over Truman's veto, and Republican candidates appeared to profit considerably in the November elections from red-baiting tactics. Communists and their liberal sympathizers were once more being hounded out of American public life.").
34. Schrecker, The Age of McCarthyism: A Brief History with Documents, *supra*, at 12–19; Caute, The Great Fear: The Anti-Communist Purge under

TRUMAN AND EISENHOWER, *supra*, at 25; Kreimer, *Sunlight, Secrets, and Scarlet Letters: The Tension between Privacy and Disclosure in Constitutional Law, supra*, at 16, 36, fn 99; HEALE, MCCARTHY'S AMERICANS: RED SCARE POLITICS IN STATE AND NATION, *supra*, at 122.

35. CAUTE, THE GREAT FEAR: THE ANTI-COMMUNIST PURGE UNDER TRUMAN AND EISENHOWER, *supra*, at 403–430 (detailing efforts by committees and commissions at the state level to generate firings of teachers and academics, most of which began by the late 1940s); Kreimer, *Sunlight, Secrets, and Scarlet Letters: The Tension between Privacy and Disclosure in Constitutional Law, supra*, at 16, 36, fn 99.

36. SCHRECKER, THE AGE OF MCCARTHYISM: A BRIEF HISTORY WITH DOCUMENTS, *supra*, at 71; HEALE, MCCARTHY'S AMERICANS: RED SCARE POLITICS IN STATE AND NATION, *supra*, at 150.

37. CAUTE, THE GREAT FEAR: THE ANTI-COMMUNIST PURGE UNDER TRUMAN AND EISENHOWER, *supra*, at 25 (as of 1945, federal and state statute books were "already bristling with anti-Communist legislation"); HEALE, MCCARTHY'S AMERICANS: RED SCARE POLITICS IN STATE AND NATION, *supra*, at 122.

38. HEALE, MCCARTHY'S AMERICANS: RED SCARE POLITICS IN STATE AND NATION, *supra*, at 125–126.

39. CAUTE, THE GREAT FEAR: THE ANTI-COMMUNIST PURGE UNDER TRUMAN AND EISENHOWER, *supra*, at 404 (noting as of 1940, twenty-one states had enacted loyalty oath requirements for teachers, and an additional fifteen would do so after 1946); SCHRECKER, THE AGE OF MCCARTHYISM: A BRIEF HISTORY WITH DOCUMENTS, *supra*, at 82 ("Besides investigating Communists, state and local politicians tried to outlaw them"). Even by 1951, McCarthyist excesses and government overreach was apparent – hence Truman's veto of the Internal Security Act (also known as the McCarran Act) in 1950, a sweeping and repressive anti-communist federal law that was ultimately passed over his veto: SCHRECKER, THE AGE OF MCCARTHYISM: A BRIEF HISTORY WITH DOCUMENTS, *supra*, at 217.

40. Freund, *The Supreme Court and Civil Liberties, supra*, at 545.

41. The Smith Act had been used to prosecute and persecute alleged communists, socialists, and their sympathizers since at least the 1940s, and would be so used for another decade after. See HEALE, MCCARTHY'S AMERICANS: RED SCARE POLITICS IN STATE AND NATION, *supra*, at 131, 147, 163 (nothing that by the end of 1956 over 100 Communist Party leaders had been convicted under the Smith Act); SCHRECKER, THE AGE OF MCCARTHYISM: A BRIEF HISTORY WITH DOCUMENTS, *supra*, at 49–52 (detailing the trails and court battles of the communist leader Smith Act prosecutions).

42. Freund, *The Supreme Court and Civil Liberties, supra*, at 545. The Supreme Court would fail this test, upholding the Smith Act prosecutions of communist leaders in Dennis v. United States, 341 U.S. 494, 501 (1951); SCHRECKER, THE AGE OF MCCARTHYISM: A BRIEF HISTORY WITH DOCUMENTS, *supra*, at 49–52. However, in a series of decisions in the late 1950s, the Court would reverse course and curtail the scope of the Act: HEALE, MCCARTHY'S AMERICANS: RED SCARE POLITICS IN STATE AND NATION, *supra*, at 194–196.

43. CAUTE, THE GREAT FEAR: THE ANTI-COMMUNIST PURGE UNDER TRUMAN AND EISENHOWER, *supra*, at 406, 407–420 (detailing extensive state and federal investigations into university professors, leading to over 600 dismissals).

44. PAUL F. LAZARSFELD & WASNER THIELENS, JR., THE ACADEMIC MIND: SOCIAL SCIENTISTS IN A TIME OF CRISIS 78, 195 (1958); Kreimer, *Sunlight, Secrets, and Scarlet Letters: The Tension between Privacy and Disclosure in Constitutional Law, supra*, at 20.

45. Justice William J. Brennan, Jr., Lewis F. Powell, Jr., Archibald Cox, James Vorenberg, & Anthony Lewis, *In Memoriam: Paul A. Freund*, 105 HARV. L. REV. 1, 3 (1992).

46. Freund was classmates with Justice William Brennan at Harvard and the late Justice would also entrust Freund with picking his law clerks for the first decade of his time on the Supreme Court on the suggestion of fellow Justice Felix Frankfurter: Stephen Wermiel, *Justice Brennan and His Law Clerks*, 98 MARQUETTE L. REV. 367, 369 (2014). Justice Felix Frankfurter, also on the Court at this time, had been one of Freund's professors at Harvard, teaching him administrative law during those years; and both Justices William Brennan and Justice Lewis Powell, Jr., wrote tributes to Freund on his death: Brennan et al., *In Memoriam: Paul A. Freund, supra*, at 1, 3.

47. Brennan et al., *In Memoriam: Paul A. Freund, supra*, at 3.

48. 344 U.S. 183 (1952).

49. 344 U.S. 183 (1952).

50. *Id.*, at 195.

51. Times Film Corp. v. City of Chicago, 365 U.S. 43, 75 (1961) (Warren, J., dissenting).

52. *Id.*, at 74, fn 11.

53. Souter et al., *In Memoriam: William J. Brennan, supra*, at 41, 44 (per Professor Lawrence Tribe: "William J. Brennan, Jr., was one of the greatest Justices of all time… Whether or not one agrees with all of Justice Brennan's views, the magnitude of his achievement is undeniable. Even Justice Scalia has described him as 'probably the most influential justice of the century'.").

54. Souter et al., *In Memoriam: William J. Brennan, supra*, at 27–28, 47.

55. Penney, *Chilling Effects: Online Surveillance and Wikipedia Use, supra*, at 125–126; Penney, *Understanding Chilling Effects, supra*; Neil Richards, *The Dangers of Surveillance*, 126 HARV. L. REV. 1934, 1964 (2013); NEIL RICHARDS, INTELLECTUAL PRIVACY: RETHINKING CIVIL LIBERTIES IN THE DIGITAL AGE (2015); Kendrick, *Speech, Intent, and the Chilling Effect, supra* at 1636, fn 7.

56. Penney, *Chilling Effects: Online Surveillance and Wikipedia Use, supra*, at 125–126; Richards, *The Dangers of Surveillance, supra*, at 1949–1950; Kendrick, *Speech, Intent, and the Chilling Effect, supra*, at 1636; Jennifer M. Kinsley, Chill, 48 LOY. U. CHI. L.J. 253, 255 (2016).

57. *New York Times v. Sullivan*, 376 U.S. 254 (1964).

58. *Id.*, at 254–262.

59. *Id.*, at 254.

60. Mike Fox, *Frederick Schauer Receives Honorary Doctorate from WU Vienna*, UNIVERSITY OF VIRGINIA NEWS (Oct. 29, 2019), https://www.law.virginia.edu/news/201910/frederick-schauer-receives-honorary-doctorate-wu-vienna; Staff, *Schauer appointed director of Safra Foundation Center*, HARVARD GAZETTE (April 5, 2007), https://news.harvard.edu/gazette/story/2007/04/schauer-appointed-director-of-safra-foundation-center/

61. See generally: Schauer, *Fear, Risk, and the First Amendment: Unraveling the Chilling Effect, supra*.

62. *See*, for example, Fred C. Zacharias, *Flowcharting the First Amendment*, 72 CORNELL L. REV. 936 (1987); Amy Pomerantz Nickerson, *Coercive Discovery and the First Amendment: Towards a Heightened Discoverability Standard*, 57 UCLA L. REV. 841, 869–872 (2010).

63. Büchi et al., *The Chilling Effects of Algorithmic Profiling: Mapping the Issues, supra*, at 4; Cohen, *A Right to Read Anonymously: A Closer Look at "Copyright Management" in Cyberspace, supra*, at 1011 n. 117; Kinsley, *Chill, supra*.

64. Eli Salzberger, *The Economic Analysis of Law: The Dominant Methodology for Legal Research?*, 4 HAIF. L. REV. 207, 217 (2007) (noting that law and economics became a "significant branch" of legal theory in the 1960s, but the "important impetus" for the "movement" came in the 1970s, thanks to the work of influential scholar Richard Posner). By 1978s, law and economics was predominant in the legal academy: Robert A.

Prentice, *Chicago Man, K-T Man, and the Future of Behavioral Law and Economics*, 56 VAND. L. REV. 1663, 1666 (2003); Jennifer Arlen, *The Future of Behavioral Economic Analysis of Law*, 51 VAND. L. REV. 1765 (1998) (noting the same); Anne C. Dailey, *The Hidden Economy of the Unconscious*, 74 CHI.-KENT L. REV. 1599, 1600 (1999).

65. Schauer, *Fear, Risk, and the First Amendment: Unraveling the Chilling Effect, supra*, at 695.

66. Katie Steele & H. Orri Stefánssont, Decision Theory, *in* Stanford Encyclopedia of Philosophy (2020), https://plato.stanford.edu/entries/decision-theory/; Thomas S. Ulen, Rational Choice Theory in Law and Economics, in ENCYCLOPEDIA OF LAW AND ECONOMICS 791 (Boudwijn Bockaert & Gerrit De Geest eds., 1999).

67. Frederick Schauer, *On the Relationship between Chapters One and Two of John Stuart Mill's on Liberty*, 39 CAP. U. L. REV. 571 (2011).

68. Schauer, *Fear, Risk, and the First Amendment: Unraveling the Chilling Effect, supra*, at 691–692, n. 35.

69. See JOHN STUART MILL, ON LIBERTY (David Bromwich & George Kateb, eds., 2003) (1859).

70. Schauer, *On the Relationship between* Chapters One and Two *of John Stuart Mill's on Liberty, supra*, at 575–576; Schauer, *Fear, Risk, and the First Amendment: Unraveling the Chilling Effect, supra*, at 693–694.

71. Schauer, *Fear, Risk, and the First Amendment: Unraveling the Chilling Effect, supra*, at 692, fn35. RICHARDS, INTELLECTUAL PRIVACY: RETHINKING CIVIL LIBERTIES IN THE DIGITAL AGE, *supra*, at 10 (discussing classical rationales for First Amendment).

72. Schauer, *Fear, Risk, and the First Amendment: Unraveling the Chilling Effect, supra*, at 693–694.

73. MILL, ON LIBERTY, *supra*, at 80; Paul Horwitz, *The First Amendment's Epistemological Problem*, 87 Wash. L. Rev. 445 (2012)

74. MILL, *id.*, at 81; Schauer, *On the Relationship between* Chapters One and Two *of John Stuart Mill's on Liberty, supra*, at 575.

75. Schauer, *Fear, Risk, and the First Amendment: Unraveling the Chilling Effect, supra*, at 693–694.

76. See RICHARDS, INTELLECTUAL PRIVACY: RETHINKING CIVIL LIBERTIES IN THE DIGITAL AGE, *supra*, at 10.

77. Andrew V. Papachristos et al., *Why Do Criminals Obey the Law?* 102 J. CRIM. L. & CRIMINOLOGY (1973) 397 (2012).

78. A. Robert Prentice, *Chicago Man, K-T Man, and the Future of Behavioral Law and Economics*, 56 VAND. L. REV. 1663, 1666–1667, 1667 no. 6 (2003).

79. Paul H. Robinson & John M. Darlow, *Does Criminal Law Deter? A Behavioral Science Investigation*, 24 OXFORD J. LEGAL STUD. 173, 173–200 (2004); Janice Nadler, *Expressive Law, Social Norms, and Social Groups*, 42 LAW & SOC. INQUIRY 60, 62–63 (2017); Prentice, *Chicago Man, K-T Man, and the Future of Behavioral Law and Economics, supra*, at 1666–1667, 1667 n. 6. See also W. Jonathan Cardi, Randall D. Penfield, & Albert H. Yoon, *Does Tort Law Deter Individuals? A Behavioral Science Study*, 9 J. EMPIRICAL LEGAL STUD. 567, 568–570 (2012); Lucas Miotto, The Good, The Bad, and The Puzzled: Coercion and Compliance, *in* CONCEPTUAL JURISPRUDENCE: METHODOLOGICAL ISSUES, CONCEPTUAL TOOLS, AND NEW APPROACHES (Jorge Fabra-Zamora & Gonzalo Villa Rosas, eds., 2019).

80. Nadler, *Expressive Law, Social Norms, and Social Groups, supra*, at 62–63; Robinson & Darlow, *Does Criminal Law Deter? A Behavioral Science Investigation, supra*, at 173–200; Prentice, *Chicago Man, K-T Man, and the Future of Behavioral Law and Economics, supra*, at 1666–1667, 1667 n. 6. See also Cardi et al., *Does Tort Law Deter Individuals? A Behavioral Science Study, supra*, at 568–570.

81. Robinson & Darlow, *Does Criminal Law Deter? A Behavioral Science Investigation*, *supra*, at 173 (stating that evidence suggests criminal law does not deter and in the few studies where there is a deterrent effect it is small and unpredictable); Nadler, *Expressive Law, Social Norms, and Social Groups*, *supra*, at 63; Tom R. Tyler, *Legitimacy and Criminal Justice: The Benefits of Self-Regulation*, 7 Ohio St. J. Crim. L. 307, 309 (2009); Raymond Pasternoster, *How Much Do We Really Know about Deterrence?* 100 J. Crim. Law & Criminology (1973-) 765 (2010); Paul H. Robinson, *The Role of Deterrence in the Formulation of Criminal Law Rules: At Its Worst When Doing Its Best*, 91 Geo. L.J. 949 (2003); Travis C. Pratt et al., *The Empirical Status of Deterrence Theory: A Meta-Analysis*, *in* Taking stock: The status of criminological theory 367, 383 (Francis T. Cullen et al., eds., 2008); Ana M. Martin et al., *Why Ordinary People Comply with Environmental Laws: A Structural Model on Normative and Attitudinal Determinants of Illegal Anti-ecological Behavior*, 19 Legal & Criminological Psychol. 80, (2014); Tom R. Tyler, *Understanding the Force of Law*, 51 Tulsa L. Rev. 507, 507 (2016). See also generally: Tom Tyler, Why People Obey the Law (2006). Though not tested as comprehensively, these findings also apply to deterrence in a civil or tort based context: Cardi et al., *Does Tort Law Deter Individuals? A Behavioral Science Study*, *supra*, at 570.
82. Tyler, *Understanding the Force of Law*, *supra*, at 507 ("There is a large body of social science evidence showing that social norms, moral values, and judgments about legitimacy all influence law-related behavior and, relying upon it, social scientists generally suggest that while sanctions matter sanction-independent forces are central to and often dominate the factors shaping people's law-related behaviors").
83. Pratt et al., *The Empirical Status of Deterrence Theory: A Meta-Analysis*, *supra*, at 383; Raymond Paternoster, *How Much Do We Really Know about Criminal Deterrence?*, *in* Deterrence 57–115 (Thom Brooks, ed., 2019).
84. Martin et al., *Why Ordinary People Comply with Environmental Laws: A Structural Model on Normative and Attitudinal Determinants of Illegal Anti-ecological Behavior*, *supra*, at 82–83. For a discussion of specific conditions required for deterrence to be effective, see: Terrie E. Moffitt, *The Learning Theory Model of Punishment: Implications for Delinquency Deterrence*, 10 Criminal Justice and Behavior 131–158 (1983); Martin Sundel & Sandra S. Sundel, Behavior Change in the Human Services: Behavioral and Cognitive Principles and Applications 155–156 (2018).
85. Robinson & Darlow, *Does Criminal Law Deter? A Behavioral Science Investigation*, *supra*, at 173.
86. See Penney, *Understanding Chilling Effects*, *supra*, at 1460–1463 (and accompanying notes) (discussing extensive array of empirical studies on chilling effects).
87. Penney, *Chilling Effects: Online Surveillance and Wikipedia Use*, *supra*, at 134–135.
88. For discussion of media coverage, see: David Lyon, Surveillance, Snowden, and Big Data: *Capacities, Consequences, Critique*, 1 Big Data & Soc'y 1, 2 (2014). See also Amy Wu et al., *"Whistleblower or Leaker?" Examining the Portrayal and Characterization of Edward Snowden in USA, UK, and HK Posts*, *in* New Media, Knowledge Practices & Multiliteracies 53 (Will W. K. Ma et al. eds., 2014); Vian Bakir, *Agenda Building, and Intelligence Agencies: A Systematic Review of the Field from the Discipline of Journalism, Media, and Communications*, 20 Int'l J. Press/Pol. 131 (2015); Keir Giles & Kim Hartmann, *Socio-political Effects of Active Cyber Defence Measures*, 6th Int'l Conf. on Cyber Conflict (CyCon 2014) (2014); Jie Qin, *Hero on Twitter, Traitor on News: How Social Media and Legacy News Frame Snowden*, 20 Int'l J. Press/Pol. 166 (2015).

89. Timothy B. Lee, *Here's Everything We Know about PRISM to Date*, WASH. POST (June 12, 2013), https://www.washingtonpost.com/news/wonk/wp/2013/06/12/ heres-everything-we-know-about-prism-to-date/.

90. Penney, *Chilling Effects: Online Surveillance and Wikipedia Use, supra*, at 141.

91. Segmented regression analysis was employed along with an interrupted time series research design. I also accounted for outliers in my analysis, using conventional statistical tests to identify outlier data points. The "Hamas" Wikipedia article was one such extreme outlier, with many million more views for that article in November 2012 and July 2014, two months where Israel conducted military operations in Gaza against the Hamas militant group. Not surprisingly, media coverage of these controversial operations drove more internet traffic to the "Hamas" Wikipedia article: Penney, *Chilling Effects: Online Surveillance and Wikipedia Use, supra*, at 137–138, 149–150.

92. Penney, *Chilling Effects: Online Surveillance and Wikipedia Use, supra*, at 157–161.

93. Penney, *Chilling Effects: Online Surveillance and Wikipedia Use, supra*, at 157–158.

94. Alex Marthews & Catherine Tucker, *Government Surveillance and Internet Search Behavior, in* CAMBRIDGE UNIVERSITY HANDBOOK ON SURVEILLANCE LAW (David Gray et al., eds., 2017).

95. *Id.,* at 446.

96. *Id.,* at 449–451.

97. *Id.,* at 446–447, 452–454.

98. See for example: Penney, *Internet Surveillance, Regulation, and Chilling Effects Online: A Comparative Case Study, supra* (finding evidence of corporate surveillance chilling effects on a range of online activities, including sharing, speech, and search).

99. Schauer, *Fear, Risk, and the First Amendment: Unraveling the Chilling Effect, supra,* at 686–687 n. 10, 691–692.

100. Robert Post & Amanda Shanor, *Adam Smith's First Amendment*, 128 HARV. L. REV. F. 165 (2014); Mila Sohoni, *The Trump Administration and the Law of Lochner*, 107 GEO. L.J. 1323, 1383–1384 (2019); Jeremy K. Kessler, *The Early Years of First Amendment Lochnerism*, 116 COLUMB. L. REV. 1915, 1917–1918 & accompanying notes (2018); Amanda Shanor, *The New Lochner*, 2016 WIS. L. REV. 133, 135–136 and accompanying notes (2016); Samuel R. Bagenstos, *The Unrelenting Libertarian Challenge to Public Accommodations Law*, 66 STAN. L. REV. 1205 (2014); Richard Blum, *Labor Picketing, the Right to Protest, and the Neoliberal First Amendment*, 42 N.Y.U. REV. L. & SOC. CHANGE 595 (2019). I use "neo-liberal" in the same sense as Blum (at 631 n. 162): DAVID HARVEY, A BRIEF HISTORY OF NEOLIBERALISM 64 (2005). See also Jedediah Purdy, *Neoliberal Constitutionalism: Lochnerism for a New Economy*, 77 L. & CONTEMP PROBS. 195 (2014); Timothy K. Kuhner, *Citizens United as Neoliberal Jurisprudence: The Resurgence of Economic Theory*, 18 VA. J. SOC. & L. 395, 397 (2011).

101. 558 U.S. 310 (2010). See also Erica Goldberg, *First Amendment Cynicism and Redemption*, 88 U. CIN. L. REV. 959, 963, n. 15 (2019) (noting the decision was controversial).

102. CITRON, HATE CRIMES IN CYBERSPACE, *supra,* at 6–8; Mary Anne Franks, *Sexual Harassment 2.0*, 71 MD. L. REV. 655, 657–658 (2012). See generally PEW RESEARCH CTR., ONLINE HARASSMENT (2014); Citron & Penney, *When Law Frees Us to Speak, supra,* at 2319.

103. CITRON, HATE CRIMES IN CYBERSPACE, *supra,* at 5–6; Citron & Penney, *When Law Frees Us to Speak, supra,* at 2319.

104. See generally Citron & Penney, *When Law Frees Us to Speak, supra.*

2 PRIVACY'S USEFUL BUT LIMITED THEORY

1. Daniel Solove, *A Taxonomy of Privacy*, 154 U. PENN. L. REV. 477, 487 (2006); Daniel Solove, *The First Amendment as Criminal Procedure*, 82 N.Y.U. L. REV. 112, 152 (2007); Daniel Solove, *I've Got Nothing to Hide and Other Privacy Misunderstandings*, 44 SAN DIEGO L. REV. 745 (2007); Neil M. Richards, *Intellectual Privacy*, 87 TEX. L. REV. 387 (2008); DANIEL SOLOVE, UNDERSTANDING PRIVACY (2010). See also Daniel J. Solove, *Conceptualizing Privacy*, 90 CALIF. L. REV. 1087 (2002); Richards, *The Dangers of Surveillance, supra,* at 1964; RICHARDS, INTELLECTUAL PRIVACY: RETHINKING CIVIL LIBERTIES IN THE DIGITAL AGE, *supra.* See also Penney, *Understanding Chilling Effects, supra.*

2. Anita L. Allen, *Coercing Privacy*, 40 WM. & MARY L. REV. 723, 754–755, 729–730 (1999) (concerned about the "rapid erosion of expectations of personal privacy" and attributing it to an "avalanche" of new technologies").

3. Cohen, *Examined Lives: Informational Privacy and the Subject as Object, supra,* at 1426; Jerry Kang, *Information Privacy in Cyberspace Transactions*, 50 STAN. L. REV. 1193 (1997); Paul M. Schwartz, *Privacy and Democracy in Cyberspace*, 52 VAND. L. REV. 1607 (1999) ("[P]erfected surveillance of naked thought's digital expression short-circuits the individual's own process of decisionmaking"); JEFF ROSEN, THE UNWANTED GAZE: THE DESTRUCTION OF PRIVACY IN AMERICA 8–12 (2000); DANIEL J. SOLOVE, *Privacy and Power: Computer Databases and Metaphors for Information Privacy*, 53 STAN. L. REV. 1393 (2001).

4. DAVID LYON, THE CULTURE OF SURVEILLANCE: WATCHING AS A WAY OF LIFE (2018); David Lyon, 9/11, *Synopticon and Scopophilia: Watching and Being Watched, in* THE NEW POLITICS OF SURVEILLANCE AND VISIBILITY 35 (Kevin Haggerty & Richard Ericson, eds., 2006); David Lyon, *Surveillance, Snowden, and Big Data: Capacities, Consequences, Critique*, 1 BIG DATA & SOC'Y 1, 8–11 (2014); Jonathon W. Penney, *Chilling Effects and Transatlantic Privacy*, 25 EUR. L.J. 122, 126–127 (2019).

5. Solove, *Conceptualizing Privacy, supra,* at 1100–1102 (noting their "right to be left alone" merely spoke to one dimension of privacy, possibly to privacy in the "private sphere," as a form of "seclusion"); Solove, *A Taxonomy of Privacy, supra,* at 549 (noting Blackstone and other writers' concern with intrusion into private spaces). See also Neil M. Richards, *The Puzzle of Brandeis, Privacy, and Speech*, 63 VAND. L. REV. 1295, 1304–1305 (2010) (noting how Warren and Brandeis' account of privacy was influenced by the "Gilded Age" conceptions of the private sphere).

6. LYON, THE CULTURE OF SURVEILLANCE: WATCHING AS A WAY OF LIFE, *supra,* at 31 (noting that the term "surveillance society" was coined in the late twentieth century to coincide with the emergence of new threats to privacy in the public sphere like camera surveillance and commercial practices, like loyalty cards, tracking people's activities in public places). See also Solove, *A Taxonomy of Privacy, supra,* at 495–496 (noting surveillance impacts both public and private spaces); Richards, *The Dangers of Surveillance, supra,* at 1935.

7. Paul De Hert & Serge Gutwirth, *Privacy, Data Protection and Law Enforcement. Opacity of the Individual and Transparency of Power, in* PRIVACY AND THE CRIMINAL LAW 72–73 (Serge Gutwirth, Antony Duff, & Erik Claes, eds., 2006); Mihály Szivos, *From Individual Privacy to the Privacy of Groups and Nations: An Approach to the Problems of the Structure of the European Public Sphere*, 16 EUI WORKING PAPERS 29 (1992); Penney, *Chilling Effects and Transatlantic Privacy, supra,* at 126–127.

8. HANNAH ARENDT, THE HUMAN CONDITION 58 (2nd ed., 1998, 1958).

9. *Id.*

10. Ryan Calo, *The Boundaries of Privacy Harm*, 86 Ind. L.J. 1131, 1146–1147 (2011) ("This is the exact lesson of the infamous Panopticon. The tower is always visible, but the guard's gaze is never verifiable … prisoners behave not because they are actually being observed, but because they believe they might be"); David Lyon, *The Search for Surveillance Theories*, in Theorizing Surveillance: The Panopticon and beyond 3–4 (David Lyon, ed., 2006).

11. Maša Galič, Tjerk Timan, & Bert-Jaap Koops, *Bentham, Deleuze and beyond: An Overview of Surveillance Theories from the Panopticon to Participation*, 30 Philos. Technol. 9 (2017); Gino Canella, *Racialized Surveillance: Activist Media and the Policing of Black Bodies*, 11(3) Communication, Culture and Critique 378, 382 (2018); Mary D. Fan, *Smarter Early Intervention Systems for Police in an Era of Pervasive Recording*, 30 U. Ill. L. Rev. 1705, 1712 (2018).

12. Lyon, *9/11, Synopticon and Scopophilia: Watching and Being Watched, supra*, at 40–41; Penney, *Chilling Effects and Transatlantic Privacy, supra*, at 126–127.

13. Solove, *The First Amendment as Criminal Procedure, supra*; Solove, *A Taxonomy of Privacy, supra*.

14. Calo, *The Boundaries of Privacy Harm, supra*, at 1139, fn.41; Ryan Calo, *Privacy Harm Exceptionalism*, 12 J. Telecomm. & High Tech. L. 361 (2014).

15. Calo, *The Boundaries of Privacy Harm, supra*, at 1139–1141.

16. Calo, *The Boundaries of Privacy Harm, supra*, at 1139–1141.

17. Solove, *A Taxonomy of Privacy, supra*, at 487–488.

18. Solove, *A Taxonomy of Privacy, supra*, at 487–488.

19. Solove, *A Taxonomy of Privacy, supra*, at 487.

20. Solove, *A Taxonomy of Privacy, supra*, at 487, 495.

21. Solove, *A Taxonomy of Privacy, supra*, at 487.

22. Solove, *A Taxonomy of Privacy, supra*, at 495, 498–499.

23. Solove, *The First Amendment as Criminal Procedure, supra*, at 170, 157.

24. *Id.*, at 1139–1141.

25. Solove, *A Taxonomy of Privacy, supra*, at 488, n.45.

26. Solove, *A Taxonomy of Privacy, supra*, at 488.

27. See for example: Cohen, *A Right to Read Anonymously: A Closer Look at "Copyright Management" in Cyberspace, supra*; Richards, Intellectual Privacy: Rethinking Civil Liberties in the Digital Age, *supra*; Richards, *The Dangers of Surveillance, supra*; Calo, *The Boundaries of Privacy Harm, supra*.

28. Cohen, *Examined Lives: Informational Privacy and the Subject as Object, supra*, at 1425–1426 ("A realm of autonomous, unmonitored choice, in turn, promotes a vital diversity of speech and behavior. The recognition that anonymity shelters constitutionally-protected decisions about speech, belief, and political and intellectual association – decisions that otherwise might be chilled by unpopularity or simple difference – is part of our constitutional tradition"); Cohen, *A Right to Read Anonymously: A Closer Look at "Copyright Management" in Cyberspace, supra*, at 1006–1014.

29. Richards, Intellectual Privacy: Rethinking Civil Liberties in the Digital Age, *supra*, at 5, 95–96.

30. Richards, Intellectual Privacy: Rethinking Civil Liberties in the Digital Age, *supra*, at 95–96. See generally Richards, *The Dangers of Surveillance, supra*.

31. Solove, *The First Amendment as Criminal Procedure, supra*, at 154–155; Solove, *I've Got Nothing to Hide and Other Privacy Misunderstandings, supra*, at 758.

32. Solove, *I've Got Nothing to Hide and Other Privacy Misunderstandings, supra*, at 765.

33. Solove, *The First Amendment as Criminal Procedure, supra*, at 157; Solove, *A Taxonomy of Privacy, supra*, at 484, 487, 499, 515, 529.
34. Cohen, *Studying Law Studying Surveillance, supra*, at 99.
35. Cohen, *Studying Law Studying Surveillance, supra*, at 94–96.
36. Alessandro Acquisti, *The Economics and Behavioral Economics of Privacy*, in PRIVACY, BIG DATA, AND THE PUBLIC GOOD: FRAMEWORKS FOR ENGAGEMENT 85–86 (Julia Lane et al., eds., 2014) (reviewing the literature on point). See also Alessandro Acquisti & Ralph Gross, *Imagined Communities: Awareness, Information Sharing, and Privacy on the Facebook*, PROC. 6TH WORKSHOP ON PRIVACY ENHANCING TECHNOLOGIES (2006); J. Alessandro Acquisti, *Privacy in Electronic Commerce and the Economics of Immediate Gratification*, PROC. 5TH ACM CONF. ON ELECTRONIC COMMUNICATION (2004); Bettina Berendt, Oliver Günther, & Sarah Spiekermann, *Privacy in E-commerce: Stated References vs. Actual Behavior*, 48 COMM. ACM 101, 104 (2005).
37. Alessandro Acquisti, Leslie K. John, & George Loewenstein, *What Is Privacy Worth?*, 42 J. LEGAL STUD. 249, 267–270 (2013).
38. Costas Panagopoulos & Sander van der Linden, *The Feeling of Being Watched: Do Eye Cues Elicit Negative Affect?*, 19(1) N. AM. J. PSYCHOL. 113, 113 (2017); Stefan Pfattheicher & Johannes Keller, *The Watching Eyes Phenomenon: The Role of a Sense of Being Seen and Public Self-Awareness*, 45(5) EURO. J. SOC. PSYCHOL. 560, 560–561 (2015); Costas Panagopoulos & Sander van der Linden, *Conformity to Implicit Social Pressure: The Role of Political Identity?* 11 SOC. INFLUENCES 177 (2016) (finding a watching eye effect concerning political identity and voter mobilization); Ryo Oda, Yuta Kato, & Kai Hiraishi, *The Watching-Eye Effect on Prosocial Lying*, 13(3) EVOLUTIONARY PSYCHOL. 1, 1–2 (2015); Costas Panagopoulos, *I've Got My Eyes on You: Implicit Social-Pressure Cues and Prosocial Behavior*, 35(1) POLITICAL PSYCHOL. 23 (2014). Recently, some have questioned the watching eye effect at least concerning pro-social behavior like donations after failed replication studies: Stefanie B. Northover et al., *Artificial Surveillance Cues Do Not Increase Generosity: Two Meta-Analyses*, 38 EVOLUTION AND HUMAN BEHAVIOR 144 (2017). However, subsequent studies and meta-analysis have confirmed its effect on donation/generosity where participants are provided cues as to the social norm: Ryo Oda, *Was the Watching Eye Effect a Fluke?*, 10 LETTERS ON EVOL. BEHAV. SCI. 4, 4–5 (2019). And on antisocial behavior contexts: Kevin Dear et al., *Do "Watching Eyes" Influence Antisocial Behavior? A Systematic Review & Meta-Analysis*, 40(3) EVOL. & HUM. BEHAV. 269 (2019). See also Costas Panagopoulos & Sander van der Linden, *Political Identity Moderates the Effect of Watchful Eyes on Voter Mobilization: A Reply to Matland and Murray*, 14 SOC. INFLUENCES 152 (2019) (replying to criticisms in replication studies); Alex Bradley, Claire Lawrence, & Eamonn Ferguson, *Does Observability Affect Prosociality?*, PROC. R. SOC. B 1, 1 (2018) (noting Northover et al. excluded certain studies from their meta-analysis that may have led to different results).
39. Oda et al., *The Watching-Eye Effect on Prosocial Lying, supra*, at 1–2; Pfattheicher & Keller, *The Watching Eyes Phenomenon: The Role of a Sense of Being Seen and Public Self-Awareness, supra*, at 560; Panagopoulos et al., *The Feeling of Being Watched: Do Eye Cues Elicit Negative Affect?, supra*, at 113–114.
40. Pfattheicher & Keller, *The Watching Eyes Phenomenon: The Role of a Sense of Being Seen and Public Self-Awareness, supra*, at 560.
41. Eugene Volokh, *Freedom of Speech and Information Privacy: The Troubling Implications of a Right to Stop People from Speaking about You*, 52 STAN. L. REV. 1049 (2000).
42. Volokh, *Freedom of Speech and Information Privacy: The Troubling Implications of a Right to Stop People from Speaking about You, id.*, at 1109, 1098.

43. Neil M. Richards, *Reconciling Data Privacy and the First Amendment*, 52 UCLA L. REV. 1149 (2005) (arguing Volokh's First Amendment argument on information privacy should be rejected); Paul M. Schwartz, *Free Speech vs. Information Privacy: Eugene Volokh's First Amendment Jurisprudence*, 52 STAN. L. REV. 1559 (2000) (critiquing Volokh's approach).

44. Kinsley, *Chill, supra*, at 269 ("The Supreme Court, too, has acknowledged that the chilling effect doctrine is merely a prediction about how speakers will behave and that, at some point, courts may lack confidence in its assumptions"). See Broaderick v. Oklahoma, 413 U.S. 601, 615 (1973).

3 SOCIAL CHILLING EFFECTS

1. Cohen, *Studying Law Studying Surveillance, supra*, at 91, 92.
2. Ari Waldman, *Privacy as Trust Sharing Personal Information in a Networked World*, 69 U. MIAMI L. REV. 559, 561 (2015). See also ARI WALDMAN, PRIVACY AS TRUST: INFORMATION PRIVACY FOR AN INFORMATION AGE 35 (2018) (noting some use of social theories in privacy, but they are only "the beginning" and "do not go far enough").
3. Schauer, *Fear, Risk, and the First Amendment: Unraveling the Chilling Effect, supra*, at 731.
4. MARTIN PETERSON, AN INTRODUCTION TO DECISION THEORY 1 (2009) ("Decision theory is the theory of rational decision making"); Steele & Stefánssont, *Decision Theory, supra*; Thomas S. Ulen, *Rational Choice Theory in Law and Economics, in* ENCYCLOPEDIA OF LAW AND ECONOMICS 791 (Boudwijn Bockaert & Gerrit De Geest, eds., 1999) (noting "rational choice theory" is "at the heart of modern economic theory and in the disciplines contiguous to economics" including "decision theory").
5. By 1978, law and economics was predominant in the legal academy: Robert A. Prentice, *Chicago Man, K-T Man, and the Future of Behavioral Law and Economics*, 56 VAND. L. REV. 1663, 1666 (2003); Jennifer Arlen, *The Future of Behavioral Economic Analysis of Law*, 51 VAND. L. REV. 1765 (1998) (noting the same).
6. Anne C. Dailey, *The Hidden Economy of the Unconscious*, 74 CHI.-KENT L. REV. 1599, 1600 (1999).
7. Richard H. McAdams & Eric Rasmusen, *Norms and the Law, in* HANDBOOK OF LAW AND ECONOMICS: VOL. 2 1609 (A. Mitchell Polinsky & Steven Shavell, eds., 2007).
8. Salzberger, *The Economic Analysis of Law: The Dominant Methodology for Legal Research?, supra*, at 208–209.
9. RICHARD A. POSNER, ECONOMIC ANALYSIS OF LAW 3–4 (5th ed., 1998).
10. McAdams & Rasmusen, Norms and the Law, *supra*; Amitai Etzioni, *Social Norms: Internalization, Persuasion, and History*, 34 LAW & SOC'Y REV. 157, 159 (2000).
11. W. Bradley Wendel, *Mixed Signals: Rational-Choice Theories of Social Norms and the Pragmatics of Explanation*, 77 IND. L.J. 1, 8 (2002) ("[T]he rational-choice vision of the human predicament has achieved unparalleled dominance in the legal academy in thinking about individual and social behavior").
12. Salzberger, *The Economic Analysis of Law: The Dominant Methodology for Legal Research?, supra*, at 219.
13. McAdams & Rasmusen, *Norms and the Law, supra*, at 1609 (noting that law and economics had "ignored" both "social norms and conventions" for its "first two decades" but then "discovered" them in the 1990s. Before then, law and economics embraced the idea that law was the "only set of enforced rules"). See also Etzioni, *Social Norms: Internalization, Persuasion, and History, supra*, at 157–158 and generally: Robert C. Ellickson, *Law and Economics Discovers Social Norms*, 27 J. LEGAL STUD. 537 (1998).

14. Richard A. Posner, *The Future of Law and Economics: A Comment on Ellickson*, 65 CHICAGO-KENT L. REV. 57, 62 (1989). Posner's work was a "central impetus" for the law and economics movement in the 1970s: McAdams & Rasmusen, *Norms and the Law*, *supra*, at 217.

15. McAdams & Rasmusen, *Norms and the Law*, *supra*, at 1609; Etzioni, *Social Norms: Internalization, Persuasion, and History*, *supra*, at 157–158.

16. ROBERT ELLICKSON, ORDER WITHOUT LAW: HOW NEIGHBORS SETTLE DISPUTES vii (1991). Robert C. Ellickson, *Of Coase and Cattle: Dispute Resolution among Neighbors in Shasta County*, 38 STAN. L. REV. 623, 624–625 (1986).

17. *See* Ronald Coase, *The Problem of Social Cost*, 3 J.L. & ECON. 1 (1960); ELLICKSON, ORDER WITHOUT LAW: HOW NEIGHBORS SETTLE DISPUTES, *supra*, at vii; Ellickson, *Of Coase and Cattle: Dispute Resolution among Neighbors in Shasta County*, *supra*, at 624–625.

18. Ellickson, *Of Coase and Cattle: Dispute Resolution among Neighbors in Shasta County*, *supra*, at 624; ELLICKSON, ORDER WITHOUT LAW: HOW NEIGHBORS SETTLE DISPUTES, *supra*, at 2.

19. William A. Fischel, *Order without Law: How Neighbors Settle Disputes by Robert C. Ellickson* (Book Review), 69 LAND ECON. 113, 113–114 (1993); Ellickson, *Of Coase and Cattle: Dispute Resolution among Neighbors in Shasta County*, *supra*, at 624; ELLICKSON, ORDER WITHOUT LAW: HOW NEIGHBORS SETTLE DISPUTES, *supra*, at 2.

20. Fischel, *Order without Law: How Neighbors Settle Disputes by Robert C. Ellickson*, *supra*, at 113–114; Ellickson, *Of Coase and Cattle: Dispute Resolution among Neighbors in Shasta County*, *supra*, at 624; ELLICKSON, ORDER WITHOUT LAW: HOW NEIGHBORS SETTLE DISPUTES, *supra*, at 2.

21. John Brigham, *Review: Order without Lawyers: Ellickson on How Neighbors Settle Disputes*, 27 LAW & SOCIETY REVIEW 609, 609 (1993); Ellickson, *Of Coase and Cattle: Dispute Resolution among Neighbors in Shasta County*, *supra*, at 624–625; ELLICKSON, ORDER WITHOUT LAW: HOW NEIGHBORS SETTLE DISPUTES, *supra*, at 2, 6–7.

22. Ellickson, *Of Coase and Cattle: Dispute Resolution among Neighbors in Shasta County*, *supra*, at 626–627; ELLICKSON, ORDER WITHOUT LAW: HOW NEIGHBORS SETTLE DISPUTES, *supra*, at 3.

23. Ellickson, *Of Coase and Cattle: Dispute Resolution among Neighbors in Shasta County*, *supra*, at 629–653, 654–655; ELLICKSON, ORDER WITHOUT LAW: HOW NEIGHBORS SETTLE DISPUTES, *supra*, at 40, fn. 1.

24. ELLICKSON, ORDER WITHOUT LAW: HOW NEIGHBORS SETTLE DISPUTES, *supra*, at 40.

25. Ellickson, *Of Coase and Cattle: Dispute Resolution among Neighbors in Shasta County*, *supra*, at 687 ("The book will explain why proposed closed-range ordinances generate so much political heat in Shasta County even though trespass law is itself practically irrelevant"); ELLICKSON, ORDER WITHOUT LAW: HOW NEIGHBORS SETTLE DISPUTES, *supra*, at 141.

26. ELLICKSON, ORDER WITHOUT LAW: HOW NEIGHBORS SETTLE DISPUTES, *supra*, at 141 ("County residents badly misperceive the substantive law that applies to road accidents").

27. Robert Cialdini & Melanie Trost, *Social Influence: Social Norms, Conformity, and Compliance*, in HANDBOOK OF SOCIAL PSYCHOLOGY 151, 152 (Daniel T. Gilbert, Susan T. Fiske, & Gardner Lindzey, eds., 1998); WOLFGANG STROEBE & MILES HEWSTONE, AN INTRODUCTION TO SOCIAL PSYCHOLOGY 295 (7th ed., 2020); SAUL KASSIN, STEVEN FEIN, & HAZEL ROSE MARKUS, SOCIAL PSYCHOLOGY 268–269 (10th ed., 2016); Amir N. Licht, *Social Norms and the Law – Why Peoples Obey the Law*, 4(3) REVIEW OF

LAW AND ECONOMICS 715, 727 (2008); Cass R. Sunstein, *Social Norms and Social Roles,* 96 COLUM. LAW REV. 903, 914 (1996); CASS SUNSTEIN, CONFORMITY: THE POWER OF SOCIAL INFLUENCES (2019).

28. ELLICKSON, ORDER WITHOUT LAW: HOW NEIGHBORS SETTLE DISPUTES, *supra,* at 52–53; Ellickson, *Of Coase and Cattle: Dispute Resolution among Neighbors in Shasta County, supra,* at 623–629.

29. ELLICKSON, ORDER WITHOUT LAW: HOW NEIGHBORS SETTLE DISPUTES, *supra,* at 52–53; Ellickson, *Of Coase and Cattle: Dispute Resolution among Neighbors in Shasta County, supra,* at 623–629.

30. ELLICKSON, ORDER WITHOUT LAW: HOW NEIGHBORS SETTLE DISPUTES, *supra,* at 53.

31. *Id.,* at 78.

32. *Id.,* at 251.

33. *Id.,* at 60.

34. *Id.,* at 57; Ellickson, *Of Coase and Cattle: Dispute Resolution among Neighbors in Shasta County, supra,* at 677–678; McAdams & Rasmusen, *Norms and the Law, supra,* at 1589.

35. ELLICKSON, ORDER WITHOUT LAW: HOW NEIGHBORS SETTLE DISPUTES, *supra,* at 57; Ellickson, *Of Coase and Cattle: Dispute Resolution among Neighbors in Shasta County, supra,* at 677–678.

36. ELLICKSON, ORDER WITHOUT LAW: HOW NEIGHBORS SETTLE DISPUTES, *supra,* at 58–59.

37. Ellickson, *Of Coase and Cattle: Dispute Resolution among Neighbors in Shasta County, supra,* at 537–540.

38. STROEBE & HEWSTONE, AN INTRODUCTION TO SOCIAL PSYCHOLOGY, *supra,* at 344 ("social influence refers to change of attitudes, beliefs, opinions, values, and behavior as a result of being exposed to other individuals' attitudes, beliefs, opinions, values, and behaviors"); TOM GILOVICH ET AL., SOCIAL PSYCHOLOGY 271 (5th ed., 2018); ROBERT CIALDINI, INFLUENCE: SCIENCE AND PRACTICE 109 (Int'l. ed., 2013) (defining the related concept of "social proof," as a "weapon of influence," wherein we "view a behavior as correct in a given situation to the degree that we see others performing it"); ELLIOTT ARONSON, THE SOCIAL ANIMAL 6 (8th ed., 1999)(defining "social influence" as the "influences that people have upon the beliefs or behavior of others"); Robert B. Cialdini & Noah J. Goldstein, *Social influence: Compliance and Conformity,* 55 ANN. REV. PSYCHOL. 591, 606 (2004); Cialdini & Trost, *Social Influence: Social Norms, Conformity, and Compliance, supra,* at 151, 155; LEE ROSS & RICHARD NESBITT, THE PERSON AND THE SITUATION: PERSPECTIVES OF SOCIAL PSYCHOLOGY (2011).

39. Cialdini & Goldstein, *Social Influence: Compliance and Conformity, supra,* at 592; GILOVICH ET AL., SOCIAL PSYCHOLOGY, *supra,* at 271.

40. GILOVICH ET AL., SOCIAL PSYCHOLOGY, *supra,* at 271; Cialdini & Goldstein, *Social Influence: Compliance and Conformity, supra,* at 592–606.

41. Cialdini & Goldstein, *Social Influence: Compliance and Conformity, supra,* at 606; GILOVICH ET AL., SOCIAL PSYCHOLOGY, *supra,* at 271.

42. The term is most often used by lawyers, journalists, and policymakers. There are exceptions, most notably among communications scholars. See, for example, Stoycheff, *Under Surveillance: Examining Facebook's Spiral of Silence Effects in the Wake of NSA Internet Monitoring, supra;* Stoycheff et al., *Privacy and the Panopticon: Online Mass Surveillance's Deterrence and Chilling Effects, supra* (experimental study finding an online government surveillance chilled behavioral intentions); Büchi et al., *The Chilling Effects of Algorithmic Profiling: Mapping the Issues, supra;* Yoan Hermstrüwer & Stephen Dickert, *Sharing Is Daring: An Experiment on Consent, Chilling Effects and a Salient Privacy Nudge,* 51 INTERNATIONAL REVIEW OF LAW AND ECONOMICS 38, 39 (2017);

Meg Leta Ambrose, *It's about Time: Privacy, Information Life Cycles, and the Right to Be Forgotten*, 16 STAN. TECH. L. REV. 369, 371 (2013).

43. Kiki J. Chu, *Power of the Eyes: Deterring Sexual Harassment in Tokyo Subways Using Images of Watchful Eyes*, BEHAVIORAL PUBLIC POLICY 1, 2–4 (2019); Pfattheicher & Keller, *The Watching Eyes Phenomenon: The Role of a Sense of Being Seen and Public Self-Awareness, supra*, at 560.

44. Panagopoulos & van der Linden, *The Feeling of Being Watched: Do Eye Cues Elicit Negative Affect?, supra*, at 113–114.

45. Shanahan et al., *The Spiral of Silence: A Meta-Analysis and Its Impact, in* MASS MEDIA EFFECTS RESEARCH: ADVANCES THROUGH META-ANALYSIS 415–427 (Raymond W. Preiss, Barbara Mae Gayle, Nancy Burrell, Mike Allen, & Jennings Bryant, eds., 2007) (providing an extensive review of the research); Stoycheff, *Under Surveillance: Examining Facebook's Spiral of Silence Effects in the Wake of NSA Internet Monitoring, supra*, at 297 ("extensively tested"). See also Keith N. Hampton et al., *Social Media and the "Spiral of Silence,"* PEW RESEARCH CENTER 8, 23 (2014), www.pewresearch.org/internet/2014/08/26/social-media-and-the-spiral-of-silence/.

46. See for example: Stoycheff, *Under Surveillance: Examining Facebook's Spiral of Silence Effects in the Wake of NSA Internet Monitoring, supra.* Ben Marder et al., *The Extended "Chilling" Effect of Facebook: The Cold Reality of Ubiquitous Social Networking*, 60 COMPUTERS IN HUM. BEHAV. 582 (2016).

47. Solomon E. Asch, *Studies of Independence and Conformity: A Minority of One against a Unanimous Majority*, 70 PSYCHOL. MONOGRAPHS 416 (1956).

48. GILOVICH ET AL., SOCIAL PSYCHOLOGY, *supra*, at 276–277; KASSIN ET AL., SOCIAL PSYCHOLOGY, *supra*, at 269–270; STROEBE & HEWSTONE, AN INTRODUCTION TO SOCIAL PSYCHOLOGY, *supra*, at 308–309.

49. GILOVICH ET AL., SOCIAL PSYCHOLOGY, *supra*, at 276–277.

50. Rod Bond & Peter Smith, *Culture and Conformity: A Meta-Analysis of Studies Using Asch's Line Judgment Task*, 119 PSYCHOL. BULLETIN 111, 116 (1996); SUNSTEIN, CONFORMITY: THE POWER OF SOCIAL INFLUENCES, *supra*, at 16–17.

51. Bond & Smith, *Culture and Conformity: A Meta-Analysis of Studies Using Asch's Line Judgment Task, supra*, at 128; SUNSTEIN, CONFORMITY: THE POWER OF SOCIAL INFLUENCES. *supra*, at 16–17.

4 A CONFORMITY THEORY OF CHILLING EFFECTS

1. Tom R. Tyler, *Understanding the Force of Law*, 51 TULSA L. REV. 507, 507 (2016); Ellickson, *Law and Economics Discovers Social Norms, supra*, at 539–541 (discussing socialization and social norms as influential). Also, see generally TOM TYLER, WHY PEOPLE OBEY THE LAW (2006).

2. Nadler, *Expressive Law, Social Norms, and Social Groups, supra*, at 60.

3. Nadler, *Expressive Law, Social Norms, and Social Groups, supra*, at 60.

4. The term "Hawthorne effect" was coined by Henry A. Landsberger in 1958: HENRY A. LANDSBERGER, HAWTHORNE REVISITED (1958). The original study was described in FRITZ J. ROETHLISBERGER & WILLIAM J. DICKSON, MANAGEMENT AND THE WORKER (1939); KASSIN ET AL., SOCIAL PSYCHOLOGY, *supra*, at 557. A recent comprehensive review found evidence of the "Hawthorne effect" in studies across multiple disciplines and domains: Jim McCambridge et al., *Systematic Review of the Hawthorne Effect: New Concepts are Needed to Study Research Participation Effects*, 67(3) J. CLIN. EPIDEMIOL. 267 (2014).

5. KASSIN ET AL., SOCIAL PSYCHOLOGY, *supra*, at 557.

6. KASSIN ET AL., SOCIAL PSYCHOLOGY, *supra*, at 557.

7. Kirsten Christiansen, *The Conquest of Space: New York City's New Frontier of Social Control*, *in* SURVEILLANCE AND GOVERNANCE: CRIME CONTROL AND BEYOND – SOCIOLOGY OF CRIME, LAW, AND DEVIANCE VOL. 10 57, 71 (Mathieu Deflam, ed., 2008).

8. Alex Bradley, Claire Lawrence, & Eamonn Ferguson, *Does Observability Affect Prosociality?* PROC. R. SOC. B 1, 1 (2018).

9. John R. Aiello & Carol M. Svec, *Computer Monitoring of Work Performance: Extending the Social Facilitation Framework to Electronic Presence*, 23 J. APPLIED SOC. PSYCHOL. 537 (1993); See Delbert M. Nebeker & B. Charles Tatum, *The Effects of Computer Monitoring, Standards, and Rewards on Work Performance, Job Satisfaction, and Stress*, 23 J. APPLIED SOC. PSYCHOL. 499 (1993); John R. Aiello & Kathryn J. Kolb, *Electronic Performance Monitoring and Social Context: Impact on Productivity and Stress*, 80 J. APPLIED SOC. PSYCHOL. 339 (1995).

10. Aiello & Svec, *Computer Monitoring of Work Performance: Extending the Social Facilitation Framework to Electronic Presence*, *supra*, at 538–539.

11. *Id.*, at 538–539.

12. ALAN WESTIN, PRIVACY AND FREEDOM 33–34, 37–38 (1967).

13. Ruth Gavison, *Privacy and the Limits of Law*, 89 YALE L.J. 421, 447 (1980).

14. Calo, *The Boundaries of Privacy Harm*, *supra*, at 1144.

15. Solove, *A Taxonomy of Privacy*, *supra*, at 493; Solove, *The First Amendment as Criminal Procedure*, *supra*.

16. Solove, *A Taxonomy of Privacy*, *supra*, at 493.

17. The term was coined by Roger Clarke in the 1980s as shorthand for data surveillance: Roger Clarke, *Information Technology and Dataveillance*, 31(5) COMMUN. ACM (May 1988), www.anu.edu.au/people/Roger.Clarke/DV/CACM88.html; Roger Clarke, *Dataveillance – 15 Years On*, 28 PRIVACY ISSUES FORUM (2003), https://citeseerx.ist .psu.edu/document?repid=rep1&type=pdf&doi=. For more recent research on dataveillance, see for example: BORGESIUS, IMPROVING PRIVACY PROTECTION IN THE AREA OF BEHAVIOURAL TARGETING, *supra*; Büchi et al., *The Chilling Effects of Digital Dataveillance: A Theoretical Model and an Empirical Research Agenda*, *supra*; Raley, *Dataveillance and Countervailance*, *supra*; Büchi et al., *The Chilling Effects of Algorithmic Profiling: Mapping the Issues*, *supra*; Kappeler et al., *Qualitative Evidence of Chilling Effects – How Users Imaginaries of Dataveillance Lead to Inhibited Digital Behavior*, *supra*; Strycharz & Segijn, *The Future of Dataveillance in Advertising Theory and Practice*, *supra*; Strycharz & Segijn, *Consumer Differences in Chilling Effects*, *supra*.

18. Büchi et al., *The Chilling Effects of Algorithmic Profiling: Mapping the Issues*, *supra*, at 7–8; Büchi et al., *The Chilling Effects of Digital Dataveillance: A Theoretical Model and an Empirical Research Agenda*, *supra*, at 5.

19. Büchi et al., *The Chilling Effects of Digital Dataveillance: A Theoretical Model and an Empirical Research Agenda*, *supra*, at 6.

20. Büchi et al., *The Chilling Effects of Digital Dataveillance: A Theoretical Model and an Empirical Research Agenda*, *supra*, at 6.

21. Hiroshi Mamiya, Arash Shaban-Nejad, & David L. Buckeridge, *Online Public Health Intelligence: Ethical Considerations at the Big Data Era*, PUBLIC HEALTH INTELLIGENCE AND THE INTERNET 129, 142 (2017).

22. CIALDINI, INFLUENCE: SCIENCE AND PRACTICE, *supra*, at 119; Adrienne Chung & Rajiv N. Rimal, *Social Norms: A Review*, 4 REV. COMM. RESEARCH 1 (2016); Rajiv N. Rimal & Maria K. Lapinski, *A Re-explication of Social Norms, Ten Years Later*, 25 COMM. THEORY 393 (2015); Morton Deutsch & Harold B. Gerard, *A Study of Normative and Informational Social Influences upon Individual Judgment*, 51 J. ABNORMAL & SOC. PSYCHOL. 629, 635

(1955); Cialdini & Trost, *Social Influence: Social Norms, Conformity, and Compliance,* *supra*; Cialdini & Goldstein, *Social Influence: Compliance and Conformity, supra,* at 606; KASSIN ET AL., SOCIAL PSYCHOLOGY, *supra,* at 268–270.

23. MUZAFER SHERIF, THE PSYCHOLOGY OF SOCIAL NORMS (1936); THOMAS HEINZEN & WIND GOODFRIEND, SOCIAL PSYCHOLOGY 437 (2019); Chung & Rimal, *Social Norms: A Review, supra,* at 2–3; KASSIN ET AL., SOCIAL PSYCHOLOGY, *supra,* at 268–270.

24. SHERIF, THE PSYCHOLOGY OF SOCIAL NORMS, *supra,* at 91–109; HEINZEN & GOODFRIEND, SOCIAL PSYCHOLOGY, *supra,* at 437; Chung & Rimal, *Social Norms: A Review, supra,* at 2–3; KASSIN ET AL., SOCIAL PSYCHOLOGY, *supra,* at 258.

25. SHERIF, THE PSYCHOLOGY OF SOCIAL NORMS, *supra,* at 91–109; HEINZEN & GOODFRIEND, SOCIAL PSYCHOLOGY, *supra,* at 437; Chung & Rimal, *Social Norms: A Review, supra,* at 2–3; Kenworthey Bilz & Janice Nadler, *Law, Psychology, and Morality,* 50 PSYCHOLOGY OF LEARNING AND MOTIVATION 101, 108–109 (2009).

26. HEINZEN & GOODFRIEND, SOCIAL PSYCHOLOGY, *supra,* at 437, 439; Chung & Rimal, *Social Norms: A Review, supra,* at 2–3; Bilz & Nadler, *Law, Psychology, and Morality, supra,* at 108–109.

27. HEINZEN & GOODFRIEND, SOCIAL PSYCHOLOGY, *supra,* at 438.

28. David Lyon, *9/11, Synopticon and Scopophilia: Watching and Being Watched, in* THE NEW POLITICS OF SURVEILLANCE AND VISIBILITY 44 (Kevin Haggerty & Richard Ericson, eds., 2006).

29. Han Baltussen & Peter J. Davis, *Parrhêsia, Free Speech, and Self-Censorship, in* THE ART OF VEILED SPEECH: SELF CENSORSHIP FROM ARISTOPHANES TO HOBBES 1–2, 9–10 (Han Baltussen & Peter J. Davis, eds., 2015).

30. Baltussen & Davis, *Parrhêsia, Free Speech, and Self-Censorship, supra,* at 1–2, 9–10.

31. Megan Cassidy-Welch, *"Dixit quod nunquam vidit hereticos": Dissimulation and Self-Censorship in Thirteenth-Century Inquisitorial Testimonies, in* THE ART OF VEILED SPEECH: SELF CENSORSHIP FROM ARISTOPHANES TO HOBBES 251, 256–263 (Han Baltussen & Peter J. Davis, eds., 2015).

32. Sagi Elbaz et al., *Self-Censorship of Narratives of Political Violence in the Media, in* SELF-CENSORSHIP IN CONTEXTS OF CONFLICT: THEORY AND RESEARCH 119, 129 (Daniel Bar-Tal et al., eds., 2017) (describing journalists who keep "silent regarding sensitive and delicate issues for fear for their personal safety. These fears may include arrests, torture, and even murder of state officials by private citizens. In South America, several journalists have been murdered or have disappeared following investigative reporting into drug-related deals").

33. CITRON, HATE CRIMES IN CYBERSPACE, *supra,* at 5–8; Mary Anne Franks, *Sexual Harassment 2.0,* 71 MD. L. REV. 655, 657–658 (2012); Alice E. Marwick, *Scandal or Sex Crime? Gendered Privacy and the Celebrity Nude Photo Leaks,* 19 ETHICS INF. TECHNOL. 179 (2017).

34. Damien R. Murray et al., *Threat(s) and Conformity Deconstructed: Perceived Threat of Infectious Disease and Its Implications for Conformist Attitudes and Behavior,* 42(2) EUR. J. SOC. PSYCHOL. 180, 180 (2012); Steven Neuberg et al., *Evolutionary Social Psychology, in* HANDBOOK ON SOCIAL PSYCHOLOGY, Vol. 1 761, 778–779 (5th ed., Susan T. Fiske et al., eds., 2010); Matthew Gailliot et al., *Mortality Salience Increases Adherence to Salient Norms and Values,* 34(7) PERS. & SOC. PSYCHOL. BULL. 993–1003 (2008); Vladas Griskevicius et al., *Going Along versus Going Alone: When Fundamental Motives Facilitate Strategic (Non) Conformity,* 91(2) JOURNAL OF PERSONALITY AND SOCIAL PSYCHOLOGY 281 (2006); Gao Yang et al., *Go with the Flow against Uncertainty about Self under Existential Threat,* 20(3) SELF AND IDENTITY 438 (2021); Jill M. Sundie et al., *The World's (Truly) Oldest Profession: Social Influence in Evolutionary Perspective,* 7(3) SOC. INFLUENCE 134 (2012).

35. Yang et al., *Go with the Flow against Uncertainty about Self under Existential Threat, supra*, at 439.
36. Neuberg et al., *Evolutionary Social Psychology, supra*, at 779.
37. Cialdini & Goldstein, *Social Influence: Compliance and Conformity, supra*, at 592. GILOVICH ET AL., SOCIAL PSYCHOLOGY, *supra*, at 597–598.
38. Jenny Saxton et al., *The Efficacy of Personalized Normative Feedback Interventions across Addictions: A Systematic Review and Meta-Analysis*, 16(4) PLoS ONE (2021).
39. Keri Dotson et al., *Stand-Alone Personalized Normative Feedback for College Student Drinkers: A Meta-Analytic Review, 2004 to 2014*, 10(10) PLoS ONE (2014); Scott Graupensperger et al., *Social Norms and Vaccine Uptake: College Students' COVID Vaccination Intentions, Attitudes, and Estimated Peer Norms and Comparisons with Influenza Vaccine*, 39(15) VACCINE 2027, 2061 (2021); Christine Wolter et al., *Finding the Right Balance: A Social Norms Intervention to Reduce Heavy Drinking in University Students*, 9 PUB. HEALTH 1 (2021); Saxton, *The Efficacy of Personalized Normative Feedback Interventions across Addictions: A Systematic Review and Meta-Analysis, supra*.
40. Cialdini & Trost, *Social Influence: Social Norms, Conformity, and Compliance, supra*, at 169, 170–172.
41. KASSIN ET AL., SOCIAL PSYCHOLOGY, *supra*, at 291–301; Cialdini & Trost, *Social Influence: Social Norms, Conformity, and Compliance, supra*, at 169, 170–172; HEINZEN & GOODFRIEND, SOCIAL PSYCHOLOGY, *supra*, at 461–468.
42. KASSIN ET AL., SOCIAL PSYCHOLOGY, *supra*, at 291–301; HEINZEN & GOODFRIEND, SOCIAL PSYCHOLOGY, *supra*, at 461–468.
43. KASSIN ET AL., SOCIAL PSYCHOLOGY, *supra*, at 291–301; Cialdini & Trost, *Social Influence: Social Norms, Conformity, and Compliance, supra*, at 169, 170–172; HEINZEN & GOODFRIEND, SOCIAL PSYCHOLOGY, *supra*, at 461–468.
44. Neuberg et al., *Evolutionary Social Psychology, supra*, at 778.
45. Neuberg et al., *Evolutionary Social Psychology, supra*, at 778.
46. STANLEY MILGRAM, OBEDIENCE TO AUTHORITY: AN EXPERIMENTAL VIEW 113–115 (1974).
47. Ruthie Pliskin et al., *Speaking Out and Breaking the Silence, in* SELF-CENSORSHIP IN CONTEXTS OF CONFLICT: THEORY AND RESEARCH 243, 250 (Daniel Bar-Tal et al., eds., 2017); Karen Sharvit, *Speaking Self-Censorship: Emerging Themes and Remaining Questions, in* SELF-CENSORSHIP IN CONTEXTS OF CONFLICT: THEORY AND RESEARCH 269, 274–275 (Daniel Bar-Tal et al., eds., 2017).
48. Thomas Blass, *The Roots of Stanley Milgram's Obedience Experiments and Their Relevance to the Holocaust*, 20(1) ANALYSE & KRITIK 46, 49–50 (1998); KASSIN ET AL., SOCIAL PSYCHOLOGY, *supra*, at 15.
49. Blass, *The Roots of Stanley Milgram's Obedience Experiments and Their Relevance to the Holocaust, supra*, at 49; KASSIN ET AL., SOCIAL PSYCHOLOGY, *supra*, at 292–293.
50. Blass, *The Roots of Stanley Milgram's Obedience Experiments and Their Relevance to the Holocaust, supra*, at 49; KASSIN ET AL., SOCIAL PSYCHOLOGY, *supra*, at 292–293.
51. There is reason to believe that Eichmann was a committed Nazi and lifelong anti-Semite who had constructed the impression of a faceless bureaucrat for trial: BARBARA TUCHMAN, PRACTICING HISTORY: SELECTED ESSAYS 121 (1981).
52. Cialdini & Trost, *Social Influence: Social Norms, Conformity, and Compliance, supra*, at 155; CIALDINI, INFLUENCE: SCIENCE AND PRACTICE, *supra*, at 127–128.
53. Cialdini & Trost, *Social Influence: Social Norms, Conformity, and Compliance, supra*, at 155; Cialdini & Goldstein, *Social Influence: Compliance and Conformity, supra*, at 606; HEINZEN & GOODFRIEND, SOCIAL PSYCHOLOGY, *supra*, at 441.

54. Kassin et al., Social Psychology, *supra*, at 271–272; Cialdini & Goldstein, *Social Influence: Compliance and Conformity*, *supra*, at 606; Heinzen & Goodfriend, Social Psychology, *supra*, at 441.

55. Brent Simpson & Robb Willer, *Beyond Altruism: Sociological Foundations of Cooperation and Prosocial Behavior*, 63 Annu. Rev. Sociol. 41, 45–46, 55 (2015).

56. Cialdini & Trost, *Social Influence: Social Norms, Conformity, and Compliance*, *supra*, at 168.

57. Neuberg et al., *Evolutionary Social Psychology*, *supra*, at 778.

58. Pliskin et al., *Speaking Out and Breaking the Silence*, *supra*, at 250.

59. Neuberg et al., *Evolutionary Social Psychology*, *supra*, at 778; Kassin et al., Social Psychology, *supra*, at 271–272.

60. Neuberg et al., *Evolutionary Social Psychology*, *supra*, at 778.

61. Neuberg et al., *Evolutionary Social Psychology*, *supra*, at 778; Kassin et al., Social Psychology, *supra*, at 271–272.

62. See Neil Richards, Why Privacy Matters 79–80 (2022).

63. Richards, Why Privacy Matters, *supra*, at 79.

64. Francis T. McAndrew & Sara S. Koehnke, *On the Nature of Creepiness*, 43 New Ideas in Psychology 10 (2016); Margo C. Watt, Rebecca A. Maitland, & Catherine E. Gallagher, *A Case of the "Heeby Jeebies": An Examination of Intuitive Judgements of "Creepiness,"* 49(1) Canadian Journal of Behavioural Science/Revue canadienne des sciences du comportement 58 (2017); Francis T. McAndrew, *The Psychology, Geography, and Architecture of Horror: How Places Creep Us Out*, 4(2) Evolutionary Studies in Imaginative Culture 47 (2020); Jessie N. Doyle, Margo C. Watt, Melissa Howse, Karen Blair, & Petra Hauf, *What Is Creepiness? The Underlying Role of Ambiguity*, 54(3) Canadian Journal of Behavioural Science/ Revue canadienne des sciences du comportement 173 (2022).

65. Yang et al., *Go with the Flow against Uncertainty about Self under Existential Threat*, *supra*, at 439.

66. Neuberg et al., *Evolutionary Social Psychology*, *supra*, at 778.

67. See generally Daniel Kahneman, Thinking, Fast and Slow (2011); Kassin et al., Social Psychology, *supra*, at 123–124.

68. Kahneman, Thinking, Fast and Slow, *supra*, at 20–21; Kassin et al., Social Psychology, *supra*, at 123.

69. Kahneman, Thinking, Fast and Slow, *supra*, at 21; Kassin et al., Social Psychology, *supra*, at 123.

70. Kahneman, Thinking, Fast and Slow, *supra*, at 24; Kassin et al., Social Psychology, *supra*, at 123.

71. Cialdini, Influence: Science and Practice, *supra*, at 222.

72. Cialdini, Influence: Science and Practice, *supra*, at 222.

73. Cialdini & Goldstein, *Social Influence: Compliance and Conformity*, *supra*, at 606–611; Daniel Bar-Tal, *Self-Censorship as a Socio-political-psychological Phenomenon: Conception and Research*, 38 Advances in Polit. Psychol. 37, 50 (2017).

74. Nadler, *Expressive Law, Social Norms, and Social Groups*, *supra*, at 63, n.1.

75. Jennifer D. Campbell et al., *Conformity and Attention to the Stimulus: Some Temporal and Contextual Dynamics*, 51(2) J. Personality & Soc. Psychol. 315 (1986) (finding social pressure and uncertainty had "additive effects" on conformity).

76. Clark McCauley, *The Nature of Social Influence in Groupthink: Compliance and Internalization*, 57(2) J. Personality & Soc. Psychol. 250, 251 (1989) (noting there are "multiple and additive" sources of groupthink). See also Julian A. Oldmeadow et al., *Self-Categorization, Status, and Social Influence*, Soc. Psychol. Q. 138, 141 (2003) (finding that social status and identity both impacted social influence, but together

had an "additive" effect); Gordon W. Meyer, *Social Information Processing and Social Networks: A Test of Social Influence Mechanisms*, 47(9) HUMAN RELATIONS 1013, 1013 (1994) (finding that "multiple mechanisms" operate "simultaneously" in impacting social influence).

77. Cialdini & Trost, *Social Influence: Social Norms, Conformity, and Compliance, supra*, at 155; Cialdini & Goldstein, *Social Influence: Compliance and Conformity, supra*, at 606; HEINZEN & GOODFRIEND, SOCIAL PSYCHOLOGY, *supra*, at 441.

78. Deutsch & Gerard, *A Study of Normative and Informational Social Influences upon Individual Judgment, supra*, at 634.

79. CHARLES STANGOR, SOCIAL GROUPS IN ACTION AND INTERACTION 150–151 (2nd ed., 2016).

80. Kaminski & Witnov, *The Conforming Effect: First Amendment Implications of Surveillance, Beyond Chilling Speech, supra*, at 500.

81. Stanley Milgram, *Some Conditions of Obedience and Disobedience to Authority*, 18(1) HUMAN RELATIONS 57–76, 75 (1965).

82. Pliskin et al., *Speaking Out and Breaking the Silence, supra*, at 250; Sharvit, *Speaking Self-Censorship: Emerging Themes and Remaining Questions, supra*, at 274–275.

83. Some like philosopher R. M. Simpson have criticized my broader definition of chilling effects, arguing that I have essentially made chilling effects synonymous with conformity, causing a "radically expand" the definitional scope of chilling effects to include any garden variety social conformity: Robert Mark Simpson, Self-Censorship: *The Chilling Effect and the Heating Effect*, 2 Political Philosophy 345, 350 (2024). As this chapter has argued, however, while conformity theory is essential to understanding chilling effects, they are nevertheless qualitatively and quantitatively different in scale, complexity, and scope. As such, chilling effects deserve their own independent treatment and terminology.

5 A TAXONOMY OF CHILLING EFFECTS

1. In this sense, I am guided by Daniel Solove and his very influential taxonomy of privacy. One of his key aims in doing was to provide a "more pluralistic understanding of privacy": SOLOVE, UNDERSTANDING PRIVACY, *supra*, at 101.

2. Julia Carrie Wong, *The Cambridge Analytica Scandal Changed the World. But It Didn't Change Facebook*, THE GUARDIAN (Mar. 17, 2019), https://www.theguardian.com/technology/2019/mar/17/the-cambridge-analytica-scandal-changed-the-world-but-itdidnt-change-facebook.

3. SCHNEIER, DATA AND GOLIATH: THE HIDDEN BATTLES TO COLLECT YOUR DATA AND CONTROL YOUR WORLD, *supra*, at 4.

4. DAVID LYON, SURVEILLANCE STUDIES 14 (2014).

5. See RICHARDS, WHY PRIVACY MATTERS, *supra*, at 138.

6. Clarke, Information Technology and Dataveillance, *supra*; Clarke, *Dataveillance – 15 Years On, supra*.

7. Clarke, *Information Technology and Dataveillance, supra*.

8. Clarke, *Information Technology and Dataveillance, id.*; ORWELL, ANIMAL FARM, BURMESE DAYS, A CLERGYMAN'S DAUGHTER, COMING UP FOR AIR, KEEPING THE ASPIDISTRA FLYING, NINETEEN EIGHTY-FOUR, *supra*, at 744.

9. Clarke, *Information Technology and Dataveillance, supra*.

10. Clarke, *Information Technology and Dataveillance, id.*

11. DAVID LYON, THE ELECTRONIC EYE: THE RISE OF SURVEILLANCE SOCIETY 48, 58 (1994); Raley, *Dataveillance and Countervailance, supra*, at 124.

12. Lyon, The Electronic Eye: The Rise of Surveillance Society, *supra*, at 40; Raley, *Dataveillance and Countervailance, supra*, at 124; Clarke, *Information Technology and Dataveillance, supra*.

13. Roger Clarke, *Risks Inherent in the Digital Surveillance Economy: A Research Agenda*, 34(1) Journal of Information Technology 59, 59–60 (2019).

14. Zuboff, The Age of Surveillance Capitalism: The Fight for a Human Future at the New Frontier of Power, *supra*.

15. Lyon, *9/11, Synopticon and Scopophilia: Watching and Being Watched, supra*, at 44.

16. Lyon, The Culture of Surveillance: Watching as a Way of Life, *supra*, at 31–34.

17. Zygmunt Bauman & David Lyon, Liquid Surveillance: A Conversation (2013).

18. Ayse Ceyhan, *Surveillance as Biopower, in* Routledge Handbook of Surveillance Studies 38, 41 (Kirstie Ball, Kevin Haggarty, & David Lyon, eds., 2012).

19. Paul M. Schwartz, *Privacy and Democracy in Cyberspace*, 52 Vand. L. Rev. 1609, 1683 (1999).

20. Solove, *A Taxonomy of Privacy, supra*, at 520.

21. DeHashed lets you search for your IP address in a database of over 14 billion compromised addresses, https://www.dehashed.com. The website "Have I Been PWNED?" allows you to search for your email or phone number through a database with details on nearly 12 billion compromised accounts: https://haveibeenpwned.com.

22. Richards, Why Privacy Matters, *supra*, at 145–162.

23. Dia Kayyali, *The History of Surveillance and the Black Community*, Electronic Frontier Foundation (Feb. 13, 2014), https://www.eff.org/deeplinks/2014/02/history-surveillance-and-black-community; David Garrow, *The FBI and Martin Luther King*, The Atlantic (July 2002), https://www.theatlantic.com/magazine/archive/2002/07/the-fbi-and-martin-luther-king/302537/; David J. Garrow, The FBI and Martin Luther King, Jr.: From "Solo" to Memphis (1981); *More about FBI Spying*, Am. C.L. Union (Jan. 22, 2013), https://www.aclu.org/other/more-about-fbi-spying.

24. Kayyali, *The History of Surveillance and the Black Community, supra*.

25. Jonathon Penney et al., *Advancing Human Rights in the Dual Use Technology Industry*, 71 Colum. J. Int'l Aff. 103, 105–107 (2018).

26. Philip Di Salvo, *Information Security and Journalism: Mapping a Nascent Research Field*, 16(3) Sociology Compass 1, 2 (2022); Matthew A. Wasserman, *First Amendment Limitations on Police Surveillance: The Case of the Muslim Surveillance Program*, 90 N.Y.U. L. Rev. 1786, 1787 (2015); Karin Wahl-Jorgensen, Lucy K. Bennett, & Jonathan Cable, *Surveillance Normalization and Critique*, 5(3) Digital Journalism 386, 400 (2017) (finding "many" of the journalist participants in the study had personal experience with surveillance and "believe that the targeted surveillance of journalists has had a chilling effect on reporting practices").

27. Helen Nissenbaum, *Privacy as Contextual Integrity*, 79 Wash. L. Rev. 119, 127, 127 fn.28 (2004); Marcy Peek, *The Observer and the Observed: Re-imagining Privacy Dichotomies in Information Privacy Law*, 8 Nw. J. Tech. & Intell. Prop. 51, 52–53 (2009).

28. Richards, *Intellectual Privacy, supra*, at 413; Daniel J. Solove, *Privacy and Power: Computer Databases and Metaphors for Information Privacy*, 53 Stan. L. Rev. 1393, 1395–1397 (2001). See also Lora Kelley, *When "Big Brother" Isn't Scary Enough*, N.Y. Times (2019), https://www.nytimes.com/2019/11/04/opinion/surveillance-big-brother.html.

29. Kirstie Ball, Kevin Haggarty, & David Lyon, *Introduction: Surveillance as Sorting, in* Routledge Handbook of Surveillance Studies 119, 119 (Kirstie Ball, Kevin Haggarty, & David Lyon, eds., 2012).

30. Kirstie Ball, *All Consuming Surveillance: Surveillance as Marketplace Icon*, 20(2) CONSUMPTION MARKETS & CULTURE 95, 95 (2017).

31. SCHNEIER, DATA AND GOLIATH: THE HIDDEN BATTLES TO COLLECT YOUR DATA AND CONTROL YOUR WORLD, *supra*, at 222–223; Barton Gellman & Laura Poitras, *U.S., British Intelligence Mining Data from Nine U.S. Internet Companies in Broad Secret Program*, WASH. POST (June 6, 2013), https://www.washingtonpost.com/investigations/us-intelligence-mining-data-from-nine-us-internet-companies-in-broad-secret-program/2013/06/06/3a0coda8-cebf-11e2-8845-d970ccb04497_story.html.

32. COHEN, BETWEEN TRUTH AND POWER: THE LEGAL CONSTRUCTIONS OF INFORMATIONAL CAPITALISM, *supra*; ZUBOFF, THE AGE OF SURVEILLANCE CAPITALISM: THE FIGHT FOR A HUMAN FUTURE AT THE NEW FRONTIER OF POWER, *supra*; Sarah Myers West, *Data Capitalism: Redefining the Logics of Surveillance and Privacy*, 58(1) BUSINESS & SOCIETY 20, 20 (2019).

33. Bruce Schneier, *Spy Agencies Are Addicted to Corporate Data Load: Bruce Schneier*, BLOOMBERG BUSINESS WEEK (Aug. 1, 2013), https://www.bloomberg.com/opinion/articles/2013-07-31/the-public-private-surveillance-partnership.

34. JOSEPH TUROW, THE DAILY YOU 17 (2011).

35. 38 U.S.C. § 5727. See also Sasha Romanosky, David Hoffman, & Alessandro Acquisti, *Empirical Analysis of Data Breach Litigation*, 11(1) JOURNAL OF EMPIRICAL LEGAL STUDIES 74, 79 (2014) (defining data breach "broadly" as the "unauthorized disclosure of personal information by an organization"); Daniel Solove, *Are People Really Harmed by a Data Security Breach?*, CONCURRING OPINIONS (Sep. 22, 2010), http://web.archive.org/web/20110317204514/http://www.concurringopinions.com/archives/2010/09/are-people-really-harmed-by-a-data-security-breach.html.

36. Bakerhostetler, *Is Your Organization Compromise Read?*, 2016 DATA SECURITY INCIDENT RESPONSE REPORT 1–2 (2016), https://s3.amazonaws.com/f.datasrvr.com/fr1/516/11618/BakerHostetler_2016_Data_Security_Incident_Response_Report.pdf; Aaron Wynhausen, *The Eighth Circuit Further Complicates Plaintiff Standing in Data Breach Cases*, 84 MO. L. REV. 1, 1 (2019).

37. Bakerhostetler, *Is Your Organization Compromise Read?*, *supra*, at 1–2; Wynhausen, *The Eighth Circuit Further Complicates Plaintiff Standing in Data Breach Cases*, *supra*, at 1.

38. Wynhausen, *The Eighth Circuit Further Complicates Plaintiff Standing in Data Breach Cases*, *supra*, at 1.

39. Bree Fowler, *Data Breaches Break Record in 2021*, CNET NEWS (Jan. 24, 2022), https://www.cnet.com/news/privacy/record-number-of-data-breaches-reported-in-2021-new-report-says/.

40. *Id.*

41. Daniel J. Solove & Danielle Keats Citron, *Risk and Anxiety: A Theory of Data-Breach Harms*, 96 TEX. L. REV. 737, 744–745 (2017).

42. Solove & Citron, *Risk and Anxiety: A Theory of Data Breach Harms*, *supra*, at 744–745.

43. Solove & Citron, *Risk and Anxiety: A Theory of Data Breach Harms*, *supra*, at 759.

44. Calo, *The Boundaries of Privacy Harm*, *supra*, at 1148.

45. Solove, *A Taxonomy of Privacy*, *supra*, at 520.

46. Kiel Brennan-Marquez, *The Constitutional Limits of Private Surveillance*, 66 U. KAN. L. REV. 485, 497 (2018). See generally HELEN NISSENBAUM, PRIVACY IN CONTEXT: TECHNOLOGY, POLICY, AND THE INTEGRITY OF SOCIAL LIFE (2010) (developing a privacy theory based on the "integrity" of its context, that is, expectations around how information will flow in different contexts).

47. Yoan Hermstrüwer & Stephan Dickert, *Sharing is Daring: An Experiment on Consent, Chilling Effects and a Salient Privacy Nudge*, 51 INTER'L REV. L. & ECON. 38, 39 (2017).

48. *Id.*, at 39–40.

49. *Id.*, at 40, 42–43, 45–46.

50. *Id.*, at 45.

51. Solove, *A Taxonomy of Privacy*, *supra*, at 488 (defining information processing). Solove also defined data mining as "excavating repositories of personal data to glean nuggets of new information" that often involves "combining different pieces of information [that] can yield new insights into an individual's personality and behavior": SOLOVE, UNDERSTANDING PRIVACY, *supra*, at 191.

52. Sagiroglu & Sinanc, *Big Data: A Review*, *supra*, at 42; Hariri et al., *Uncertainty in Big Data Analytics: Survey, Opportunities, and Challenges*, *supra*, at 1.

53. Hideyuki Matsumi & Daniel J. Solove, *The Prediction Society: AI and the Problems of Forecasting the Future*, 1 U. ILL. L. REV. 1–2 (2025). For more on the prediction society, see also AJAY AGRAWAL, JOSHUA GANS, & AVI GOLDFARB, PREDICTION MACHINES: THE SIMPLE ECONOMICS OF ARTIFICIAL INTELLIGENCE (2018).

54. SOLOVE, UNDERSTANDING PRIVACY, *supra*, at 194.

55. Matsumi & Solove, *The Prediction Society: AI and the Problems of Forecasting the Future*, *supra*, at 35–36.

56. See for example: BORGESIUS, IMPROVING PRIVACY PROTECTION IN THE AREA OF BEHAVIOURAL TARGETING, *supra*; Raley, *Dataveillance and Countervailance*, *supra*, at 123–124; Büchi et al., *The Chilling Effects of Algorithmic Profiling: Mapping the Issues*, *supra*; Büchi et al., *The Chilling Effects of Digital Dataveillance: A Theoretical Model and an Empirical Research Agenda*, *supra*; Kappeler et al., *Qualitative Evidence of Chilling Effects – How Users Imaginaries of Dataveillance Lead to Inhibited Digital Behavior*, *supra*; Elana Zeide & Helen Nissenbaum, *Learner Privacy in MOOCs and Virtual Education*, 16(3) THEORY & RESEARCH IN EDUC. 280–307 (2018).

57. Sagiroglu & Sinanc, *Big Data: A Review*, *supra*, at 45; Hariri et al., *Uncertainty in Big Data Analytics: Survey, Opportunities, and Challenges*, *supra*, at 8–13; Ike Kavas, *AI and Data Mining: Do You Have the Keys to the Castle?*, FORBES (July 26, 2022), https://www.forbes.com/sites/forbestechcouncil/2022/07/26/ai-and-data-mining-do-you-have-the-keys-to-the-castle/?sh=671af50f5cc5. See also DANIEL T. LAROSE & CHANTAL D. LAROSE, DISCOVERING KNOWLEDGE IN DATA: AN INTRODUCTION TO DATA MINING (2014); David J. Hand, *Principles of Data Mining*, 30(7) DRUG SAFETY 621 (2007); IAN H. WITTEN ET AL., DATA MINING 21–22 (3rd ed., 2011).

58. Konstantinos V. Katsikopoulos & Marc C. Canellas, *Decoding Human Behavior with Big Data? Critical, Constructive Input from the Decision Sciences*, 43 AI MAGAZINE 126, 126 (2022); Helen Susannah Moat et al., *Using Big Data to Predict Collective Behavior in the Real World*, 37(1) BEHAVIORAL AND BRAIN SCIENCES 92, 92–93 (2014).

59. Katsikopoulos & Canellas, *Decoding Human Behavior with Big Data? Critical, Constructive Input from the Decision Sciences*, *supra*, at 128, 131; Moat et al., *Using Big Data to Predict Collective Behavior in the Real World*, *supra*, at 92–93; Chris Anderson, *The End of Theory: The Data Deluge Makes the Scientific Method Obsolete*, 16(7) WIRED MAGAZINE 16, 16–17 (2008); Danielle Keats Citron & Frank Pasquale, *The Scored Society: Due Process for Automated Predictions*, 89 WASH. L. REV. 1 (2014) (noting predictive algorithms are being used in finance, housing, employment, and consumer contexts); Wang Hai et al., *Towards Felicitous Decision Making: An Overview on Challenges and Trends of Big Data*, 367 INFORMATION SCI. 747 (2016) (reviewing countless studies); Martin Hilbert, *Big Data for Development: A Review of Promises and Challenges*, 34(1) DEV. POL'Y REV. 135 (2016) (reviewing countless big data behavioral prediction applications). See also Andrew D. Selbst, *Disparate Impact in Big Data Policing*, 52 GA. L.

REV. 109, 109 (2017) (noting big data driven advancements in a range of domains, including predictive policing); Sean D. Young, *Behavioral Insights on Big Data: Using Social Media for Predicting Biomedical Outcomes*, 22(1) TRENDS IN MICROBIOL. 601 (2014); Giles C. Oatley, *Themes in Data Mining, Big Data, and Crime Analytics*, 12 WIREs DATA MINING KNOWL. DISCOV. 1 (2021).

60. Katsikopoulos & Canellas, *Decoding Human Behavior with Big Data? Critical, Constructive Input from the Decision Sciences, supra*, at 126; Moat et al., *Using Big Data to Predict Collective Behavior in the Real World, supra*.

61. Mark G. Cooper, *The Contradictions of Minority Report*, 28(2) FILM CRITICISM 24, 24 (2002); David Sims, *Minority Report Tried to Warn Us about Technology*, THE ATLANTIC (June 2022), https://www.theatlantic.com/culture/archive/2022/06/minority-report-spielberg-movie-tom-cruise/661274/.

62. Cooper, *The Contradictions of Minority Report, supra*; Sims, *Minority Report Tried to Warn Us about Technology, supra*.

63. Cooper, *The Contradictions of Minority Report, supra*; Sims, *Minority Report Tried to Warn Us about Technology, supra*.

64. Cooper, *The Contradictions of Minority Report, supra*, at 24; Sims, *Minority Report Tried to Warn Us about Technology, supra*. See also Deitmar Kammerer, *Video Surveillance in Hollywood Movies*, 2(2/3) SURVEILLANCE & SOCIETY 464 (2004); Christopher Wehner, *"What I Did Was Ignore the Hardware" – Scott Frank on Minority Report*, CREATIVE SCREENWRITING (Feb. 24, 2015), https://www.creativescreenwriting.com/what-i-did-was-ignore-the-hardware-scott-frank-on-minority-report/.

65. Before filming, Spielberg assembled a coterie of "self-styled futurists" at the Massachusetts Institute of Technology. These ideas were key themes of discussion at this "think tank summit": Ian Rothkerch, *Will the Future Really Look Like "Minority Report"?*, SALON (July 10, 2002), https://www.salon.com/2002/07/10/underkoffler_belker/.

66. Seungjin Whang, *"Sense and Respond" Tailors Message to Customers*, INSIGHTS BY STANFORD BUSINESS (May 1, 2005), https://www.gsb.stanford.edu/insights/sense-respond-tailors-message-customers.

67. Matsumi & Solove, *The Prediction Society: AI and the Problems of Forecasting the Future, supra*, at 1, 12–22; Hideyuki Matsumi, *Predictions and Privacy: Should There Be Rules about Using Personal Data to Forecast the Future*, 48 CUMB. L. REV. 149, 149–150 (2017); Daniel J. Solove, *Data Is What Data Does: Regulating Based on Harm and Risk Instead of Sensitive Data*, 118 Nw. U. L. REV. 1081 (2023).

68. Matsumi, *Predictions and Privacy: Should There Be Rules about Using Personal Data to Forecast the Future, supra*, at 149.

69. Charles Duhigg, *How Companies Learn Your Secrets*, N.Y. TIMES MAGAZINE (Feb. 16, 2012), https://www.nytimes.com/2012/02/19/magazine/shopping-habits.html.

70. *Id.*

71. Eric Siegel, *When Does Predictive Technology Become Unethical?*, HARVARD BUSINESS REVIEW (Oct. 23, 2020), https://hbr.org/2020/10/when-does-predictive-technology-become-unethical.

72. *Id.*

73. Matt Stroud, *Heat Listed*, THE VERGE (May 24, 2021), https://www.theverge.com/c/22444020/chicago-pd-predictive-policing-heat-list; Chris Gilliard, *Crime Prediction Keeps Society Stuck in the Past?*, WIRED (Jan. 2, 2022), https://www.wired.com/story/crime-prediction-racist-history/.

74. Stroud, *Heat Listed, supra*; Gilliard, *Crime Prediction Keeps Society Stuck in the Past?, supra*.

75. Stroud, *Heat Listed, supra*; Gilliard, *Crime Prediction Keeps Society Stuck in the Past?*, *supra*.

76. Stroud, *Heat Listed, supra*; Gilliard, *Crime Prediction Keeps Society Stuck in the Past?*, *supra*.

77. Stroud, *Heat Listed, supra*; Gilliard, *Crime Prediction Keeps Society Stuck in the Past?*, *supra*.

78. Michal Kosinski et al., *Private Traits and Attributes Are Predictable from Digital Records of Human Behavior*, 110 PROC. NAT. ACAD. SCI. U.S. AM. 5802, 5802–5803 (2013).

79. Solove, *Data Is What Data Does: Regulating Based on Harm and Risk Instead of Sensitive Data, supra*, at 21–22; Alicia Solow-Niederman, *Information Privacy and the Inference Economy*, 117 NW. L. REV. 357 (2022).

80. Matsumi & Solove, *The Prediction Society: AI and the Problems of Forecasting the Future, supra*, at 12–14, 18–19; Kate Crawford & Jason Schultz, *Big Data and Due Process: Toward a Framework to Redress Predictive Privacy Harms*, 55 B.C. L. REV. 93, 96–109 (2014).

81. Matsumi & Solove, *The Prediction Society: AI and the Problems of Forecasting the Future, supra*, at 12–21. Though Stroud notes in his reporting that Chicago began experimenting with data-based policing as early as the 1990s: Stroud, *Heat Listed, supra*.

82. Matsumi & Solove, *The Prediction Society: AI and the Problems of Forecasting the Future, supra*, at 1, 36. For more on the prediction society, see also AGRAWAL, GANS, & GOLDFARB, PREDICTION MACHINES: THE SIMPLE ECONOMICS OF ARTIFICIAL INTELLIGENCE, *supra*.

83. Büchi et al., *The Chilling Effects of Algorithmic Profiling: Mapping the Issues, supra*, at 7–8; Büchi et al., *The Chilling Effects of Digital Dataveillance: A Theoretical Model and an Empirical Research Agenda, supra*, at 5.

84. Duhigg, *How Companies Learn Your Secrets, supra*.

85. Jeremy Gorner, *Chicago Police Use "Heat List" as Strategy to Prevent Violence*, THE CHICAGO TRIBUNE (Aug. 21, 2013), https://www.chicagotribune.com/news/ct-xpm-2013-08-21-ct-met-heat-list-20130821-story.html.

86. Gorner, *Chicago Police Use "Heat List" as Strategy to Prevent Violence, id.*; Stroud, *Heat Listed, supra*.

87. Gorner, *Chicago Police Use "Heat List" as Strategy to Prevent Violence, supra*.

88. Gorner, *Chicago Police Use "Heat List" as Strategy to Prevent Violence, id.*

89. Büchi et al., *The Chilling Effects of Algorithmic Profiling: Mapping the Issues, supra*, at 7–8; Büchi et al., *The Chilling Effects of Digital Dataveillance: A Theoretical Model and an Empirical Research Agenda, supra*, at 5.

90. DANIEL SOLOVE, THE DIGITAL PERSON: TECHNOLOGY AND PRIVACY IN THE DIGITAL AGE 36–37, 226 (2004).

91. Ivan Manokha, *Surveillance, Panopticism, and Self-Discipline in the Digital Age*, 16(2) SURVEILLANCE & SOCIETY 219, 232 (2018).

92. FRANK PASQUALE, THE BLACK BOX SOCIETY: THE SECRET ALGORITHMS THAT CONTROL MONEY AND INFORMATION 6–8 (2015).

93. *Id.*, at 8.

94. Victoria Hollis et al., *On Being Told How We Feel: How Algorithmic Sensor Feedback Influences Emotion Perception*, 2(3) PROCEEDINGS OF THE ACM ON INTERACTIVE, MOBILE, WEARABLE AND UBIQUITOUS TECHNOLOGIES 1, 1–2 (2018). See also Caitlin Lustig, *Algorithmic Authority: The Case of Bitcoin*, 48TH HAWAII INTERNATIONAL CONFERENCE ON SYSTEM SCIENCES, IEEE 743 (2015).

95. Danielle Keats Citron, *Technological Due Process*, 85 WASH. UNIV. LAW REV. 1249, 1271 (2008).

96. Sonia K. Katyal, *Private Accountability in an Age of Artificial Intelligence, in* THE CAMBRIDGE HANDBOOK OF ALGORITHMS 47 (Woodrow Barfield, ed., 2021) (noting courts all too often defer to AI decision-making and deny defendants access to source code for software). See also Thomas Grote & Philipp Berens, *On the Ethics of Algorithmic Decision-Making in Healthcare,* 46(3) J. MED. ETHICS 205 (2020).
97. Sandra Wachter, *Affinity Profiling and Discrimination by Association in Online Behavioral Advertising,* 35 BERKELEY TECH. L.J. 367, 369–370 (2020); Elspeth A. Brotherton, *Big Brother Gets a Makeover: Behavioral Targeting and the Third-Party Doctrine,* 61 EMORY L.J. 555, 558 (2012).
98. Wachter, *Affinity Profiling and Discrimination by Association in Online Behavioral Advertising, supra,* 369–370; RICHARDS, WHY PRIVACY MATTERS, *supra,* at 145–162. See also generally: Crawford & Schultz, *Big Data and Due Process: Toward a Framework to Redress Predictive Privacy Harms, supra.*
99. RICHARDS, WHY PRIVACY MATTERS, *supra,* at 145–162.
100. Hu, *Cambridge Analytica's Blackbox, supra,* at 2.
101. This is similar to the forms of "system chill" we will talk about later in the chapter.
102. Manokha, *Surveillance, Panopticism, and Self-Discipline in the Digital Age, supra,* at 232.
103. Joanne Hinds, Emma J. Williams, & Adam N. Joinson, *"It Wouldn't Happen to Me": Privacy Concerns and Perspectives following the Cambridge Analytica Scandal,* INTERNATIONAL JOURNAL OF HUMAN-COMPUTER STUDIES 10, 10 (2020).
104. Yuval Feldman & Doron Teichman, *Are All Legal Probabilities Created Equal,* 84 N.Y.U.L. REV. 980, 985 (2009).
105. *Id.,* at 985.
106. Schauer, *Fear, Risk, and the First Amendment: Unraveling the Chilling Effect, supra,* at 687.
107. YUVAL FELDMAN, THE LAW OF GOOD PEOPLE: CHALLENGING STATES' ABILITY TO REGULATE HUMAN BEHAVIOR 1185 (2018).
108. Lauren B. Edelman, *Legal Ambiguity and Symbolic Structures: Organizational Mediation of Civil Rights Law,* 97(6) AM. J. SOCIOL. 1531, 1542 (1992).
109. Yuval Feldman & Alon Harel, *Social Norms, Self-Interest and Ambiguity of Legal Norms: An Experimental Analysis of the Rule vs. Standard Dilemma,* 4 REV. L. & ECON. 81, 81–82 (2008).
110. *Id.,* at 81–82.
111. Feldman & Teichman, *Are All Legal Probabilities Created Equal, supra,* at 985.
112. Licht, *Social Norms and the Law, supra,* at 717, 727; McAdams & Rasmusen, *Norms and the Law, supra,* at 1606.
113. McAdams & Rasmusen, *Norms and the Law, supra,* at 1591, 1606; Licht, *Social Norms and the Law, supra,* at 717.
114. Licht, *Social Norms and the Law, supra,* at 717, 736–737; Tyler, *Understanding the Force of Law, supra,* at 507; Ellickson, *Law and Economics Discovers Social Norms, supra,* at 539–541.
115. Kinsley, *Chill, supra,* at 272–273.
116. Kinsley, *Chill, supra,* at 261; Brian Calabrese, *Fear-Based Standing: Cognizing an Injury-in-Fact,* 68 WASH. & LEE L. REV. 1445, 1460–1461 (2011).
117. Martin et al., *Why Ordinary People Comply with Environmental Laws: A Structural Model on Normative and Attitudinal Determinants of Illegal Anti-ecological Behavior, supra,* at 82–83.
118. ERIC BARENDT ET AL., LIBEL AND THE MEDIA: THE CHILLING EFFECT (2007); Stephen M. Renas, Charles J. Hartmann, & James L. Walker, *An Empirical Analysis of*

the *Chilling Effect, in* THE COST OF LIBEL: ECONOMIC AND POLICY IMPLICATIONS 41 (Everette E. Dennis & Eli M. Noam, eds., 1989); Michael Massing, *The Libel Chill: How Cold Is It Out There?*, COLUM. JOURNALISM REV. 31 (May–June 1985) (citing 150 interviews with editors and attorneys); Elizabeth K. Hansen & Roy L. Moore, *Chilling the Messenger: Impact of Libel on Community Newspapers*, 11(2) NEWS. RES. J. 86 (1990).

119. Massing, *The Libel Chill: How Cold Is It Out There?*, *supra*; Hansen & Moore, *Chilling the Messenger: Impact of Libel on Community Newspapers*, *supra*.

120. Anthony A. Braga et al., *Focused Deterrence Strategies and Crime Control: An Updated Systematic Review and Meta-Analysis of the Empirical Evidence*, AMERICAN SOCIETY OF CRIMINOLOGY 205, 205, 209 (2018) (discussing results of research meta-analysis of "person-focused" crime deterrence strategies that target "individuals" and "groups" and finding focused deterrence strategies are associated with an "overall statistically significant, moderate crime reduction effect"). See also ANTHONY A. BRAGA & DAVID M. KENNEDY, A FRAMEWORK FOR ADDRESSING VIOLENCE AND SERIOUS CRIME: FOCUSED DETERRENCE, LEGITIMACY, AND PREVENTION 3–4 (2020).

121. Braga, *Focused Deterrence Strategies and Crime Control: An Updated Systematic Review and Meta-analysis of the Empirical Evidence*, *supra*, at 205.

122. Kevin D. Haggerty & Richard V. Ericson, *The Surveillant Assemblage*, 51(4) BRITISH JOURNAL OF SOCIOLOGY 605, 611 (2000).

123. *Id.*

124. Sarah Brayne, *Surveillance and System Avoidance: Criminal Justice Contact and Institutional Attachment*, 79 AM. SOC. REV. 367 (2014); SARAH BRAYNE, SURVEIL AND PROTECT: DATA, DISCRETION, AND THE FUTURE OF POLICING 115 (2020).

125. BRAYNE, SURVEIL AND PROTECT: DATA, DISCRETION, AND THE FUTURE OF POLICING, *supra*, at 115.

126. BRAYNE, SURVEIL AND PROTECT: DATA, DISCRETION, AND THE FUTURE OF POLICING, *id.*, at 115. Karen Levy has used the term "justice-involved" to refer to these people. See: Karen Levy, *Chilling Effects and Unequal Subjects: A Response to Jonathon Penney's Understanding Chilling Effects*, 106 MINN. L. REV. Headnotes 392, 394 (2022).

127. BRAYNE, SURVEIL AND PROTECT: DATA, DISCRETION, AND THE FUTURE OF POLICING, *supra*, at 115.

128. Sarah Lageson & Shadd Maruna, Digital Degradation: Stigma Management in the Internet Age, 20(1) PUNISHMENT & SOCIETY 113 (2018); Sarah Lageson, *Found Out and Opting Out: The Consequences of Online Criminal Records for Families*, 665(1) ANNALS OF THE AMERICAN ACADEMY OF POLITICAL AND SOCIAL SCIENCE 127 (2016).

129. Levy, *Chilling Effects and Unequal Subjects: A Response to Jonathon Penney's Understanding Chilling Effects*, *supra*, at Headnotes 392.

130. Levy, *Chilling Effects and Unequal Subjects: A Response to Jonathon Penney's Understanding Chilling Effects*, *id.*, at 394–395; KAREN LEVY, DATA DRIVEN: TRUCKERS, TECHNOLOGY, AND THE WORKPLACE SURVEILLANCE (2022).

131. Levy, *Chilling Effects and Unequal Subjects: A Response to Jonathon Penney's Understanding Chilling Effects*, *supra*, at 394–395.

132. Lageson, *Found Out and Opting Out: The Consequences of Online Criminal Records for Families*, *supra*, at 133.

133. Levy, *Chilling Effects and Unequal Subjects: A Response to Jonathon Penney's Understanding Chilling Effects*, *supra*, at 394–395.

134. Emily A. Vogels, *The State of Online Harassment*, PEW RESEARCH CENTER (Jan. 13, 2021).

135. *Id.*
136. Siyi Wang & Nelsy Affoum, *Cyber Harassment: A Growing Concern in the Age of COVID*, WORLD BANK BLOG (Dec. 9, 2021), https://blogs.worldbank.org/developmenttalk/cyber-harassment-growing-concern-age-covid; Miriam Berger, *Gender-Based Online Abuse Surged during the Pandemic. Laws Haven't Kept Up, Activists Say*, WASHINGTON POST (Nov. 24, 2021), https://www.washingtonpost.com/world/2021/11/24/online-abuse-surged-during-pandemic-laws-havent-kept-up-activists-say/; Bianca Nogrady, *"I Hope You Die": How the COVID Pandemic Unleashed Attacks on Scientists*, NATURE (Oct. 13, 2021).
137. CITRON, HATE CRIMES IN CYBERSPACE, *supra*, at 5–8, 29; Danielle Keats Citron, *Sexual Privacy*, 128 YALE L. J. 1870, 1875 (2019); Mary Anne Franks, *Sexual Harassment 2.0*, 71 MD. L. REV. 655, 657–658 (2012).
138. Mary Anne Franks, *Beyond "Free Speech for the White Man": Feminism and the First Amendment, in* RESEARCH HANDBOOK ON FEMINIST JURISPRUDENCE 29 (Cynthia Bowman et al., eds., 2018)("evidence abounds of the chilling effects of harassment and other forms of abuse"); Marwick, *Scandal or Sex Crime? Gendered Privacy and the Celebrity Nude Photo Leaks, supra*, at 179 (noting online abuse has "a chilling effect where women and LGB individuals are less likely to contribute content and more likely to self-censor"); Danielle Keats Citron & Mary Anne Franks, *Criminalizing Revenge Porn*, 49 WAKE FOREST L. REV. 345, 385 (2014) ("the nonconsensual disclosure of a person's sexually explicit images chills private expression").
139. Pliskin et al., *Speaking Out and Breaking the Silence, supra*, at 129 (describing journalists who keep "silent regarding sensitive and delicate issues for fear for their personal safety. These fears may include arrests, torture, and even murder of state officials by private citizens. In South America, several journalists have been murdered or have disappeared following investigative reporting into drug-related deals").
140. See generally Danielle Keats Citron, *Spying Inc.*, 72 WASH. & LEE L. REV. 1243 (2015).
141. Jennifer Rand, *Online Harassment against Women in the Trump Era*, HUFFINGTON POST (Dec. 5, 2016), https://www.huffpost.com/entry/online-harassment-against-women-in-the-trump-era_b_58446a1de4b0cf3f64558af0.
142. ZEYNEP TUFEKCI, TWITTER AND TEAR GAS: THE POWER AND FRAGILITY OF NETWORKED PROTEST 239 (2017); Zeynep Tufekci, *It's the (Democracy Poisoning) Golden Age of Free Speech*, WIRED (Jan. 16, 2018), https://www.wired.com/story/free-speech-issue-tech-turmoil-new-censorship/.
143. Tim Wu, *Is the First Amendment Obsolete*, 117 MICH. L. REV. 547 (2018).

6 THE DANGERS OF CHILLING EFFECTS

1. MICHEL FOUCAULT, POWER/KNOWLEDGE: SELECTED INTERVIEWS AND OTHER WRITINGS1972–1977 118–119 (Colin Gordon et al., trans., 1980).
2. *Id.*, at 118–119.
3. *Id.*, at 121–122.
4. MICHEL FOUCAULT, DISCIPLINE AND PUNISHMENT: THE BIRTH OF THE PRISON 194 (2nd ed., 1995).
5. Jonathan R. Siegel, *Chilling Injuries as a Basis for Standing*, 98 YALE L.J. 905, 914 (1989) (citing New York Times Co. v. Sullivan, 376 U.S. 254, 270 (1964)).
6. JOSEPH RAZ, THE MORALITY OF FREEDOM 368 (1986); Paul M. Schwartz, *Privacy and Democracy in Cyberspace*, 52 VAND. L. REV. 1607, 1655–1656 (1999).

232   *Notes to pages 96–99*

7. Cohen, *What Privacy Is for, supra*, at 1908.
8. Cohen, *What Privacy Is for, supra*, at 1908.
9. Cohen, *What Privacy Is for, supra*, at 1908.
10. Cohen, *What Privacy Is for, supra*, at 1908.
11. Cohen, *What Privacy Is for, supra*, at 1908.
12. Erving Goffman, Interaction Ritual 84–85 (1967); George Herbert Mead, Mind, Self, and Society 152–164 (1934). *See also* Robert C. Post, *The Social Foundations of Defamation Law: Reputation and the Constitution*, 74 Calif. L. Rev. 691 707–719 (1986) (discussing the social foundations of the "dignity" interest in defamation law).
13. David Shulman, *Self Presentation: Impression Management in the Digital Age, in* The Routledge International Handbook of Goffman Studies 26, 27 (Michael Hviid Jacobsen & Greg Smith, eds., 2022).
14. Goffman, Interaction Ritual, *supra*, at 84–85; Post, *The Social Foundations of Defamation Law: Reputation and the Constitution, supra*, at 708–709.
15. Goffman, Interaction Ritual, *supra*, at 84–85; Erving Goffman, The Presentation of Self in Everyday Life 75, 132–137, 253 (1959).
16. Mead, Mind, Self, and Society, *supra*, at 178, 173.
17. Goffman, Interaction Ritual, *supra*, at 84; Post, *The Social Foundations of Defamation Law: Reputation and the Constitution, supra*, at 710.
18. Goffman, Interaction Ritual, *supra*, at 84; Post, *The Social Foundations of Defamation Law: Reputation and the Constitution, supra*, at 710.
19. Cohen, *What Privacy Is for, supra*, at 1932.
20. Cohen, *What Privacy Is for, supra*, at 1910.
21. Cohen, *Examined Lives: Informational Privacy and the Subject as Object, supra*, at 1426.
22. Cohen, *Examined Lives: Informational Privacy and the Subject as Object, supra*, at 1426.
23. Richards, Intellectual Privacy: Rethinking Civil Liberties in the Digital Age, *supra*, at 95–96, 98–99.
24. Richards, Why Privacy Matters, *supra*, at 114–115, 118.
25. Richards, Why Privacy Matters, *supra*, at 114–115.
26. Richards, Why Privacy Matters, *supra*, at 115.
27. Mead, Mind, Self, and Society, *supra*, at 178,173. Goffman, The Presentation of Self in Everyday Life, *supra*, at 111–119.
28. Richards, Why Privacy Matters, *supra*, at 130.
29. Jonathon W. Penney, *Internet Access Rights: A Brief History and Intellectual Origins*, 38 Wm. Mitchell L. Rev. 10, 23–34 (2011).
30. Keith N. Hampton et al., *Social Media and the "Spiral of Silence,"* Pew Res. Ctr. 4 (2014). Other Pew Internet surveys found similar chilling effects. See: Lee Rainie et al., *Americans' Privacy Strategies Post-Snowden*, Pew Res. Internet Project 4 (Mar. 16, 2015); Lee Rainie et al., *Anonymity, Privacy, and Security Online*, Pew Res. Ctr. (2013); FDR Group & PEN American Center, *Chilling Effects: NSA Surveillance Drives U.S. Writers to Self-Censor* 3–4 (2013); FDR Group & PEN American Center, *Global Chilling: The Impact of Mass Surveillance on International Writers* (2015).
31. Julian Hattem, *Many Say NSA News Changed Their Behavior*, The Hill (Apr. 4, 2014), https://thehill.com/policy/technology/202434-poll-nearly-half-say-nsa-news-affected-behaior/.
32. Mark Rosso, Abm Nasir, & Mohsen Farhadloo, *Chilling Effects and the Stock Market Response to the Snowden Revelations*, 22 New Media & Soc'y 1976 (2020) (finding NSA surveillance revelations chilling effects in search engine use); Andrea Forte, Nazanin Andalibi, & Rachel Greenstadt, *Privacy, Anonymity, and Perceived Risk in Open Collaboration: A Study of Tor Users and Wikipedians*, CSCW 1800 (2017).

33. See for example: Penney, *Understanding Chilling Effects, supra*, at 1453 (and accompanying footnotes).
34. Elizabeth Stoycheff, *Under Surveillance: Examining Facebook's Spiral of Silence Effects in the Wake of NSA Internet Monitoring, supra*.
35. Stoycheff et al., *Privacy and the Panopticon: Online Mass Surveillance's Deterrence and Chilling Effects, supra*, at 608–609.
36. Penney, *Internet Surveillance, Regulation, and Chilling Effects Online: A Comparative Case Study, supra*.
37. Aleecia McDonald & Lorrie Faith Cranor, *Beliefs and Behaviors: Internet Users' Understanding of Behavioral Advertising*, TPRC (2010).
38. Strycharz & Segijn, *Consumer Differences in Chilling Effects, supra*.
39. Kappeler et al., *Qualitative Evidence of Chilling Effects – How Users Imaginaries of Dataveillance Lead to Inhibited Digital Behavior, supra*.
40. Büchi et al., *The Chilling Effects of Digital Dataveillance: A Theoretical Model and an Empirical Research Agenda, supra*, at 6.
41. Cohen, *Examined Lives: Informational Privacy and the Subject as Object, supra*, at 1426.
42. *Id.*, at 129–130.
43. Richards, Why Privacy Matters, *supra*, at 119. See also Julie Cohen, Configuring the Networked Self 149 (2012).
44. Jason Blakely, *Radicalizing and De-radicalizing Charles Taylor*, 29(5) Inter'l J. of Philos. Stud. 689, 690 (2021); Gilberto Hoffmann Marcon & Reinaldo Furlan, *The Issue of Identity in Postmodernity: Authenticity and Individualism in Charles Taylor*, 31 Psicologia USP 1, 1 (2020).
45. Charles Taylor, The Ethics of Authenticity 33 (1991).
46. Joseph Woelfel, *Significant Others, in* The Blackwell Encyclopedia of Sociology 1, 1 (George Ritzer, ed., 2023).
47. Rachel Kleinfeld, *The Rise in Political Violence in the United States and Damage to Our Democracy*, Carnegie Endowment for International Peace Blog (Mar. 31, 2021); *Social Media and Political Extremism*, Homeland Security and Emergency Preparedness Blog, L. Douglas Wilder School of Government and Public Affairs, Virginia Commonwealth University (Feb. 28, 2023); Paul Barrett, Justin Hendrix, & Grant Sims, *How Tech Platforms Fuel US Political Polarization and What Government Can Do about It*, Brookings Institute Commentary (Sep. 27, 2021).
48. Sunstein, Conformity: The Power of Social Influences, *supra*, at ix.
49. Kassin et al., Social Psychology, *supra*, at 269–270.
50. Cass Sunstein, #Republic: Divided Democracy in the Age of Social Media 75–76 (2017).
51. See for example: Markus Kaakinen et al., *Impulsivity, Internalizing Symptoms, and Online Group Behavior as Determinants of Online Hate*, 15(4) PLoS One 1, 3 (2020) ("Self-stereotyping and conformity to emergent group norms can make hostile online behavior more prevalent"); Wai Yen Tang & Jesse Fox, *Men's Harassment Behavior in Online Video Games: Personality Traits and Game Factors*, 42 Aggress. Behav. 513 (2016); Jesse Fox & Wai Yen Tang, *Sexism in Online Video Games: The Role of Conformity to Masculine Norms and Social Dominance Orientation*, 33 Computers in Hum. Behav. 314 (2014); Jonas Colliander, *"This Is Fake News": Investigating the Role of Conformity to Other Users' Views When Commenting on and Spreading Disinformation in Social Media*, 97 Computers in Hum. Behav. 202, 208 (2019) (finding social conformity to impact people's willingness to share false news and disinformation online).

52. For examples, see generally: SUNSTEIN, #REPUBLIC, *supra*; CASS SUNSTEIN, REPUBLIC. COM 2.0 (2007); CASS SUNSTEIN, GOING TO EXTREMES: HOW LIKE MINDS UNITE AND DIVIDE (2009).

53. SUNSTEIN, CONFORMITY: THE POWER OF SOCIAL INFLUENCES, *supra*, at 85–86; SUNSTEIN, REPUBLIC.COM 2.0, *supra*, at 60–61.

54. Sunstein maintains that conformity and group polarization are distinct phenomena, which they are, and in earlier works argued that the former cannot explain the latter: Cass R. Sunstein, *The Law of Group Polarization*, 91 JOHN M. OLIN PROGRAM IN L. & ECON. WORKING PAPER 1, 12–13, 13 n.56 (1999). He was right to the extent that conformity cannot explain group polarization in its entirety but it is unquestionably a central factor: John T. Jost, Delia S. Baldassarri, & James N. Druckman, *Cognitive–Motivational Mechanisms of Political Polarization in Social-Communicative Contexts*, 1 NAT. REV. PSYCHOL. 560, 560–561 (2022) (reviewing the literature and noting that one of the two leading explanations of group polarization relies on social comparison processes and conformity). See also Yizhou Zhang, Yibao Wang, Tinggui Chen, & Jiawen Shi, *Agent-Based Modeling Approach for Group Polarization Behavior Considering Conformity and Network Relationship Strength*, 32(14) CONCURRENCY & COMPUTATION: PRACT. & EXPER. 1, 2 (2020). In more recent works, Sunstein himself cites "reputational" considerations and the "spiral of silence" as key contributors to group polarization, and conformity is central to understanding both: SUNSTEIN, #REPUBLIC, *supra*, at 72–73.

55. SUNSTEIN, #REPUBLIC, *supra*, at 76–83.

56. SUNSTEIN, #REPUBLIC, *supra*, at 76–77.

57. SUNSTEIN, #REPUBLIC, *supra*, at 71–72; SUNSTEIN, REPUBLIC.COM 2.0, *supra*, at 65–66; RICHARDS, WHY PRIVACY MATTERS, *supra*, at 124–125.

58. ELI PARISER, THE FILTER BUBBLE: WHAT THE INTERNET IS HIDING FROM YOU (2011); RICHARDS, WHY PRIVACY MATTERS, *supra*, at 124–125.

59. SUNSTEIN, #REPUBLIC, *supra*, at 76.

60. Murdoch Watney, *Intensifying State Surveillance of Electronic Communications: A Legal Solution in Addressing Extremism or Not?*, 2015 IEEE 10TH INTERNATIONAL CONFERENCE ON AVAILABILITY, RELIABILITY AND SECURITY 367 (2015).

61. Dominic Abrams, Margaret Wetherell, Sandra Cochrane, Michael A. Hogg, & John C. Turner, *Knowing What to Think by Knowing Who You Are: Self-Categorization and the Nature of Norm Formation, Conformity and Group Polarization*, 29(2) BRIT. J. SOC. PSYCHOL. 97, 98 (1990).

62. Kyounghee Hazel Kwon & Raghav Rao, *Cyber-Rumor Sharing under a Homeland Security Threat in the Context of Government Internet Surveillance: The Case of South-North Korea Conflict*, 34(2) GOV. INFO. Q. 307, 310 (2017).

63. See generally: SIMONE BROWN, DARK MATTERS: ON SURVEILLANCE OF BLACKNESS (2015); Barton Gelman & Sam Adler-Bell, *The Disparate Impact of Surveillance*, THE CENTURY FOUNDATION (2017), https://policycommons.net/artifacts/1329125/the-disparate-impact-of-surveillance/1932415/.

64. MUDASSAR TOPPA & PRINCESS MASILUNGAN, STRUGGLE FOR POWER: THE ONGOING PERSECUTION OF THE BLACK MOVEMENT BY THE U.S. GOVERNMENT 1 (2021); KEEANGA-YAMAHTTA TAYLOR, FROM #BLACKLIVESMATTER TO BLACK LIBERATION (2016); BUD SCHULTZ & RUTH SHULTZ, IT DID HAPPEN HERE: RECOLLECTIONS OF POLITICAL REPRESSION IN AMERICA xviii (1989); George Joseph, *Exclusive: Feds Regularly Monitored Black Lives Matter since Ferguson*, THE INTERCEPT (July 24, 2015), https://theintercept.com/2015/07/24/

documents-show-department-homeland-security-monitoring-black-lives-matter-since-ferguson/; Nicole Ozer, *Police Use of Social Media Surveillance Software Is Escalating, and Activists Are in the Digital Crosshairs*, ACLU (Sep. 16, 2022), www.aclu.org/news/privacy-technology/police-use-social-media-surveillance-software; Bud Schultz & Ruth Shultz, *Final Word, in* IT DID HAPPEN HERE: RECOLLECTIONS OF POLITICAL REPRESSION IN AMERICA 409, 410–411 (Bud Schultz & Ruth Schultz, eds., 1989); Barry Friedman et al., *Policing Police Tech: A Soft Law Approach*, 37 BERK. TECH. L.J. 101, 112 (2022).

65. Schultz & Shultz, *Final Word, supra*, at 412. The left continues to be targeted today: Charlie Savage, *Justice Department Demands Data on Visitors to Anti-Trump Website, Sparking Fight*, N.Y. TIMES (Aug. 15, 2017), www.nytimes.com/2017/08/15/us/politics/justice-department-trump-dreamhost-protests.html?_r=0.

66. Terry Pender, *The Gaze on Clubs, Native Studies, and Teachers at Laurentian University, 1960s-1970s, in* WHOSE NATIONAL SECURITY?: CANADIAN STATE SURVEILLANCE AND THE CREATION OF ENEMIES 110 (Gary William Kinsman et al., eds., 2000); Ahrum Joy Kwak, *The Depth of Our Denial: The History of Discriminatory Policing in Canada*, MCGILL INTERNATIONAL REVIEW (2020); Jane Gerster, *The Dark Side of the RCMP*, THE WALRUS (Oct. 20, 2021), https://thewalrus.ca/can-the-rcmp-be-saved/.

67. Stephanie Wood, *For Activists, CSIS-Spying Revelations Were Cold Comfort*, NATIONAL OBSERVER (Aug. 29, 2019), www.nationalobserver.com/2019/08/29/news/activists-csis-spying-revelations-were-cold-comfort.

68. BROWN, DARK MATTERS: ON SURVEILLANCE OF BLACKNESS, *supra*; Alvaro M. Bedoya, *The Color of Surveillance*, SLATE (Jan.21, 2016); Dia Kayyali, *The History of Surveillance and the Black Community*, ELECTRONIC FRONTIER FOUNDATION (Feb. 13, 2014); Mary A. Franks, *Democratic Surveillance*, 30 HARV. J.L. & TECH. 425, 441 (2017) ("The surveillance of marginalized populations has a long and troubling history. Race, class, and gender have all helped determine who is watched in society, and the right to privacy has been unequally distributed according to the same factors"); Scott Skinner-Thompson, *Performative Privacy*, 50 U.C. DAVIS L. REV. 1673, 1738 (2017).

69. RUHA BENJAMIN, RACE AFTER TECHNOLOGY: ABOLITIONIST TOOLS FOR THE NEW JIM CODE (2019); Brown, DARK MATTERS: ON SURVEILLANCE OF BLACKNESS, *supra*; Safiya Nobel, ALGORITHMS OF OPPRESSION (2018); Vincent M. Southerland, *The Intersection of Race and Algorithmic Tools in the Criminal Legal System*, 80 MD. L. REV. 487, 498 (2021); Ngozi Okidegbe, *Discredited Data*, 107 CORNELL L. REV. 2007 (2021); Andrew Guthrie Ferguson, *Persistent Surveillance*, 74 ALABAMA L. REV. 1 (2022).

70. Scott Skinner-Thompson, *Privacy's Double Standards*, 93 WASH. L. REV. 2051, 2055 (2018).

71. Kiel Brennan-Marquez, *The Constitutional Limits of Private Surveillance*, 66 U. KAN. L. REV. 485, 495 (2018).

72. The Muslim American Civil Liberties Coalition (MACLC) et al., *Mapping Muslims: NYPD Spying and Its Impact on American Muslims* (2013). See also Conor Friedersdorf, *The Horrifying Effects of NYPD Ethnic Profiling on Innocent Muslim Americans*, THE ATLANTIC (Mar. 28, 2013), www.theatlantic.com/politics/archive/2013/03/the-horrifying-effects-of-nypd-ethnic-profiling-on-innocent-muslim-americans/274434/ (discussing the report's findings).

73. MACLC, MAPPING MUSLIMS: NYPD AND ITS IMPACT ON AMERICAN MUSLIMS, *supra*, at 4; Citron & Penney, *When Law Frees Us to Speak, supra*, at 2319–2320.

74. Citron & Penney, *When Law Frees Us to Speak, supra*, at 2319–2320; CITRON, HATE CRIMES IN CYBERSPACE, *supra*, at 13–19; Citron, *Sexual Privacy, supra*, at 1875.

75. Citron, *Sexual Privacy, supra*, at 1875.

76. See Penney, *Internet Surveillance, Regulation, and Chilling Effects Online: A Comparative Case Study, supra*; Jonathon Penney, *Whose Speech Is Chilled by Surveillance?*, SLATE (July 7, 2017), https://slate.com/technology/2017/07/women-young-people-experience-the-chilling-effects-of-surveillance-at-higher-rates.html.

77. BARENDT ET AL., LIBEL AND THE MEDIA: THE CHILLING EFFECT, *supra*; Renas, Hartmann, & Walker, *An Empirical Analysis of the Chilling Effect, supra*; Massing, *The Libel Chill: How Cold Is It Out There?, supra*, at 31 (citing 150 interviews with editors and attorneys); Hansen & Moore, *Chilling the Messenger: Impact of Libel on Community Newspapers, supra*, at 86.

78. HEINZEN & GOODFRIEND, SOCIAL PSYCHOLOGY, *supra*, at 437; KASSIN ET AL., SOCIAL PSYCHOLOGY, *supra*, at 451–452.

79. See generally, BROWN, DARK MATTERS: ON SURVEILLANCE OF BLACKNESS, *supra*.

80. Marit Hammond, *Democratic Innovations after the Post-democratic Turn: Between Activation and Empowerment*, 15(2) CRITICAL POLICY STUDIES 174, 177–178 (2021); Stephen Elstub, *The Third Generation of Deliberative Democracy*, 8 POLITICAL STUDIES REVIEW 291, 291 (2010).

81. Hammond, *Democratic Innovations after the Post-democratic Turn: Between Activation and Empowerment, supra*, at 177.

82. Hammond, *Democratic Innovations after the Post-democratic Turn: Between Activation and Empowerment, supra*, at 177.

83. Simone Chambers, *Deliberative Democratic Theory*, 6(1) ANN. REV. POLIT. SCI. 307, 307 (2003).

84. *Id.*, at 307–308.

85. Dennis F. Thompson, *Deliberative Democratic Theory and Empirical Political Science*, 11 ANNU. REV. POLIT. SCI. 497, 497 (2008).

86. Hammond, *Democratic Innovations after the Post-democratic Turn: Between Activation and Empowerment, supra*, at 177; Peter Dahlgren, *The Internet, Public Spheres, and Political Communication: Dispersion and Deliberation*, 22(2) POLIT. COMM. 147 (2015).

87. RICHARDS, INTELLECTUAL PRIVACY: RETHINKING CIVIL LIBERTIES IN THE DIGITAL AGE, *supra*, at 95–96, 98–99.

88. Schauer, *Fear, Risk, and the First Amendment: Unraveling the Chilling Effect, supra*, at 687, 693.

89. Kris Dunn & Shane P. Singh, *Pluralistic Conditioning: Social Tolerance and Effective Democracy*, 21(1) DEMOCRATIZATION 1 (2014).

90. Amartya Sen, *Violence and Civil Society, in* PEACE AND DEMOCRATIC SOCIETY 1, 1 (Amartya Sen, ed., 2011); Amartya Sen, *We Can Best Stop Terror by Civil, Not Military Means*, THE GUARDIAN (Nov. 9, 2007).

91. See generally CASS SUNSTEIN, WHY SOCIETIES NEED DISSENT (2003); Steven SHIFFREN, Dissent, INJUSTICE, AND THE MEANINGS OF AMERICA (1999).

92. Schneier, among others, has made this point: SCHNEIER, DATA AND GOLIATH: THE HIDDEN BATTLES TO COLLECT YOUR DATA AND CONTROL YOUR WORLD, *supra*, at Ch. 7.

93. RICHARDS, WHY PRIVACY MATTERS, *supra*, at 143.

94. Sunstein gives the example of Nelson Mandela. See: SUNSTEIN, WHY SOCIETIES NEED DISSENT, *supra*, at 6.

95. LAWRENCE CAPPELLO, NONE OF YOUR DAMN BUSINESS: PRIVACY IN THE UNITED STATES FROM THE GILDED AGE TO THE DIGITAL AGE 121 (2019). SCHRECKER, THE AGE OF MCCARTHYISM: A BRIEF HISTORY WITH DOCUMENTS, *supra*, at 104–105.

7 WHAT CHILLING EFFECTS THEORY IS FOR

1. Texas Heartbeat Act, 87th Leg., R.S., S.B. 8 (Tex. 2021) (codified at TEX. HEALTH & SAFETY CODE ANN. §§ 171.201–171.212).

2. Rhodes & Wasserman, *Solving the Procedural Puzzles of the Texas Heartbeat Act and Its Imitators: The Potential for Defensive Litigation, supra*; Peter N. Salib, *Ban Them All; Let the Courts Sort Them Out. Saving Clauses, the Texas Abortion Ban, and the Structure of Constitutional Rights*, 100 TEX. L. REV. ONLINE 13 (2021); Kimberley Harris, *How Do You Solve a Problem Like SB 8? Flagrantly Unconstitutional Laws, Procedural Scheming, and the Need for Pre-enforcement Offensive Litigation*, 89 TENN. L. REV. 829 (2021); Randy Beck, *Popular Enforcement of Controversial Legislation*, 57 WAKE FOREST L. REV. 553 (2022).

3. Rhodes & Wasserman, *Solving the Procedural Puzzles of the Texas Heartbeat Act and Its Imitators: The Potential for Defensive Litigation, supra*, at 189; Salib, *Ban Them All; Let the Courts Sort Them Out. Saving Clauses, the Texas Abortion Ban, and the Structure of Constitutional Rights, supra*, at 15.

4. 410 U.S. 113 (1973).

5. Dobbs v. Jackson Women's Health Org., 142 S. Ct. 2228 (2022). The decision has been described as the "most consequential case in modern history": Aaron Tang, *After Dobbs: History, Tradition, and the Uncertain Future of a Nationwide Abortion Ban*, 75 STAN. L. REV. 1091 (2023).

6. Beck, *Popular Enforcement of Controversial Legislation, supra*; Rhodes & Wasserman, *Solving the Procedural Puzzles of the Texas Heartbeat Act and Its Imitators: The Potential for Defensive Litigation, supra*, at 190; Salib, *Ban Them All; Let the Courts Sort Them Out. Saving Clauses, the Texas Abortion Ban, and the Structure of Constitutional Rights, supra*, at 14.

7. TEX. HEALTH & SAFETY CODE ANN. § 171.208 (2021); Rhodes & Wasserman, *Solving the Procedural Puzzles of the Texas Heartbeat Act and Its Imitators: The Potential for Defensive Litigation, supra*, at 190; Salib, *Ban Them All; Let the Courts Sort Them Out. Saving Clauses, the Texas Abortion Ban, and the Structure of Constitutional Rights, supra*, at 14.

8. Whole Woman's Health v. Jackson, 141 S. Ct. 2494, 2498 (2021) (Sotomayor, J., dissenting).

9. Whole Woman's Health v. Jackson, 142 S. Ct. 522, 545 (2021) (Sotomayor, J., dissenting).

10. Whole Woman's Health v. Jackson, 142 S. Ct. 522, 545 (2021) (Sotomayor, J., dissenting).

11. Whole Woman's Health v. Jackson, 142 S. Ct. 522, 538 (2021) (Gorsuch J., delivering the opinion of the Court).

12. Nadler, *Expressive Law, Social Norms, and Social Groups, supra*, at 60.

13. Licht, *Social Norms and the Law, supra*, at 717, 736–737; Tyler, *Understanding the Force of Law, supra*, at 507; Ellickson, *Law and Economics Discovers Social Norms, supra*, at 539–541.

14. Frank Fagan, *Systemic Social Media Regulation*, 16 DUKE L. & TECH. REV. 393 (2017); Roxana Radu et al., *Normfare: Norm Entrepreneurship in Internet Governance*, 45(6) TELECOMM. POL'Y 1 (2021).

15. United States v. Texas, No. 1:21-CV-796-RP, 2021 WL 4593319, at *81 (footnote 54) (W.D. Tex. Oct. 6, 2021).

16. United States v. Texas, *id.*, at *80–85.

17. United States v. Texas, *id.*, at *81 (footnote 56).

18. United States v. Texas, *id.*

19. United States v. Texas, *id.*, at *80.

20. United States v. Texas, *id.*, at *81 (footnote 54).

21. United States v. Texas, *id.*

22. Whole Woman's Health v. Jackson, 142 S. Ct. 522, 544 (2021) (Roberts C.J., concurring in part, dissenting in part).

23. Jeremy Blackman, *Seed for Texas Abortion Ban Was Planted 20 Years Ago, in Louisiana*, HOUSTON CHRONICLE (Sep. 9, 2021), https://www.houstonchronicle.com/politics/texas/article/Abortion-Origins-16446584.php; Esther Wang, *Inside the Plan to End Legal Abortion*, JEZEBEL (May 22, 2020), https://www.jezebel.com/inside-the-plan-to-end-legal-abortion-1843155358; Eleanor Klibanoff, *Anti-abortion Lawyers Target Those Funding the Procedure for Potential Lawsuits under New Texas Law*, THE TEXAS TRIBUNE (Feb. 23, 2022), https://www.texastribune.org/2022/02/23/texas-abortion-sb8-lawsuits/; Maggie Q. Thomas, *Architect of "Bounty-Hunter" Abortion Ban Wants List of Abortion Seekers*, THE AUSTIN CHRONICLE (Sep. 29, 2023), https://www.austinchronicle.com/daily/news/2023-09-29/architect-of-bounty-hunter-abortion-ban-wants-list-of-abortion-seekers/.

24. Sarah McCammon, *He Helped Craft the "Bounty Hunter" Abortion Law in Texas. He's Just Getting Started*, NATIONAL PUBLIC RADIO (May 8, 2023), https://www.npr.org/2023/05/08/1174552727/jonathan-mitchell-abortion-texas-sb8-roe-v-wade-dobbs.

25. *Id.*

26. Blackman, *Seed for Texas Abortion Ban Was Planted 20 Years Ago, in Louisiana, supra.*

27. McCammon, *He Helped Craft the "Bounty Hunter" Abortion Law in Texas. He's Just Getting Started, supra* (quoting Mitchell on this point).

28. Susan Rinkunas, *Anti-abortion Lawyer Wants Names of People Who Donated to 9 Texas Abortion Funds*, JEZEBEL (Sep. 29, 2023), www.jezebel.com/texas-abortion-fund-donor-names-lawsuit-1850884550; Caitlin Cruz, *A Man Sued His Ex's Friends for Helping Her Get Abortion Pills. They're Countersuing*, JEZEBEL (May 2, 2023), www.jezebel.com/a-man-sued-his-exs-friends-for-helping-her-get-abortion-1850395804.

29. 143 S. Ct. 2106 (2023).

30. 143 S. Ct. 2106, 2112–2113 (2023).

31. 143 S. Ct. 2106, 2112–2113, 2118–2119 (2023).

32. 143 S. Ct. 2106, 2117–2119 (2023).

33. Citron, *From Bad to Worse: Stalking, Threats, and Chilling Effects, supra*, at 5–6; Mary Anne Franks, *How Stalking Became Free Speech*, GEORGE WASHINGTON L. REV. DOCKET (July 28, 2023), https://www.gwlr.org/how-stalking-became-free-speech-counterman-v-colorado-and-thesupreme-courts-continuing-war-on-women/; Mary Anne Franks, *The Supreme Court Just Legalized Stalking*, SLATE (July 6, 2023), https://slate.com/news-and-politics/2023/07/supreme-court-legalized-stalking-counterman-colorado.html; Evelyn Douek & Genevieve Lakier, *The Supreme Court Seems Poised to Decide an Imaginary Case*, THE ATLANTIC (Apr. 26, 2023), https://www.theatlantic.com/ideas/archive/2023/04/supreme-court-social-media-stalking-case-colorado/673849/.

34. Clapper v. Amnesty Int'l, 133 S. Ct. 1138 (2013); Laird v. Tatum, 408 U.S. 1, 6 (1972).

35. Jameel Jaffer, Joshua Faust, & Eric Posner, *Is the N.S.A. Surveillance Threat Real or Imagined?*, NEW YORK TIMES ROOM FOR DEBATE (June 9, 2013), https://www.nytimes.com/roomfordebate/2013/06/09/is-the-nsa-surveillance-threat-real-or-imagined.

36. *Id.*

37. *Id.*

38. *Id.*

39. Sklansky, *Too Much Information: How Not to Think about Privacy and the Fourth Amendment, supra*, at 1069, 1094, 1097, 1099.

40. Sklansky, *Too Much Information: How Not to Think about Privacy and the Fourth Amendment, supra*, at 1101.

41. Jaffer, Faust, & Posner, *Is the N.S.A. Surveillance Threat Real or Imagined?, supra*.
42. See for example: Kinsley, *Chill, supra*, at 276 (arguing that with people already aware of "potentially limitless" surveillance and disclosure of their online activities, chilling effects are unlikely as the surveillance is normalized – any chill has "already arrived"); Sandro Nickel, *The Double-Edged Effects of Social Media Terror Communication: Interconnection and Independence vs. Surveillance and Human Rights Calamities, in* NEW OPPORTUNITIES AND IMPASSES: THEORIZING AND EXPERIENCING POLITICS 255, 263 (Zeynep Guler, ed., 2014).
43. Evan Selinger & Hyo Joo Judy Rhee, *Normalizing Surveillance*, 22(1) SATS 49, 57–58 (2021); Anupam Chander & Uyen P. Le, *Free Speech*, 100 Iowa L. Rev. 501, 546 (2015).
44. *See* Jonathon W. Penney, *(Mis)conceptions about the Impact of Surveillance*, FREEDOM TO TINKER BLOG (Feb. 14, 2018), https://freedom-to-tinker.com/2018/02/14/misconceptions-about-the-impact-of-surveillance/.
45. Büchi et al., *The Chilling Effects of Digital Dataveillance: A Theoretical Model and an Empirical Research Agenda, supra*, at 6.
46. Lina Dencik, Arnge Hintz, & Jonathan Cable, *Towards Data Justice? The Ambiguity of Anti-surveillance Resistance in Political Activism*, BIG DATA & SOC'Y 1 (2016) (qualitative study finding political activists were chilled from certain activities post-Snowden revelations); Lina Dencik & Jonathan Cable, The Advent of Surveillance Realism: Public Opinion and Activist Responses to the Snowden Leaks, 11 INTER'L J. COMM. 763 (2017) (similar findings). See also Kiran Kappeler, Noemi Festic, & Michael Latzer, *Dataveillance Imaginaries and Their Role in Chilling Effects Online*, 179 INT. J. HUM.-COMPUTER STUD. 1 (2023) (qualitative study finding evidence of both chilling effects and behavior akin to surveillance realism among participants).
47. Orwell's Big Brother was inspired by Stalinist Russia and Nazi Germany. See George Orwell, *George Orwell's Letter on Why He Wrote "1984,"* THE DAILY BEAST (Jan. 22, 2019), www.thedailybeast.com/george-orwells-letter-on-why-he-wrote-1984; David Aaronovitch, *1984: George Orwell's Road to Dystopia*, BBC NEWS (Feb. 8, 2013), www.bbc.com/news/magazine-21337504.
48. Alex C. Geisinger & Michael Ashley Stein, *Expressive Law and the Americans with Disabilities Act*, 114 MICH. L. REV. 1061, 1061–1062 (2016).
49. Geisinger & Stein, *Expressive Law and the Americans with Disabilities Act, supra*, at 1061–1062. See for example: Frederick Schauer, The Force of Law (2015); Paternoster, *How Much Do We Really Know about Criminal Deterrence?, supra*, at 765.
50. SCHAUER, THE FORCE OF LAW, *supra*.
51. Geisinger & Stein, *Expressive Law and the Americans with Disabilities Act, supra*, at 1061. See for example: Tom Tyler, Why People Obey the Law (1990); Janice Nadler, Flouting the Law, 83 Tex. L. Rev. 1399, 1402, 1404–1410 (2005).
52. Geisinger & Stein, *Expressive Law and the Americans with Disabilities Act, supra*, at 1062; RICHARD H. MCADAMS, THE EXPRESSIVE POWERS OF LAW: THEORIES AND LIMITS 4 (2015).
53. CAPPELLO, NONE OF YOUR DAMN BUSINESS: PRIVACY IN THE UNITED STATES FROM THE GILDED AGE TO THE DIGITAL AGE, *supra*, at 121; Edward S. Herman, Freedom of Expression in the West: Myth and Reality, *in* Human Wrongs: Reflections on Western Global Dominance and Its Impact upon Human Rights 178 (1996).
54. SOLOVE, UNDERSTANDING PRIVACY, *supra*, at 13, 29–34.
55. SOLOVE, UNDERSTANDING PRIVACY, *supra*, at 44 (noting the influence of the article); WALDMAN, PRIVACY AS TRUST: INFORMATION PRIVACY FOR AN INFORMATION

AGE, *supra*, at 18 (noting that Warren and Brandeis linked their conception of privacy to the idea of "inviolate personality," which concerned a form of autonomy and dignity: "the dignity owed us as fully formed, autonomous individuals"). See also Samuel Warren & Louis Brandeis, *The Right to Privacy*, 4 HARV. L. REV. 193 (1890); Edward J. Bloustein, *Privacy as an Aspect of Human Dignity: An Answer to Dean Prosser*, 39 N.Y.U. L. REV. 962, 971 (1964) (explaining "inviolate personality" in terms of autonomy, self-determination, and dignity).

56. RICHARDS, WHY PRIVACY MATTERS, *supra*, at 17 (citing the US Supreme Court's famous decisions in Katz v. United States, 389 U.S. 347 (1967); Roe v. Wade, 410 U.S. 113 (1973); and Griswold v. Connecticut, 381 U.S. 479 (1965)). *Katz* remains good law, but *Roe* has since been overturned by the US Supreme Court in its recent *Dobbs* decision.

57. Paul M. Schwartz, *Privacy and Democracy in Cyberspace*, 52 VAND. L. REV. 1607, 1613, 1650–1653 (1999).

58. Ruth Gavison, *Privacy and the Limits of Law*, 89 YALE L.J. 421, 455 (1980); Cohen, *Examined Lives: Informational Privacy and the Subject as Object*, *supra*, at 1426–1427; RICHARDS, WHY PRIVACY MATTERS, *supra*, at 157; RICHARDS, INTELLECTUAL PRIVACY: RETHINKING CIVIL LIBERTIES IN THE DIGITAL AGE, *supra*, at 99–100.

59. Danielle Keats Citron & Daniel J. Solove, *Privacy Harms*, 102 B.U. L. REV. 793, 845 (2022).

60. Schwartz, *Privacy and Democracy in Cyberspace*, *supra*, at 1655–1656.

61. *Id.*, at 1655–1656.

62. Gavison, *Privacy and the Limits of Law*, *supra*, at 446–447, 449–450.

63. *Id.*, at 450.

64. SOLOVE, UNDERSTANDING PRIVACY, *supra*, at 13.

65. James Q. Whitman, The Two Western Cultures of Privacy: Dignity versus Liberty, 113 Yale L.J. 1151, 1161 (2004); SOLOVE, UNDERSTANDING PRIVACY, *supra*, at 29–30.

66. GOFFMAN, INTERACTION RITUAL, *supra*, at 84–85; Robert C. Post, *The Social Foundations of Defamation Law: Reputation and the Constitution*, 74 CALIF. L. REV. 691, 707–719 (1986).

67. GOFFMAN, INTERACTION RITUAL, *supra*, at 84; Post, *The Social Foundations of Defamation Law: Reputation and the Constitution*, *supra*, at 710.

68. Jeremy Waldron, *How Law Protects Dignity*, 71(1) CAMBRIDGE L. J. 200 (2012).

69. Robert C. Post, *Three Concepts of Privacy*, 89 GEO. L.J. 2087, 2092 (2001).

70. Quoted in: SOLOVE, UNDERSTANDING PRIVACY, *supra*, at 29–30.

71. Lon L. Fuller, The Morality of Law 108 (1964).

72. Daniel Susser, Beate Roessler, & Helen Nissenbaum, *Online Manipulation: Hidden Influences in a Digital World*, 4 GEO. L. TECH. REV. 1, 15 (2019); Cass R. Sunstein, The Ethics of Influence: Government in the Age of Behavioral Science 82 (2016).

73. SUNSTEIN, THE ETHICS OF INFLUENCE: GOVERNMENT IN THE AGE OF BEHAVIORAL SCIENCE, *supra*, at 84; Susser et al., *Online Manipulation: Hidden Influences in a Digital World*, *supra*, at 16–17, 39 fn.130.

74. SUNSTEIN, THE ETHICS OF INFLUENCE: GOVERNMENT IN THE AGE OF BEHAVIORAL SCIENCE, *supra*, at 82–84.

75. Citron & Solove, *Privacy Harms*, *supra*, at 845–846.

76. Neil Richards, *The Social Dimensions of Privacy*, WORKING PAPER (forthcoming 2025) (manuscript on file with the author).

77. *Id.*; Ignacio Cofone, The Privacy Fallacy: Harm and Power in the Information Economy (2024).

78. Neil Richards & Woodrow Hartzog, *Taking Trust Seriously in Privacy Law*, 19 STAN. TECH. L. REV. 431, 452–457, 513 (2016).

79. WALDMAN, PRIVACY AS TRUST: INFORMATION PRIVACY FOR AN INFORMATION AGE, *supra*, at 52.

80. Danielle K. Citron, *Why Sexual Privacy Matters for Trust*, 96 WASH. U. L. REV. 1189, 1199 (2019).

81. Citron, *Why Sexual Privacy Matters for Trust, supra*, at 113.

82. HELEN NISSENBAUM, PRIVACY IN CONTEXT: TECHNOLOGY, POLICY, AND THE INTEGRITY OF SOCIAL LIFE 3 (2010).

83. *Id.*, at 3.

84. COFONE, THE PRIVACY FALLACY: HARM AND POWER IN THE INFORMATION ECONOMY, *supra*, at 6–7.

85. WOODROW HARTZOG, PRIVACY'S BLUEPRINT: THE BATTLE TO CONTROL THE DESIGN OF NEW TECHNOLOGIES 134 (2018).

86. Lyon, *The Search for Surveillance Theories, supra*, at 3, 4; Kevin D. Haggerty, *Tear Down the Walls: On Demolishing the Panopticon, in* THEORIZING SURVEILLANCE THE PANOPTICON AND BEYOND 23, 23–24 (David Lyon, ed., 2006); Kirstie Ball, Kevin Haggerty, & David Lyon, *Introducing Surveillance Studies, in* ROUTLEDGE HANDBOOK OF SURVEILLANCE STUDIES 1 (Kirstie Ball, Kevin Haggerty, & David Lyon, eds., 2012).

87. Michel Foucault, Discipline and Punish: The Birth of the Prison 200 (Alan Sheridan, trans., 1995).

88. Calo, *The Boundaries of Privacy Harm, supra*, at 1146–1147 ("This is the exact lesson of the infamous Panopticon. The tower is always visible, but the guard's gaze is never verifiable ... prisoners behave not because they are actually being observed, but because they believe they might be").

89. FOUCAULT, DISCIPLINE AND PUNISH: THE BIRTH OF THE PRISON, *supra*, at 200.

90. Lyon, *The Search for Surveillance Theories, supra*.

91. FOUCAULT, DISCIPLINE AND PUNISHMENT: THE BIRTH OF THE PRISON, *supra*, at 171–172; Gary Gutting & Johanna Oksola, *Michel Foucault, in* STANFORD ENCYCLOPEDIA OF PHILOSOPHY (2022), https://plato.stanford.edu/entries/foucault/; Haggerty, *Tear Down the Walls: On Demolishing the Panopticon, supra*, at 25; François Ewald, *Norms, Discipline, and the Law*, 30(1) REPRESENTATIONS 138–161, at 148 (1990).

92. ZUBOFF, THE AGE OF SURVEILLANCE CAPITALISM: THE FIGHT FOR A HUMAN FUTURE AT THE NEW FRONTIER OF POWER, *supra*, at 8.

93. Kapczynski, *The Law of Information Capitalism, supra*, at 1473–1474; ZUBOFF, THE AGE OF SURVEILLANCE CAPITALISM: THE FIGHT FOR A HUMAN FUTURE AT THE NEW FRONTIER OF POWER, *supra*, at 8, 11.

94. ZUBOFF, THE AGE OF SURVEILLANCE CAPITALISM: THE FIGHT FOR A HUMAN FUTURE AT THE NEW FRONTIER OF POWER, *supra*, at 94–95, 201; Kapczynski, *The Law of Information Capitalism, supra*, at 1469.

95. COHEN, BETWEEN TRUTH AND POWER: THE LEGAL CONSTRUCTIONS OF INFORMATIONAL CAPITALISM, *supra*, at 6.

96. COHEN, BETWEEN TRUTH AND POWER: THE LEGAL CONSTRUCTIONS OF INFORMATIONAL CAPITALISM, *supra*, at 6; Kapczynski, *The Law of Information Capitalism, supra*, at 1480.

97. Kapczynski, *The Law of Information Capitalism, supra*, at 1473–1474; ZUBOFF, THE AGE OF SURVEILLANCE CAPITALISM: THE FIGHT FOR A HUMAN FUTURE AT THE NEW FRONTIER OF POWER, *supra*, at 11.

98. Kapczynski, *The Law of Information Capitalism, supra*, at 1473–1474.

99. Sauvik Das et al., *Self-Censorship on Facebook*, CSCW '13 Proc. of the 2013 Conf. on Compu. Supported Coop. Work 793 (2013); Marder et al., *The Extended "Chilling" Effect of Facebook: The Cold Reality of Ubiquitous Social Networking, supra*.
100. Zuboff, The Age of Surveillance Capitalism: The Fight for a Human Future at the New Frontier of Power, *supra*, at Ch. 16.

8 A FRAMEWORK FOR HARD CASES

1. Andrew Koppelman, *Revenge Pornography and First Amendment Exceptions*, 65 Emory L.J. 661, 667 (2016).
2. Nissenbaum, Privacy in Context: Technology, Policy, and the Integrity of Social Life, *supra*.
3. Nissenbaum, Privacy in Context: Technology, Policy, and the Integrity of Social Life, *supra*, at 128.
4. Nissenbaum, Privacy in Context: Technology, Policy, and the Integrity of Social Life, *supra*, at 128, 161–162.
5. Aliza Chasan, *What Is a Target Letter? What to Know about the Document Trump Received from DOJ Special Counsel Jack Smith*, CBS News (July 19, 2023), www.cbsnews.com/news/donald-trump-what-is-a-target-letter-meaning-doj-special-counsel-jack-smith/.
6. Pratt et al., *The Empirical Status of Deterrence Theory: A Meta-Analysis, supra*, at 384.
7. *Id.*, at 384.
8. Gregory M. Zimmerman & Bob Vasquez, *Deterrence Theory: A Meta-Analysis*, in Criminology and Criminal Justice: Theory, Research Methods, and Statistics 23 (Sean Maddan & Jeffery T. Walker, eds., 2011).
9. Zimmerman & Vasquez, *Deterrence Theory: A Meta-analysis, supra*, at 23.
10. Richards, Intellectual Privacy: Rethinking Civil Liberties in the Digital Age, *supra*.
11. Citron, *Sexual Privacy, supra*; Citron, The Fight for Privacy: Protecting Dignity, Identity, and Love in the Digital Age, *supra*.
12. Nissenbaum, Privacy in Context: Technology, Policy, and the Integrity of Social Life, *supra*.
13. danah boyd & Nicole Ellison, *Social Network Sites: Definition, History, and Scholarship*, 13(1) J. Computer-Mediated Comm. 210, 222 (2007); Marder et al., *The Extended "Chilling" Effect of Facebook: The Cold Reality of Ubiquitous Social Networking, supra*.
14. Lyon, The Culture of Surveillance: Watching as a Way of Life, *supra*, at 31–34.
15. Penney, *Internet Surveillance, Regulation, and Chilling Effects Online: A Comparative Case Study, supra* (finding evidence of government and corporate surveillance chilling effects on a range of online activities, including sharing and speech).
16. Roslyn Layton, *The 10 Problems of the GDPR*, American Enterprise Institute Report (Mar. 12, 2019).
17. C-131/12, Google Spain SL & Google Inc. v. Agencia Española de Protección de Datos & Mario Costeja González, 2014 EUR-Lex CELEX LEXIS 317, ss. 89–99 (imposing a "right to be forgotten" derived from the EU Directive against Google under the European Charter of Fundamental Rights and Freedoms).
18. Eugenia Politou, Efthimios Alepis, & Constantinos Patsakis, *Forgetting Personal Data and Revoking Consent under the GDPR: Challenges and Proposed Solutions*, 20(1) Journal of Cybersecurity 1, 9 (2018).

19. Politou, Alepis & Patsakis, *Forgetting Personal Data and Revoking Consent under the GDPR: Challenges and Proposed Solutions, supra,* at 9, 11.
20. Politou, Alepis & Patsakis, *Forgetting Personal Data and Revoking Consent under the GDPR: Challenges and Proposed Solutions, supra,* at 9.
21. Hermstrüwer & Dickert, *Sharing Is Daring: An Experiment on Consent, Chilling Effects and a Salient Privacy Nudge, supra,* at 39; Meg Leta Ambrose, *It's about Time: Privacy, Information Life Cycles, and the Right to Be Forgotten,* 16 STAN. TECH. L. REV. 369, 371 (2013).
22. Hermstrüwer & Dickert, *Sharing Is Daring: An Experiment on Consent, Chilling Effects and a Salient Privacy Nudge, supra,* at 39; Ambrose, *It's about Time: Privacy, Information Life Cycles, and the Right to Be Forgotten, supra,* at 376 ("This information haunts the individual, causing undesirable repercussions for the subject, as well as society which may be chilled by the prospect of permanence").
23. See for example: Jeff Rosen, *The Right to Be Forgotten,* 64 STAN. L. REV. ONLINE 88, 91 (2011) (arguing the right "could lead data controllers to opt for deletion in ambiguous cases, producing a serious chilling effect"); Emily A. Shoor, *Narrowing the Right to Be Forgotten: Why the European Union Needs to Amend the Proposed Data Protection Regulation,* 39 BROOK. J. INT'L L. 487, 489 (2014); Robert Lee III Bolton, *The Right to Be Forgotten: Forced Amnesia in a Technological Age,* 31 J. MARSHALL J. INFO. TECH. & PRIVACY L. 132, 137, 142 (2015); Kris Lahiri, *How Could a GDPR-Like US Law Raise Constitutional Concerns?,* EGNYTE BLOG (June 21, 2018); Layton, *The 10 Problems of the GDPR, supra;* Danielle Bernstein, *Why the "Right to Be Forgotten" Won't Make It to the United States,* MTLR BLOG (Feb. 2020).
24. Brooke Auxier, *Most Americans Support Right to Have Some Personal info Removed from Online Searches,* PEW RESEARCH CENTER (Jan. 20, 2020); Rebecca Heilweil, *How Close Is an American Right-to-Be-Forgotten?,* FORBES (Mar. 4, 2018), www .forbes.com/sites/rebeccaheilweil1/2018/03/04/how-close-is-an-american-right-to-be-forgotten/#a649f14626ef.
25. Dawen Zhang, Pamela Finckenberg-Broman, Thong Hoang, Shidong Pan, Zhenchang Xing, Mark Staples, & Xiwei Xu, *Right to Be Forgotten in the Era of Large Language Models: Implications, Challenges, and Solutions,* ARXIV PREPRINT ARXIV:2307.03941 (2023); Alfonso Maruccia, *Right to Be forgotten in the Era of AI and Large Language Models,* TECHSPOT (July 14, 2023), www.techspot.com/news/99402-navigating-complexity-right-forgotten-era-large-language-models.html.
26. Glen A. Brown, *Consumers' "Right to Delete" under US State Privacy Laws,* PRIVACY WORLD (BLOG) (Mar. 3, 2021), www.privacyworld.blog/2021/03/consumers-right-to-delete-under-us-state-privacy-laws/.
27. Duane Pozza and Joan Stewart, *GDPR-Like Privacy Rights May Get a Little Closer to Home,* JDSUPRA (Dec. 18, 2020), www.jdsupra.com/legalnews/gdpr-like-privacy-rights-may-get-a-15052/; Paul Karp, *Australia to Consider European-Style Right to Be Forgotten Privacy Laws,* THE GUARDIAN (Jan. 18, 2023), www.theguardian.com/australia-news/2023/jan/19/right-to-be-forgotten-australia-europe-gdpr-privacy-laws.
28. Michael L. Rustad & Sanna Kulevska, *Reconceptualizing the Right to Be Forgotten to Enable Transatlantic Data Flow,* 28 HARV. TECH. L.J. 349, 409 (2015).
29. Hermstrüwer & Dickert, *Sharing Is Daring: An Experiment on Consent, Chilling Effects and a Salient Privacy Nudge, supra,* at 39.
30. Rosen, *The Right to Be Forgotten, supra,* at 90–91; Shoor, *Narrowing the Right to Be Forgotten: Why the European Union Needs to Amend the Proposed Data Protection Regulation, supra,* at 507–511.

31. Rosen, *The Right to Be Forgotten, supra,* at 90–91; Shoor, *Narrowing the Right to Be Forgotten: Why the European Union Needs to Amend the Proposed Data Protection Regulation, supra,* at 507–511.

32. See generally: Clay Calvert & Mary-Rose Papandrea, *The End of Balancing? Text, History & Tradition in First Amendment Speech Cases after Bruen,* 18 DUKE J. CONST. L. & PUB. POL'Y 59 (2023). See also DAVID GRAY, THE FOURTH AMENDMENT IN AN AGE OF SURVEILLANCE 96–97 (2017).

33. Neil Richards offers some of the policy reasons against a RTBF but concludes that more modest versions are likely constitutional: RICHARDS, INTELLECTUAL PRIVACY: RETHINKING CIVIL LIBERTIES IN THE DIGITAL AGE, *supra,* at 91–92. In the Canadian context, Michael Geist offers similar policy criticism: Michael Geist, *Why a Canadian Right to Be Forgotten Creates More Problems than It Solves,* THE GLOBE AND MAIL (Jan. 26, 2023), www.theglobeandmail.com/report-on-business/rob-commentary/why-a-canadian-right-to-be-forgotten-creates-more-problems-than-it-solves/article37757704/.

34. Citron & Penney, *When Laws Free Us to Speak, supra,* at 2319; Danielle Keats Citron, *From Bad to Worse: Stalking, Threats, and Chilling Effects,* 2023(1) SUP. CT REV. 175–212 (2024).

35. Lisa Ilene Steinman, *Despite Anti-stalking Laws, Stalkers Continue to Stalk: Are These Laws Constitutional and Effective,* 6 ST. THOMAS L. REV. 213, 229 (1993); Robert P. Faulkner & Douglas H. Hsiao, *Where You Go I'll Follow: The Constitutionality of Antistalking Laws and Proposed Model Legislation,* 31 HARV. J. ON LEGIS. 1, 17 (1994); John A. Humbach, *The Constitution and Revenge Porn,* 35 PACE L. REV. 215, 217 (2014); Michal Buchhandler-Raphael, *Overcriminalizing Speech,* 36 CARDOZO L. REV. 1667 (2015); Eugene Volokh, *Challenge to Maryland Law Banning Speech That Intentionally Seriously Distresses Minors,* WASHINGTON POST (Volokh Conspiracy Blog) (June 29, 2016), www.washingtonpost.com/news/volokh-conspiracy/wp/2016/06/29/challenge-to-maryland-law-banning-speech-that-intentionally-seriously-distresses-minors/; Lindsay Byers, Stalking or Talking? An Analysis of State v. Shackelford, Stalking, and the First Amendment, 19 FIRST AMEND. L. REV. 99, 120 (2020); Katherine G. Foley, "But, I Didn't Mean to Hurt You": Why the First Amendment Does Not Require Intent-to-Harm Provisions in Criminal "Revenge Porn" Laws, 62 B.C. L. REV. 1365, 1389 (2021).

36. See for example: Byers, *Stalking or Talking? An Analysis of State v. Shackelford, Stalking, and the First Amendment, supra,* at 119–120 (discussing chilling effect challenges to anti-stalking laws); Cheeyein Yang, *Minnesota Revenge Porn Law: A Look at the State v. Casillas Decisions,* 47 MITCHELL HAMLINE L. REV. 1216, 1216 (2021) (similar challenges to revenge porn laws).

37. 143 S. Ct. 2106, 2112 (2023).

38. 143 S. Ct. 2106, 2112 (2023).

39. People v. Counterman, 497 P.3d 1039, 1043 (2021) (Colorado Court of Appeals, Div. II).

40. 143 S. Ct. 2106, 2112 (2023).

41. 143 S. Ct. 2106, 2112 (2023); P.3d 1039, 1043 (2021).

42. 143 S. Ct. 2106, 2112 (2023).

43. 497 P.3d 1039, 1043 (2021).

44. 497 P.3d 1039, 1043 (2021).

45. Laurence Miller, *Stalking: Patterns, Motives, and Intervention Strategies,* 17(6) AGGRESSION & VIOLENT BEHAV. 495, 497 (2012); Mary P. Brewster, *Power and Control Dynamics in Prestalking and Stalking Situations,* 18 J. FAM. VIOLENCE 207 (2003).

46. 143 S. Ct. 2106, 2112 (2023).

47. 143 S. Ct. 2106, 2112 (2023).

48. Here is how Whalen described the experience, in her own words: "The thousands of unstable messages sent to me were life threatening and life altering. I was terrified that I was being followed and could be hurt at any moment; I had no choice but to step back from my dream, a music career that I had worked very hard to build": Coles Whalen, *Statement on Counterman v. Colorado*, www.coleswhalen.com.

49. Franks, *The Supreme Court Just Legalized Stalking, supra.*

50. 143 S. Ct. 2106, 2118–2119 (2023).

51. Citron & Penney, *When Laws Free Us to Speak, supra,* at 2319.

52. 143 S. Ct. 2106, 2118–2119 (2023).

53. 143 S. Ct. 2106, 2118–2119 (2023).

54. SCHNEIER, DATA AND GOLIATH: THE HIDDEN BATTLES TO COLLECT YOUR DATA AND CONTROL YOUR WORLD, *supra,* at 4, 7, 170–171.

55. Robert M. Chesney, *State Secrets and the Limits of National Security Litigation*, 75 GEO. WASH. L. REV. 1249, 1314 (2006) ("The state secrets privilege as it currently stands strikes a balance among security, justice for individual litigants, and democratic accountability that is tilted sharply in favor of security, tolerating almost no risk to that value despite the costs to the competing concerns").

56. DAVID GRAY, THE FOURTH AMENDMENT IN AN AGE OF SURVEILLANCE 16–17, 97–98 (2017).

57. Chesney, *State Secrets and the Limits of National Security Litigation, supra,* at 1249, 1314.

58. Wikimedia 2021. See also Wikimedia 2017.

59. Wikimedia 2017, *supra,* at 202.

60. Wikimedia 2017, *supra,* at 209–2013.

61. Gene R. Nichol, Jr., *Standing for Privilege: The Failure of Injury Analysis*, 82 B.U. L. REV. 301, 326 (2002) ("[M]uch of the rationale for access to the courthouse likely lies in ideology").

62. Wikimedia 2021, *supra,* at 209–213.

63. United States v. Reynolds, 345 U.S. 1, 10, 73 S. Ct. 528, at 528.

64. Chesney, *State Secrets and the Limits of National Security Litigation, supra,* at 1249.

65. Chesney, *State Secrets and the Limits of National Security Litigation, supra,* at 1289–1291.

66. Chesney, *State Secrets and the Limits of National Security Litigation, supra,* at 1249.

67. Chesney, *State Secrets and the Limits of National Security Litigation, supra,* at 1308–1314.

68. A slide in an NSA presentation on the PRISM surveillance program leaked by Snowden explicitly referenced Wikipedia as a target. See Wales & Tretikov, *Stop Spying on Wikipedia Users, supra.*

69. SCHNEIER, DATA AND GOLIATH: THE HIDDEN BATTLES TO COLLECT YOUR DATA AND CONTROL YOUR WORLD, *supra,* at 136–140.

70. SCHNEIER, DATA AND GOLIATH: THE HIDDEN BATTLES TO COLLECT YOUR DATA AND CONTROL YOUR WORLD, *supra,* at 136–137.

9 TRANSFORMING CHILLING EFFECTS DOCTRINE

1. My recommendations assume courts approach these issues both informed by the social theory and social science set out here, and in good faith. I am, however, not naïve about the Roberts Court and the biases and ideology that can drive its outcomes.

2. This point was argued extensively in Chapter 1. Indeed, in the very first chilling effect cases, deterrence was central. See for example: Times Film Corp. v. City of Chicago, 365 U.S. 43, 75 (1961) (Warren, J., dissenting) ("[T]he fear of the censor by the composer of ideas acts as a substantial deterrent to the creation of new thoughts"). See also

Kinsley, *Chill*, *supra*, at 272–283 (describing the "law of chilling effects" as based on the "notion that laws regulating speech may act as a deterrent to expression factors into First Amendment free speech"); Kendrick, *Speech, Intent, and the Chilling Effect*, *supra*, at 1637–1638 ("A claim of a chilling effect necessarily rests upon suppositions about the deterrent effects of law"); Penney, *Chilling Effects: Online Surveillance and Wikipedia Use*, *supra*, at 125–126.

3. Alex Abdo, *Why Rely on the Fourth Amendment to Do the Work of the First?*, 127 YALE L.J. FORUM 444, 449–445 (2017–2018); Matthew Tokson, *The Normative Fourth Amendment*, 104 MINN. L. REV. 741, 741–742, 758–762 (2019).

4. Tokson, *The Normative Fourth Amendment*, *supra*, at 741–742; Abdo, *Why Rely on the Fourth Amendment to Do the Work of the First?*, *supra*, at 446, 453.

5. See generally: Paul Ohm, *The Fourth Amendment in a World without Privacy*, 81 MISS. L.J. 1309, 1325–1326 (2012).

6. Tokson, *The Normative Fourth Amendment*, *supra*, at 742; Ohm, *The Fourth Amendment in a World without Privacy*, *supra*, at 1325–1326.

7. See for example: ERIC Barendt, LAURENCE Lustgarten, KENNETH Norrie, & HUGH Stephenson, Libel and the Media: The Chilling Effect 189–190 (1997); Michael Massing, The Libel Chill: How Cold Is It Out There?, COLUM. JOURNALISM REV. 31 (May/June, 1985) (concluding after interviews with 150 editors, reporters, and press lawyers that "a chill has indeed set in").

8. David Kohler, *Forty Years after New York Times v. Sullivan: The Good, the Bad, and the Ugly*, 83 OR. L. REV. 1203, 1203–1212, 1218–1219 (2004) (while noting libel chill remains a reality for the press due to the threat of defamation claims, the problem is much improved thanks to *Sullivan*); Kendrick, *Speech, Intent, and the Chilling Effect*, *supra*, at 1649–1650.

9. See Time v. Hill, 385 U.S. 374 (1967) (citing New York Times v. Sullivan, 376 U.S. 254 (1964)). See generally Neil Richards, *The Limits of Tort Privacy*, 9 J. ON TELECOM. & HIGH TECH. L. 357 (2011).

10. For example, in the 1971 case Dietemann v. Time, Inc., 449 F.2d 245 (9th Cir. 1971), the Ninth Circuit found in favor of the plaintiff's intrusion upon seclusion privacy tort claim, and justified its application to the facts – photographs surreptitiously taken in the privacy of the plaintiff's home without his consent and later published in a magazine – based on an implicit concern for chilling effects: "A different rule could have a most pernicious effect upon the dignity of man and it would surely lead to guarded conversations and conduct where candor is most valued, e.g., in the case of doctors and lawyers" (at 249). See also SOLOVE, UNDERSTANDING PRIVACY, *supra*, 164–165.

11. This point has been demonstrated at length by leading privacy scholars. See Danielle Keats Citron, *Mainstreaming Privacy Torts*, 98 CALIF. L. REV. 1805, 1824 (2010); Richards, *The Limits of Tort Privacy*, *supra*; Daniel J. Solove & Neil M. Richards, *Prosser's Privacy Law: A Mixed Legacy*, 98 CAL. L. REV. 1887 (2010).

12. Richards, *The Dangers of Surveillance*, *supra*, at 1942; Daniel J. Solove & Danielle Keats Citron, *Standing and Privacy Harms: A Critique of TransUnion v. Ramirez*, 101 B.U. L. REV. ONLINE 62, 69 (2021).

13. Kaminski, *Standing after Snowden: Lessons on Privacy Harm from National Security Surveillance Litigation*, *supra*, at 425; Kinsley, *Chill*, *supra*, at 257.

14. Kinsley, *Chill*, *supra*, at 256.

15. See Laird v. Tatum, 408 U.S. 1, 11 (1972) ("In recent years this Court has found in a number of cases that constitutional violations may arise from the deterrent, or "chilling," effect of governmental regulations that fall short of a direct prohibition against the exercise of First Amendment rights").

16. See Virginia v. Am. Booksellers Ass'n, 484 U.S. 383, 392–393 (1988) (discussing "pre-enforcement fear" injury as "one of self-censorship," that is, an "inhibition from acting in a particular manner"). See also Brian Calabrese, *Fear-Based Standing: Cognizing an Injury-in-Fact*, 68 WASH. & LEE L. REV. 1445 (2011).

17. See White v. United States, 601 F.3d. 545, 550–551 (6th Cir. 2010).

18. See Clapper v. Amnesty Int'l, 133 S. Ct. 1138, 1152–1153 (2013).

19. Clapper, *supra*, at 1152–1153, footnote 5.

20. See Babbitt v. United Farm Workers Nat'l Union, 442 U.S. 289, 298 (1979) (citing Doe v. Bolton, 410 U.S. 179, 188 (1973)). See also Susan B. Anthony List, 134 S. Ct. at 2346 (holding that a demonstration of threatened future enforcement of a law is sufficient for Article III standing).

21. See Kinsley, *Chill, supra*, at 261; Calabrese, *Fear-Based Standing: Cognizing an Injury-in-Fact, supra*, at 1456–1464.

22. Calabrese, *Fear-Based Standing: Cognizing an Injury-in-Fact, supra*, at 1456–1464.

23. Kinsley, *Chill, supra*, at 255.

24. Fred C. Zacharias, *Flowcharting the First Amendment*, 72 CORNELL L. REV. 936, 989 (1986–1987).

25. Solove & Citron, *Privacy Harms, supra*, at 854–855; Kaminski & Witnov, *The Conforming Effect: First Amendment Implications of Surveillance, beyond Chilling Speech, supra*, at 479–482; Felix T. Wu, *How Privacy Distorted Standing Law*, 66 DePaul L. Rev. 439 (2017).

26. Kinsley, *Chill, supra*, at 257–258; Calabrese, *Fear-Based Standing: Cognizing an Injury-in-Fact, supra*, at 1456–1464; Solove & Citron, *Privacy Harms, supra*, at 854–855.

27. Penney, Chilling Effects: Online Surveillance and Wikipedia Use, supra, at 120–121 (describing skepticism of the US Supreme Court in the Laird and Clapper decisions); Kaminski & Witnov, The Conforming Effect: First Amendment Implications of Surveillance, beyond Chilling Speech, supra, at 478–482; Jonathan R. Siegel, *Chilling Injuries as a Basis for Standing*, 98 YALE L.J. 905 (1989).

28. Laird v. Tatum, 408 U.S. 1, 6 (1972).

29. *Id.*, at 13–15.

30. *Id.*, at 13–15.

31. [2004] 3 S.C.R. 432, 2004 SCC 67 (hereinafter Tessling).

32. Tessling, *supra*, at paras. 4–6.

33. Tessling, *supra*, at paras. 3, 65.

34. Tessling, *supra*, at para. 55.

35. [1986] 2 S.C.R. 637, at p. 657.

36. See for example: Corp. of Canadian Civil Liberties Assn. v. Canada (Attorney General), 8 OR (3d) 289 – 91 DLR (4th) 38 (ONSC) (finding allegations of chilling effects via testimony are merely "subjective chill" and nonjusticiable); Canadian Broadcasting Corporation v. Attorney General of Ontario, 2015 ONSC 3131 (rejecting testimony from victims explaining how they were chilled by police surveillance as too "subjective" and thus insufficient to recognize).

37. 214 CCC (3d) 399; 42 CR (6th) 348 at paras. 54–58. See also J. L. Savarese, *Warming up the Chilling Effect: A Comment on the Motive Clause Discussions in R v Khawaja (2010) and R v Khawaja (2013)*, 30 WINDSOR Y.B. ACCESS JUST. 199, 201 (2012).

38. 103 O.R. (3d) 321, at paras. 119–120.

39. 2012 SCC 69 at paras. 76–84.

40. Khawaja, *supra*, at paras 76–84.

41. It should be noted that some judges of the Supreme Court of Canada, past and present, have been far more open-minded about the chill of privacy threats, including Justices Rosalie Abella and Gérard La Forest (both now retired). Justice Abella, for instance, wrote a concurring judgment in *Vice Media Canada* that was more open about presuming chilling effects due to privacy threats. Also Justice Sheilah Martin, currently in the Supreme Court of Canada, has raised chilling effect concerns in a number of cases, including *R. v. Mills*, 2019 SCC 22, at paras. 99–100 (speaking to new empirical studies documenting the chilling effect of government surveillance on online behavior and citing this author's empirical research on point).

42. Schauer, *Fear, Risk, and the First Amendment: Unraveling the Chilling Effect, supra*, at 730; Vincent Blasi, *The Pathological Perspective and the First Amendment*, 85 COLUM. L. REV. 449, 482 (1985); Kendrick, *Speech, Intent, and the Chilling Effect, supra*, at 1657; Kinsley, *Chill, supra*, at 256.

43. See Toni M. Massaro, *Chilling Rights*, 88 U. COLO. L. REV. 33, 65–66 (2017) ("There is little doubt that national security apprehensions affect judicial willingness to second-guess government conduct in ways that can skew case law"); Richard H. Fallon, Jr., *The Fragmentation of Standing*, 93 TEX. L. REV. 1061, 1095–1096 (2015); Mark C. Rahdert, *Forks Taken and Roads Not Taken: Standing to Challenge Faith-Based Spending*, 32 CARDOZO L. REV. 1009, 1015–1016 (2011); Gene R. Nichol, Jr., *Standing for Privilege: The Failure of Injury Analysis*, 82 B.U. L. REV. 301, 326 (2002).

44. TransUnion LLC v. Ramirez, 141 S. Ct. 2190, 2204 (2021).

45. 481 U.S. 465, 467–468 (1987).

46. *Id.*, at 473–474.

47. *Id.*, at 475–476.

48. Kaminski, *Standing after Snowden: Lessons on Privacy Harm from National Security Surveillance Litigation, supra*, at 425; Kinsley, *Chill, supra*, at 257.

49. Grayned v. City of Rockford, 408 U.S. 104, 108–109 (1972); Kendrick, *Speech, Intent, and the Chilling Effect, supra*, at 1652–1653; Kinsley, *Chill, supra*, at 262.

50. Kendrick, *Speech, Intent, and the Chilling Effect, supra*, at 1653; Kinsley, *Chill, supra*, at 263.

51. Kendrick, *Speech, Intent, and the Chilling Effect, supra*, at 1653–1654.

52. In her important book, Mary Anne Franks similarly critiques existing chilling effects doctrine.: Mary Anne Franks, Fearless Speech: Breaking Free from the First Amendment (2024).

53. Nadler, *Expressive Law, Social Norms, and Social Groups, supra*, at 62–63 ("Knowledge of the relevant legal rule is often weak, even among those who have reasons to know the rules"); Robinson & Darlow, *Does Criminal Law Deter? A Behavioral Science Investigation, supra*, at 175–178.

54. Yuval Feldman & Alon Harel, *Social Norms, Self-Interest and Ambiguity of Legal Norms: An Experimental Analysis of the Rule vs. Standard Dilemma*, 4 REV. L. & ECON. 81, 81–84 (2008).

55. *Id.*, at 81–84.

56. Penney, *Internet Surveillance, Regulation, and Chilling Effects Online: A Comparative Case Study, supra*.

57. Danielle Keats Citron & Jonathon Penney, *Empowering Speech by Moderating It*, 153(3) DAEDALUS 31–44 (2024) (discussing empirical findings); Danielle Citron, Jonathon Penney, & Alexis Shore Ingber, *Platforms, Privacy, and Power: Examining Predictors of Intimate Information Disclosure and Expression*, COMMUNICATIONS LAW & POLICY (under peer review).

58. U.S. CONST. art. III, § 2, cl. 1. See also Brian Calabrese, Fear-Based Standing: Cognizing an Injury-in-Fact, supra, at 1445; Matthew A. Wasserman, *First Amendment Limitations on Police Surveillance: The Case of the Muslim Surveillance Program*, 90 N.Y.U. L. REV. 1786 (2015); Kaminski, Standing after Snowden: Lessons on Privacy Harm from National Security Surveillance Litigation, supra, at 425; Courtney M. Cox, *Risky Standing: Deciding on Injury*, 8 N.E. U. L.J. 75 (2016); Margot E. Kaminski, *Privacy and the Right to Record*, 97 B.U. L. REV. 167 (2017).

59. Lujan v. Defenders of Wildlife, 504 U.S. 555, 560 (1992); Friends of the Earth Inc. v. Laidlaw Envt'l Sys. (TOC), Inc., 528 U.S. 167 (2000).

60. Richard Pierce, *Standing Law Is Inconsistent and Incoherent*, YALE J. REG. NOTICE & COMMENT (Sep. 7, 2021), www.yalejreg.com/nc/standing-law-is-inconsistent-and-incoherent/.

61. Kimberly Wehle, *The Squishiness of Federal Courts' "Standing" Doctrine*, THE BULWARK (Dec.23,2020),www.thebulwark.com/the-squishiness-of-federal-courts-standing-doctrine/.

62. Abram Chayes, The Supreme Court 1981 Term – Foreword: Public Law Litigation and the Burger Court, 96 HARV. L. REV. 4, 22–23 (1982). See also SCOTT R. ANDERSON, REVISING STANDING DOCTRINE: RECENT DEVELOPMENTS, POLICY CONCERNS, AND POSSIBLE SOLUTIONS, BROOKINGS INSTITUTE (GOVERNANCE STUDIES REPORT) (Sept. 29, 2022).

63. 136 S. Ct. 1540 (2016).

64. In *TransUnion*, the Court held that the plaintiff needed to prove a "harm" even though Congress had created a legal right to sue for a privacy violation with no such requirement: TransUnion LLC v. Ramirez, *supra*, at 2200. See also Solove & Citron, *Standing and Privacy Harms: A Critique of TransUnion v. Ramirez, supra*, at 64.

65. Spokeo, *supra*, at 340; TransUnion LLC v. Ramirez, *supra*, at 2198; Solove & Citron, *Privacy Harms, supra*, at 803.

66. In the words of Justice Brandeis, standing required showing a "legal injury, actual or threatened": Edward Hines Yellow Pine Trs. v. United States, 263 U.S. 143, 148 (1923); Andrew F. Hessick, *Standing, Injury in Facts, and Private Rights*, 93 CORNELL L. REV. 275, 292, n.104 (2007).

67. 381 U.S. 301, 307 (1965).

68. 381 U.S. 301, 308–309 (1965).

69. Richard H. Fallon, Jr., *The Fragmentation of Standing*, 93 TEX. L. REV. 1061, 1065–1066 (2015). See also Cass R. Sunstein, *What's Standing after Lujan? Of Citizen Suits, "Injuries," and Article III*, 91 MICH. L. REV. 163, 183–192 (1992); William A. Fletcher, *The Structure of Standing*, 98 YALE L.J. 221 (1988).

70. Fallon, Jr., *The Fragmentation of Standing, supra*, at 1061–1062.

71. 738 F.2d 1375, 1378–1379 (D.C. Cir. 1984) ("some who have successfully challenged governmental action on 'chilling effect' grounds have themselves demonstrably not suffered the harm of any chill, since they went ahead and violated the governmental proscription anyway").

72. Broadrick v. Oklahoma, 413 U.S. 601, 612 (1973).

73. Meese v. Keene, *supra*, at 473–474.

74. Friends of the Earth, Inc. v. Laidlaw Envtl. Servs., *supra*, at 181–182.

75. *Id.*, at 183–184.

76. Others have proposed this same interpretation. See for example: Kaminski, *Standing after Snowden: Lessons on Privacy Harm from National Security Surveillance Litigation, supra*, at 425; Wasserman, *First Amendment Limitations on Police Surveillance: The Case of the Muslim Surveillance Program, supra*, at 1786.

10 THE FUTURE OF CHILLING EFFECTS
AND HOW TO STOP IT

1. This chapter, its title, and its future-oriented focus and proposal for reforms, are inspired by Jonathan Zittrain's earlier work on the internet, which similarly offered critical ideas for understanding threats to freedom, today and tomorrow, and offered a vision and proposals on how to respond. See generally JONATHAN ZITTRAIN, THE FUTURE OF THE INTERNET AND HOW TO STOP IT (2008).

2. In 2024, renowned security expert Bruce Schneier and I hypothesized and wrote about the implications of a system just like this: Jonathon Penney & Bruce Schneier, *A.I. Microdirectives Could Soon Be Used for Law Enforcement*, SLATE (July 17, 2024), https://slate.com/technology/2023/07/artificial-intelligence-microdirectives.html.

3. Anthony J. Casey & Anthony Niblett, *The Death of Rules and Standards*, 92 IND. L.J. 1401 (2016); Anthony Casey & Anthony Niblett, *Self-Driving Laws*, 66 U. TORONTO L.J. 429 (2016); Anthony J. Casey & Anthony Niblett, *Micro-Directives and Computational Merger Review*, 1 STANFORD COMPUTATIONAL TRUST 132 (2021).

4. Cass R. Sunstein, *Deciding by Default*, 162 U. PA. L. REV. 1, 57 (2013) ("[P]ersonalized default rules are the wave of the future. We should expect to see a significant increase in personalization as greater information becomes available about the informed choices of diverse people"); Ariel Porat & Lior Jacob Strahilevitz, *Personalizing Default Rules and Disclosure with Big Data*, 112 MICH. L. REV. 1417 (2014); Benjamin Alarie, Anthony Niblett & Albert H. Yoon, *Law in the Future*, 66 U. TORONTO L.J. 423 (2016); Timothy Endicott & Karen Yeung, *The Death of Law? Computationally Personalized Norms and the Rule of Law*, 72 U. TORONTO L.J. 72, 373 (2022) (observing that new forms of personalized law are coming, including microdirectives, but arguing they likely will be the death of law); Lance Eliot, *Robustness and Overcoming Brittleness of AI-Enabled Legal Micro-Directives: The Role of Autonomous Levels of AI Legal Reasoning*, ARXIV PREPRINT ARXIV:2009.02243 (2020); Colin Harrison, *Autonomous Decentralised Systems and Global Social Systems*, 101(8) IEICE TRANSACTIONS ON COMMUNICATIONS 1753 (2018); Megan Ma et al., *Deconstructing Legal Text: Object-Oriented Design in Legal Adjudication*, MIT COMPUTATIONAL LAW REPORT (2020).

5. Hartzog et al., *Inefficiently Automated Law Enforcement, supra*, at 1763; Frank Pasquale & Glyn Cashwell, *Four Futures of Legal Automation*, 63 UCLA L. REV. DISC. 26, 36, 39 (2015); Shay et al., *Confronting Automated Law Enforcement, supra*, at 235 (noting chilling effects likely caused by automated legal systems).

6. Penney & Schneier, *A.I. Microdirectives Could Soon Be Used for Law Enforcement, supra*.

7. Digital Millennium Copyright Act of 1998, Pub. L. No. 105-304, § 103, 112 Stat. 2860, 2863–2876 (1998) (codified at 17 U.S.C. §§ 1201–1202 (2000)).

8. Maayan Perel & Niva Elkin-Koren, *Accountability in Algorithmic Copyright Enforcement*, 19 STAN. TECH. L. REV. 473, 481 (2016); Niva Elkin-Koren, *Fair Use by Design*, 64 UCLA L. REV. 1082, 1084 (2017).

9. Mack DeGeurin, *How Law Enforcement Agencies around the Globe Are Using Robo-Dogs*, GIZMODO (Feb. 11, 2022), https://gizmodo.com/law-enforcement-agencies-robot-dogs-spot-1848525601/4; Joe Anuta, *Watch Your Step: A New Robot Will Police the NYC Subways*, POLITICO (Sep. 22, 2023), www.politico.com/news/2023/09/22/nyc-mayor-unveils-robot-to-police-subway-station-00117619; Robin Mitchell, *Robots on Patrol: The Future of Crime Prevention*, ELECTRO PAGES (Sep. 27, 2023), www.electropages.com/blog/2023/09/police-robots-safety-solution-or-risk.

10. Matthew Field, *Google Backs London AI Law Firm in £9.5m Funding Round*, THE TELEGRAPH (Apr. 15, 2024), www.telegraph.co.uk/business/2024/04/15/google-backs-london-ai-legal-startup-lawhive/; News, *The Legal Industry Reacts to Amazon Investing up to $4bn in Anthropic*, LEGAL IT INSIDER (Sep. 26, 2023), https://legaltechnology .com/2023/09/26/the-legal-industry-reacts-to-amazon-investing-up-to-4bn-in-anthropic/; Mark Kleinman, *Microsoft Venture Arm M12 Backs UK Legal Tech Start-Up Definely*, SKY NEWS (Sep. 10, 2021), https://news.sky.com/story/microsoft-venture-arm-m12-backs-uk-legal-tech-start-up-definely-12403697; Keith Porcaro, *Robot Lawyers Are about to Flood the Courts*, WIRED (Apr. 13, 2023), www.wired.com/story/generative-ai-courts-law-justice/.

11. Lisa Fickensher, *Retailers Busting Thieves with Facial-Recognition Tech Used by MSG's James Dolan*, NEW YORK POST (Feb. 12, 2023), https://nypost .com/2023/02/12/retailers-busting-thieves-with-facial-recognition-tech-used-at-msg/; Leslie Gaydos, *AI Is Helping Businesses Stop Shoplifting in Their Stores*, NBC NEWS (BOSTON) (Mar. 20, 2024), www.nbcboston.com/investigations/consumer/ ai-is-helping-small-businesses-stop-shoplifting-in-their-stores/3314063/.

12. Adam Satariano & Kashmir Hill, *Barred from Grocery Stores by Facial Recognition*, N.Y. TIMES (June 23, 2023), www.nytimes.com/2023/06/28/technology/facial-recognition-shoplifters-britain.html; Gaydos, *AI Is Helping Businesses Stop Shoplifting in Their Stores*, *supra*; Mark Townsend, *Home Office Secretly Backs Facial Recognition Technology to Curb Shoplifting*, THE GUARDIAN (July 29, 2024), www.theguardian.com/technology/2023/ jul/29/home-office-secretly-backs-facial-recognition-technology-to-curb-shoplifting.

13. Ryan Mac et al., *Police in at Least 24 Countries Have Used Clearview AI. Find Out Which Ones Here*, BUZZFEED NEWS (Aug. 25, 2021), www.buzzfeednews.com/article/ ryanmac/clearview-ai-international-search-table; Drew Harwell, *Facial Recognition Firm Clearview AI Tells Investors It's Seeking Massive Expansion beyond Law Enforcement*, WASHINGTON POST (Feb. 16, 2022), www.washingtonpost.com/technology/2022/02/16/ clearview-expansion-facial-recognition/; Vera Bergengruen, *Ukraine's "Secret Weapon" against Russia Is a Controversial U.S. Tech Company*, TIME MAGAZINE (Nov. 14, 2023), https://time.com/6334176/ukraine-clearview-ai-russia/; Yuval Abraham, *"Lavender": The AI Machine Directing Israel's Bombing Spree in Gaza*, +972 MAGAZINE (Apr. 3, 2024), www.972mag.com/lavender-ai-israeli-army-gaza/.

14. Paul Mozur, Muyi Xiao, & John Liu, *"An Invisible Cage": How China Is Policing the Future*, N.Y. TIMES (June 25, 2022), www.nytimes.com/2022/06/25/technology/china-surveillance-police.html; Charlie Campbell, *How China Is Using "Social Credit Scores" to Reward and Punish Its Citizens*, TIME MAGAZINE (2019), https://time.com/collection/ davos-2019/5502592/china-social-credit-score/; Eunsun Cho, *The Social Credit System: Not Just Another Chinese Idiosyncrasy*, J. PUB. & INTER'L AFF. (May 1, 2020), https://jpia .princeton.edu/news/social-credit-system-not-just-another-chinese-idiosyncrasy.

15. Mozur et al., *"An Invisible Cage": How China Is Policing the Future*, *supra*.

16. Mozur et al., *"An Invisible Cage": How China Is Policing the Future*, *id*.

17. Cho, *The Social Credit System: Not Just Another Chinese Idiosyncrasy*, *supra*; Campbell, *How China Is Using "Social Credit Scores" to Reward and Punish Its Citizens*, *supra*; Stacey Vabek Smith & Cardiff Garcia, *What It's Like to Be on the Blacklist in China's New Social Credit System*, NATIONAL PUBLIC RADIO (Oct. 31, 2018), www.npr.org/2018/10/31/662696776/ what-its-like-to-be-on-the-blacklist-in-chinas-new-social-credit-system.

18. Campbell, *How China Is Using "Social Credit Scores" to Reward and Punish Its Citizens*, *supra*; Cho, *The Social Credit System: Not Just Another Chinese Idiosyncrasy*, *supra*; Smith & Garcia, *What It's Like to Be on the Blacklist in China's New Social Credit System*, *supra*.

19. Smith & Garcia, *What It's Like to Be on the Blacklist in China's New Social Credit System, supra*; Campbell, *How China Is Using "Social Credit Scores" to Reward and Punish Its Citizens, supra*.
20. Campbell, *How China Is Using "Social Credit Scores" to Reward and Punish Its Citizens, supra*; Cho, *The Social Credit System: Not Just Another Chinese Idiosyncrasy, supra*; Smith & Garcia, *What It's Like to Be on the Blacklist in China's New Social Credit System, supra*.
21. UNESCO, *Silk Roads: Initial Section of the Silk Roads, the Routes Network of Tian-shan Corridor: China Section*, UNESCO SILK ROADS PROGRAMME, https://en.unesco.org/silkroad/countries-alongside-silk-road-routes/china#.
22. FOUCAULT, POWER/KNOWLEDGE: SELECTED INTERVIEWS AND OTHER WRITINGS 1972–1977, *supra*, at 121–122.
23. Casey & Niblett, *The Death of Rules and Standards, supra*, at 1405, 1441–1445.
24. Niva Elkin-Koren & Michal Gal, *The Chilling Effect of Governance-by-Data on Data Markets*, 86 U. CHI. L. REV. 403, 406 (2019); De Filippi and Hassan raise similar concerns: Samer Hassan & Primavera De Filippi, *The Expansion of Algorithmic Governance: From Code Is Law to Law Is Code*, 17 FIELD ACTIONS SCIENCE REPORTS 88 (2017).
25. Shay et al., *Confronting Automated Law Enforcement, supra*, at 30 (noting chilling effects likely caused by automated legal systems); Hartzog et al., *Inefficiently Automated Law Enforcement, supra*, at 1789–1790; see generally, M. RYAN CALO, ROBOTS AND PRIVACY, IN ROBOT ETHICS: THE ETHICAL AND SOCIAL IMPLICATIONS OF ROBOTICS 491, 491–505 (Patrick Lin, George Bekey, & Keith Abney, eds. 2011).
26. Yuval Feldman and Yotam Kaplan, *Differentiated Regulation across People and Situations: A Behavioral Ethics Perspective to Personalized Law*, SSRN WORKING PAPER 30 (2018).
27. Vikas Hassija et al., *Interpreting Black-Box Models: A Review on Explainable Artificial Intelligence*, 16(1) COGNITIVE COMPUTATION 45 (2024); Yavar Bathaee, *The Artificial Intelligence Black Box and the Failure of Intent and Causation*, 31 HARV. J.L. & TECH. 889 (2017); Sandra Wachter, Brent Mittelstadt, & Chris Russell, *Counterfactual Explanations without Opening the Black Box: Automated Decisions and the GDPR*, 31 HARV. J.L. & TECH. 841 (2017); Finale Doshi-Velez et al., Accountability of AI under the Law: The Role of Explanation, arXiv preprint arXiv:1711.01134 (2017); FRANK PASQUALE, THE BLACK BOX SOCIETY: THE SECRET ALGORITHMS THAT CONTROL MONEY AND INFORMATION (2015).
28. Solon Barocas and Andrew D. Selbst, *Big Data's Disparate Impact*, 104 CALIF. L. REV. 671 (2016); Xavier Ferrer et al., *Bias and Discrimination in AI: A Cross-Disciplinary Perspective*, 40(2) IEEE TECHNOLOGY AND SOCIETY MAGAZINE 40, 72 (2021). See also generally: SOLON BAROCAS, MORITZ HARDT, & ARVIND NARAYANAN, FAIRNESS AND MACHINE LEARNING: LIMITATIONS AND OPPORTUNITIES (2023).
29. PASQUALE, THE BLACK BOX SOCIETY: THE SECRET ALGORITHMS THAT CONTROL MONEY AND INFORMATION, *supra*, at 8. The term originated with Clay Shirky. See Clay Shirky, *A Speculative Post on the Idea of Algorithmic Authority*, MEDIUM (Nov. 23, 2009), https://stoweboyd.medium.com/a-speculative-post-on-the-idea-of-algorithmic-authority-clay-shirky-c248019a0921.
30. Springsteen's 1978 classic "Darkness on the Edge of Town" is particularly apt here, given the looming dark future presented by superveillance and similarly chilling emerging technologies: "Where no one asks any questions // Or looks too long in your face // In the darkness on the edge of town // In the darkness on the edge of town": BRUCE

SPRINGSTEEN, DARKNESS ON THE EDGE OF TOWN (Columbia Records Inc., 1978). But see: Mark Tushnet, *Darkness on the Edge of Town: The Contributions of John Hart Ely to Constitutional Theory*, 89 YALE L.J. 1037 (1980) (using the reference in an entirely different legal context!).

31. Daniel Laufer & Sebastian Meineck, *A Polish Company Is Abolishing Our Anonymity*, NETZPOLITIK.ORG (July 10, 2020), https://netzpolitik.org/2020/pimeyes-face-search-company-is-abolishing-our-anonymity/; Linda Morrish, *A Face Recognition Site Crawled the Web for Dead People's Photos*, WIRED (Mar. 13, 2023); Mara Hvistendahl, *Facial Recognition Search Engine Pulls Up "Potentially Explicit" Photos of Kids*, THE INTERCEPT (July 16, 2022), https://theintercept.com/2022/07/16/facial-recognition-search-children-photos-privacy-pimeyes/.

32. Morrish, *A Face Recognition Site Crawled the Web for Dead People's Photos*, *supra*; Hvistendahl, *Facial Recognition Search Engine Pulls Up "Potentially Explicit" Photos of Kids, supra*.

33. Ramish Cheema, *10 Leading Social Media Companies in the Artificial Intelligence Theme*, YAHOO FINANCE (Oct. 5, 2023), https://finance.yahoo.com/news/10-leading-social-media-companies-160217412.html; Gerrit De Vynck & Naomi Nix, *Big Tech Keeps Spending Billions on AI. There's No End in Sight*, WASHINGTON POST (Apr. 25, 2024), www.washingtonpost.com/technology/2024/04/25/microsoft-google-ai-investment-profit-facebook-meta/; KASHMIR HILL, YOUR FACE BELONGS TO US: A SECRETIVE STARTUP'S QUEST TO END PRIVACY AS WE KNOW IT 111 (2023).

34. Hill, *The Secretive Company That Might End Privacy as We Know It*, *supra*.

35. Zeya Yang, *The World's Biggest Surveillance Company You've Never Heard of*, MIT TECHNOLOGY REVIEW (June 22, 2022), www.technologyreview.com/2022/06/22/1054586/hikvision-worlds-biggest-surveillance-company/.

36. Yang, *The World's Biggest Surveillance Company You've Never Heard of*, *supra*.

37. COHEN, BETWEEN TRUTH AND POWER: THE LEGAL CONSTRUCTIONS OF INFORMATIONAL CAPITALISM, *supra*, at 6, 225–228, 264–268 (2019); ZUBOFF, THE AGE OF SURVEILLANCE CAPITALISM: THE FIGHT FOR A HUMAN FUTURE AT THE NEW FRONTIER OF POWER, *supra*, at 389–394.

38. NICK DYER-WITHEFORD ET AL., INHUMAN POWER: ARTIFICIAL INTELLIGENCE AND THE FUTURE OF CAPITALISM 3 (2019); see generally, Pieter Verdegem, *Dismantling AI Capitalism: The Commons as an Alternative to the Power Concentration of Big Tech*, 39(2) AI & SOCIETY 727 (2024).

39. See, generally: DYER-WITHEFORD ET AL., INHUMAN POWER: ARTIFICIAL INTELLIGENCE AND THE FUTURE OF CAPITALISM, *supra*, at 1010; Verdegem, *Dismantling AI Capitalism: The Commons as an Alternative to the Power Concentration of Big Tech, supra*. See also Pieter Verdegem, Critical AI Studies Meets Critical Political Economy, *in* HANDBOOK OF CRITICAL STUDIES OF ARTIFICIAL INTELLIGENCE 302 (Simon Lindgren, ed., 2023); Dieuwertje Luitse & Wiebke Denken, *The Great Transformer: Examining the Role of Large Language Models in the Political Economy of AI*, 8(2) BIG DATA & SOC'Y 1, 3 (2021); SIMON LINDGREN, CRITICAL THEORY OF AI 105–110 (2024); MARK COECKELBERGH, THE POLITICAL PHILOSOPHY OF AI: AN INTRODUCTION 49–50 (2022).

40. COHEN, BETWEEN TRUTH AND POWER: THE LEGAL CONSTRUCTIONS OF INFORMATIONAL CAPITALISM, *supra*, at 264–268; ZUBOFF, THE AGE OF SURVEILLANCE CAPITALISM: THE FIGHT FOR A HUMAN FUTURE AT THE NEW FRONTIER OF POWER, *supra*, at 393.

41. Kelsey McCune et al., *Evidence for Personality Conformity, Not Social Niche Specialization in Social Jays*, 29(4) BEHAV. ECOLOGY 910, 915 (2018).

42. Martha S. Zlokovich, Daniel P. Corts, & Mary Moussa Rogers, *Descriptive and Inferential Statistics, in* THE CAMBRIDGE HANDBOOK OF RESEARCH METHODS AND STATISTICS FOR THE SOCIAL AND BEHAVIORAL SCIENCES 468, 481–482 (Austin Nichols & John Edlund, eds., 2023).

43. GANGADHARRAO S. MADDALA, INTRODUCTION TO ECONOMETRICS 89 (1992). Roberta Bortolotti, *Data Prep 2-3: Outlier Handling, in* HANDBOOK OF STATISTICAL ANALYSIS AND DATA MINING 515 (Robert Nisbet et al., eds., 2018). It also impacts the predictions of machine learning systems: Sayali Sandbhor & N. B. Chaphalkar, Impact of Outlier Detection on Neural Networks Based Property Value Prediction, *in* INFORMATION SYSTEMS DESIGN AND INTELLIGENT APPLICATIONS 481 (Suresh Satapathy et al., eds., 2019); Kaushik Choudhury, *Are Outliers Ruining Your Machine Learning Predictions? Search for an Optimal Solution,* TOWARD DATA SCIENCE (Aug. 11, 2020).

44. OSCAR H. GANDY, THE PANOPTIC SORT: A POLITICAL ECONOMY OF PERSONAL INFORMATION 2 (1993); Lyon, *The Search for Surveillance Theories, supra,* 6, 13–17.

45. JAMES C. SCOTT, SEEING LIKE A STATE: HOW CERTAIN SCHEMES TO IMPROVE THE HUMAN CONDITION HAVE FAILED (1998).

46. SCOTT, SEEING LIKE A STATE: HOW CERTAIN SCHEMES TO IMPROVE THE HUMAN CONDITION HAVE FAILED, *supra,* at 183.

47. KATE CRAWFORD, THE ATLAS OF AI: POWER, POLITICS, AND THE PLANETARY COSTS OF ARTIFICIAL INTELLIGENCE 57 (2021).

48. RICHARDS, WHY PRIVACY MATTERS, *supra,* at 213 ("Without a doubt, in the evolving information society that we live in, privacy has become the whole ball game").

49. WALDMAN, INDUSTRY UNBOUND: THE INSIDE STORY OF PRIVACY, DATA, AND CORPORATE POWER, *supra,* at 239.

50. Woodrow Hartzog & Evan Selinger, *Facial Recognition is the Perfect Tool for Oppression,* MEDIUM (Aug. 2, 2018), https://medium.com/@hartzog/facial-recognition-is-the-perfect-tool-for-oppression-bc2a08fofe66; Lindsey Barrett, *Ban Facial Recognition Technologies for Children – and for Everyone Else,* 26 B.U. J. SCI. & TECH. L. 223 (2020); Tate Ryan-Mosley, *The Movement to Limit Face Recognition Tech Might Finally Get a Win,* MIT TECHNOLOGY REVIEW (July 20, 2023), www.technologyreview.com/2023/07/20/1076539/face-recognition-massachusetts-test-police/.

51. Regulation (EU) 2024/1689 of the European Parliament and of the Council of 13 June 2024 Laying Down Harmonised Rules on Artificial Intelligence and Amending Regulations (EEC No. 300/2008, (EU) No. 167/2013, (EU) No. 168/2013, (EU) 2018/858, (EU) 2018/1139 and (EU) 2019/2144 and Directives 2014/90/EU, (EU) 2016/797 and (EU) 2020/1828, 2024 O.J. (L) 1 (hereinafter AI Act).

52. Sandra Wachter, *Limitations and Loopholes in the EU AI Act and AI Liability Directives: What This Means for the European Union, the United States, and beyond,* 26 YALE J. OF LAW & TECH. 671, 676 (2024); Felix Busch et al., *Navigating the European Union Artificial Intelligence Act for Healthcare,* 7(210) NPJ DIGITAL MEDICINE 1, 1 (2024).

53. AI Act, *supra,* at art. 5; Wachter, *Limitations and Loopholes in the EU AI Act and AI Liability Directives: What This Means for the European Union, the United States, and beyond, supra,* at 678; Busch et al., *Navigating the European Union Artificial Intelligence Act for Healthcare, supra,* at 1.

54. AI Act, *supra,* at art. 5(1); Wachter, *Limitations and Loopholes in the EU AI Act and AI Liability Directives: What This Means for the European Union, the United States, and beyond, supra,* at 678–679; Busch et al., *Navigating the European Union Artificial Intelligence Act for Healthcare, supra,* at 3.

55. Bruce Schneier, *We're Banning Facial Recognition. We're Missing the Point*, N.Y. TIMES (Jan. 10, 2020).

56. See Commission Regulation 2016/679 of the European Parliament and of the Council of 27 April 2016 on the Protection of Natural Persons with Regard to the Processing of Personal Data and on the Free Movement of Such Data, and Repealing Directive 95/46/EC (General Data Protection Regulation) art. 22, 2016 O.J. (L 119) 1, 49 (hereinafter GDPR).

57. Wachter, *Limitations and Loopholes in the EU AI Act and AI Liability Directives: What This Means for the European Union, the United States, and beyond, supra*, at 676.

58. Dan Simmons, *17 Countries with GDPR-Like Data Privacy Laws*, COMFORTE BLOG (Jan. 13, 2022), https://insights.comforte.com/countries-with-gdpr-like-data-privacy-laws.

59. Jonathon Penney, *Chilling Effects and Transatlantic Privacy*, 25 EUR. L.J. 122, 132–135 (2019).

60. Cohen, Between Truth and Power: The Legal Constructions of Informational Capitalism, *supra*, at 262; Waldman, Industry Unbound: The Inside Story of Privacy, Data, and Corporate Power, *supra*, at 61. For a discussion of privacy-as-control, see generally Daniel J. Solove, *Introduction: Privacy Self-Management and the Consent Dilemma*, 126 HARVARD L. REV. 1880 (2013).

61. Matt Burgess, *We Need to Fix GDPR's Biggest Failure: Broken Cookie Notices*, WIRED (May 28, 2020), www.wired.com/story/gdpr-cookie-consent-eprivacy/.

62. WALDMAN, INDUSTRY UNBOUND: THE INSIDE STORY OF PRIVACY, DATA, AND CORPORATE POWER, *supra*, at 120–121, 212–215.

63. Neil Richards & Woodrow Hartzog, *A Duty of Loyalty for Privacy Law*, 99 WASH. U. L. REV. 961 (2021); Woodrow Hartzog & Neil Richards, *The Surprising Virtues of Data Loyalty*, 71 EMORY L.J. 985 (2022); Woodrow Hartzog & Neil Richards, *Legislating Data Loyalty*, 97 NOTRE DAME L. REV. REFLECTION 356 (2022).

64. Hartzog & Richards, *The Surprising Virtues of Data Loyalty, supra*, at 986–987, fn.1; Emily Laidlaw, The Diligent Online Platform, *in* PLATFORM GOVERNANCE IN CANADA 1, 1–2 (Taylor Owen & Heidi Tworek, eds., forthcoming 2025); SSRN Draft (Mar. 20, 2024), https://papers.ssrn.com/sol3/papers.cfm?abstract_id=4735876. See also: Liliane Langevin et al., *Canada's Bill C-63: Online Harms Act Targets Harmful Content on Social Media*, LEXOLOGY (Feb. 29, 2024), www.lexology.com/library/detail.aspx?g=a491f559-2503-44c0-af2d-7bc3798ccb3e; Emily B. Laidlaw, *Mis- Dis- and Mal-Information and the Convoy: An Examination of the Roles and Responsibilities of Social Media*, PUBLIC ORDER EMERGENCY COMMISSION REPORT (Sep. 2022). Elettra Bietti has also argued convincingly for decentralizing platforms and treating them as public utilities: Elettra Bietti, *A Geneology of Digital Platform Regulation*, 7 GEO. L. TECH. REV. 1 (2023).

65. Balkin first proposed the idea in 2014, and has since developed it in a series of papers. See Jack M. Balkin, *Information Fiduciaries in the Digital Age*, BALKINIZATION (Mar. 5, 2014), https://balkin.blogspot.com/2014/03/information-fiduciaries-in-digital-age.html; Lina M. Khan & David E. Pozen, *A Skeptical View of Information Fiduciaries*, 133 HARV. L. REV. 497, 499 (2019).

66. Richards & Hartzog, *A Duty of Loyalty for Privacy Law, supra*, at 966.

67. Richards & Hartzog, *A Duty of Loyalty for Privacy Law, supra*, at 966.

68. Richards & Hartzog, *A Duty of Loyalty for Privacy Law, supra*, at 966.

69. Paulina Perlin, *ACLU v. NSA: How Greater Transparency Can Reduce the Chilling Effects of Mass Surveillance*, MFIA BLOG, Yale Law School (Dec. 6, 2017), https://law.yale.edu/mfia/case-disclosed/aclu-v-nsa-how-greater-transparency-can-reduce-chilling-effects-mass-surveillance.

70. Laidlaw, *The Diligent Online Platform, supra*, at 1–2.

71. Laidlaw, *The Diligent Online Platform, supra*, at 1–2.

72. Richards & Hartzog, *A Duty of Loyalty for Privacy Law, supra*, at 1008.
73. Waldman, Industry Unbound: The Inside Story of Privacy, Data, and Corporate Power, *supra*, at 238.
74. Penney & Schneier, *A.I. Microdirectives Could Soon Be Used for Law Enforcement, supra*.
75. Sunstein, *Deciding by Default, supra*, at 5; Porat & Strahilevitz, *Personalizing Default Rules and Disclosure with Big Data, supra*, generally.
76. Sunstein, *Deciding by Default, supra*, at 57.
77. See for example: Citron, Hate Crimes in Cyberspace, *supra*, generally; Mary Anne Franks, *Sexual Harassment 2.0*, 71 Md. L. Rev. 655 (2012).
78. Communications Decency Act, 47 U.S.C. § 230(c)(1)(2) (1996). For reforms, see Danielle Keats Citron & Benjamin Wittes, *The Internet Will Not Break: Denying Bad Samaritans § 230 Immunity*, 86 Fordham Law Review 414 (2017); Mary Anne Franks, *The Lawless Internet? Myths and Misconceptions about CDA Section 230*, Huffington Post (Feb. 17, 2014), www.huffpost.com/entry/section-230-the-lawless-internet_b_4455090; Carrie Goldberg, *Herrick v. Grindr: Why Section 230 of the Communications Decency Act Must Be Fixed*, Lawfare (Aug. 14, 2019), www.lawfareblog.com/herrick-v-grindr-why-section-230-communications-decency-act-must-be-fixed.
79. Citron, The Fight For Privacy: Protecting Dignity, Identity, and Love in the Digital Age, *supra*, at 84–90.
80. Laidlaw, *The Diligent Online Platform, supra*, at 2–3.
81. Citron & Penney, *When Law Frees Us to Speak, supra*.
82. See Danielle Citron, Jonathon W. Penney, & Alexis Shore Ingber, *Platforms, Privacy, and Power: Examining Predictors of Intimate Information Disclosure and Expression*, Communications Law & Policy (forthcoming 2025). For a discussion of some of the preliminary results see: Citron & Penney, *Empowering Speech by Moderating It, supra*.
83. Richards has made a compelling case for this claim: Richards, Why Privacy Matters, *supra*, at Ch. 2.
84. Owen, *On the Coming Merger of Tech and State Power, supra*.
85. Lisa M. Austin, Enough about Me: Why Privacy Is about Power, Not Consent (or Harm), *in* A World without Privacy: What Law Can and Should Do? 131 (Austin Sarat, ed., 2015); Richards, Why Privacy Matters, *supra*, at 3; Carissa Véliz, Privacy Is Power: Why and How You Should Take Back Control of Your Data (2020).
86. Waldman, Industry Unbound: The Inside Story of Privacy, Data, and Corporate Power, *supra*, at 238.
87. Kiel Brennan-Marquez, *Extremely Broad Laws*, 61 Ariz. L. Rev. 641 (2019).
88. Laura Lee Prather, *SLAPP Suits: An Encroachment on Human Rights of a Global Proportion and What Can Be Done about It*, 22 Nw. UJ Int'l Hum. Rts. 49, 87–91 (2023); David L. Hudson Jr., *Anti-SLAPP Coverage and the First Amendment: Hurdles to Defamation Suits in Political Campaigns*, 69 Am. UL Rev. 1541, 1542–1543 (2019).
89. Sophie Hurwitz, *The Bipartisan Bill Fighting Trump's Attempts to Silence Critics*, Mother Jones (Dec. 12, 2024), www.motherjones.com/politics/2024/12/trump-raskin-slapp-federal-law/.
90. Waldman has described the differences between more "moderate" privacy reforms – that would similarly balance privacy protections with data monetization – and more "radical" or sweeping reforms that would seek to undermine the entire business model of data and information capitalism: Ari Ezra Waldman, *Privacy's Rights Trap*, 117 Nw. UL Rev. Online 88, 104–106 (2022).
91. Richards, Why Privacy Matters, *supra*, at Ch. 6.

92. Jonathon W. Penney, Protecting Information Consumers, *in* MODELS FOR PLATFORM GOVERNANCE: A CIGI ESSAY SERIES 69 (Taylor Owen, ed., 2019).
93. The DAIS and Centre for Media, Technology and Democracy (McGill University), *Submission to the House of Commons Standing Committee for Industry & Technology Study on Bill C-27: Digital Charter Implementation Act*, THE DAIS AND CENTRE FOR MEDIA, TECHNOLOGY AND DEMOCRACY REPORT 13 (Nov. 2023) (the author was a contributor to this report).
94. Dale Smith, *The Future of Competition Law*, CBA NATIONAL MAGAZINE (Jan. 11, 2024); Keldon Bester, *Proposed Amendments to Canada's Competition Act Should Go Further*, CENTRE FOR INTERNATIONAL GOVERNANCE INNOVATION (Oct. 18, 2023).
95. DEIBERT, RESET: RECLAIMING THE INTERNET FOR CIVIL SOCIETY, *supra*, at 24–26; Di Salvo, *Information Security and Journalism: Mapping a Nascent Research Field*, *supra*, at 2.
96. See for example: Bill Marczak & John Scott-Railton, *The Million Dollar Dissident: NSO Group's iPhone Zero-Days Used against a UAE Human Rights Defender*, THE CITIZEN LAB (Aug. 24, 2016); John Scott-Railton et al., *Reckless Exploit: Mexican Journalists, Lawyers, and a Child Targeted with NSO Spyware*, THE CITIZEN LAB (June 19, 2017); Azam Ahmed & Nicole Perlroth, *Using Texts as Lures, Government Spyware Targets Mexican Journalists and Their Families*, N.Y. TIMES (June 19, 2017), www.nytimes .com/2017/06/19/world/americas/mexico-spyware-anticrime.html; Jakub Dalek et al., *Planet Netsweeper*, THE CITIZEN LAB (Apr. 25, 2018); Bill Marczak, *The Kingdom Came to Canada: How Saudi-Linked Digital Espionage Reached Canadian Soil*, THE CITIZEN LAB (Oct. 1, 2018).
97. COHEN, BETWEEN TRUTH AND POWER: THE LEGAL CONSTRUCTIONS OF INFORMATIONAL CAPITALISM, *supra*, at 90–91, 174–175; RICHARDS, WHY PRIVACY MATTERS, *supra*, at 91, 169–170; WALDMAN, INDUSTRY UNBOUND: THE INSIDE STORY OF PRIVACY, DATA, AND CORPORATE POWER, *supra*, at 232–233; 240–242; Daniel J. Solove & Woodrow Hartzog, *The FTC and the New Common Law of Privacy*, 114 COLUM. L. REV. 583 (2014).
98. Ryan Calo, *Robotics and the Lessons of Cyberlaw*, 103 CALIF. L. REV. 513, 556–557 (2015).

CONCLUSION

1. FREEDOM HOUSE, THE GLOBAL EXPANSION OF AUTHORITARIAN RULE – FREEDOM IN THE WORLD REPORT (2022).
2. Tirana Hassan, *The Signs of Diminishing Democracy*, HUMAN RIGHTS WATCH (Nov. 18, 2024); Marie Lamensch, *Evolving Surveillance Tech Whets the Authoritarian Impulse to See and Know All*, CENTRE FOR INTERNATIONAL GOVERNANCE INNOVATION (CIGI) ONLINE (Aug. 28, 2024); Amy Slipowitz et al., *No Way in or out: Authoritarian Controls on the Freedom of Movement*, FREEDOM HOUSE REPORT (2024); Bengisu Gulsen Kosarhan, *A New World Order? Digital Authoritarianism*, DEMOCRATIC EROSION CONSORTIUM (Jan. 5, 2023); Adrian Shahbaz, *The Rise of Digital Authoritarianism*, FREEDOM HOUSE REPORT (2018).
3. Gram Slattery et al., *Donald Trump Wants to Control the Justice Department and FBI. His Allies Have a Plan*, REUTERS (May 29, 2024); Robert Tait, *DoJ and FBI Officials Consult Lawyers Amid Threats of Trump Legal Retribution*, THE GUARDIAN (Nov. 18, 2024); Thor Benson, *How Donald Trump Could Weaponize US Surveillance in a Second Term*, WIRED (June 3, 2024).

4. Gerrit De Vynck & Nitasha Tiku, *Silicon Valley Eyes a Windfall from Trump's Plans to Gut Regulation*, Washington Post (Nov. 14, 2024); Virginie Berger, *How Donald Trump's AI Deregulation Could Reshape the Music Industry*, Forbes (Nov. 13, 2024).

5. See Penney, Citron, & Shore Ingber, *The Chilling Effects of Dobbs, supra*.

6. See generally: Karl Polanyi, The Great Transformation: The Political and Economic Origins of Our Time (1957). See also Cohen, Between Truth and Power: The Legal Constructions of Informational Capitalism, *supra*, at 268–271.

7. Deibert, Reset: Reclaiming the Internet for Civil Society, *supra*, at 6–7.

8. Penney, Citron, & Shore Ingber, *The Chilling Effects of Dobbs, supra*. For instance, Nathan Matias' Citizens and Technology (CAT) Lab at Cornell University, with whom I have collaborated, is doing cutting edge research on the large scale chilling effects of automated enforcement of the law: J. Nathan Matias, Jonathon W. Penney, Merry Ember Mou, and Maximilian Klein, Do Law Enforcement Bots Reduce Freedom of Expression Online? Study Results, Citizens and Technology (CAT) Lab Report (September, 2020), https://citizensandtech.org/2020/09/chilling-effect-automated-law-enforcemen. As for impacts on discrete and marginal groups see, for instance, Kendra Albert's work with sex workers: Kendra Albert, Five Reflections from Five Years of FOSTA/SESTA, 40 Cardozo Arts & Ent. LJ 413(2022).

9. Waldman, Industry Unbound: The Inside Story of Privacy, Data, and Corporate Power, *supra*, at 234.

10. Penney, *Understanding Chilling Effects, supra*, at 1476, 1529–1530; Cohen, Between Truth and Power: The Legal Constructions of Informational Capitalism, *supra*, at 89–93; Waldman, Industry Unbound: The Inside Story of Privacy, Data, and Corporate Power, *supra*, at 64–65.

11. Waldman, Industry Unbound: The Inside Story of Privacy, Data, and Corporate Power, *supra*, at 237.

12. Cohen, *Surveillance vs. Privacy: Effects and Implications, supra*.

13. Citron & Penney, *When Law Frees Us to Speak, supra*.

Index

Printed by Integrated Books International,
United States of America